Central American Recovery and Development

Task Force Report to the International Commission

for Central American Recovery and Development

Edited by William Ascher and Ann Hubbard

Duke University Press   Durham and London 1989

Library of Congress Cataloging-in-Publication Data
Central American Recovery and Development Task Force.
Central American Recovery and Development Task Force
report to the International Commission for Central
American Recovery and Development.
Includes index.
1. Central America—Economic policy. 2. Central
America—Social policy. I. International Commission
for Central American Recovery and Development. II. Title.
HC141.C379 1989 338.972 89-7695
ISBN 0-8223-0905-X

Table of Contents

Preface

The purpose of this volume is to make available to the public a set of critical essays on Central America prepared for the International Commission for Central American Recovery and Development. The essays collected in this book were written by members of a Study Task Force composed of experts in Central American development, economics, politics, and administration.

The International Commission for Central American Recovery and Development was created in 1987 to undertake a comprehensive analysis of development prospects in Central America and formulate a set of recommendations for the region's governments and for the international community. The commission is made up of forty-seven commissioners from twenty countries in Latin America, North America, Asia, and Europe. This volume is published as a companion volume to the commission's report, which consists of the commission's own assessment and its proposals for a Central American development plan.

When the commission was established, Duke University's Center for International Development Research also set up a Study Task Force to provide analyses for the commission. Study Task Force members were not asked to undertake field research on Central America's problems, but rather to synthesize existing knowledge on the prospects for aid, trade, and institutional reform for Central America and to air creative approaches to the problems facing the region. While the International Commission is responsible for making recommendations regarding the feasibility of various policy options, the Study Task Force's diagnoses and suggestions have been important inputs for the commission's deliberations.

For the purpose of these studies "Central America" has been defined as the five original republics that grew out of the Central American Federation: Costa Rica, El Salvador, Guatemala, Honduras, and Nicaragua. Although some of the diagnoses and recommendations may hold for Belize and Panamá, and some statistics include these countries as part of Central America, these cases were studied only incidentally. As always, generalizations beyond the five core nations of Central America are hazardous, especially in light of the special economic and political links that Panamá and Belize have with both the United States and Great Britain.

Contributors

Sergio Aguayo is currently a SSRC-MacArthur Foundation fellow in International Peace and Cooperation and a visiting professor at the Instituto Latinoamericano de Estudios Trasnacionales in Mexico City. He holds a Ph.D. from the School of Advanced International Studies at Johns Hopkins University and has done research on Central American refugees in Mexico. He was a founding member of the Mexican Academy of Human Rights.

His recent publications include a forthcoming book coauthored with Astri Surhrki and Aristede Coolberg, *Escape from Violence: Refugees and Social Violence in the Third World.*

Gustavo Arcia is an agricultural economist in the Center for Development Policy at the Research Triangle Institute. He has led, advised, and evaluated numerous AID projects in Central America. Prior to his work at RTI, Arcia was a research economist in the division of agricultural insurance and credit at the Inter-American Institute for Cooperation on Agriculture in Panama. Since receiving his Ph.D. from the University of Missouri in 1980, he has conducted extensive research in Central American agriculture policy and development and written numerous papers and reports.

Colin Bradford, Jr., the associate director of the Yale Center for International and Area Studies since 1978, is also a research economist at the National Bureau of Economic Research, International Studies Program. He received his Ph.D. in economics from Columbia University in 1970 and has served on the senior economics staff at the Inter-American Committee of the Alliance for Progress as a legislative assistant, as director of the Office of Multilateral Development Banks, and as director of graduate studies in international relations at Yale University. He has published numerous books, articles, and essays in professional journals.

Philip L. Brock, an assistant professor of economics at Duke University, received his Ph.D. from Stanford University in 1982. In addition to many awards and grants he has received to conduct research in Latin America, he received a Fulbright fellowship for research on the 1981–83 Chilean financial collapse and the Tinker Foundation travel research grant in 1987 for research on the growth of the Chilean fruit industry. He has published articles on economic and trade liberalization in less-developed countries for U.S. and Latin American publications.

Richard E. Feinberg is vice president of the Overseas Development Council. He has worked as a Latin American specialist at the

Department of State and as an international economist for the Treasury Department and the House Banking Committee.

John Jacob Freiberger is currently an assistant professor of anesthesiology at Duke University Medical Center. While completing a clinical fellowship in medicine and later in anesthesiology at Harvard Medical School, he served as an intern at Cambridge Hospital from 1979 to 1980 and resident at Massachusetts General Hospital, 1981–83. He has worked as acting chief and chief of anesthesiology services at the Durham Veterans Administration Medical Center and has published chapters in three books.

Claudio Gonzalez Vega has been a professor of economics at Ohio State University since 1982. Formerly, he had been dean of the faculty of economics and professor of economics at the University of Costa Rica. Both a lawyer and economist, he has been a consultant for many major international organizations including the World Bank, IMF, Inter-American Development Bank, and USAID. His most recent book is *Economic Reform and Stabilization in Latin America* (Praeger, 1987).

Robert J. Healy is senior associate of The Conservation Foundation in Washington, D.C. Currently a visiting professor of resource and environmental policy in the School of Forestry and Environmental Studies at Duke University, he has taught land-use policy in graduate schools of urban planning and forestry at the University of California, Los Angeles, and Harvard University. Healy works on natural resources, land-use and environmental regulation, and the economic effects of public policies. He has research experience in Latin

America and is author or coauthor of numerous articles and six books on land-related subjects.

Eduardo Lizano Fait has been a professor of economics at the University of Costa Rica in San José. He is currently serving as president of Central Bank of Costa Rica and is the author of two books, *Agricultura y desarrollo economico* (1980) and *Cambio social en Costa Rica* (1975).

Cassio Luiselli is assistant deputy director for operations, Inter-American Institute for Cooperation on Agriculture (IICA). He previously held the post of assistant director at the UN Economic Commission for Latin America and the Caribbean. Luiselli worked as a Kellogg Foundation fellow at the University of California, Berkeley, on a project on food security and macroeconomic policy. He is the author or coauthor of several books and numerous articles, papers, and chapters in magazines and professional journals.

Richard McCall is presently the foreign policy assistant to Senator John Kerry of Massachusetts. Previously he had been the deputy staff director of foreign and defense policy at the Senate Democratic Policy Committee and in 1980 left the Senate briefly to accept the post of assistant secretary of state for international organization affairs. He is author of the chapter "From Monroe to Reagan: An Overview of U.S. Latin American Relations" in *From Gunboats to Diplomacy*.

Lars Schoultz is director of the Institute of Latin American Studies and a professor of political science at the University of North Carolina at Chapel Hill. A recipient of many awards and grants, he has held fellowships from the USIA Binational Center in Bucaramanga, Colombia, NDFL, Fulbright. His field research in Bogotá, Buenos Aires, and Washington, D.C., has focused on urbanization and electoral behavior and U.S. policy toward Latin America. He has written three books and published numerous articles and essays for books and political journals. Since 1979 Schoultz has served as a member of the Latin American Studies Association's Committee on Human Rights and Academic Freedom and chaired the committee between 1983–85.

Alan Stoga joined Kissinger Associates, Inc., in May 1984 as senior associate with responsibility for international economic and financial consulting, research, and client relations. From 1977 to 1984 he was vice president and head of the country risk management division at the First National Bank of Chicago, responsible for the overall analysis of international economic, political, and social developments which affected the bank's overseas portfolio. In the last few years he has worked

extensively on the international debt problem, U.S. policy in Central America, and U.S.-Mexican relations. His articles on international economic and financial issues have appeared in numerous popular and professional publications.

Stuart K. Tucker is a fellow at the Overseas Development Council. Prior to joining ODC, he was a research consultant for the Inter-American Development Bank, the Urban Institute, and the Roosevelt Center for American Policy Studies. He has written on U.S. international trade policy, the debt crisis and trade, U.S. costs of Third World recession, and the Caribbean Basin Initiative.

Sally W. Yudelman is a joint fellow at the Overseas Development Council and the International Center for Research on Women. She was an officer at the Inter-American Foundation and was Central American/Caribbean planning and program officer for the Peace Corps.

Introduction

From the international community, we solicit respect and help. We
have Central American roads to peace and development, but we need
help to make them come true. We ask for an international response
that will guarantee development so that the peace we are seeking can
be a lasting one. We firmly reiterate that peace and development are
inseparable.
Declaration of Central American Presidents
Esquipulas, Guatemala, August 1987

By signing the Esquipulas peace accords in August 1987, the five Central
American presidents affirmed their governments' urgent desire for peace
after eight years of civil war. The agreement called for not only an end to
hostilities, but also democracy, economic development, regional cooperation
on a broad range of issues, and economic assistance from the international
community. The presidents put particular emphasis on the link between
peace and development: without peace economic recovery cannot proceed;
without equitable economic development peace cannot endure.

Central America's political and social struggles have propelled the region
into the world spotlight, but economic factors form the antecedent for
understanding the region's crisis. Central America's severe economic and
social problems are not the result of grossly insufficient rates of economic
growth; gross domestic product (GDP) grew at a healthy 5 percent per year
between 1950 and 1980. The problems came because that growth was marked
by harsh inequities and massive distortions. Large sectors of the population—
women, subsistence farmers, indigenous peoples—were excluded from the
benefits of growth. Their dissatisfaction has fueled the region's conflicts.

In this decade the economies deteriorated, and social tensions heightened. Three of the five Central American countries—El Salvador, Guatemala, Nicaragua—have been ravaged by military conflicts that have claimed the lives of 160,000 people over the last eight years and seriously damaged the nations' infrastructure and productive sectors. All five countries have suffered from social and economic turbulence, exacerbated by the fighting in the region. Even Costa Rica, so often the bright exception to the region's problems of inequality and political instability, has felt the economic deterioration resulting from the collapse of intraregional trade and the burden of a large refugee population. For the region as a whole, efforts to reverse marked economic deterioration have not succeeded: in 1987 per capita income for the region as a whole had fallen to the level of two decades earlier. The region has grown increasingly dependent on external aid, but that aid has also helped promote polarization and support militarization.

Despite the obstacles to recovery, Central America clearly possesses the potential for growth. The region is endowed with sufficient natural resources relative to its current population, a favorable climate for agriculture, the human resources required for light manufacturing, and a geographical position well suited for trade and tourism. Through the signing of the peace plan and through ongoing efforts to forge closer regional economic and political ties, Central Americans have demonstrated their will for peace and economic development. The international community is showing an increased awareness of the need to provide the region with aid that is linked to lasting economic development, not just short-term economic stabilization and national security. The old model of political exclusion of large population segments, which exacerbated unbalanced economic growth and social and political polarization, is dramatically less viable as a strategy of political control. New actors such as political parties, nongovernmental organizations, and religious groups are entering the political arena to press claims for their constituents and members. This certainly does not guarantee the stability required for economic development; in fact the mobilization of previously excluded groups has been an obvious element in the turmoil in the region. Yet *if* a more fully participatory Central America can find stable political formulas and workable models of sustained economic development, then democracy and equitable development can reinforce one another.

The region needs a coordinated regional economic strategy built on concerted international support. There is growing support for such a regional development plan in Central America and throughout the world. The United Nations Development Programme has drawn up a special plan for economic cooperation with Central America, based in part on the Central American Vice Presidents' Plan of Immediate Action. Above all, the Esquipulas peace accords have set forth the conditions for meaningful action on Central America.

The International Commission for Central American Recovery and Development

The International Commission for Central American Recovery and Development was formed in 1987 to help the Central American nations achieve their desire for equitable and sustained economic development. With forty-seven members from twenty countries in Latin America, North America, Europe, and Asia, the commission provides a forum for collaboration between Central Americans and the international community, whose assistance is a prerequisite for economic recovery and development. The political diversity of the Central American members of the commission demonstrates the commission's firmly held belief that lasting development must rest on a stable social consensus. The commission first met in San José, Costa Rica in December 1987 and released its final recommendations in Guatemala in February 1989.

The commission formulated its plan under the leadership of Central Americans; it was not a plan imposed on the region from the outside. Now the commission is working to influence the international community to support its recommendations for advancing peace and balanced economic growth in the region, within the framework of the Esquipulas peace accords and the Contadora initiative rather than as the focus of an international geopolitical struggle.

The Study Task Force

To help prepare the commission for its work, a Study Task Force was assembled in 1987 to analyze and suggest fresh prescriptions for a set of the most serious problems facing Central America. Members of the multidisciplinary task force include specialists in Central American development, economics, politics, and administration. The topics addressed in this volume's essays range from health care systems to currency convertibility to rural development. The seemingly disparate topics are bound together by a complex set of linkages, some of which will be set forth later in this introduction.

Goals and Perspectives of the Commission

The commission looked at the immediate needs of the poorest sectors of the Central American population and at the requirements for the transition to long-term, sustainable economic growth. It also examined the region's external debt profile, the strengths and weaknesses of Central America's financial institutions, the opportunities for democratic participation, and the prospects for diversifying the region's export markets.

The commission recognized from the outset that economic progress must go far beyond improvements in economic aggregates like the gross national product (GNP) and the balance of trade. Economic equity and poverty alleviation are not only of great intrinsic importance, they are also critical for the long-term prospects of political stability and the consolidation of democracy.

In the case of Central America, equity need not come at the expense of efficiency. Many of the obstacles to sustained economic development in Central America stem from poverty and the lack of access to resources by large segments of the populations. Agricultural development has been held back by lack of access to credit, general productivity has been constrained by low educational and health levels (except in Costa Rica), and home-market industrial expansion has been limited by the inability of many families to afford major manufactured items. Therefore, the work of the commission has emphasized the importance of exploring "growth with equity" strategies while not taking their success for granted.

As important as economic growth *and* distribution are, the commission also recognized that a plan for recovery and development would have to be far more than an economic program—even one that addressed economic justice and poverty alleviation. Just as economic equity is important for its own sake as well as to avert the political instability born of dissatisfaction and economic polarization, broad political participation is important as both a basic facet of democracy and a safeguard of the gains made toward equity and poverty alleviation. Therefore, the chapters of this volume look at both the economic and the participatory potentials of institutions within Central America, in recognition of the close connections between economic benefits and participation.

Finally, the commission recognized the futility of debating whether a plan for recovery and development ought to focus on immediate needs *or* on long-term development prospects. A successful strategy must do both. There is likely to be a distinct period of transition from war to peace that will present economic opportunities but also increased economic burdens. Potential opportunities include an end to the war damage and the disruption of agriculture and industry, combined with the restoration of regional trade, the redirection of external aid and domestic resources from defense to productive investment, and eventually the return of flight capital. These opportunities may be countered by the possibility of continued disorder in the regional trade and monetary system, the lack of employment for returning refugees and internally displaced persons, further deterioration of the Nicaraguan economy, and cutbacks in external aid. During this transition period it is imperative to address the *immediate* needs of the most vulnerable segments of Central American populations. These include refugees and persons displaced within their own countries, with an emphasis on the biologically vulnerable—young children, pregnant and nursing women, and the elderly—and the extremely poor, who are faced with even greater than usual economic hardships. Unless these immediate needs are met, the short-term transition phase may crumble, jeopardizing the movement toward sustained democracy and setting back Central America's socioeconomic conditions even further. Clearly, Central America's long-term prospects for stability would suffer if the region had to face a permanent underclass of refugees and displaced persons who cannot integrate productively into either new settings or their original communities. Disease and illiteracy are no less dangerous for sustained economic and political progress.

Yet the commission also recognized another level of need equally important for long-term progress: the "basic" need of reasonable access to economic opportunity, health care, nutrition, education, and housing beyond the barest necessities for survival. Even if peace, economic growth, and the formal procedures of democracy were reestablished, they would be particularly fragile in a context of extreme inequality and poverty. One lesson of the Costa Rican success story is that a relatively high degree of income equity and broad coverage of social benefits may not be sufficient conditions for genuine, sustained democracy—but they can help enormously. Therefore, several Study Task Force essays assess both immediate needs and longer-term basic needs. They avoid, however, the pitfall of searching for *the* single answer to the question of how, and at what pace, these needs must be addressed.

The Study Task Force Essays

The task force essays explore the form that Central American recovery should take. Which sectors and which institutions have the capacity to lead the way to recovery? What role can regional institutions play in recovery? How should foreign aid be channeled? How can this aid contribute to alleviating the inequities that give rise to the conflicts?

Some of the essays, such as Richard Feinberg's study of debt and Lars Schoultz's analysis of aid conditionality, deal primarily with relations between Central America and the international community. Colin Bradford offers a possible economic strategy for the Central American states, focusing on the interaction between international trade and aid and national economic policy. He explores a scenario in which prudent national policies make optimal use of foreign flows and foreign markets. Two essays address different aspects of past and present efforts to strengthen regional ties: Philip Brock looks at currency convertibility and the breakdown of intraregional trade, and Eduardo Lizano Fait analyzes past efforts and current prospects for regional economic integration.

Several essays examine the relations between government policies and key economic and social sectors, in particular, agriculture. Whatever one's long-term vision of the Central American economy might be, agriculture will remain a crucial sector for many years to come. In 1985 agricultural production accounted for 25 percent of GDP, compared to 27 percent a decade earlier, while industry's 22 percent share in 1975 remained the same in 1985 (Gallardo and López, 1986: 61, 71). In 1979 agricultural-sector exports (raw agricultural products, agro-industry products, leather, and wood) from Central America accounted for 40 percent of all of the region's exports. By 1985 agricultural-sector exports had risen to 52 percent, due largely to the decline in export-oriented industry (Lindenberg, 1987: 58–59).

Two essays examine in detail sectoral and macroeconomic policies that affect agriculture. Gustavo Arcia reviews the governments' agricultural policies and the structure of rural institutions. Cassio Luiselli focuses on those general government policies that are not commonly recognized as agricultural policies but nonetheless have an enormous impact on the agricultural sector: exchange rates, investment incentives, credit policies, and other macroeconomic policies. Both essays reveal economic discrimination against the agricultural sector despite its preeminence in the region's economies. Claudio Gonzalez Vega, assessing the performance and weaknesses of the region's financial institutions, discovers that one important aspect of such discrimination is the rural population's very limited access to credit, particularly for the smaller landowners and would-be entrepreneurs with small nonfarm businesses.

In light of Central America's heavy reliance on natural resources, Robert Healy surveys the contemporary resources and environmental situation in Central America and offers suggestions for sustainable resource-based development. Healy also examines links between the environment and other forms of economic activity, such as tourism, fishing, and forestry, and assesses the environmental impact of rapid urbanization.

Several essays examine the direct impact of past policies and the dislocation of war on the socioeconomic problems of Central America's most vulnerable populations. Sergio Aguayo evaluates the magnitude and effects of the migration and internal displacement caused by the armed conflict in Central America. John Freiberger reviews the dramatic deterioration of the region's health care systems and suggests that cooperation on health care issues can serve as a foundation for regional cooperation on a broader range of issues. In her essay on access and opportunity for women in Central America, Sally Yudelman outlines how past policies have marginalized women and explores ways to promote greater economic benefits and democratic participation for women.

Finally, three task force essays discuss past development programs for Latin America and the Caribbean. Richard McCall evaluates the Alliance for Progress, Alan Stoga examines the results of the Kissinger Commission's efforts, and Stuart Tucker looks at the Caribbean Basin Initiative. This group of essays provides the commission with an overview of the strengths and weaknesses of past aid efforts.

All of these essays share the assumption that there is an integral link between promoting more equitable economic structures and revitalizing the region's economies. The debate over the best development path for each of the Central American nations can and should be conducted in broad political and philosophical terms. However, the strictly economic dimensions of the debate cannot be ignored. As many of these essays point out, economic efficiency and equity are complementary in a number of areas: land reform (Arcia); redress of the urban, industrial, male-oriented credit and development bias (Gonzalez Vega and Yudelman); labor-intensive development strategies (Bradford); and reduced subsidization of industrial production at the expense of the agricultural sector (Brock and Lizano).

The task force has paid particularly close attention to the institutions that will have to mediate economic activity in one form or another. Gonzalez Vega's essay scrutinizes the region's banking systems, which will have to provide access to financial services for large segments of the population from owners of microenterprises to owners of middle-size farms. Philip Brock examines the Central American Clearing House, which is responsible for ensuring currency convertibility between the five Central American nations. These mediating institutions must function properly if Central America is to enjoy an economic recovery.

Current Conditions in Central America

The Central American nations have long been highly dependent on events taking place beyond their borders. The export sector has always been the main engine of growth for these economies, as well as the main source of capital accumulation and employment opportunities. During the 1960s and 1970s a rapid process of industrial growth based on the substitution of imports was initiated under the aegis of Central American economic integration. The export sector became increasingly diversified, but rates of growth continued to depend on the performance of the traditional export sector. For the region as a whole, exports as a proportion of GDP rose from less than 19 percent in 1950 to over 30 percent in 1980. Imports went from 16 percent to over 35 percent during the same period. World prices for key raw material exports, such as sugar, fruits, and cotton, were high but volatile. Intraregional trade registered impressive gains, reaching a total of $1 billion by 1980. This figure represented over 20 percent of the region's total external trade, up from 6.5 percent twenty years earlier.

During the period of growth the Central American nations built a set of regional institutions to manage the economic boom: the Secretariat of the

Treaty on Central American Integration (SIECA), the Central American Bank for Economic Integration (CABEI), the Monetary Council, the Central American Clearing House (CACH), and others, including sectoral institutions. Together, these specific institutions constitute the "Central American Common Market."

The integration model began to unravel in the late 1970s. The region faced external economic shocks, including higher oil prices, high real interest rates on foreign debt, and depressed commodity prices for its principal exports (including coffee, sugar, and bananas). Trade fell sharply and intraregional commerce suffered an even more severe decline. By 1986 trade within the region was down to U.S. $389 million, a 60 percent reduction, according to Philip Brock's essay. The region also began accumulating a large external debt, totaling $17 billion by 1987 and drawing off interest payments equal to over 20 percent of both Nicaragua's and Costa Rica's export revenues. National savings rates fell to 10 percent for the region, down from 19 percent in 1977. Gross domestic product for the region fell steadily from 1979 to 1987.

The regional institutions lost their effectiveness. By 1981 all five nations had imposed new taxes on imports in order to avoid devaluation. As Nicaragua and El Salvador began to run up large debts with the other three nations (particularly Costa Rica), the creditor nations began to impose trade restrictions. In 1981 the Central American Clearing House (CACH) handled all commercial payments between the five nations. By 1986, only 45 percent of official transactions went through CACH. The unpaid balances have become the central obstacle to overcoming the contraction of intraregional trade. The essays by Brock and Lizano in this volume chronicle the decline in regional commerce.

The region's economic crisis, in conjunction with the military conflicts, has also had a profound social impact. It has created new problems such as massive population migrations and exacerbated existing problems such as inadequate health care. Sergio Aguayo writes that between 1.8 and 2.8 million Central Americans have been displaced by the wars and the economic dislocations. The commission has identified these refugees and internally displaced persons, together with the biologically vulnerable (including pregnant and nursing women, young children, and the elderly), as the sectors of the population most in need of immediate aid if Central America is to move forward.

The refugee problem has placed an additional burden on the countries' already-fragile health care systems. In his chapter on Central America's health systems John Freiberger notes that 40 percent of Central Americans have no access to organized health care and 50 percent lack access to safe drinking water. Health—along with education—has also suffered as a consequence of the fiscal shortfalls. Macroeconomic problems compound already serious difficulties, especially in health. The shortage of foreign exchange restricts the purchase of medical technology, spare parts, and medicines. The Central American nations have inadequate funds to train auxiliary medical personnel, such as nurses and X-ray technicians, or to pay salaries high enough to attract sufficient numbers of people into those fields. Central America's overall shortage of physicians is exacerbated by this severe lack of auxiliary medical personnel.

Structural Weaknesses. Beneath the economic and social statistics are *institutional* weaknesses that are carefully dissected in the essays of this volume. To some degree the vulnerability of the Central American economies to the swings in international trade and monetary conditions stems from internal weaknesses of these economies—although few economies of indebted developing countries could have weathered the combination of low commodity prices and unprecedented increases in world interest rates that occurred in the 1980s.

All the essays touch on some form of bias or distortions that have promoted inequities and lessened efficiency. These include favoring urban development over rural development, discrimination against women in education, credit and access to land, foreign aid that benefits the few, inadequate access to credit for owners of small and medium-sized farms and for entrepreneurs in the informal sector, and the perpetuation of a two-tiered economy populated by large commercial farmers on the one hand and land-poor peasants and rural laborers on the other. The list is long and ranges from macroeconomic distortions such as overvalued exchange rates to institutional weaknesses such as inadequate mechanisms for establishing land titles.

The economic model that generated such rapid growth in the 1960s has been exposed as deeply flawed. While the region was growing, structural weaknesses went unrecognized or were ignored. For example, the banking systems (with the possible exception of Costa Rica's) remained underdeveloped, allowing credit to be rationed to industrial and agricultural concerns on the basis of connections rather than economic productivity. Although the governments will have to weigh the costs and benefits of trying to fine-tune credit policy as an instrument for promoting particular sectors or regions, Gonzalez Vega documents how Central American credit systems, at least in El Salvador, Guatemala, and Honduras, are so skewed that the first order of business is simply to move closer to income and regional neutrality in the availability of credit.

Similarly, some of the industrial development under the tariff protection of the Central American Common Market lacked the efficiency to compete on a more open basis. Tax structures remained ineffective and inequitable. The large peasant populations generally remained outside the economic mainstream of the "modern sector." For Central America to achieve sustained peace and development, the basic model, along with its attendant institutions, must be altered.

External Assistance. As demonstrated in several of this volume's chapters— Richard Feinberg's on the debt, Eduardo Lizano's on regional integration, and Philip Brock's study of intraregional trade and currency convertibility— Central America will need external support if it is to recover. But, for some of the reasons cited in the previous section, underlying structural and institutional problems must be addressed before proposing a program for external assistance or trade openings.

Three Study Task Force essays examine past aid initiatives for Latin America or the Caribbean Basin. The Alliance for Progress, discussed by Richard McCall, began its life operating with a new development principle that stressed social reform and democratic political processes as much as economic growth. But in response to forces in the United States and in Latin America, the Alliance shortly became "just another aid program," promoting economic growth but following the recipient country's existing pattern of income distribution.

The Alliance approach also contained a largely unexamined bias in favor of industrialization and manufacturing over agricultural development, which contributed to inequality and too-rapid urbanization by widening the rural-urban income gap. Ironically, the Alliance was noted for its emphasis on land reform, but this was a matter—albeit a very important one—of distribution *within* the rural sector. This unbalanced development also created barriers to an effective export orientation necessary to balance foreign trade and restrain foreign indebtedness. The waste and inequity involved in the Alliance for Progress boom reveal the pitfalls of major aid infusions, but they are avoidable pitfalls.

The Kissinger Commission in 1984 identified many of the same problems addressed by the International Commission for Central American Recovery and Development. Alan Stoga writes that the Kissinger Commission's effectiveness was reduced because it failed to sell its program to the U.S. bureaucracy that would have to implement the initiatives. Although much of the economic and security assistance urged by the Kissinger Commission has been disbursed, that aid has focused on short-term stabilization and military concerns, while its longer-term development initiatives remain dormant. Another problem is that Central Americans did not participate in drafting the plan, and Central American governments did not comply with many of the conditions of U.S. aid for long-term development. Again, this very complicated issue of providing aid with conditions attached is analyzed in Lars Schoultz' essay, which illuminates the dilemmas of both the Alliance for Progress and the Kissinger Commission plan. Moreover, the Kissinger Commission was working at a time when a lasting peace permitting coherent long-term plans was not foreseeable. That situation has now changed. So too has the old order in which the United States was more or less the only significant foreign donor and lender to Central America. The very active participation of Europeans, Japanese, and Canadians in the commission's work is but one indication of the increased importance of Central America to these nations and of their greater willingness to cooperate in bringing stability and prosperity to the region.

As several of the essays point out, even large amounts of financial aid will not help the region as much as the revival of international trade and the opening of markets in North America, Western Europe, and Japan. The Reagan administration's Caribbean Basin Initiative (CBI) has attempted to use trade openings to promote growth in the region, but, as Stuart Tucker points out, the trade concessions respond more to U.S. security concerns than to the region's development needs. What limited successes the CBI has had demonstrate the potential effectiveness of a broader liberalization of U.S. trade. Tucker adds that trade alone is not sufficient for regional economic recovery. The United States and other donor countries must support the reconstruction of Central America's infrastructure and the revitalization of regional trade and coordination through the Central American

Bank for Economic Integration and the Central American Common Market.
Meanwhile, as noted by Luiselli and Arcia, some type of short-term
commodity stabilization scheme is needed.

The essays in this volume help to clarify the relationships among aid,
trade, and institutional reform. Aid that does not spur sustainable development is only recycled to meet the region's debt payments. Additional external
aid will have few long-term benefits if Central America cannot find new
markets for its goods. Small economies depend heavily on trade, and although
the Lizano essay is an eloquent argument for the revitalization of Central
American by strengthening regional economic institutions, extraregional
trade will undoubtedly remain crucial to both recovery and long-term
development. Indeed, Lizano notes that the most thoughtful architects of
the Central American Common Market viewed it as a mechanism for
promoting Central America's insertion into the world market rather than as
a pretext for protectionism that would permanently insulate inefficient
Central American industry from outside competition. Yet for trade to
flourish, foreign markets must be open at any given point in time, but there
must also be enough certainty that those markets will remain open so as to
attract the necessary investment to build Central America's export potential.

Institutional and policy reforms are in turn linked to the effectiveness of
aid in taking advantage of these trade opportunities and other potentials for
economic recovery. The distortions in the provision of credit and investment
incentives not only perpetuate inequality, they also impede economic efficiency. Aid will be of limited effectiveness if it is not accompanied by
institutional reform, as demonstrated by McCall's essay on the Alliance for
Progress and by the Arcia and Gonzalez Vega essays on rural development
and credit mechanisms, respectively. Donor countries will certainly attach
conditions to any aid to Central America. What is important is that these
conditions focus not on short-term stabilization, but on longer-term reform
of the region's credit institutions, agricultural institutions, and regional
monetary facilities.

Just as the need for policy reform is not confined to the Central American
governments, but rather extends to the trade and aid policies of the industrial
countries, so too the *institutions* through which the industrial nations interact
with Central America require rethinking. The essays by Schoultz and McCall
call into question the predominantly bilateral thrust of aid to Central America.
The complexity of Central America's development challenges and the

multiplicity of outside agents (national governments, nongovernmental organizations, and international organizations such as the World Bank, United Nations Development Programme, and the Inter-American Development Bank) call for greater coordination of aid, trade policy, and development program implementation.

Prospects for Reform, Recovery, and Sustained Development

It is outside the scope of this volume to speculate on the prospects for peace in the near future. Certainly the Central American nations, backed by the international community, have taken some important steps toward achieving peace and laying the foundation for postwar Central America. If peace does come soon, the five Central American countries will be in a position to tap into new forces in the region that will help promote balanced growth and the continuation of recent political openings. If the wars continue, the nations will almost certainly not be able to pull themselves out of their economic decline. Yet, to put these essays into perspective, it is important to return to the question of the long-range economic outlook and to link the economic possibilities to political and military scenarios.

The Study Task Force essays confirm the commission's premise that economic recovery and sustained, equitable development are critical requirements for any stable future for Central America. No matter what interpretation is given to the origins of the political instability and armed conflict in the region, the current economic stagnation and the precariousness of many segments of the Central American population present serious obstacles to regional peace and stability. It is fair to conclude that economic prosperity with equity for Central America is both beneficial in its own right *and* essential for peace.

If this formula is separated into its three components- -economic recovery, long-term sustainability, and equity—there is some basis for optimism. Although Central America has clearly been going through a downward economic spiral, the prospects for recovery are bolstered by the demonstrated potential of intraregional trade to propel some growth. The Central American Common Market, whatever its weaknesses and ultimate limitations, was responsible for the considerable increases in production and regional trade that have all but disappeared over the past decade. The resumption of that exchange, even without going beyond what the Central American Common

Market had accomplished before, would contribute considerably to growth in the entire region.

The prospects for recovery are also bolstered by the fact that cessation of hostilities will eliminate the enormous drag on the Central American economies resulting from the destruction of crops and roads, the diversion of resources away from productive investment into defense and the care of refugees, and the abysmal investment climate of a war-torn region. The economic levels reached in the 1970s were not flukes—Central America was not "living beyond its means" through massive external borrowing channeled into consumption, as were certain other Latin American countries. Therefore, the aggregate economic performances reached before 1980 reflect plausible targets for short-term recovery that would nonetheless constitute impressive improvements over today's situation. Nor is the debt situation a dead end for Central American recovery. As Richard Feinberg argues in his essay, only Costa Rica and Nicaragua have massive debts relative to their export potentials, and sensible, case-by-case approaches to debt management by the Central American governments and the creditors can do much to resolve the debt problems.

The question of the sustainability of economic development is much thornier. One side of sustainability is the natural resource endowment that is so important for countries with such large agricultural sectors. Robert Healy's assessment of Central America's ecological issues points to deforestation, the conversion of cropland into low-yielding pasture, greater demands on water and other resources, and other environmental stresses as potentially serious constraints on long-term development.

The other side of sustainability is the issue of population pressure. Sally Yudelman's essay on the plight of women in Central America should be read not only as an assessment of the problems of women and the young children who depend on them, but also as a chilling diagnosis of why population planning has largely failed in Central America. When parents are insecure about their economic or physical well-being and about their children's prospects for survival, they tend to have more children, so that it is more likely that some will survive to support them. Thus the sources of poverty outlined by Aguayo, Arcia, Gonzalez Vega, and Yudelman are directly relevant to the population pressures that have already had a very negative impact on economic progress in El Salvador.

The issues of poverty and inequality are, of course, equally troubling, all the more so because of the politically explosive nature of such redistributive questions. In one ironic sense the prospects for addressing poverty and inequality are better for the lack of progress made thus far in this area. Undoubtedly Central American leaders have drawn lessons from more than a decade of war and economic deterioration. In Esquipulas the leaders of Central America have explicitly recognized the connections between lasting peace and the social and economic reforms that can provide the basis for more stable political arrangements. The Nicaraguan revolution is an obvious example of how dissatisfaction over political and economic injustice can lead to the overthrow of even a long-entrenched regime.

Yet there are at least three very troubling scenarios. One is the possibility that if an economic growth spurt occurs, perhaps due to little more than a reduction in armed conflict or a surge in intraregional trade without any fundamental policy or institutional reforms, the reforms may be postponed indefinitely so as not to risk what seems to be a healthy recovery. Although current policies and structures place great constraints on long-term economic growth, as demonstrated by the studies in this volume, this may not be apparent or politically palatable to policymakers.

Even if rapid economic recovery occurs, it will undoubtedly be accompanied by such "growing pains" as inflation, rising imports, and (particularly if aid is reduced) government deficits. Will the management of these problems make the marginal populations worse off? The reader may find it useful to review the essays on debt and conditionality, and on the past experiences of Central America's relations with the outside world, with an eye to the question of whether "stabilization with a human face"—i.e., sober economic management that does not increase the burden on the poor—is politically and institutionally viable.

Second, the absolute deterioration in the living standards of the most vulnerable populations may make their situations seem hopeless to policymakers concerned with the promotion of immediate growth. The gravest danger lies in the possibility that the governments will write off the marginal populations, leaving another source of future political eruption. The problems do not disappear with the end of military conflict. With respect to refugees and displaced persons, Aguayo points out that some families will never go back; others will return only to find themselves dispossessed of their land. Unless generous aid is forthcoming for refugees and internally displaced people, the results of emigration and internal dislocation (as outlined in

Aguayo's essay) will include both the irreversible destruction of communities, because some skilled community members will never return, and the permanence of refugee settlements, many offering little prospect of economic productivity or adequate government services.

Failure to rebuild the infrastructure of health and sanitation holds the same perils. As tragic as the collapse of the health infrastructure is in sheer human terms, it is also a potential economic catastrophe in terms of reduced future labor productivity and the long-term health care costs to treat the consequences of malnutrition (documented in Arcia's essay), the spread of infectious diseases (documented by Freiberger), and substandard maternal and child care (assessed by Yudelman).

Third, the one new ominous possibility that has not been manifested in the decline over the last decade is the possibility that the withdrawal of economic and military aid from economies increasingly dependent on such aid will create new problems. Given that recovery will be costly—refugees will have to be repatriated or resettled, soldiers will have to be reintegrated into other employment, infrastructure will have to be repaired—the reduction of aid for a region of decreased "strategic risk" is a sobering possibility. To be sure, the impressive interest in Central America on the part of Canadian and Western European leaders bodes well for the willingness of other governments to fill the vacuum that could result if the United States decreases its aid. And in light of the risk that Central American governments may be prone to disregard the marginal populations, donors may well focus their aid efforts on these groups.

Conclusion

As an adjunct to the International Commission for Central American Recovery and Development, the Study Task Force addressed essentially the same question faced by the commission: Can a plausible scenario of peace and economic progress be written for Central America? The answer seems to be yes, but the hoped-for emergence of peace will not provide it automatically. In a very powerful sense, the diagnoses of the essays in this volume reinforce the need for the kind of comprehensive blueprint that the commission has undertaken. An important motive of both efforts has been to demonstrate that peace is indeed consistent with economic prosperity, given that the current military buildup entailing considerable foreign aid might be jeopardized if peace "breaks out." Some fear that peace will bring economic collapse and that it therefore constitutes a dangerous potential obstacle to the resolution of Central America's conflicts. Therefore, in asking whether a plausible scenario of peace and economic progress can be written for Central America, both the commission and the Study Task Force are asking what this scenario would require in terms of trade opportunities and economic aid from the donor countries. What sorts of changes are necessary in national, regional, and international institutions? The commission's vision of a postwar Central America hinges on support from industrial countries—in the form of aid, more attractive lending, and improved trade—for both greater economic efficiency and greater equity. It also includes, through a series of reforms at key institutions, a more active role for women's groups, indigenous groups, labor unions, nongovernmental organizations, and peasants. Thus, although the essays in this volume do not provide a comprehensive overview of all the issues concerning Central American development, they do provide insights into the linkages among external relations, policy changes, institutional reform, and the need to broaden economic and political participation in Central America.

References

Gallardo, María, and José López (1986). *Centroamérica: La crisis en cifras*. San José, Costa Rica: Instituto Interamericano de Cooperación para la Agricultura and Facultad Latinoaméricana de Ciencias Sociales.

Lindenberg, Marc (1987). "La recuperación económica de Centro América: Mito y realidad," in Forrest Colburn, ed. *Centroamérica: Estrategias de desarrollo*. San José, Costa Rica: Editorial Universitaria Centroamericana.

Part 1

Central America's Domestic Problems and Potentials

Chapter 1

Displaced Persons and Central American Recuperation and Development

Sergio Aguayo

Introduction

The cessation of hostilities in Central America will not automatically bring about a return to normal life. Central America has changed profoundly. Ten years of war have devastated the economies, altered the political systems, displaced societies and modified international relations. Peace—a gradual and irregular process—requires reconstruction and development, and these present enormous challenges.

The number of displaced persons is immense. Estimates run from 1.8 million to 2.8 million people. This represents varying percentages of each country's population: between 3 and 7.5 percent of Guatemalans and between 25 and 29 percent of Salvadorans. Their existence presents us with difficult challenges in humanitarian, economic, political, legal, and international terms.

This chapter is based on a simple assumption: peace does not automatically resolve the problems of this displaced population. Undoubtedly peace is the basis for any lasting solution, but the duration and scale of the demographic movements have given them autonomy. The violence could diminish or cease, but the Central American demographic map has been modified—in some ways irreversibly. The implications of these changes are as yet difficult to determine.

In the past few years great efforts have been made to identify and understand the characteristics of this phenomenon, and the literature is vast and diverse. There are newspaper articles, reports of all kinds, and some fifty academic works on the subject of demographic changes involving Central America, Mexico and the United States.[1] The accumulated knowledge is considerable but still insufficient. To begin with, there is a fundamental problem: we do not know the exact number of displaced persons. Except for the 116,008 refugees recognized by the United Nations High Commissioner for Refugees (UNHCR),[2] estimates are based upon mere appraisals.

On the other hand, the existing works have been dedicated, above all, to describing the phenomenon and defending the Central Americans. Therefore, they have emphasized the political, international, and legal aspects of the refugees. Few works review the economic impact of the displacements of people, and those that exist are not sufficient to permit valid generalizations in terms of all countries.

In the literature about the massive flow of Central Americans, it is correctly assumed that the best solution for the displaced is the return to their place of origin. Nonetheless, the studies on this and other migrations have emphasized the situation in the receiving countries even though the conditions in the countries of origin will determine repatriation.[3] The return to peace and the reconstruction of economies and communities are the central factors.

In the following discussion (which presents only the broadest and most general concepts), the variety of situations and the great number of actors involved in the phenomenon should also be taken into account. In the arena of the displaced Central Americans, the participants include regional and European governments, international organizations like the United Nations High Commissioner for Refugees (UNHCR), political institutions, religious groups, and private development agencies.

In view of the above, it is difficult to establish recommendations for the future. Still, it is essential to begin to explore the links between displaced persons and reconstruction and development. Achieving a satisfactory response to the challenges presented by the displaced Central American population would be an historic step forward that could serve in confronting the phenomenon of massive displacements common in other parts of the world.

Review of a Decade of Displacement

In order to assess the impact of the displaced and to recommend responses, we must first look at what has taken place in a decade of peoples being displaced within their countries and abroad. Observers and students of the phenomenon have estimated that between 1.8 million and 2.8 million have left their place of residence in recent years. Of these, about 1 million are displaced in four countries (El Salvador, Guatemala, Nicaragua, and Honduras); the rest are dispersed throughout at least 11 countries. UNHCR estimates that there are some 300,000 residing outside their own country (not including those in the United States), but it has recognized and protected only 116,000.

Those Displaced Within Their Own Countries

Those considered to be displaced within their own countries are people who have changed their place of residence within their own borders for reasons connected with the conflict. The country most affected is El Salvador, followed by Nicaragua and Guatemala. A special case worthy of mention is Honduras. Although the conflict within Honduras is minor, 35,000 people are displaced by the Nicaraguan counterrevolution; for many years the Honduran government has denied the existence of these contras in Honduras.

The primary factors causing displacement are the violence of certain military campaigns that do not discriminate between combatant and civilian populations, and the economic devastation caused by the conflicts. In fact, a direct correlation exists between the number of people displaced and the intensity of the counterinsurgency campaigns (in Guatemala, 1982 estimates reached 1 million, while now they are at 250,000).[4]

Another cause of displacement is that some people or groups foresee the possibility (actual or potential) of being affected by the confrontation. A third factor is forced relocation for military reasons. This practice has been followed by the governments of three countries: the *Plan Mil* ("Plan One Thousand") of the Christian Democratic Party of El Salvador, the *Aldeas Modelos* ("Model Villages") and the *Polos de Desarrollo* ("Development Areas") of Guatemala, and the relocation carried out by the Sandinista Army in some parts of Nicaragua.[5]

Displaced persons are in a difficult situation both because they receive little protection and because the majority do not receive material assistance. In El Salvador, of the estimated 500,000 displaced persons, only 17 or 18 percent are given aid. Of those, 60 percent receive the help of a government more interested in controlling them than in resolving their situation. The other 40 percent are assisted by private international agencies.[6]

This lack of attention has various explanations. First, the violent situation causes displaced persons to remain scattered and hidden. Second, the attention given those displaced within their own borders is outside the jurisdiction of many humanitarian organizations (including UNHCR). Third, and perhaps most important, the possibility of helping displaced persons depends upon the will of their government. In Guatemala, for example, the authorities are not inclined to permit the presence of international organizations that wish to maintain a certain independence from official control. Managua allows greater freedom to operate, and for that reason there are dozens of organizations working in Nicaragua with the displaced.[7]

Those displaced within their own countries are, on the other hand, a potential (reserve) of international refugees. In studies on refugees, one of the most difficult problems is to determine the causes that lead individuals or groups to leave their countries. When we are able to understand these dynamics (for example, determining how many of those actually recognized as refugees were previously displaced in their own countries), it will be easier to establish the importance of attending to this community. Actually, some private international agencies have been expanding their mandates to include internally displaced persons. These agencies maintain that it is better to help the displaced while they are in their own country, before they become refugees.

There is no doubt that because of the great number of people affected, any plan for reconstruction and development must include the displaced. The central problem, however, is that this requires the collaboration of the local governments, which is difficult to obtain as long as they do not form part of a global plan for pacification and reconciliation. I will return to this point later.

Those Displaced Abroad

Estimates are that almost 2 million Salvadorans, Guatemalans, and Nicaraguans are living outside their own countries. What we are witnessing is a migration from Central America to North America. Between 87 and 88 percent of the Central Americans who have left their countries are now in Mexico and the United States, countries that for a variety of economic, political, and geographic factors have become the principal receiving countries for Central Americans. This implies that, from the start, these two countries must participate in the search for any possible solution to the refugee problem.

The same factors that lead to internal displacement also influence those who decide to leave their country. To these factors must be added the influence of economic distinctions between countries and the existence of migratory networks. Migration from Central America to North America has been possible because land travel is inexpensive and because the borders have been relatively open. This last element is ignored in the studies on the topic, despite its fundamental importance. I will therefore discuss it further.

In Central America there is an old migratory tradition among countries. With the war in the region, migration has been reoriented toward North America. This destination is encouraged because Salvadorans, Nicaraguans, and Hondurans do not need a visa to enter into Guatemala. They arrive easily at the Mexican border, for which they do need a visa but into which they can enter without papers through the region of El Soconusco (level ground of some 70 kilometers between the Pacific and the mountains). Due to a series of economic and political factors El Soconusco is an open border that is virtually impossible to seal. Once in Mexico, ethnic and linguistic similarities allow for their integration into the local population. Those who decide to continue the trip to the United States—in part compelled by the Mexican economic crisis—make use of the existence of a sophisticated and old migratory tradition between Mexico and the United States (another border equally easy to cross).

Part of the reason for the precarious conditions facing the displaced is that the number of those recognized and protected as refugees by UNHCR is very limited. It follows, then, that recognition is one of the central problems of this community. I will return to the legal questions, but for the moment I will note a central issue: some institution or government must decide who is a refugee, who a displaced person, and who is a migrant for economic reasons. The criterion used most often is an evaluation of the conditions of the country of origin. As a result, the prevailing political and ideological influences of the region are factors even when the problem of the displaced is eminently humanitarian.

The Response to the Central Americans

Reactions to the massive arrival of Central Americans have been diverse. Despite this, two basic tendencies can be identified within each country and on a regional basis: on the one hand, there is a humanitarian position that has sought to resolve the problems of this community, and on the other, efforts have been made not to receive the people but to expel them and to encourage them to go to other countries.

These two tendencies have been neither exclusive nor constant. Generally they coexist within a single country, although there are cycles in which humanitarianism or restrictive tendencies are dominant. For example, in 1981 the Mexican government deported Guatemalan peasants under the premise that they did not qualify individually for asylum. Months later the government allowed them to stay, and in 1984 it agreed to let some of them participate in self-sufficiency projects. At the same time, Mexico promoted a generous regional solution, while refusing to recognize the majority of Central Americans within its borders. Still, it maintained a certain flexibility.

Ambiguities of this kind are repeated in other countries because in responding to the displaced, a good number of actors intervene for humanitarian, ideological, political, and economic reasons. In other words, even when the phenomenon of the displaced should be governed by humanitarian considerations, it cannot escape political reality.

This is evident if we review the case of the UNHCR, an institution created by the international community to address the phenomenon of refugees and displaced persons. Its mandate is humanitarian but must be adapted to the reality in which it operates. This is revealed in the numerical estimates that it produces. It estimates that there are 300,000 Central American refugees, but for political reasons does not include the United States, where the greatest number of Central Americans are concentrated. It could then be argued (and is by many) that the number of refugees is much higher.

Another problem appears when determining who qualifies as a refugee. The international community has created two criteria: the narrow or "classical" one and the broad one. The former recognizes specific persons who have escaped persecution against them or who have a well-founded fear of suffering persecution. In this case the situation of each individual is the determining factor. The broad criteria (prima facie) protects mass migrations to neighboring countries and is based on evaluations of the general conditions of a country or the regions of a country.[8]

UNHCR uses both definitions in Central America, although it has favored the broad criteria; 80 percent of those recognized as refugees come under this category (especially those who are actually in camps). The other 20 percent, especially those who have traveled individually or in small groups, meet the "classical" criteria. In some circumstances UNHCR does not use any definition because it does not protect the refugees. In Mexico it responds only to those soliciting asylum in the capital, ignoring some outlying regions with a strong Central American presence. More disturbing—although politically understandable—is that UNHCR carries out minimal protective activity in the United States, where the greatest number of Central Americans are concentrated.

Of course in some countries UNHCR has had an exceptionally protective role. I would like to emphasize that the work of UNHCR has not taken place in a political vacuum, but rather is conditioned by nonhumanitarian interests. With more or less intensity, these politicizing influences have appeared in the reactions of governments and private institutions.

The Hospitable Response

The hospitable response has various explanations. First is the old tradition of asylum in Latin American countries, the United States, and Canada. Next would be political reasons (solidarity with some parts of the conflict) and economic reasons (the desire of some employers to count on a reserve of cheap labor). The result is that Central Americans have come upon sectors within the bureaucracy and groups within the society that have become their protectors.

This hospitality is supported and strengthened by the influence of external actors such as UNHCR, some nongovernmental organizations, and interested governments. It is fitting to wonder what would have happened with the Salvadoran refugees in Honduras (given the historical resentment these two countries hold toward each other) or with the Guatemalans in Mexico if it were not for this external factor.

Hospitality implies protection, which has legal, material, and political dimensions. Before discussing these dimensions, it is necessary to briefly place them in a time frame. Between approximately 1977 and 1983, the response and the proposals were oriented toward resolving the most immediate problems, because it was generally assumed that the phenomenon would be of short duration. When the perception of the conflict changed in 1983–84 and it became evident that there would be no immediate peace, long-term solutions were sought and some of the more structural aspects of the Central American conflict were explored.

The ideal situation would be for the international community to decide, through UNHCR and using some of the previously mentioned criteria, that an individual or group is or are refugees. Those selected would acquire a legal status entitling them to receive emergency support, to participate in economic self-sufficiency projects, and to have support when they decide to return to their countries.

The ideal, however, often clashes with the political and economic realities of each country, resulting in different interpretations and manifestations of this protection. To shed light upon a complex history, let us take the legal aspect in Mexico and the United States. In Mexico, the defenders of the Central Americans have never been very concerned with making changes in existing legislation, in which the refugee does not figure. Interest was concentrated on reaching a political decision that would allow the refugees to stay. In the United States, to the contrary, a good portion of the defense has been in the legal arena.

Emergency assistance incorporates all the emergency material provided to refugees to enable them to regain some degree of control over their daily lives. Legal recognition is not always essential in order for assistance to be given; many programs attend to the unrecognized.

Emergency assistance presents the risk that, if extended for a long time, it feeds the syndrome of dependency common in refugee camps. To avoid this, the most logical answer is the economic self-sufficiency programs that require accepting a certain permanence. There are all kinds of experiences of this nature in the region.

Nicaragua has developed the most positive policies. Even the U.S. State Department acknowledges that it "provides the refugees with residency and work permits and accords them treatment essentially like that enjoyed by Nicaraguan citizens." Accepting permanent residents as described is the exception rather than the rule. Integrating them into their new setting has usually been avoided, the objective being that they return to their place of origin.

There are, however, a number of self-sufficiency programs. The experience in the region is disparate. Among larger self-sufficiency programs, one finds both the unsuccessful "Los Angeles" project in Costa Rica for Salvadorans, and the relatively successful self-sufficiency programs for some 20,000

Guatemalans in Campeche and Quintana Roo (Mexico). Similarly, there are both successes and failures in microprojects implemented throughout the region.

What is certain is that the implementation of lasting solutions is technically and politically complex. The most constant problem has been that when the implementing agencies formulate programs, they rarely consider the experience and desires of the refugees. When active participation of the refugees is included in all the stages of the projects, the possibilities for success are notably enhanced.[9]

Restrictive Tendencies

The restrictive tendency originates in several factors, first of all in the very generalized belief that displaced populations have a negative impact on the receiving society. Competition for scarce jobs or a contaminating or disruptive political effect are the most commonly used arguments.

Elements in each country's particular history also contribute to a negative attitude toward refugees. In the United States, for example, the arrival of the Mariel Cubans and of Haitians and Mexicans has reinforced concern for control of the borders since the early 1980s. Similar influences are the anti-Salvadoran sentiments in Honduras or the Costa Rican anti-Sandinista sentiment generalized as also anti-Nicaraguan.

Manifestations of restrictive tendencies are facilitated because the domestic legislation of the countries of the region was shaped by a fundamentally individual tradition of asylum that allowed a certain control over the selection and integration of the newcomers. At present, however, the displaced are numerous, are generally poor, and arrive to the different territories in an uncontrolled manner.

Viewed from a strictly legal perspective, restrictive tendencies have triumphed because only 116,000 Central Americans have been recognized by the international community as refugees. In practice, however, this is not so clear. The most important receiving countries—Mexico and the United States—have maintained a certain tolerance. The reasons are different, but an important factor is that there are groups that defend the Central Americans. These groups may not have achieved recognition for them, but they have avoided mass deportation.

In a certain sense one can speak of a standstill that has drawn the countries of the region, with the exception of Nicaragua, into inaction or temporary and insufficient solutions. The problem is recognized, but a definitive position is avoided. For example, in the United States the displaced Central Americans are illegal, but there have been no campaigns of massive deportations; in Costa Rica they are recognized as refugees but their work permits are restricted for several years.

A Regional Perspective

Since 1986 there have been important qualitative changes. In November of that year the Congress of the United States approved a new immigration law. Although it is still not possible to determine the actual effect of this law, apparently sanctions against employers and greater control of the border could substantially modify the nature of the border between the United States and Mexico (especially considering increased drug traffic control). This law, adopted for domestic reasons, accelerated restrictive attitudes that were already appearing in the region. Since 1985 the Mexican government has tried to improve control over its southern border, and in October 1986 the Mexican consulates in Central America tightened visa requirements. In February 1987 Canada announced that it would no longer accept requests for territorial asylum; this was a response to the arrival of thousands of Central Americans fearful of the effects of the immigration law in the United States. Guatemala and Costa Rica are also reevaluating their migration policies. In other words, the open nature of regional borders is slowly being modified.

At this time it is impossible to say whether or not restrictive tendencies will overrule hospitable ones. This is true mostly because a regional search for collective and generous solutions and the phenomenon of displacement appear simultaneously. This attitude forms part of the pacifist spirit initiated in Contadora and continued in Esquipulas and the Arias Plan. Among the pacifist actions of the Contadora Group is a whole chapter of the Peace and Cooperation Act dedicated to the refugee problem.[10]

More important for the objectives of this paper is the Cartagena Declaration, adopted in November 1984 by UNHCR and the governments of the region (excluding the United States, which was not invited). In this declaration a very broad definition of who qualifies as a refugee was adopted. In contrast to the traditional definition, in which the central criteria is that there be a well-founded fear of persecution, this one considers refugees to be persons who have "fled their countries because their life, security, or liberty have been threatened by general violence, foreign aggression, internal conflicts, massive violation of human rights, or other circumstances that have seriously disturbed public order."[11]

The force of this declaration is more symbolic than real, but it represents an important doctrinal advance in the need to modernize the tradition of Latin American asylum upon the appearance of massive tides of population. It is equally significant that the initiative had continuity with a series of discussions in May 1987 by a group of eight experts invited by UNHCR. Although they were invited as individuals, six of them are high Central American and Mexican government officials.[12] Among their conclusions are support for a peaceable solution to the conflict, a reaffirmation of the Cartagena Declaration, a call for respect for human rights, an expression of support for efforts toward repatriation, and a recommendation that the demographic dimension of the displaced be better evaluated.[13]

Another manifestation of the search for solutions to the refugee situation is the creation of tripartite commissions—or of bilateral negotiations—to begin handling the desires of different refugee groups for repatriation. To date, commissions have operated, with greater or lesser success, between Nicaragua and Honduras, Nicaragua and Costa Rica, Honduras and El Salvador, and Mexico and Guatemala. In each of these UNHCR has played an important role as catalyst.

Thus in each of the countries and in the region as a whole we find the clash between humanitarian and restrictive tendencies. Efforts to understand the phenomenon of the displaced from a broader perspective are also in evidence. In this vein, it must be pointed out that these efforts are gradually becoming integrated into the framework of the search for peace. Nonetheless, none of the abovementioned documents elaborates the potential nexus between the displaced peoples and development. In part this is because there is little knowledge of the real impact of the displaced community.

The Impact of the Displaced

One of the most important and difficult questions to answer is: What impact have the displaced had on development? This assessment must form the basis of any proposal encouraging the displaced to participate in development.

Unfortunately, this is the aspect of displacement about which the least research has been done. It is generally said that although displaced persons affect the receiving country, the greatest effects are felt by the displaced and the countries of origin. To facilitate analysis I will once again divide the discussion of the impact on the displaced.

Those Displaced Within Their Own Country

Although this section is based on research on those displaced within El Salvador and Guatemala, certain conclusions could also apply to Nicaragua. In Central America, the displaced population is made up of peasants expelled to urban areas (in El Salvador 85 percent of a group surveyed came from rural areas). Among these the majority are children, women, and the elderly.[14] The effects and problems presented by this population can be synthesized as follows:

(a) The distribution of the Central American population between rural and urban areas is changing radically. As time goes on, the possibility of their returning to their places of origin diminishes. This indicates a process of progressive deruralization in societies that are fundamentally agrarian.

(b) The rate of growth and the pyramid population structure are changing. In El Salvador the age pyramid is becoming recessive for males and for those between 15 and 35 years old, while the dependent portion of the population is growing.

(c) Urban unemployment and subemployment are growing markedly more acute (for example, 73.6 percent of a sample of displaced people surveyed in El Salvador were unemployed).

(d) The number of precarious, marginal settlements is increasing in the cities. This implies reduced access to educational and health services. The rate of illiteracy is also on the rise.

(e) Their very status as displaced persons accentuates conditions of permanent insecurity (having fled their place of origin makes many of them suspicious to security forces). The fact that sometimes they do not have their papers available heightens their sense of insecurity and facilitates the exploitation to which they are often subjected.

(f) These and other elements have intensified mental health problems, especially among children who feel great social isolation because they are discriminated against or excluded. In Guatemala very clear distinctions are made between those who escaped to Mexico and those who remained in their place of origin.

(g) The creation of strong control mechanisms in the countryside have profoundly altered the nature of economic activities. In the *Aldeas Modelos* ("Model Communities") and the *Polos de Desarrollo* ("Development Areas") in Guatemala, for example, the population is concentrated, has difficulty getting to the farmland, and cannot leave the area for long, which prevents the traditional migration to the coast.

(h) In El Salvador unemployment fosters the militarization of the society, because often the only source of income for a family is through the enlistment of some of its members in the armed forces. In Guatemala, the forced integration into the Civil Patrol system, which consists of 1 million men out of a population of 8 million, is a break from the traditional community-based structure.

(i) The war and generalized inflation also alter the conditions of normal life: the prices of agricultural products increase, and the number of domestic animals is reduced. In Guatemala the loss of one or two harvests has affected an already precarious diet.

(j) In some regions the agrarian property structure, already inequitable, is suffering changes. The forced abandonment of land means that the land can be occupied by peasants who are loyal to one of the sides, or by individuals with more political or economic power.

(k) In the case of the displaced who receive help, a relationship of dependency on the offering organization is seen to develop.

These consequences of displacement—some of which also affect those who are abroad—must be further studied, including what is happening in Nicaragua and Honduras.

Refugees and Displaced Persons Abroad

In the case of the recognized refugees some positive effects have been identified. One obvious one is that the flow of international assistance has been a relief to the local economies. In 1987 the UNHCR budget for Costa Rica, Honduras, and Mexico rose to some $30 million.[15] The local populations also avail themselves of the pool of less expensive and easily exploitable labor. An additional benefit, though a less tangible one, is that the governments that accept refugees acquire prestige in the eyes of the international community.

There are also some negative elements. Some studies carried out in Mexico demonstrate that the presence of refugees lowers salaries, causes inflation, and has a negative ecological effect. For example, in Chiapas, Mexico refugees accepted a salary of 40 percent of the legal minimum wage, and the pressure on the land and water came to create serious problems.[16]

Moreover, the presence of refugees has become a disruptive issue in the domestic and international politics of different countries. In the United States, for example, the presence of Central Americans has generated a bitter domestic debate. The same is true of Mexico, where the presence of refugees has contributed to the strong tensions between its government and that of Guatemala.

The impact of the unrecognized Central Americans is more difficult to evaluate. Studies show that they have great difficulty in being included in the job market of the zones of refuge.[17] Despite this, we can only suppose that they compete with the most marginated of the people in minimal subsistence activities.

On the other hand, the high concentration of Central Americans in the United States means that they have a positive economic impact on their country of origin. The importance of the money they send periodically to El Salvador and Guatemala was demonstrated when, before the imminent execution of some of the provisions of the new immigration law of the United States (November 1986), the presidents of El Salvador and Guatemala asked Washington to suspend the deportation of their citizens.

The major impact of these displacements, however, falls directly on the displaced. Exile is creating enormous problems with cultural identity, mental health, and civil status. Many of these problems have already been identified and can serve as a basis for the design of possible solutions that nonetheless must be based upon this reality: the effects of these displacements are, in many senses, irreversible and represent changes in the regional demographic map.

Conclusions and Recommendations

The enormous complexity of the phenomenon described briefly in the preceding pages makes it difficult to make recommendations. The 1945 commentary of Fred K. Hoehler (director of the Displaced Persons Division of the United Nations) on the Europeans uprooted by World War II is still valid in 1988 in reference to Central America:

> The road back home for these displaced persons is not a short or easy one; it will probably be years before the last of them will have found their rightful places again in society. Bringing them back to normal existence is not just a simple matter of providing emergency medical care, food, clothing, and the trucks and railway cars to carry them to their countries of origin or to new locations. They pose problems of rehabilitation that go far deeper into human psychology and sociology.[18]

In Central America the situation is still more complicated because the conflicts have not ended. That is to say, we are discussing possible solutions before peace is restored, but it is the characteristics of normalization that will determine how the displaced are integrated into the reconstruction process. In my opinion, pacts or partial solutions are more viable in the near future than is total regional peace.

There is another equally fundamental obstacle. The conflicts arose because of distortions in the existing order, and the reforms necessary to resolve these conflicts and to promote stability have not been achieved.

In spite of this and other obstacles it is worthwhile to link the phenomenon of the displaced peoples with the peace process, and, in turn, to connect the peace process to a process of reconstruction and development that includes the displaced. The effort is new in that, it might be recalled, the Marshall Plan in Europe separated the reconstruction process from that of the resettlement of displaced persons. If successful—as partial as such success might be—this effort will make a useful contribution toward the resolution of similar problems in other parts of the world.

Based on these brief comments, I will make a series of recommendations on the dimensions that seem to me most important.

Research Work on the Subject

Although there are important gaps in the research on displaced Central Americans, the fast pace at which the principal traits of the phenomenon have been understood is encouraging. Studies now underway include a profile of the unrecognized persons, natural integration processes, and the mental health implications of displacement.[19]

Still, there is a subject that is not being investigated despite its crucial importance: establishing more precisely the number of displaced. The existing estimates are quite insufficient. The recommendation is, therefore, that a regional interdisciplinary study be realized using existing censuses, but also including birth projections in the most affected regions and, most important, the registers of migratory entrances to and exits from the various countries of the region. A more realistic determination of the magnitude of displacement would facilitate the formulation of policies.

The Problem of Recognition

The lack of numerical estimates of refugees is due, in part, to the illegal standing of almost all of this community. This illegal status puts these people in an extremely vulnerable position. Although this is a political problem, it is also a legal problem: adequate criteria to deal with a massive flux of people do not exist.

Political will notwithstanding, national legislation should adjust to this new reality. Given that the problem is regional, an inter-American focus is necessary, which will give rise to a new regional convention on the subject. In this vein, UNHCR must clarify and unify the criteria it uses in the region.

In this potential regional effort, special attention should be given to the problem of the temporary nature of recognition, an aspect that is not considered in the Cartagena Declaration. In practice, the governments of the region have looked for domestic formulas that avoid definitive settlement for the refugees. Given the political sensitivity of offering permanent status for refugees, legal ways to allow the Central Americans to be protected in an explicitly temporal sense should be explored. This is not an ideal solution for the refugees, but in the short term, it seems to be the only one that is politically viable.

Emergency Assistance

In 1988 it seems that there is a certain stability in the massive flux of people and that emergency relief is no longer so urgent. Of course, this appraisal is premised on the condition that violence does not worsen. In any case, a vigorous effort should be made to find ways to redirect outright relief efforts, which have perpetuated a situation of dependency among the Salvadorans in Honduras, the Nicaraguans in Costa Rica, and the Guatemalans in Chiapas, Mexico.

Integration and Self-Sufficiency Projects

Wherever possible, relief programs should be replaced by integration and economic self-sufficiency. This is a difficult undertaking because it is costly and because it entails an implicit acknowledgment that not all refugees are on the verge of returning home. The region's governments are reticent, but criteria should be established to encourage this solution in cases of prolonged exile.

The necessity of allowing the refugees a voice in all stages of the planning and implementation of these projects is demonstrated by the experience of recent years.

Repatriation

This is one of the most desirable solutions, but also the most difficult because it is highly dependent on the achievement of peace. To date, very few recognized refugees have returned. Those who have returned have confronted the political problem of protection and the economic problem of reconstruction.

On the other hand, there will someday be peace, and the question that rises is how many of the displaced will want to return or be able to return. We do not know, in part because we do not know how many refugees there are and in part because the studies on the intentions of these groups are still under way.

My belief is that a good percentage will not return. In order for the largest possible number to do so, the problems of protection and the cost of programs of reinstatement must be addressed. The subject of protection for displaced persons who return to their country of origin is tricky because it touches upon the sovereignty of the governments and the limited mandates of international organizations. Can an organization like UNHCR or Catholic Relief Services extend its protection to refugees who return to a region in

El Salvador that is in conflict? Should they at least have access to the returnees?

In this section I avoid making estimates on the possible costs of a repatriation program because the situations vary widely. For example, the transportation costs of Guatemalans returning from Chiapas will be infinitely less than that of Salvadorans returning from Washington, D.C., the cost of reinstatement varies between rural or urban communities, and the costs of repatriating or resettling Nicaraguan counterrevolutionaries varies depending upon how many go to Miami and how many return to Nicaragua. In this light, it is best to judge case by case and make use of institutions like UNHCR that have considerable experience in managing these programs.

The Regional Solution

There are various problems with the preceding considerations and recommendations. First, they are general due to the lack of information. Second, even while problems of displacement, development, and war are interrelated, the links have not been firmly established. Finally, ideal solutions must confront reality. In other words, the phenomenon of displaced peoples should be approached with humanitarian and realistic policies based on hard research, policies that might make exile tolerable while resolving conflicts and preparing the necessary conditions for return.

In contrast to this obligation stands daily practice. All these years, and even today, forces are operating in favor of and against a humanitarian solution. It is the daily action of individuals, groups, parties, organizations, and governments that will shape the final solution for the Central American peoples. There are no ideal solutions or magic recipes.

Despite this, a promising way to advance the implementation of some of the preceding recommendations is through a very concrete regional accord. The International Conference on Refugees and Displaced Peoples scheduled to take place in May 1989 can provide the basis for greater regional and international cooperation on this issue. UNHCR will participate, as will the governments of the region and other "interested governments." Whereas the Cartagena Declaration of 1984 required no obligation from the parties, more concrete compromises are now necessary. This meeting may serve as a forum in which possible solutions are discussed and adopted.

In order for this meeting to be of consequence, the participation of Mexico and the United States is necessary. Mexico is participating in the process. Washington, on the other hand, has not participated in the regional initiative and has been careful to endorse the broad definition of Cartagena. United States officials believe privately that humanitarianism should prevail, but in the countries of the region.[20] Getting the United States to participate in a constructive manner continues to be one of the most difficult problems.

The nongovernmental organizations (NGOs) have been present in all the steps of this long process, and on most occasions they have played a fundamental role. Among other things, they have fought for the legal protection of the Central Americans, offered emergency assistance, created economic self-sufficiency projects, and have used their good offices before different institutions and governments.

A coincidence of objectives has caused a gradual convergence among organizations from different countries. This improvement in communication has evidenced itself in collaboration on very specific problems, in informational interchanges, and in binational and regional meetings such as those organized by the International Council of Voluntary Agencies (ICVA).

As part of this process, the NGOs have also programmed an international meeting for March 1989 in which organizations from Central America, Mexico, Belize, the United States, Canada, and Europe will meet to discuss the legal, economic, and political plight of the displaced and the role that the NGOs can play in their resolution.

Both forums are steps in the slow and arduous search for a consensus regarding humanitarian and realistic solutions. The International Commission for Central American Recovery and Development can contribute by fostering understanding of the links that exist among displaced persons, peace, and development.

Notes

1. A research project that systemizes this academic output is O'Dogherty (1987).

2. UNHCR (1987).

3. Bach (1985).

4. See, among other documents, Americas Watch Committee (1984) and Americas Watch Committee and Lawyers Committee for International Human Rights (1984). The annual reports of the United Nations Commission on Human Rights and Amnesty International also provide information on this subject.

5. In the case of El Salvador see Moore (1984). On Guatemala see Government of Guatemala (1985) and USAID (1984). In Nicaragua a Sandinista official asserted that the "resettlement [of people] is part of a whole strategic concept". *La Jornada* (Mexico), May 18, 1987.

6. Cauas (1985).

7. Interviews with members of private international organizations, San José, Costa Rica, September 1986.

8. The augmentation of the UNHCR mandate came from United Nations General Assembly resolutions 39/140 (December 14, 1984), 35/46 (November 25, 1980), or 32/67 (December 8, 1977).

9. Central American University (1986) and Aguayo, Christensen, O'Dogherty, and Varesse (1987).

10. Among other points, this chapter recommends that countries adhere to the Convention of 1951 and the Protocol of 1967, adopt their terminology, support UNHCR, respect the human rights of the refugees, etc.

11. For the complete text and the papers presented at that meeting, see UNHCR (1984).

12. Besides officials of UNHCR, other participants in this meeting include Alejandro Bendaña, secretary-general of the Nicaraguan Ministry of Foreign Affairs; Carmen Rosa de León, president of the Special Commission for Attention to Guatemalan Repatriates; Oscar Gonzalez, general coordinator of the Mexican Commission for Help to Refugees in Mexico; Danilo Jiménez Veiga, minister, adviser to the president of the Republic of Costa Rica; Joaquín Alex Maza Martelli, vice-minister of foreign affairs of El Salvador; Leo Valladares Lanza, adviser to the minister of foreign affairs of Honduras; Hector Gros Espiell, judge on the Inter-American Court on Human Rights; and Sergio Aguayo, researcher with El Colegio de México.

13. "Informe del Grupo de Consulta sobre Posibles Soluciónes a los Problemas de los Refugiados Centroamericanos", Geneva, May 25–27, 1987.

14. This section on the impact of those displaced within their own countries is a synthesis of the following works and of interviews with members of private Central American organizations: Americas Watch—Lawyers Committee for International Human Rights (1984), Central American University (1986); Manz (1986), and Motes (1984).

15. The exact figures (in U.S. dollars) of the UNHCR budget for 1987 are $7,616,400 to attend to 19,260 refugees in Costa Rica, $14,263,200 for 47,300 refugees in Honduras, and $7,846,000 for 46,232 refugees in Mexico.

16. These statements are based mainly on Aguayo et al. (1987) and the Comisión Mexicana de Ayuda a Refugiados (1985).

17. See, for example, Marmora (1985). I also base this on an unpublished research project by Joanne Gauthier, and on those being carried out by Laura O'Dogherty and Juan García with Central American migrants in Mexico City.

18. Hoehler (1945), p. 10.

19. Some of the institutions doing this work are the Center for Immigration Programs and Refugee Assistance of Georgetown University, the Programa de Estudios de Refugiados of the Academia Mexicana de Derechos Humanos, and the Universidad Centroamericana.

20. The reasons for this policy are basically domestic: to back the process while also limiting the unilateral aspect of direct action would give weight to the groups that support the Central Americans in the United States. What is at play is the decision concerning whether or not the United States forms part of the region.

References

Aguayo, Sergio, Hanne Christensen, Laura O'Dogherty, and Stefano Varesse (1987). *Guatemalan Refugees in Campeche and Quintana Roo.* Geneva: UNRISD/El Colegio de México.

Americas Watch Committee (1984). *Human Rights in Guatemala: No Neutrals Allowed.* New York: AW.

Americas Watch Committee and Lawyers Committee for International Human Rights (1984). *El Salvador's Other Victims: The War on the Displaced.* New York: AWC.

Bach, Robert (1985). *Western Hemisphere Immigrants to the United States: A Review of Selected Research Trends.* Washington: Center for Immigration Policy and Refugee Assistance.

Cauas, José Simeón (1985). "The Displaced and Refugees, Preliminary Version." San Salvador: Central American University.

Central American University (1986). *El Salvador 1986: En Busca de Soluciónes para los Desplazados.* San Salvador: UCA.

Comisión Mexicana de Ayuda a Refugiados (1985). "Diagnóstico-Campamentos de Chiapas." Mexico. May.

Guatemala, Government of (1985). *Revista Cultural del Ejército.* Guatemala: Ministerio de la Defensa Nacional. January–February.

Hoehler, Fred K. (1945). *Europe's Homeless Millions.* Headline Series, No. 54. New York: Foreign Policy Association, November–December.

"Informe del Grupo de Consulta sobre Posibles Soluciónes a los Problemas de los Refugiados Centroamericanos." Geneva, May 25–27, 1987.

La Jornada (Mexico). May 18, 1987.

Manz, Beatriz (1986). *Guatemala: Community Changes, Displacement and Repatriation.* Cambridge, Mass.: Harvard University Press.

Marmora, Lelio (1985). *Migraciónes Laborales e Integración del Refugiado en Costa Rica.* Buenos Aires: ILO-UNHCR.

Moore, L. R. (1984). "El Salvador: Estrategias de Integración Social para Poblaciónes Desplazados y Marginadas: Labores Realizadas, Conclusiónes, Recomendaciónes. Informe de Misión." El Salvador: Programa de Naciónes Unidas para el Desarrollo, Proyecto ELS/83/004.

Motes, Segundo (1984). "La situación de los salvadoreños desplazados y refugiados." *Estudios Centroamericanos* 29:434.

O'Dogherty, Laura (1987). "The Hidden Face of the War: Trend Report on the Research of Central American Displaced and Refugees." Mexico. Unpublished manuscript.

United Nations High Commissioner on Refugees (1984). *La Protección internacional de los refugiados en América Central, México y Panamá: Problemas jurídicos y humanitarios: Memorias del Coloquio de Cartagena de Indias*. Bogotá: UNHCR/Center for Third World Studies/National University of Colombia.

United Nations High Commissioner on Refugees (1987). "Number of Refugees as of 31 May 1987." Geneva: UNHCR. June.

United States Agency for International Development (1984). "Guatemalan Displaced Persons Needs Survey Covering Huehuetenango, Quiché, Western Petén and Playa Grande: Final Report." USAID Project No. DR-520-84-04.

Chapter 2

Assessment of Rural Development in Central America
Gustavo Arcia

Executive Summary

Central American food production has remained stable over the last decade, despite substantial domestic turmoil, declining world commodity prices, and large external debt. However, the value of agricultural production has declined or remained stagnant because of reduced export revenues, increased export taxes, and currency devaluations. If Central America is to move out of its present state of transition, significant improvements will have to be made in the policies and the institutions affecting the farm sector.

In the area of agricultural production a number of policies will need to be reformed. Price policies for basic grains and actions by state monopolies in charge of food imports and exports need to be modified to reduce excessive protection to large commercial producers and excessive consumer subsidies in urban areas. Food security for most of the urban population has been achieved at the cost of increased budget deficits and external debt. Because of unfavorable interest rates and high transaction costs, credit institutions have become dependent on external funds. This dependence inhibits the establishment of a self-sustaining credit system and the mobilization of savings in rural areas. Land reform has been instituted only intermittently and should be refocused to favor land titling and the development of small commercial farms. Landless laborers and subsistence farmers have not been absorbed by production activities or land reform. They should be encouraged to participate in farmers' cooperatives or should be incorporated into nonfarm activities in rural areas. Farm labor is growing faster than food or export crop production and needs to be channeled into the rural labor force. Hence, the development of secondary and tertiary cities is crucial for creating new jobs at the lowest possible cost. Agricultural marketing has become an important vehicle for sectoral growth. There is potential for the region to feed itself, but export growth can only be achieved by improving the marketing channels within the region. Terminal markets, product packing, quality control, and a better transportation network are some of the areas of investment that could increase agricultural exports and augment the demand for labor in the rural-urban fringe.

Institutions in the area could also use some reforms. Institutional management is suffering from built-in deterrents to personnel advancement. For institutions to become more dynamic, administration priorities must shift toward both professional and salary advancement policies based on performance and more flexible field operations. Moreover, institutions' effectiveness would improve greatly if their actions were to be coordinated with macroeconomic policies. Finally, agricultural research systems will need to revise their research agendas to respond to new technological needs. Rural income growth could then be accelerated by promoting rapid technological change in the production of poultry and nontraditional exports such as fruits and vegetables, and by improving agricultural marketing.

Introduction

The objective of this chapter is to review rural development in Central America and to offer alternatives for improvement within a context of peace. This analysis concentrates on two instruments of rural development: food policy and rural institutions. The first includes price supports for farm products, subsidized inputs, direct and indirect taxes on agriculture, and protectionist measures. The second includes institutions that affect rural welfare, such as land tenure, labor, credit, marketing, and technology.

The goals of agricultural policy in Central America are practically the same in each of the five countries: to increase income and employment in rural areas and to increase production and productivity in the agricultural sector. The benefits of these goals are self-explanatory but it is important to differentiate in terms of the beneficiaries. Increments in agricultural production are intended to help consumers in urban areas since the abundance of agricultural products imply low food prices and higher real incomes for the urban poor. Increments in productivity tend to benefit producers and consumers; however, more often than not the benefits of increasing agricultural productivity go to the richer producers. Increments in income and employment can be direct consequences of increasing production and productivity. Thus, even if a farm policy has desirable goals, its benefits may not be as evenly distributed as might be desired. The empirical evidence in Central America shows that the effect of agricultural policy on income and employment has had negative equity considerations that now are at the crux of the social and economic problems of rural areas.

Challenges of Rural Development in Central America

Managing Effects of Internal Unrest

The main challenge faced by planners in Central America is to predict economic performance in the rural sector within an environment of violence and social unrest. The well-defined armed conflicts in El Salvador and Nicaragua, the long-term political uncertainty in Guatemala and Honduras, and the adverse spillover effects in Costa Rica have created a difficult environment for rural development. Economically, these factors have decreased private investment, induced capital flight, and contributed to the exit of well-trained farmers and agriculturists. Socially, the present instability has increased expectations about the risk of investing and about the length of the transition period that always follows a drastic change in the social structure.

Adjusting Policies and Institutions for Peacetime

The second challenge for Central American planners is to design policy and institutional alternatives that will produce fast and effective results in the advent of peace. Whereas the current climate of high risk and uncertainty in the farm sector yields one set of problems, a peace effort also brings expectations of its own. And with these two environments to be accounted for, any policy and institutional actions must be clearly defined and implemented or run the risk of being ignored by the rural sector.

Coping with External Adversity

The two challenges described above are internal. A third challenge, and a very important one, is to plan within an adverse external environment. Two negative factors must be considered. First, commodity prices are low and will continue to be low for a long time, because most developing countries are depending on export revenues to improve their economies and will tend to increase production of their export crops all at the same time. Second, many developed countries (including the United States) are becoming increasingly protectionist in foreign trade. Hence, Central American countries should expect no drastic changes in quotas for products such as sugar and meat. At the same time, these countries can expect to find themselves competing with many other developing countries for a larger share of the North American market.

Coordinating Macroeconomic Policies

A last challenge faced by planners is the design and implementation of agricultural policies within a good macroeconomic environment. No micro-economic policies will be successful unless foreign exchange rates are kept at appropriate levels, budget deficits are kept under control, debt service is negotiated on more favorable terms, and the effects of external shocks (such as further reductions in commodity prices or oil price hikes) are kept to a minimum.

Review of Sectoral Performance

Growth in the agricultural sector during the last five years has been uneven. In terms of physical output, production of basic grains (rice, corn, beans) and export crops (coffee, bananas, sugar, beef, cotton) has increased despite droughts throughout the region and war in Nicaragua and El Salvador. Agriculture export revenues, however, have declined significantly as a result of low world prices for the region's export crops and political conflict in Nicaragua and El Salvador. As a consequence, the growth rate of the agriculture sector in 1986 declined significantly in El Salvador (− 2.1 percent) and Nicaragua (− 5.4 percent), remained stagnant in Costa Rica (0.0 percent) and Guatemala (− 0.2 percent), and increased only slightly (1.6 percent) in Honduras.

Most of the growth came from export crops, which were exported in greater quantities but faced a drop in price of 20 percent for sugar, 17 percent for corn, 5.9 percent for cocoa, and 5.2 percent for beef. Food crops are still being produced in sufficient quantities to feed the population. The present adverse economic climate, however, will hamper future performance in the food crops sector unless measures are taken to revitalize the institutional sector.

Agricultural Price Policy in Central America

The orientation of agricultural policy in Central America has been fairly straightforward: increasing the access of farmers to land and capital resources, promoting technological change, and improving market access. However, the implementation of agricultural policy has been more problematic: incomplete efforts at land reform, inefficient credit institutions, low investment on agricultural research, inadequate marketing channels, and overly distorted agricultural prices. The result is a sector in which small farmers are practically left out of most of the benefits of agricultural policy. In addition, the good intentions associated with agricultural policies have been neutralized by macroeconomic variables and political events out of the control of microeconomic incentives. For example, the budget deficits found among all five countries, along with the decline in the gross domestic product caused by droughts, low export prices, and political unrest have diminished the importation of food and capital goods to the extent that price inflation has now become the main economic problem faced by households.

The microeconomic environment in the agricultural sector of Central America has not been devoid of action on the part of the governments. Rather, the efforts at policymaking and institution building have been ill-conducted, sporadic, and uncoordinated. Since the relative imperfections found among the policy instruments of the farm sector help explain the inequities faced by small farmers, the policies examined in the rest of the paper will be reviewed against a backdrop of recommendations intended to make policies and institutions in the farm sector more efficient and equitable.

Support Prices

Support prices for basic grains traditionally have formed the cornerstone of price policy in the region. The main intent behind the price supports has been the provision of economic incentives to producers of corn, beans, and rice. Thus, official producer prices for basic grains generally have been set at slightly higher levels than border prices. In combination with official control of grain imports, price supports have served as a protectionist measure in favor of local producers. Until 1983, agricultural product prices were too high in almost all the countries in the region because of the countries' overvalued currencies. This had two unintended consequences. First, parastatal institutions in charge of grain marketing had an incentive to import basic grains at prices artificially lower than domestic prices, thus competing against the small farmers they were supposed to help. Second, the benefits of high domestic grain prices generally benefited those farmers with the best access to the consumer and institutional markets. Not surprisingly, the richest farmers and those with larger farms received most of the benefits from high support prices. The unrealistic exchange rates also affected the farm sector indirectly and negatively by encouraging capital flight and reducing the availability of funds for agricultural investment.

Nonetheless, high support prices for basic grains—rice, corn, and beans—have been effective in increasing food supplies when used in combination with the government monopoly in charge of agricultural marketing. In general, the quantity of basic grains purchased at the official support price has not exceeded 20 percent of total production. The marketing institutes cannot cope with purchases larger than 20 to 25 percent of total production of basic grains because of their insufficient capital and storage capacity. However, the price leadership exerted by the institutions, coupled with their ability to import basic grains, seem to have satisfied most of the domestic demand. In cases where grains have been imported in massive amounts, however, basic grains producers have been affected negatively.

Although the use of high support prices has meant a fairly stable and adequate supply of basic grains in the region, it has also brought about an increase in budget deficits and a failure to distribute the price gains among the smaller farm producers.

Taxes on Agriculture

The cost of food security during the last decade has been underwritten by external loans, by government deficits, and by the implicit taxation of rural producers with very few alternatives for subsistence. In all cases the high cost can be traced to increases in budgetary deficits financed with external loans, inefficiencies in the operation of the marketing institutions (the official institutions in charge of implementing price support, marketing, and storage are not self-sustaining), the high cost of storage, and most importantly, a net deterrent to small commercial producers of basic grains. Furthermore, the need for additional government revenues has led to excessive taxation on export crops, creating a net deterrent to investment in productive inputs. Although most governments in the region are looking closely at the cost of government intervention in food markets, they cannot afford to deregulate the market completely because of the short-term political cost.

In the case of export crops, each of the countries has monopolized the export of commodities in order to collect export taxes, which are the main source of hard currency revenue. The current debt crisis and the decline in world prices (which reduce export taxes) have induced governments to increase the taxes on exports even more (IDB, 1987). This increase in taxation of agriculture, coupled with political uncertainty, has created a climate of austerity which is bound to reduce agricultural investment in the near future.

Effects on Consumption

Price and marketing policies in the region have resulted in food security for most urban consumers. However, adequate nutrition for the rural population has not been achieved. For example, in Honduras, more than 90 percent of the rural population and about 20 percent of the urban population have caloric intakes which fall short of the recommended daily allowances (RDA) (SIECA, 1982). In Costa Rica, where nutritional deficiencies are less prevalent than in the rest of Central America, almost 38 percent of all households consume less than 80 percent of the RDA for calories and 18.5 percent of the households consume less than 75 percent of the RDA for protein (SIN, 1985).

According to a recent study (Fletcher, Green, De la Cruz, and Hager, 1985), the quotient of self-sufficiency in basic grains for the Central American region exceeds 100 percent. That is, through either domestic production or the use of imports, Central American governments have been able to satisfy 100 percent of the local demand for grains during the past decade. For example, by July of 1985, four of the five countries had an exportable surplus of corn, and three out of five had a surplus of beans and rice (Fletcher et al., 1985). These levels of production have alleviated but not eliminated the problem of hunger in rural areas. USAID and SIECA studies on the consumption effects of agricultural policies for Honduras show that the level of malnutrition in the population is directly connected to household income. Thus, adequate levels of production of basic grains, which have come at a very high budgetary cost, have answered only partially the problem of hunger in rural areas.

Although market intervention by governments seems to have been successful in terms of increasing food supply, the near future does not look promising. Small and medium-sized businesses are likely to continue producing basic grains for the local market, but prospects are dim for increases in productivity because of the upcoming scarcity in capital inputs, the high cost of imported inputs, and low world prices for export crops. Unless productivity increases, taxing the agricultural sector to maintain or increase revenues will imperil agriculture in the long run.

Central American Institutions

Land Tenure

Agriculture in Central America is in danger of becoming more dualistic than ever before. In the past, one of the perceived constraints to rural development was the existence of two well-defined subsectors within agriculture: a modern subsector, with a high level of technology and capital investment, almost exclusively oriented to the export market, and a traditional subsector, mostly engaged in the production of basic grains and subsistence crops. The problem with this dualism is the disparity in numbers of people in each subsector, and the underlying problem of equity. The relatively few farmers in the modern subsector have always had access to most of the capital available for investment, as well as most of the desirable lands. In return, the modern subsector provides the central governments with export tax revenues and hard currency.

The traditional subsector, which produces most of the food crops consumed internally, is in the hands of the vast majority of the farmers. This subsector is fragmented in terms of political power, provides little in terms of government revenues, and, as a consequence, has been taxed implicitly by having to provide food to the urban masses at prices lower than the market would dictate (Fletcher et al., 1985).

The only exception to this dualistic pattern is Nicaragua, where the modern sector has been restructured to fall mostly under state control, and the benefits that used to go to the privileged owners of the export crops are now being redirected to owners of medium-size commercial farm and farmer cooperatives (Zalkin, 1987). However, the need for hard currency (under the present political conflict and under declining terms of trade and capital scarcity) will imperil this strategy in the short run. Unless capital investment in the farm sector increases, the large state holdings (those involved in export crop production) will absorb most of the capital and institutional resources and crowd out the private and reformed sectors.

The principal problem with dualism in an adverse economic environment is that it fails to address one of the main sources of political unrest in Central America: the grossly unequal distribution of wealth in the rural sector. Unless steps are taken to increase the welfare of subsistence farmers and landless laborers, peace will only be temporary.

Land ownership is one of the basic causes of the present political conflict in the region. Despite substantial redistribution of land among landless peasants and owners of small farms during the last five years, land distribution in Central America still is highly skewed in three of the five countries. In Guatemala, 83 percent of the farms have an area of less than 3.5 hectares, but their total area represents only 10.5 percent of the total for all farms. In Honduras, the number of farms under 4 hectares is 58 percent of the total, but represents only 7 percent of the total area (Fletcher et al., 1985). In Costa Rica subsistence farms comprise 32 percent of all farms and represent 4.7 percent of the total farming area (Fletcher et al., 1985).

The above distributions are significant economically because they represent what conventional wisdom considers to be subsistence farms. By the nature of their land quality and the size of the farm family, subsistence farms most likely will be outside the economic mainstream. As will be discussed later, this pattern of land ownership has substantial implications for rural labor markets in the near future.

In El Salvador and Nicaragua the political events of the last seven years have helped initiate programs of land reform. These programs include land titling and cooperatives in both countries, plus the creation of state farms in Nicaragua. Despite considerable political difficulties, the agrarian reform in El Salvador redistributed 22 percent of the total agricultural land to more than half a million individuals (18 percent of the rural population). However, the efforts at land reform in El Salvador have virtually stagnated since 1984 (Reinhardt, 1987).

In Nicaragua the efforts at land reform between 1979 and 1984 took three forms: cooperatives (19 percent of all agricultural land), state farms (8 percent of all agricultural land), and land titling (17 percent of all agricultural land), bringing 44 percent of the total area in exploitation under the reform program (Reinhardt, 1987). One explicit intent behind the policy of creating state farms in Nicaragua was to maintain or increase the level of export crop production (cotton, coffee, sugar cane) necessary to generate foreign exchange. In addition, both El Salvador and Nicaragua have made attempts to keep medium-sized commercial farms in production, since they account for most of the production surplus available to urban consumers, as well as for 60 percent of coffee and cotton production.

In both countries the issue of success of the reform effort cannot be examined in complete fairness, since land reform is one of the issues at the root of the present conflict. The slow pace at which the reform is being undertaken, however, indicates that El Salvador has encountered significant political difficulties that threaten future advances in the reform process.

The present economic difficulties and the experience of Nicaragua and El Salvador indicate that the scope of land reform needs to be drastically modified. In order for the reform process to yield the short-term results necessary for its long-term viability, land reform must address two issues: (1) increasing the collateral and decreasing the risk premium of commercial farmers, and (2) increasing rural equity.

The first issue means that for land reform to succeed, rural credit must be made affordable. Unless owners of small farms are able to increase their collateral and reduce their risk premiums, rural credit from private sources will not be forthcoming, official credit will not be self-sustaining, and rural interest rates invariably will be too expensive for owners of small commercial farms. After all, if self-sustaining financial institutions are to be desired, the price of capital needs to cover the administrative cost and the risk premium attached to a loan.

The second issue means that in terms of national priorities and improved societal welfare some groups of farmers may have to be given preference over others. At least in the short run, owners of small farms in farming areas that have the best chance of entering the mainstream of commercial agriculture or who are able to respond to institutional and market stimulus should, for the benefit of the majority, be given priority in the allocation of land titles and institutional services. The recent experience of land reform in Nicaragua shows that attempts to benefit all owners of small farms in all farming areas results in an overburdening of the managerial and budgetary resources of land and credit institutions. Hence, the land reform process may have to rely more on land titling than on comprehensive rural development packages, which are too demanding on scarce managerial resources. Moreover, the titling process may have to exclude most of the subsistence farmers and landless laborers, since they are at the greatest disadvantage in terms of technological change and commercial viability. In order to cope with the needs of these two disadvantaged groups the reform effort may have to consider the development of labor markets outside the farm but inside rural areas.

Labor and Rural Labor Markets

The presence of a large segment of the rural population in subsistence farming, especially in Guatemala, Honduras, and Costa Rica, and the shift in population from rural to urban activities make the issue of rural labor markets a compelling one. The last 30 years have seen a gradual shift in the composition of employment, transforming the rural labor force into an increasingly large urban population (table 2.1). During the last ten years

Table 2.1   Shifts in the Agricultural Labor Force, 1970–80

Country	Year	Percentage of Labor Force in Agriculture	Change in Percentage Points
Costa Rica	1970	42.6	
	1980	30.8	11.8
El Salvador	1970	56.0	
	1980	43.2	12.8
Guatemala	1970	61.3	
	1980	56.9	4.4
Honduras	1970	64.9	
	1980	60.5	4.4
Nicaragua	1970	51.6	
	1980	46.6	5.0

Source: International Labor Office, *Economically Active Population, 1950–2025*, vol. 3 (Geneva, 1986).

Costa Rica and El Salvador have experienced relatively large shifts in the agricultural labor force. Between 1970 and 1980 in Costa Rica, the proportion of the economically active population in agriculture decreased by 11.8 percentage points; El Salvador underwent a reduction in the rural labor force of 12.8 percent during the same period.

Four of the five countries have high rates of population growth (between 2.5 and 3.5 percent), so the shift from urban to rural labor is compounded by population growth pressures. The main sources of labor transfers from the rural to the urban sector are subsistence farms and landless families. Most of the laborers transferred are young and relatively unskilled in agriculture (CEPAL, 1985; Todaro, 1977). The incidence of poverty in the rural sector ranges from 30 percent of the rural population in Costa Rica to 75 percent or more in El Salvador, Honduras, and Guatemala. (Given the grossly undervalued cordoba, virtually all the rural dwellers in Nicaragua would fall under the poverty levels for Central America.) Hence, the high level of rural poverty and the subsistence farms' low capacity to absorb larger families indicate that investment in land reform programs would fail to keep pace with the growth in the rural labor force.

The high labor growth rate in rural areas and the limited scope of land reform mean that Central American countries will need to address the development of rural-urban linkages very soon. Policies must be created to encourage decentralization, to develop an infrastructure in secondary and tertiary cities, and to nurture labor demand in the rural-urban fringe. Developing demand for rural labor by exploiting the backward and forward linkages between the rural sector and secondary and tertiary cities is far less expensive and much faster than land reform.

Credit Institutions

Rural capital markets in Central America have been stagnant for most of the past decade. Rural financial institutions are relatively inefficient and have failed to reach the medium-sized farms that are the mainstay of Central American agriculture. These failures stem from ill-designed interest rate policies and the lack of managerial incentives at the institutional level.

Without exception, the five Central American countries' rural credit institutions need restructuring. Currently, most of the credit available to the farm sector goes to the larger farms and to the export crop producers. In Guatemala the rural credit system can serve only 10 percent of the effective demand for credit from owners of small and medium-sized commercial farms (IDB, 1984). Similar trends can be observed in Honduras. In all five countries the effect of low interest rates has been found to be overwhelmingly negative, either because of subsidized rates or because of fixed rates along with high levels of inflation. During the past year the rates of inflation in the consumer price index for El Salvador and Guatemala were above 30 percent, while for Nicaragua the inflation rate exceeded 680 percent. No rural credit system can be self-sustaining under these conditions in the long run.

The debt crisis and the macroeconomic measures taken by government to control national finances have compounded the gradual decapitalization of the rural financial system in Central America. New loans for agriculture in the five countries have been curtailed, and the level of private investment and the mobilization of rural saving have declined because of the high capital risks associated with the sector (IDB, 1987). In Nicaragua and El Salvador the high risk premiums associated with agriculture are easily explained by war. Clearly, the mobilization of private savings in the rural areas of these two countries will not be possible until the political conflicts are resolved.

In Guatemala, Honduras, and Costa Rica the relative inefficiency of rural financial markets may be traced to the allocation of scarce credit to the most productive sectors of the economy (e.g., a few large loans to export-crop producers or to builders), unfavorable rates of interest that keep financial institutions from being self-sustaining, and the lack of managerial incentives for personnel in public institutions. The managerial problem prevents credit institutions from reducing their operational costs and denies them the flexibility required to deal with customers efficiently.

The reform of credit institutions presents two competing forces: a tendency to lower interest rates to make credit more affordable to small farmers and a tendency to increase interest rates to make credit institutions self-sustaining. The answer to this dilemma lies in a coherent agricultural policy that aggressively promotes managerial efficiency in credit institutions (to lower the administrative cost of credit and to expand services) at the same time that it fosters technological change and increased productivity among small commercial farmers (to increase the returns to capital investment in farm production). Other operational changes need to be promoted also, such as group lending, monetization of the rural sector, land titling to increase collateral, and so forth, but the above two principles are the fundamental ones for achieving affordable credit in small farm agriculture.

Agricultural Marketing and Marketing Institutions

Government intervention in the marketing of agricultural products in Central America has fragmented and weakened private marketing systems. For example, the monopoly power that governments have exerted over both the export of primary commodities and the import of basic grains has created a long-term deterrent to the development of private market talent. As a consequence, the managerial capabilities and efficiency necessary to diversify exports are scarce or nonexistent. Guatemala and Costa Rica are the only countries in the region in which nontraditional exports have started to develop in a significant way. Guatemala now has several years of experience in exporting vegetables, fruits, and other farm products to Mexico and the United States. The vast majority of these exports are produced on family farms of an average of 0.7 hectares (IFPRI, 1987). Costa Rica has been involved in cut-flower exports for several years. Although it requires considerable capital and managerial ability, the cut-flower industry has provided Costa Rica with two badly needed elements of development: jobs for unskilled workers, and hard currency.

The examples of Guatemala and Costa Rica need to be expanded to include other products within these two countries, as well as in other countries in the region. Since the weak link seems to be the management component, all the countries in the region will have to address the issue of identifying and encouraging entrepreneurs in the rural-urban fringe.

Despite the collapse of the Central American Common Market and the current political unrest, intraregional trade has continued, although under great strain. In fact, it declined by 23 percent between 1985 and 1986 (IDB, 1987). As expected, El Salvador and Nicaragua suffered the largest reductions: -32.9 and -49.8 percent, respectively. However, with the advent of peace, the intraregional exports of these two countries would increase several times over their current volume until their currencies (in particular the cordoba) reach a proper rate of exchange with other currencies in the region. At that point intraregional trade would increase at the same pace as income growth.

In terms of market development the immediate concern should be satisfying regional markets, because there is a clear demand for food and nonfood products at the regional level currently being satisfied with products from outside the region. Exporting farm products to regional markets is certainly possible. Most of the vegetables exported by Guatemala (with the exception of snow peas) go to Mexico. Furthermore, every one of the Central American countries has been importing certain agricultural products that could be produced in the region. Although exports to the United States and Europe may be economically feasible, interregional trade within Central America, Mexico, and northern South America would have multiplier effects that could be kept within the region.

Table 2.2 presents the net trade balances for some of the agricultural products now being imported by at least one of the five countries. As the table clearly indicates, the five countries show a net trade deficit in dairy and poultry products and in animal and vegetable oils. These products, however, can be produced in any of the five countries. In Honduras, Nicaragua, and Costa Rica there are significant comparative advantages in the production of vegetable oils, while at one time El Salvador had most of the expertise in egg production. Because of climatic advantages, most of Costa Rica and Guatemala could expand the production of dairy products. Evidently, expanding production of the foods listed in table 2.2 would require adequate infrastructure development, production expertise, and managerial ability. The important point of table 2.2, however, is that

Table 2.2   Food Trade Balances in Central America, Average 1981–85, for Selected Products ($ Millions)

Country	Cereals	Meats	Dairy and Eggs	Fruits and Vegetables	Animal and Vegetable Oils
Costa Rica	−25	51	−4	229	−4
El Salvador	−39	−7	−17	−31	−22
Guatemala	−31	42	−10	89	−23
Honduras	−22	24	−14	246	−1
Nicaragua	−36	16	−12	3	−30

Source: InterAmerican Development Bank, *Economic and Social Progress in Latin America, 1987 Report*, p. 49.

intraregional agricultural trade could be expanded substantially for both the near and slightly more distant futures.

The last ingredient needed in agricultural marketing is as important as managerial expertise: adequate infrastructure. As mentioned previously, the current marketing infrastructure is grossly deficient, especially in the areas of nontraditional farm products such as fruit, vegetables, and ornamentals. The marketing components in greatest need of development are: terminal markets and storage facilities for perishables, better and more reliable transportation networks for perishables, and fast and accurate market information at the points of delivery. These marketing components can absorb substantial investments very efficiently (Rondinelli, 1987). In addition, the development of these components is entirely compatible with the idea of expanding labor markets, because developing a market infrastructure is labor intensive.

Extension and Research

Given declining agricultural prices for the region's exports and the under-employment of a significant proportion of the rural population, all countries in the region should examine gains in agricultural productivity as a way to improve income in rural areas and generate economic growth (and the subsequent demand for other goods) among commercial farmers. Without continuing research, however, increases in productivity will remain marginal. The current system of agricultural research in Central America is slowly moving into place. Although there are national research institutions in every country, as well as excellent regional research centers in Costa Rica, agricultural research in areas other than production of basic grains and export crops is sorely lacking. The agricultural research system has not yet responded to the needs for appropriate technologies for packing and trans-porting farm products, or adaptive research and extension in nontraditional products. The system should also be better managed, to coordinate research activities with long-term economic trends and government goals. The capacity of the five nations to analyze research needs and to plan solutions is very limited, particularly in coordinating the research agenda and the policy environment. Two areas in particular need improvement: the administration of research and the management skills for running an adequate research budget, especially under financial restrictions (Hanrahan et al., 1987).

Although the institutional framework already exists, and although there are good researchers in the area, improvements must be made to increase the effectiveness of the present system.

During the last five years the international donor community has become increasingly concerned over the problem of natural resource degradation. The World Bank, in particular, has started a major effort to address the problems of the deforestation of the tropics and the degradation of fragile lands. Clearly, the problem of resource degradation results from the relatively low access to land for some of the small farmers in the region, the lack of knowledge of good conservation practices, and, most importantly, the pressing need for survival that induces owners of small farms to think only in the short run. Owners of small commercial farms, for instance, are reluctant to implement conservation technologies because the payoff period exceeds their family needs or because land tenure is not secured. The relevance for research is obvious; the region greatly needs appropriate conservation technologies.

Conclusions: Guidelines for Development

Although each of the five countries has unique characteristics and problems, and although the severity of each problem varies among the five republics, some generalizations can still be made. The solutions outlined here will apply to each country with different degrees of relevance. However, the consensus among academics, external donors, and international financial institutions includes some or all of the following guidelines for major changes:

Drastic improvements in the access to land by small commercial farmers. Although complete land reform for everyone will always be welcome, the realities of the managerial and infrastructural capacity of the rural sector suggest that commercially competitive family farms should be given priority. Access to land may also include the development of land markets, land titling, and the active promotion of farmer cooperatives.

Rapid development of rural-urban linkages in secondary and tertiary cities in order to absorb the fast-growing rural population. Strategies should encourage efficiency in nonfarm enterprises and the private sector in order to maximize government efforts. Private-sector businesses

that handle urban functions in rural areas (such as transportation, input
and output trading, storage, food services, entertainment, and financial
services) should be promoted avidly.

Designing and implementing agricultural policies consistent with
private sector development and income growth in rural areas. Macroeconomic policies should include appropriate rates of foreign exchange,
fair export taxes, and elimination of the implicit taxation on agriculture.
Microeconomic policies should include appropriate support prices for
basic commodities, and no effective protection for inappropriate agricultural products.

Development of institutional incentives that allow for better administration and management of rural institutions, particularly credit and
research. These incentives should include training opportunities, flexible
personnel policies, and career and salary advancement based on performance.

Development of new research that takes into account nontraditional
agricultural products and resource conservation. For traditional and
export crops, research should include the development of technologies
to enhance food security, such as small farm irrigation and yield stability.

Rapid reform of the rural financial system to help mobilize rural
savings and activate domestic investment in the farm sector. Measures
may include group lending, financial intermediation by private sources,
and allowances for real rates of interest in competitive financial markets.

Development of markets and more efficient marketing within the
Central American region. Decentralization policies, the development of
the rural infrastructure, and the promotion of rural labor markets
combined with more efficient marketing will accelerate income growth.
Policies and actions for improving agricultural markets should include
the construction of better marketing facilities, improvements in the
transportation network, and market information. Moreover, people
involved in marketing need to be trained in packing technology, quality
control, inventory management, and delivery scheduling.

The above strategies have one very important element in common: all of
them rely heavily on the willingness of the countries themselves to adopt
reform. Because national identity seems to be as important as development
financing, the above guidelines can be implemented with as much external

involvement as the countries desire. Although each of the guidelines involves an active role for the private sector, none of them runs contrary to governmental objectives of improving the welfare of the population. In the specific case of Nicaragua, where markets are nominally more regulated than in the rest of Central America, these guidelines should be reconciled with the specific goals set by the government for its agricultural sector.

Finally, the preceding analysis and guidelines do not refer to assistance for either developing a new rural infrastructure or reconstructing the infrastructure destroyed by the wars in Nicaragua and El Salvador. Although these construction activities will affect income and employment profoundly for the next few years, they are outside the scope of this analysis. However, to be consistent with the development of rural labor markets and decentralization, these construction activities should be planned in conjunction with rural development policies.

References

Economic Commission for Latin America and the Caribbean (ECLAC) (1985). *La Pobreza en América Latina: Dimensiones y Políticas*. Report No. 54. Santiago: Estudios e Informes de la CEPAL.

Fletcher, Lehman, Duty Green, Justino de la Cruz, and Randall Hager (1985). "Situación de la Seguridad Alimentaria y Opciones de Políticas en la Región del CORECA." Report, Secretaría de Coordinación del Consejo para la Cooperación Agrícola en América Central, Panamá y la República Dominicana (CORECA), n.c.

Hanrahan, Charles, Edgar Ariza-Nino, John Tilney, and Rolando Jiron (1987). "Guidelines for Supporting Agricultural and Rural Development in Latin America and the Caribbean." Report, Agricultural Policy Analysis Project, U.S. Agency for International Development, Washington, D.C.

Inter-American Development Bank (IDB) (1984). "Informe Económico. Guatemala." Report No. DES-02. Washington, D.C.

Inter-American Development Bank (IDB) (1986, 1987). *Economic and Social Progress in Latin America*. Washington, D.C.

International Labor Office (ILO) (1986). "Economically Active Population, 1950-2050." Vol. III. Geneva.

International Food Policy Research Institute (IFPRI) (1987). *Report, 1986*. Washington, D.C.

Reinhardt, Nola (1987). "Agro-Exports and the Peasantry in the Agrarian Reforms of El Salvador and Nicaragua." *World Development*, vol. 15, no. 7, pp. 941–59.

Rondinelli, Denis (1987). "Agriculture, Employment and Enterprise: Rural-Urban Dynamics in AID Development Strategy." Report, Regional and Resources Development Division, Office of Rural and Institutional Development, Bureau for Science and Technology, U.S. Agency for International Development, Washington, D.C.

SIECA/AID/ROCAP (1982). Food Consumption and Nutrient Intakes by Socio-Economic Groups in Honduras Households. Document no. 31. U.S. Agency for International Development, Tegucigalpa.

SIN. Sistema de Información en Nutrición (1985). *Estudio de Casos Sobre la Situación Alimentaria y Nutricional de Costa Rica*. Oficina de Control de Asignaciones Familiares, San José.

Todaro, Michael (1977). *Economic Development of the Third World*. New York: Longman.

World Food Council (1986). "Food Policy Adjustments in Latin America and the Caribbean in Support of Food Security and Development." Report, Ministerial Consultation on Food Policies and Strategies in Latin America and the Caribbean, Buenos Aires, April 1986.

Zalkin, Michael (1987). "Food Policy and Class Transformation in Revolutionary Nicaragua, 1979-86." *World Development*, vol. 15, no. 7, pp. 961–84.

Chapter 3

Macroeconomic Adjustment and Agricultural Reactivation in Central America

Cassio Luiselli

I. The Outlines of Adjustment and Its Impact on Central American Agriculture

A. Introduction

The Central American crisis has deeply transformed the economics of agriculture. Determined efforts to control crises through politics of recessive adjustment, though often futile, have drastically modified the macroeconomic framework of agriculture and the relationships it maintains with other sectors. Similarly, the fall of international prices of the region's agro-exports has aggravated the politics of reactivation. These novel conditions compel us to rethink the traditional role of agriculture in development.

The current crisis in Central America is particularly deep. Since the crisis of the 1930s, Central America has gone through at least seven recessive economic cycles, none of which resembles this decade's crisis. The Central American economies are more open, and consequently are more vulnerable, than in the 1930s. The fall in international agro-export prices and the increase in oil prices in the 1970s mark two external "shocks." In addition, the agricultural sectors are markedly bimodal, with modern and subsistence subsectors. This unequal pattern of modernization should be taken into account in any policy of macroeconomic adjustment because policy affects these subsectors differently. In any case, facing strong imbalances in their foreign accounts and unable to find adequate financing through loans and investments, the Central American countries have had to undergo a highly recessive process of adjustment with deep structural impacts of social as well as economic consequence.

The macroeconomic policies of adjustment, whatever their specifics or severity, essentially sought short-term financial correction and medium-term economic adjustment. Sectoral policies, including agriculture, were subordinated, sacrificing production and growth.

The policies of adjustment, with an emphasis on financial variables and short-term urgencies (especially the balance of payments), have modified the decisionmaking processes, and the mechanisms of social harmonization have disintegrated. These policies of adjustment and the imbalances of the crisis find Central America extremely vulnerable and particularly incapable of achieving a framework for democratic and social agreement that could define a strategy to end the crisis. The urgencies of the crisis put pressure not only on the financial base, but also on the natural resources and the social structures of the productive base. That is, the necessity of financial adjustment and the maintenance of a net flow of currency into Central America have frequently caused the adoption of ecologically irrational and socially onerous policies.

The drastic policies of stabilization that have been adopted to correct external imbalances and inflationary pressures have included exchange rate devaluations, trade and price liberalization, and reduction of public spending. To succeed, those policies should be able to reassign resources from nontradable to tradable sectors and substitute domestic production for some imports while expanding exports. Nevertheless, protectionism, the fall of exchange terms, and other difficulties arising from the slow growth of the world economy make it unlikely for agricultural exportation to achieve reactivation by itself; it must be complemented by foreign exchange savings through import substitution. Yet even in this, agriculture can play an important role in global reactivation.

Devaluation, more than any other adjustment, creates an automatic stimulus for exports and discourages imports. It is, nonetheless, important to take into account that in Central America the bulk of producers in the subsistence subsector cannot rapidly adjust and produce strictly tradable goods. Poverty, subsistence consumption, the rigidity of the productive structure, and the lack of access to resources and technology impede this subsector's responsiveness. It is therefore disadvantaged in the internal reassignment of resources at a sectoral level in terms of the relative costs of inputs, services, and credit, as well as the displacement from the best lands. Thus, devaluation may stimulate agriculture, but it must also be accompanied by compensation for the neediest farmers.

Table 3.1 Central America: Share of Exports and Imports of Nonfactorial Goods and Services in GDP (%)

	1980	1981	1982	1983	1984	1985	1986
Costa Rica[a]		46	43	36	36	34	
Exports		46	43	36	36	34	
Imports		51	40	37	35	35	
El Salvador[b]							
Exports			24.6	25.4	24.3	22.1	23.9[g]
Imports			30.6	30.1	30.2	27.9	29.8
Guatemala[c]							
Exports			15	15	13	13[h]	
Imports			19	15	15	13	
Honduras[d]							
Exports		33.5	27.5	27.1	26.5		
Imports		40.1	30.5	30.8	33.2		
Nicaragua[e]							
Exports		17.6	17.1	15.3	12.1	10.2[h]	
Imports		32.6	32.9	32.6	36.4	30.6	
Panama[f]							
Exports		42.5	41.1	39.5			
Imports		44.1	38.8	38.2			

[a] Source: IMF, Costa Rica (1986), p. iv (figures rounded by the source).

[b] Source: IMF, El Salvador (1986), p. v.

[c] Source: IMF, Guatemala (1986), p. iv.

[d] Source: IMF, Honduras (1985), p. iv.

[e] Source: IMF, Nicaragua (1987), p. iv.

[f] Source: IMF, Panamá (1985), p. v.

[g] Estimated figures.

[h] Preliminary figures.

B. The New Macroeconomic Context

International prices of agricultural products have declined throughout the present decade, and it is highly unlikely that they will recover in a sustained fashion. Between 1980 and 1986, for instance, wheat prices fell by 43 percent, rice by 50 percent, and other cereals by nearly 50 percent. This decline has accelerated the secular fall in the prices of the last 100 years (with the exceptions of the Korean War and the food crisis of 1973–75). Price projections cannot reasonably be optimistic. The situation is worsened by the inconsistent protectionism of the Organization of Economic Cooperation and Development, which is currently restrictive and not very hopeful for Central American exports.

A second aspect of the current context results from the adjustment processes in almost all of the Third World countries; devaluations have typically been drastic. Economic liberalization and spending cuts, among other things, have followed these devaluations. Thus comparative advantage is redefined, at least in the short run, where technological change does not enter into the analysis. Therefore, the benefits of exchange rate changes are diminished. To this, one must add the structural inflexibilities due to Central America's agricultural dualism.

Third, the policies of stabilization and adjustment have not only changed the structure of the relative prices of tradable and nontradable goods but have also redefined the structure of costs according to the relative importance of tradable and nontradable inputs. Devaluation increases the prices of all imported inputs and has a direct effect on agricultural costs, often discriminating against the poorest producers. Real wages are also reduced notably. It is important that the units of agricultural production that are not open to the wage market and that use simple technology of low import content have tended to improve their competitive position due precisely to the adjustment programs. The cheapening of labor and land and the rise in the cost of certain capital goods favor the forms of production and technology that can well be compatible with the factor endowments and the employment needs of Central America. The productivity of these units must be favored for the sake of equity.

A final characteristic of the current agricultural situation is the drastic fall in the public's expenditure in agriculture. This includes not only subsidies, for production as well as for food consumption, but also a drastic fall in credit, investment, and infrastructure. Thus, these fiscal circumstances along with an increase in the interest rates have increased the productive and financial difficulties of the Central American farmer. The Central American governments have also tried to open their economies and reduce the role of the state in directing and programming economic activities. They have been driven above all by the policies of agencies such as the World Bank, the IMF, and USAID, which favor free trade and administer the elimination of restrictions on foreign investment.

C. The Agricultural Impact of Adjustment Policies

Exchange policy undoubtedly has been the most powerful macroeconomic instrument used in the adjustment process. Central American countries, like many others in Latin America, have effected notable nominal devaluations oriented toward elevating the real exchange rate. With the notable exception of Honduras, modifications in the exchange rate occur nowadays with more frequency in Central America, a region which for many years had abstained absolutely from modifying its parities.

Exchange policies have a contradictory effect on agriculture. On the one hand, there is a positive stimulus toward exports and import substitution; on the other hand, foreign exchange earnings that have been achieved through export promotion have not increased as expected because of the deterioration of prices. Lower prices thus deter import substitution; at the same time, the increase in the price of imported technological input results in higher production costs. Again, the production of exports is rigid. This is, for instance, the alleged reason for devaluation in countries highly dependent on the export of bananas, as in Honduras, because prices vary little with exchange rate changes. Likewise, other products of great importance in the region, such as coffee and sugar, are subject to administered prices, quotas, etc. that have less relevance in regard to the exchange rate. Other instruments of great relevance in the adjustment process are the monetary policies designed to restrict demand. These often include a reduction in credit and a decrease in preferential interest rates, which thus lose relevance for promoting production or pursuing other agricultural objectives. Moreover, the reduction of credit also signifies a partial dismantling of the related economic and technical structure associated with official credit operations. The reduction of credit has also implied the need for greater levels of self-financing, which, linked with the intrinsic insecurity of agriculture, constitutes a serious deterrent to private investment.

Fiscal policies, primarily oriented to the reduction of public spending, have had an essentially negative impact on agriculture. This is particularly serious in the case of poorer zones that could receive infrastructure invest-

Table 3.2 Central America: Total and Agricultural Economically Active
Population

	1950 000s	%	1960 000s	%	1970 000s	%	1980 000s	%
CACM								
Total	2,981	100	3,473	100	4,668	100	6,342	100
Agricultural	2,080	69.8	2,216	63.8	2,679	57.4	3,252	51.3
Costa Rica								
Total	272	100	374	100	532	100	742	100
Agricultural	149	54.8	193	51.6	224	42.1	260	35
El Salvador								
Total	653	100	815	100	1,100	100	1,495	100
Agricultural	413	63.2	502	61.6	617	56.1	754	50.4
Guatemala								
Total	968	100	1,199	100	1,638	100	2,207	100
Agricultural	660	68.2	802	66.9	999	60.9	1,211	54.9
Honduras								
Total	758	100	—	—	807	100	1,087	100
Agricultural	635	83.8	—	—	536	66.4	680	62.5
Nicaragua								
Total	330	100	490	100	591	100	811	100
Agricultural	223	67.6	302	61.6	303	51.3	347	42.8

Source: ECLAC (1986), table 32.

ments, subsidies, and some public property. Moreover, spending for infrastructure and production services that could stimulate private investment in
agriculture has been interrupted; public investment in irrigation, conservation, improvement of soils, development of harvesting of fruit and pasture,
etc. has been reduced. Likewise, spending on research and development has
decreased, affecting the long-term development potential of the region. For
example, exploitation of the enormous irrigation potential in Central America
has been cut back drastically, precisely at a time when it should have been
promoted.

Trade policies to promote exports often clash with fiscal systems that are
based to a certain extent upon export taxes. Generally the state ends up

Table 3.3 Agricultural Exports as a Share of Total Exports

	1970	1975	1979	1980	1981	1982	1983	1984	1985
Costa Rica									
Exports[a]	227	456	934	981	1,008	864	888	1,174	
Agric. Exports[b]	72.50	63.70	62.50	61.90	53.80	59.70	58.90	56.60	71.10
Coffee	31.60	19.60	33.50	24.80	24.00	27.30	27.06	27.70	33.3
Bananas	28.90	29.20	20.20	20.70	22.40	26.30	28.20	24.00	21.7
Cotton			0.10	0.20					
Beef	7.80	7.70		7.10	7.40	6.10	3.70	4.90	5.7
Others[c]	4.20	7.20	8.70	9.10					10.4
El Salvador									
Exports[a]	236	514	1,205	1,038	786	698	729	845	
Agric. Exports[b]	59.60	50.10	68.50	65.60	62.90	64.50	63.20	63.1	65.3
Coffee	49.40	35.80	59.80	57.20	56.10	57.60	55.20	61.4	60.2
Bananas									
Cotton	10.20	14.30	7.50	7.90	6.70	6.50	7.50	1.30	5.1
Beef			1.20	0.50	0.10	0.40	0.50	0.4	
Others[d]									
Guatemala									
Exports[a]	291	623	1,239	1,510	1,202	1,113	1,158	1,205	
Agric. Exports[b]	59.10	65.10	55.70	54.50	44.50	47.60	40.80	59.50	60.30
Coffee	34.50	25.90	35.40	30.50	24.90	32.00	28.30	31.90	45.60
Bananas	6.90	5.40	1.50	2.900	4.30	6.10	4.90	4.90	6.70
Cotton	8.90	11.60	15.40	10.90	13.00	8.10	6.20	6.40	7.00

Table 3.3 Agricultural Exports as a Share of Total Exports (*Continued*)

	1970	1975	1979	1980	1981	1982	1983	1984	1985
Beef	4.20	2.60	3.40	1.90	2.30	1.40	1.40	1.10	1.00
Others[e]	4.60	19.60		8.30				15.20	
Honduras									
Exports[a]	171	302	734	821	723	663	740	775	
Agric. Exports[b]	69.07	60.85	67.63	64.01	62.87	67.63	61.66	60.45	61.50
Coffee	14.90	19.40	26.00	24.00	22.10	22.60	21.80	22.10	23.00
Bananas	43.30	21.00	26.40	26.80	27.30	32.30	29.30	29.80	35.80
Cotton	0.60	1.50	1.50	1.60	1.60	1.00	0.60	1.00	
Beef	0.80	6.20	8.00	7.20	5.90	5.00	4.50	3.20	2.70
Others[f]	9.47	12.75	5.73	4.41	5.97	6.73	5.46	4.35	
Nicaragua									
Exports[a]	180	375	551	414	476	371	427	432	
Agric. Exports[b]	52.40	41.80	64.00	58.4	60.10	62.10	72.10	74.20	79.8
Coffee	18.00	12.80	25.80	36.80	27.30	30.50	35.80	31.80	40.7
Bananas	0.20	1.60	1.00	1.90	4.20	2.40	3.50	3.10	5.0
Cotton	19.20	25.50	22.00	6.70	24.40	20.90	25.50	34.70	30.1
Beef	15.00	1.90	15.20	13.00	4.20	8.30	7.30	4.60	4.0
Panamá									
Exports[a]	106	278	303	350	317	308	299	252	
Agric. Exports[b]	50.60	39.50	22.10	36.30	24.20	25.20	27.50	34.90	18.50
Coffee			2.80	2.40	4.10	3.50	4.40	2.70	
Bananas	46.80	24.60	18.70	14.60	20.10	19.10	21.90	21.30	18.50

Cotton	3.80	0.60	0.70	2.60	1.20	0.60		
Beef								
Others^h	14.90		18.60			10.30		
Central America								
Exports^a	1,212	2,548	4,966	5,114	4,510	4,017	4,242	4,683
Agric. Exports^b	56.80	44.40	55.80	50.10	50.40	53.40	53.10	53.20
Coffee	24.70	18.90	30.50	29.30	26.50	28.90	28.80	29.60
Bananas	21.00	13.60	11.30	11.20	13.00	14.40	14.60	13.90
Cotton	6.50	8.80	7.80	4.50	7.60	6.10	6.60	7.20
Beef	4.60	3.10	6.20	5.10	3.30	4.00	3.10	2.50

a Total exports in millions of U.S. dollars.
b Agricultural exports as a share of total exports (%).
c Includes cacao and nontraditional agricultural exports.
d Includes sugar and cardamom.
f Refers to lumber.
h Refers to sugar.
Source: ECLAC (1986), table 19.

losing its fiscal base in order to promote exports, precisely when fiscal resources are most necessary for reactivation and productive reinvestment.

In conclusion, the effects of macroeconomic adjustments on Central American agriculture are incomplete and contradictory. They have not been accompanied by true investment incentives because they have not been able to provide support for the neediest producers. This has a restrictive effect, not only on the capacity to export, but also on the internal market that contracts each time real wages decrease.

II. The Present Challenges in Overcoming the Crisis

A. Magnitude of the Challenge

Central American agriculture has a wide potential that can be fulfilled in spite of the challenges and obstacles mentioned earlier. But in order to fulfill the economic potential of Central America, it is necessary to have a macroeconomic and microeconomic coherence that favors vigorous expansion of the agricultural sector, allowing for greater production of food products and for a more diverse range of export products.

1. Food Demand and Nutritional Security. Food and nutritional security in Central America is more or less fulfilled, except for some areas of critical poverty, but demand will increase considerably in the immediate future. This is due to the crucial and complex interaction between the increases in population and urbanization and their effects on the volume and composition of demand. If a new era of accelerated growth arises, there will be another paradox of success: a higher than proportional increase in the demand for food products and, moreover, food products of high initial demand elasticity, especially animal protein requiring more economic resources, land, and energy. Satisfying the nutritional security of the region and substantially improving the levels of nutrition, will require enormous production efforts.

The growing qualitative and quantitative pressures to meet food requirements are closely linked with population, which has increased particularly fast in the last decades, at nearly 3 percent annually. A total population of 40 million inhabitants is projected for the year 2000, even allowing for a demographic transition that could dampen population growth. This poses a critical strain on the natural resource base. The population density, 80 inhabitants per km^2 in 1985, will exceed 92 per km^2 at the turn of the century. Rapid urbanization is expected to continue, implying a 12 percent increase on the current base of 38 percent of the population residing in cities. This natural population growth will correspond to an additional impact on the demand for food products. The effects of increases in disposable income and changes in consumption and dietary patterns are unknown.

These trends will require adjustments in order to achieve nutritional security and to allow for a continued growth, which in Central America means avoiding the rupture of foreign trade. It is estimated that the requirements of basic grains will grow from 345,000 to 543,000 tons per year just to maintain the current nutritional levels. This means that the land dedicated to production should be increased by nearly 20 percent (from 4 million to 4.8 million hectares) during this period, although this may, and should, be moderated through improved yields. In this case, the keys to adequate production and productivity are small-scale irrigation and an improved technological package of high-yielding inputs.

It is important to remember the need to supervise the ecological impact of the expansion of the agricultural frontier. On the other hand, the delicate balance of the regional nutritional system could be disrupted if a concerted effort to increase production does not take place. Failure to expand production could lead to a food deficit of nearly 20 percent.

It is also important to emphasize that the promotion of agriculture would lead, above all, to the vigorous creation of both rural and urban employment,

Table 3.4   Food Security for Central America

	Total Population (millions)	Grains Required (000s tons)	Hectares Required (thousands)	Nutritional Indices Per Capita*		
				Food	Protein	Calories
1986	26	345	4.000	90	60	97
				(72)	(48)	(80)**
2000	40	543	4.800	92	65	98

* Food = Production of foodstuffs by physical volume (74/76).

Protein = Consumption of proteins in daily grams per capita (79/81).

Calories = Consumption of calories as percentage of minimum.

**Nutritional indices in the region for the year 2000 if measures are not taken in this regard.

Note: Nutritional indices in Haiti: food = 70, protein = 45, calories = 80.

Source: IICA, based on data from ECLAC and CATIE.

thus increasing the demand for food products and some industrial products. Moreover, regional nutritional security should pursue rural development beyond agricultural production narrowly defined, since 70 percent of basic grains are produced by small-scale producers. Thus, the strengthening of nutritional security should be accompanied by development of rural infrastructure, services, and education. In this way, the strengthening of nutritional security will promote greater social equity; otherwise, the viability of small-scale production may be jeopardized.

There is no better antidote for extreme poverty than the creation of productive jobs, and this is another great challenge posed by the region's current crisis. A million and a half productive jobs must be created in the rural sector, and more than two million additional jobs in the rest of the economy, from now until the end of this century. This challenge makes it imperative that agricultural technologies be adopted to achieve productivity increases that will, at the same time, maximize employment. The social organization of jobs must also allow for access to land and productive resources by a greater number of inhabitants.

The region's economically active population in agriculture will amount to nearly 45 percent of the total in the next decade. Unemployment, underemployment, and seasonal employment are the clearest expressions of structural and technological breakdowns of the productive system in agriculture. These are long-standing structural problems in the region, and during the last three decades nearly 60 percent of agricultural workers have been unemployed or underemployed. An equivalent of 3 million people are unemployed in this sector. (See table 3.5 for actual figures of unemployment and underemployment as well as the employment requirements extrapolated to the year 2000.) These figures indicate that even if current unemployment

Table 3.5   Need for Generation of Employment in Agriculture

	Unemployment %	Underemployment %	Job Requirements (thousands)
1986	25	60	1.500
2000	12	20	1.750

Source: IICA-CEPI.

were cut in half, and underemployment decreased to only 65 percent of its current level, there still would be a greater employment deficit than the present one. This gives us an idea of the magnitude of the challenge that must be faced by employment policies. Projects in small agricultural industries, small-scale irrigation, and, in general, local agro-industrial development stimulated also by local agricultural demand, could be the basis for an unemployment strategy that also combats rural poverty.

These figures force us to be very cautious about technologies that fail to increase work productivity vis-à-vis other productive resources, thus actually discriminating against employment. It is also important that those technologies favored and promoted for agriculture increase the productivity of land and natural resources.

2. Improvement of Land Distribution. One of the major structural obstacles of the agricultural sector in Central America is the marked inequality in the distribution of agricultural property. This is linked with the limitations of access to other resources such as water, infrastructure, energy, and credit. Politically and institutionally, the solution to the agricultural problem is one of the biggest challenges faced by the countries of the region, given that it involves the interests of powerful groups in society. Nevertheless, solving this problem would overcome one of the greatest limits to economic development and internal market growth. El Salvador and Nicaragua have made important efforts in the right direction. Costa Rica, which began with an enviable equality of landholding, now faces a dangerous process of concentration of agricultural property. For the region as a whole, 95 percent of the producers occupy 38 percent of the available land in relatively small production units of less than 15 hectares (sometimes much smaller) of generally poor quality land. At the other extreme, 6 percent of the producers hold more than 60 percent of agricultural land (see table 3.6). The average size of farms larger than 15 hectares is 650 hectares.

Table 3.6   Land Distribution in Central America (1971)

% Farms	% Land	Average Size HS.
6	62	650
94	38	5

Source: IICA-CEPI, based on CATIE data.

This serious inequality has led to inefficient use that is also damaging to the resource base. On one hand, the impoverished *minifundio* (very small farms) literally digs under its base of agro-ecological sustenance and the *latifundio* (very large estates) uses its resources extensively and wastefully. Historically, land has been considered a symbol of status and an instrument of access to financial and other resources. This idea is one of the principal obstacles in the actual agricultural panorama of the region. Over the last three decades, 20 percent of the land has been dedicated to the production of basic food products, 18 percent to industrial products (exports as well as nonexports) and 61 percent for pasture. This last category, nevertheless, includes idle lands whose principal function has been speculation. Thus, the challenge faced by the Central American governments consists in harmonizing productive, social, and political objectives.

3. Equilibration of Balance of Payments. An important challenge faced by the Central American countries is to achieve a favorable payments balance. This requires a favorable current account in agricultural trade. The United Nations Economic Commission for Latin America and the Caribbean (ECLAC) has calculated that this would require annual growth rates of at least 7 percent, an increase in the volume of exports, and a growing substitution of imported inputs and agricultural imports.

4. Promotion of the "Self-sustainable" Use of Renewable Natural Resources. The promotion of the "self-sustainable" use of natural resources is particularly dramatic for all the countries of the region given that its abundant wealth of germplasm is being depleted at an accelerated rate. Likewise, soil erosion has become critical in many areas, most notably El Salvador. This is linked with soil degradation, indiscriminate felling of forests, and inappropriate agricultural practices such as the cultivation of areas containing extreme slopes or poor soil. To some extent this has been unavoidable because a very high proportion of the agricultural surface in Central America is hilly land.

The inappropriate handling of natural resources generates certain problems that are worth mentioning:

a. The loss of productive forests due to deforestation activities and to conflicts with other uses of the land. CATIE calculates that less than 60 percent of the region's area is now covered with forests. The deforestation process is accelerating at an alarming rate of 400,000 hectares per year.

b. Degradation of the fragile ecosystems of the tropical rainforests. Reduced

forest area has triggered a strong process of degradation of forest ecosystems—
a process that is difficult to reverse.

c. Decrease in the importance of trees in the agricultural systems. Small-
scale producers have been forced to use their reduced plots intensively with
soils that rapidly lose their productivity, sacrificing, gradually but increasingly, the trees on their properties.

d. Degradation of hydrographic basins. The great need for water to provide
for the urban population and to generate electricity has imposed additional
pressure on the need to reverse the degradation process of the hydrographic
basins, which is highly advanced in many cases (see table 3.7).

Thus the ecological panorama shows an important challenge to the
agricultural strategy of the region. The actual rates of deforestation leave
little hope that the demand for forest products can be met by the year 2000.
It is essential to establish proper forest management for renewable natural
resources of the region; soil, water, and forests should be integrated into a
long-term production-conservation policy. This requires productive reforestation, making reforestation compatible with the generation of jobs and the
need for exports. This is a very difficult task in the varied and fragile
ecosystems of the tropical rainforests.

5. *Revitalization of the Integration Process.* Another fundamental challenge
is to rekindle the growth based on regional integration. Integration of the
regional market would allow for economies of scale and a more rational use
of those agricultural resources that are distributed unequally among the

Table 3.7 Status of Tropical Forests in Central America

Country	Primary Forest Remaining 1983 (km²)	Current Rate of Loss of Forest/Year (km²)	Percentage Cover Lost/Year
Nicaragua	27,000	1,000	3.7
Guatemala	25,700	600	2.3
Panamá	21,500	500	2.3
Honduras	19,300	700	3.6
Costa Rica	15,400	600	3.9
El Salvador	0	0	0.0

Source: IICA-CEPI, based on CATIE data.

Central American countries. Cattle raising, irrigation, grain production, management of the agricultural frontier, and diversification of production would all be much more efficient if they were integrated into productive projects of a regional, not national, scope.

B. Principal Restrictions Due to the Potential and Response Capacity of the Central American Economies

We have already indicated that the exaggerated concentration of rural property and its irrational use present fundamental restrictions on the development process and affect the levels of rural poverty. Other factors are less visible, but equally important.

1. Access to Credit, Technology, and Technical Assistance. As a result of the factors mentioned previously, the agricultural sector displays great heterogeneity and technological levels reflecting this heterogeneity. Most cases underline the insufficiency and unproductiveness of small-scale agriculture. Nonetheless, agro-exporting activity has been developing in response to the signals and stimuli of the foreign market. This has moved small-scale farmers into a process of technological change and growing capitalization. On the other hand, the producers of basic food grains, who are discouraged by consumer subsidies and overvalued exchange rates, do not have sufficient incentives to adopt technological innovations, modernize their operations, or seek access to greater credit and financing.

This duality results in the almost exclusive concentration of scarce resources in the hands of producers who are oriented toward exports. In fact, 86 percent of credit placed by Central American banks in 1985 went to export

Table 3.8   Distribution of Land by Size of Farm (%)

Category (Ha)	Units	Average Area	Total Area
≤0.7	25	0.42	1.5
0.7–7.0	41	2.4	9.0
7.0–35.0	28	16	27.0
>350	6	650	62.5

Source: IICA-CEPI.

products, leaving less than 14 percent for products of internal consumption. The farm credit market has been at a virtual standstill during the greater part of the last decade. The institutions responsible for farm credit have demonstrated a high level of inefficiency and a lack of political will to reach the medium-scale and small-scale producers.

The duality of income reinforces the technological differentiation between producers of exports and producers of basic food grains. Without serious policy intervention, this technological breach will continue to heighten this bimodal social and economic differentiation.

"Appropriate technology" faces the needs of both subsectors. Biotechnology, for instance, should help to reduce the costs of small-scale producers *and* increase the productivity of agricultural exporters. The region's difficult institutional and financial situation makes the current technological duality a grave restriction for rechanneling Central American agriculture into elevated growth that could contribute to a favorable trade balance.

2. Exhaustion of Renewable Natural Resources. The ecological change resulting from demographic pressures and general economic tendencies is mostly a rapid deforestation of the tropical and deciduous forests of the isthmus. Two-thirds of all the forests felled from colonial times to the present have been cut down since 1950.

C. Potentiality of the Region

Throughout this study we have affirmed that Central America has great potential for a policy of rapid agricultural development. In this section we shall develop that thesis.

1. Land Availability. The Central American isthmus holds an important reserve of natural resources to maintain its economic reactivation in proportion to the population. Even though resources are distributed unequally, important opportunities exist for the development of agriculture and cattle breeding and for the recovery of forest zones. In particular, there is a large "agricultural frontier": largely uncultivated lands with quality soils capable of small- to medium-scale cultivation. Moreover, increased productivity of currently cultivated land is quite feasible.

As we have seen, the essential limits are the landholding structures prevailing in most of the countries, which result in the use of less than 30 percent of the sum total of an enormous agricultural frontier; the rest of this

Table 3.9   Rates of Growth of the Population and of Per Capita Gross Domestic
Product—Central America and Panamá

	Percentage Growth Rates					
	Guatemala	El Salvador	Honduras	Nicaragua	Costa Rica	Panamá
Population						
1970–84	3.02	2.92	3.38	3.28	2.42	2.49
1985–2000	2.77	3.00	3.12	3.14	2.04	1.92
Economically Active Population						
1970–84	3.62	3.18	3.43	3.47	3.61	3.20
1985–2000	3.17	3.47	3.64	3.63	2.37	2.54
Per Capita GDP						
1981	−2.3	−10.5	−2.3	0.5	−5.4	2.0
1982	−6.3	−8.1	−5.2	−4.5	−8.9	0.3
1983	3.2	−5.1	−3.6	1.7	—	2.0

Source: CORECA, "Situación de la Seguridad Alimentaria y Opciones de politica en la Región del CORECA" (adaptation from tables 4 and 6) (1985).

land is generally used inefficiently. The majority of the cultivable surface is found in the dry Pacific region. On the other hand, more than a third of the available land, characterized as the "agricultural frontier," is located in the region of the Atlantic Ocean. This region could be brought into production, and, in fact, into the economic, social, and political mainstream of the Central American countries. However, this would require major investments and detailed agricultural studies. In the short term, it is more feasible to develop the Pacific region, where medium-and small-scale works of irrigation are required to cover very large land areas for the production of short-cycle basic grains or fruits. Proper irrigation could thus incorporate a significant share of the two million available hectares. This would ensure the provision of sufficient food production and also promote agricultural exportation in particularly appropriate areas. ECLAC estimates that this great irrigation potential has been applied to only 16 percent of the area appropriate for irrigation. Of course, all of these irrigation efforts should take into account the delicate ecological balances in the tropical ecosystems. As for the nearly 18 million hectares of forest use, it is important to incorporate policies of sustainable production with a long-term vision.

Table 3.10   Sectoral Distribution of the Labor Force in the Central American
Isthmus 1950–80 (thousands of persons)

Country	Year	EAP				Agriculture/
		Agriculture	Industry	Service	Total	Total (%)
Costa Rica	1950	169	49	76	294	57
	1960	194	70	115	379	51
	1970	226	106	199	531	43
	1980	239	180	358	777	31
El Salvador	1950	447	106	131	684	65
	1960	517	145	179	841	61
	1970	662	170	350	1,182	56
	1980	685	308	594	1,587	43
Guatemala	1950	681	138	177	996	68
	1960	828	167	248	1,243	67
	1970	973	270	344	1,587	61
	1980	1,118	335	514	1,967	57
Honduras	1950	338	42	88	468	72
	1960	435	66	118	619	70
	1970	513	112	166	791	65
	1980	652	174	252	1,078	60
Nicaragua	1950	249	56	62	367	68
	1960	289	75	104	468	62
	1970	319	96	204	619	52
	1980	384	130	311	852	47
Panamá	1950	117	43	94	254	46
	1960	195	53	134	382	51
	1970	214	90	210	514	42
	1980	209	119	329	657	32

Source: IDB, *Economic and Social Progress in Latin America* (Washington, D.C., 1987), p. 98.

2. Proximity to Extremely Large Markets. Another evident advantage of the
Central American region is its privileged geographical location: in the south
is the Panama Canal, the natural link with South America; to the north are
Mexico, the United States, and Canada, providing an enormous market for
the countries of the region. The United States, Canada, Mexico, Colombia,

and Venezuela are very close to the region; they could, and should, be thought of as important markets for certain agricultural products for which the region offers clear comparative advantages. Consolidating these markets for Central America's agro-export supply is very important. Colombia, Venezuela, and, above all, Mexico have structural deficits in providing certain basic agricultural products for which Central America has an evident potential. With the possibility of transport through the Panama Canal, Central American products have good access to the more remote markets of Japan, other Asian countries, and Europe.

3. *Availability of Manual Labor.* There is an abundance of manual labor in the region—in fact, there is an excess of supply—that, with proper training, organizational skills, and technology, could be harnessed in a productive and competitive fashion for agricultural development. Greater rural employment in agriculture and agricultural industry will provide a larger internal market with obvious advantages of scale, efficiency, and productivity for local agriculture.

4. *Response Capacity Toward Appropriate Incentives.* In spite of the intense economic and political Central American crises, the region has gained great capacity to react to market stimuli and to launch previously restricted productive activities. Moreover, this response capacity is reflected in Third World markets, where there has been an important, although still insufficient, penetration by new Central American products.

D. Integration and Its Advantages

The creation of a large internal market through Central American integration mechanisms still offers one of the most important prospects for general economic recovery. In agriculture, and specifically in projects of agricultural reactivation (such as public works of infrastructure, irrigation, and frontier development), the regional perspective is the most appropriate basis for identifying comparative advantage. Table 3.11 displays the commercial balance of Central American agricultural products. All the countries show a deficit in dairy products, poultry, eggs, and vegetable and animal oils. Nicaragua, Costa Rica, and Honduras show comparative advantages for vegetable production, while El Salvador shows ample experience in the production of poultry and eggs. Due to their climatic advantages, Guatemala and Costa Rica could expand their production of dairy products, while, for

Table 3.11   Balance of Trade in Agricultural Products in Central America
(average 1981–85; millions of U.S. dollars)

Country	Cereal Grains	Beef	Dairy Products and Eggs	Fruits and Vegetables	Vegetable Oils and Animal Fats
Costa Rica	− 25	51	− 4	229	− 4
El Salvador	− 39	− 7	− 17	− 31	− 22
Guatemala	− 31	42	− 10	89	− 23
Honduras	− 22	24	− 14	246	− 1
Nicaragua	− 36	16	− 12	3	− 30

Source: IICA, based on data from 1987 IDB Report.

example, Nicaragua could produce more grains and oilseeds. Likewise, cattle-raising could be much more efficient on a regional basis. In addition, integration would produce a regional market adequate for stimulating efficiency and additional demand.

E. To Confront the Basic Trade-Offs: A Unimodal Policy

There is a delicate dilemma in agricultural policy concerning the balance between food crops and export-oriented cash crops. For Central America, exports have the advantages of promoting employment, securing foreign exchange, and providing fiscal resources for the state. Their negative aspects include reducing land available for the production of staples, thus eroding food security. Nevertheless, one cannot conclude that this is an inevitable trade-off. Central America has the capacity to increase both basic food and export production. Both climatic and seasonal variation allow for specialization of certain regions in one type of crop or the other. Moreover, there are some labor-intensive agro-export crops, such as the "Kenaf," which is being introduced into Central America.

In this regard, an interesting study by Von Braun and Kennedy shows favorable empirical results. In a set of more than twenty countries, there is a positive correlation between growth of area dedicated to farming and the volume of food production, because these countries have "unimodal" agricultural policies—macroeconomic policies that are consistent with the development of agriculture as a whole. The same authors have also found a positive correlation in the per capita growth of food availability and growth of agriculture as a whole. Thus it is important to put the problem of the trade-offs between agricultural exportation and basic food production into perspective.

It is important to point out the necessity for a "unimodal" policy. If agricultural reactivation is born exclusively out of an agro-export development, it will never solve the basic problems of lack of access to productive resources, generalized poverty, and market narrowness. There will not be a truly dynamic drive toward a long-term solution. On the other hand, if governments neglect present and potential export opportunities, there would be a decrease in currency flows, income, employment, and, finally, the size of the market. Thus, a selective unimodal policy should be encouraged in which small-scale farmers have the opportunity to produce new agricultural exports, especially products of high manual labor content.

III. Growth with Equity: Broad Strategy Lines

A. A New Macroeconomic Framework

Which macroeconomic policy will be consistent with growth and equity and will also incorporate nutritional security as a central ingredient?

In the first place, the new macroeconomic policy regime should follow a "unimodal" strategy. That is, it must reunify what is now a dual structure, focusing both on the productivity of the backward peasant economy and the productivity of agro-exports. Thus the macroeconomic strategy should favor, first of all, the stimulation of agriculture as a whole. But it should establish a policy of differential interest rates, prices, and even subsidies that in some way would compensate the sectors whose structural rigidity, technological backwardness, or capital endowments have not allowed them to capture the benefits of exchange rate policy or other pro-agricultural policies which thus far have benefited only commercial agro-exportation.

A fundamental requirement of macroeconomic policy should be food security for Central America. This should be understood in a broader sense as providing access to the previously defined minimum nutritional requirements to all of the Central American population. This requires a promotion of internal production, but also mechanisms for channeling imports and subsidies to certain very poor groups. This policy should be pinpointed to support marginal producers. Obviously it is possible, given the fiscal restrictions and the trade-offs of fiscal and monetary policies existing within the region, that one will not be able to accomplish these objectives simultaneously with the countries' own resources. Here it is legitimate to pose a strategic plan for foreign cooperation and aid. Even without external resources, available resources and needs can be balanced without sacrificing minimum nutritional security. It is true that exports and basic production compete for scarce resources. That is exactly where a clear and explicit definition of macroeconomic policies and a significant role for food cooperation should intervene. With this macroeconomic framework, one can aim for the design of sectoral policies that confront the severe restrictions faced by Central American agriculture. Only on this basis can one put forth a sectoral policy of growth and gradual distribution with relative prices favorable to agriculture and with a balance between exports and basic production. Let us then look at some premises for sectoral reactivation within this macroeconomic policy.

B. The Strategy of Sectoral Reactivation

The reactivation of the agricultural sector must address three fundamental objectives:

1. the nutritional security of the marginal population,
2. increased capacity to generate a positive foreign balance, and
3. increased supply of basic food products.

Obviously, the possible trade-offs of these strategies should be identified clearly in order to achieve a proper balance, and should be accompanied by a strategy to improve the *institutional* capacity to provide support services necessary to fulfill these objectives.

C. Investments in Infrastructure and Production

The broadening of an internal market has two requirements: the creation of employment and income generation in the whole population, and the establishment of conditions to facilitate additional production. That is why capital resources should be devoted to the creation of an infrastructure that will allow for the fulfillment of the basic needs of the population: health, including basic medical services, disease prevention, potable water, and sanitation; production distribution networks, including both access routes to areas of production and markets and facilities for transportation and storage; access to electricity; personal security; and basic education. Similarly, rural housing and other infrastructural support for rural communities is important.

As mentioned before, irrigation plays a strategic role in the region. This should be accompanied by technical assistance, adequate inputs, and institutions, such as the organization of users to establish and carry out efficient rules for the distribution and use of water, its conservation, and the maintenance of the infrastructure.

The placement of basic investments depends on which segments of the population are to be targeted. This favors, above all, the employment of unskilled agricultural workers, whose labor is precisely the most abundant, for the construction and maintenance of the infrastructure. This would have the additional advantage of providing a ready-made market for the greater yield. This means that there is a direct and immediate benefit obtained from investment.

Prices and Finance. Agricultural policy has many objectives: nutritional security, investment, a supply of raw materials and rural labor, and the maintenance of low and stable consumer prices. But domestic production and the desire for maximum supply sometimes clash in the short run. Short-term increases in production and productivity or in foreign-produced supply, along with the low elasticity of demand for certain agricultural products, tends to reduce producers' incomes. This is true even though the long-term increases in demand allow for expansion in the market. In order to overcome domestic supply constraints, governments have resorted to support prices for basic grains and agro-exports, subsidies for imports and specialized inputs, subsidies to producers, and the institutionalization of regulating monopolies for the management of exports and grains trading. Frequent currency overvaluation has stimulated excessive grain imports at artificially low prices, which unduly hinder domestic production. Although this policy has generally resulted in a great enough total (domestic and imported) supply to cover the demand for food products, it has hurt domestic producers, thus undermining domestic supply in the long term and reducing the possibility of a progressive decrease of prices through economies of scale and increases in productivity. At the same time, these imports increase the financial deficit.

The need to reduce the deficits has driven the governments of the region to impose greater taxes on foreign trade, in turn driving away investment in export agriculture and undermining the future capacity of production.

The remedy is to establish and maintain appropriate prices that will support the growth of production and the income of the rural sector without artificially stimulating subsidized urban consumption. For instance, the exchange rates should reflect the real costs of reacquiring foreign resources. Taxes on foreign trade should contain unequivocal and stable signals concerning the selective level of protection that is to be granted to specific goods and productive activities; the imposition of implicit taxation on agriculture should be eliminated to the point that agriculture is not taxed above other sectors. On the other hand, global policy measures should be coordinated with specific measures of the sector. This will avoid the possibility of inadequate protection of agricultural production confronted by efforts to reactivate other sectors.

The objective of establishing and maintaining relative prices favorable to the continuous flow of resources toward productive activities is precisely to strengthen the reactivation of agriculture within a unimodal or redistributive strategy. Thus, these flows should be structured to mobilize private savings from the agricultural sector itself and from commercial banks to finance productive activities. Specific rediscounts and interest rates, covering administrative costs and capital risk, are required. To reduce financial costs, policies should be coordinated with a restructuring of the financial system to promote greater efficiency and broader regional coverage with strict administrative measures. If production and market risks can also be decreased through the use of appropriate technology and better infrastructure, such costs will be reduced even further.

Support services for production and distribution, supplied at market value, will create an additional incentive for agricultural production and will strengthen the links between agricultural production and other sectors of the economy, notably agro-industry. Mobilizing private savings for agricultural production will have an additional important effect: it will free public resources to back up the construction of basic infrastructure.

The role of the public sector. The public sector should concentrate on a series of elements, including the prediction of the economic behavior of the country, and, particularly, of the agricultural sector, and the adjustment of this behavior to the changing conditions of the macroeconomic policy regime.

At the same time, the public sector should develop guidelines, norms, and appropriate incentives for the creation of labor demand inside and outside the agricultural sector. These guidelines should begin with the construction of a basic infrastructure aimed toward low-resource producers, so that they, in turn, may have greater productive potential. The public sector should stimulate the design and operation of self-sufficient production financing programs, mobilizing savings for such activities. It should also develop and execute research and technology transfers that take into account nontraditional products and forms of production and the conservation of resources, especially those belonging to the poorest farmers. Technological development ought to reinforce several objectives:

1. nutritional security through irrigation and the improvement or stabilization of economic returns,
2. development of capacities of distribution, domestic and foreign marketing, including proper infrastructure, and
3. improvement in the administration's performance and management.

D. The State, Peasant Organizations, and Promotion of the Unimodal Strategy

Action by the state to promote and support peasant organizations is necessary. "Bureaucratic hierarchy" ought to be increased, and peasant organizations ought to be accepted participants in the coordination of policies to promote production.

The contribution of the peasant economy ranges from 35.6 percent (Costa Rica) to 63.9 percent (Honduras) of production for the internal market. In Honduras and Costa Rica, peasants also produce 25 to 30 percent of agricultural exports.

From that perspective, rural development cannot be focused exclusively on the process of incorporating the peasants into production and the national economy because, in many cases, they have already been incorporated into the economic development of their respective countries although they have low levels of productivity and low shares of the benefits.

Given the weight of small-scale production within total agricultural production of the Central American countries, strengthening and organizing small productive units is indispensable for the growth of the agricultural sector. In this sense, the struggle against rural poverty should be placed within the strategy of global development and not merely as a compensatory measure. This affirmation is sustained in the following considerations:

1. Two thirds of the Central American rural population are peasant families.
2. Peasant families are consumers as well as producers; increasing their income benefits all productive sectors oriented toward this market.
3. A better distribution of idle or underutilized agricultural land among land-poor and landless peasants would contribute to better exploitation of that resource if such a measure were accompanied by rural development policies as discussed above.

Development of Differentiated Policies Targeted to Small-Scale Producers. The strengthening of peasant units in Central America requires differentiated policies targeted to small-scale production. The design of policies to support small-scale agricultural production should begin with the recognition of the characteristics that differentiate this segment from medium- and large-scale production, while taking into account that this segment is differentiated within itself.

Implementing these differentiated policies requires the revision and establishment of new administrative systems. The participation of small-scale producers in this administration should be increased, and administrative decentralization should be favored. For this reason, public agencies involved in Central American rural development should coordinate their efforts with nongovernmental agencies that generate development among small-scale producers and channel financial and technical resources to them.

Increase of Production and Productivity of Peasant Labor. The rural development of the countries of the isthmus will not be achieved until production and productivity of peasant labor are increased. For this to occur, the following conditions are necessary:

1. The Central American peasant communities must have access to lands whose quality and location will allow for their development and competitiveness in the national and international markets. The distribution and titling of land must be motivated by the objective of rural development and the creation of viable agricultural enterprises, rather than the distribution of poorly situated land of little agricultural potential. Similarly, in certain areas irrigation or drainage suitable for increasing productivity and diversification of small-scale production is imperative.

2. Priority must be given to the identification and promotion of agricultural products that will upgrade the profitability of peasant production and the exploitation of comparative advantages. Peasant production should be diversified by introducing crops requiring intensive use of land and labor. At the same time, the identification and promotion of small-scale agro-industrial, extractive, and artisan processes are required to permit fuller use of peasant labor and to increase the value added to their product.

3. Appropriate technology for small-scale agricultural production must be generated, adapted, and applied in order to increase productivity and improve managerial performance. Therefore, it is necessary to develop regional programs of agricultural research and technology transfer for the small-scale producer. These regional programs would allow the countries of the isthmus to unify their efforts and would contribute to reducing the gap between the generation of technology and its adoption by small-scale farmers.

4. Lack of access to adequate and suitable financial resources is one of the biggest obstacles facing small-scale agricultural producers. It is necessary to design flexible systems of decentralized credit in Central America in order to administer and manage credit funds and to create reserve funds.

E. Promotion of Rural Agricultural Industry

Promotion of agro-industrial production is the most efficient productive link for benefitting peasants in the region. Agro-industry improves the possibility of placing basic products into different markets; this, in turn, sets the stage for increasing and diversifying incomes. In this manner the capability to overcome restrictive market situations is increased, at least in the short and medium term. In the long term, agro-industry offers opportunities to create multiplier effects through intersectoral forward and backward linkages.

The development of agro-industry is thus a key element within a strategy to promote the reactivation of the agricultural sector. Such development must be oriented toward increasing employment, generating currency reserves, and improving the technical and economic efficiency of production.

For this reason Central American agro-industry should address three principal areas:

1. Reconversion, in those cases in which, due to market limitations or

obsolescence, structural obstacles impede expansion or continuation of productive activity. The first case will require specific actions to obtain and transfer technology effectively with current commercial viability; the second case (i.e., continuation of productive activity) would require the development of new products springing from the use of basic raw materials, byproducts, or wastes.

2. New industries, concentrating on processed, finished, and intermediate goods, with high value added.
3. Rural agro-industry, initially directed toward basic transformation of production generated by small-scale commercial agriculture.

This last thrust can focus first on the national market or on simple processing for local markets. The development of production for foreign markets could be initiated at more advanced stages. In all of these cases, the object is the producers' appropriation of a share of the additional profits generated through value added. The development of rural agro-industry should complement the development of the rest of the subsector: this will secure its eventual link with wider markets, and, at the same time, lay down the guidelines for selecting productive processes and techniques consistent with market requirements.

The promotion of agro-industry should be channeled through groups or cooperatives to facilitate technological adoption and to overcome the limitations of small-scale operations. The private sector has an important role in these developments: mobilization of savings for the financing of projects, insertion into markets (internal and external), and the creation of efficient commercial operations, taking advantage of the facilities and supports in concert with the public sector.

F. Technological Change

The existence of comparative advantages is increasingly associated with technological change, rather than with the availability of natural and human resources. For this reason, it is vital to stimulate the capacity of the countries to develop, adopt, and use adequate technology for such ends. Thus the strategy for technological development of agriculture should contain three main elements:

1. strengthening and institutionalizing minimal technological capacities,

2. reciprocal technical cooperation, particularly for small countries, and
3. development of new capacities and orientations.

The strengthening should contemplate an urgent institutional and organizational reordering to increase the effectiveness and reduce the costs—today beyond the reach of Central America—of research and development. This will require a selective concentration of public effort and resources, or of foreign aid, on the solution of problems having priority and pertinence to the reactivation. Similarly, research and development institutions must be adjusted by means of, among other things, administrative flexibility and adequate salary levels, to improve operational capacity. Government regulation of the private sector must be revised and the private sector's formal relationships with other official agencies, producers, and the wider sector of science and technology must be reexamined.

Strengthening these areas also implies the provision of resources, not only for a physical infrastructure (i.e., experimental centers and stations, laboratories, and equipment) but also for wages and salaries, operating expenses, and the formation of human resources at adequate levels. This financing must be provided through a special emergency plan that will not worsen the countries' debts. On the other hand, the participation of the private sector in the financing of specific fields will be promoted.

The development of reciprocal technical cooperation is linked to the fact that Central American countries are too small for each of them to have large enough research units in each country without incurring excessively high costs. For the same reason, the ability to capture the benefits derived from technological change are limited. At the same time, there is a certain commonality among the countries of the region in agro-ecological conditions and socioeconomic problems. These points bring out the strategic character of reciprocal technical cooperation among the countries. Through collaborative research, one would reduce per capita costs and expand the benefits of the research, achieving in addition a better allocation of resources. Therefore it is necessary to support the development of networks and joint work addressing priorities common to the region.

To develop new capacities, the region needs mostly to increase its capacities to identify, select, and incorporate international advances that will deeply transform agriculture and agricultural research. This capacity could be developed by reinforcing specific programs, including the improvement or creation of regional research centers, university centers, or both. A key aspect of this is to train professionals in the basic sciences. This strategy must be complemented by special programs, or regional specialized centers of technological development in biotechnology, in those areas where comparative advantages are deemed possible.

The application of new knowledge by small-scale farmers depends on a joint effort among producers, researchers, and extension agents, aimed at removing commonly recognized technical restrictions that are peculiar to specific agro-ecological and socioeconomic conditions. At the same time the possible solutions are subject to two critical restrictions of the producer: his capital limitations and the risk aversion arising from his socioeconomic vulnerability. To the degree that the proposed changes require an intensification of the use of industrial inputs in that sector, they require institutional support of growing intensity, to minimize or compensate for such restrictions of capital and risk. This implies:

1. increasing specific efforts directed toward small-scale producers, through research in farming and production systems, with participation of agencies and technology generation and transfer in association with the producers,
2. developing a regional service to follow the worldwide generation of technologies appropriate to the small-scale producer and to feed "technological hypotheses" to the researchers within Central America,
3. consolidating results obtained at a subregional level in order to provide feedback on experiences of successful and unsuccessful innovations, and
4. a special initiative of support and aid to the countries to formulate policies and instruments that will institutionalize, regulate, and coordinate the state's actions toward agricultural technology to ensure that these actions address the social and developmental objectives of the country. This implies a concentration of available public sector resources in the areas of greatest financial and socioeconomic priority. On the other hand, it involves the participation of other actors, particularly the private sector, in financing the remainder of the required research. This will require the development of policies and instruments, within the countries and at regional levels, that will allow the private sector to capture or reserve resources for efforts to generate and transfer technology into fields where

such research and development would provide a sufficient level of benefits; and the development of policies and mechanisms to facilitate joint efforts between the state and the private sector.

G. *Employment, Poverty, and Nutritional Security*

As we have seen, unemployment, poverty, and nutritional security are closely linked. Nutritional security, then, constitutes an objective of macroeconomic policy and not merely of agricultural policy. Central America does not pose food problems of the seriousness of many other developing regions of the world or even of other countries in Latin America, where the chronic scarcity of food products as well as chronic malnutrition are present. The food problems of Central America have more to do with market instability, insecurity of food imports, low agricultural productivity, and the fall of purchasing power of certain segments of the population. The crisis of the 1980s was caused above all by the heavy burden of foreign debt, which led to decreased investment capacity and, as a result, decreased employment creation. The lack of purchasing power for food products is intimately related to the unemployment problem analyzed earlier.

The high rates of growth of the population and labor force, combined with poor GDP per capita growth, point toward great pressures on the labor market, on the levels of well-being, and consequently on nutritional security. Urbanization has been very rapid. The rural exodus has brought people to the service sector, rather than the industrial sector, and it is within the service sector that unemployment and underemployment are greatest. There are more people in the cities who must be fed, and these people work in sectors of lower salaries. At the same time, the mass of farmers who fled to the cities was essentially formed by small-scale farmers, who were most responsible for food production. The three countries of densest population—Guatemala, El Salvador, and Honduras—have great contingents of peasant populations; in Guatemala and Honduras they represent nearly 60 percent of the total labor force.

The challenge is to achieve an increase in employment opportunities, an improvement in income levels, and greater food production. In a recent article John Mellor and Richard Adams propose a strategy to achieve these objectives. Such a strategy concentrates precisely on making the production of food by small-scale farmers economically feasible. Given such antecedents, it is clear that the strategy of unimodal development that we propose for Central America is, at its base, a strategy of rural development.

Appendix. Project Ideas in Areas Relevant to the Strategy

Based on the foregoing analysis, and as examples, following are listed a series of Project Profiles[1] prepared by IICA-CEPI and the CORECA Secretariat for the Central American governments, which cover a major part—though not all—of the areas relevant for carrying out a strategy for the recovery and development of Central American agriculture. This Appendix includes a summary of such projects. A set of project profiles has already been delivered, via CORECA, to the respective governments.

This presentation is a preliminary step in a subsequent stage of identification, harmonization, and prioritizing of technical cooperation and investment projects for productive and social purposes to contribute to the equitable development of agriculture in Central America.

The Projects are:

1. Planning of Agricultural Production.
2. Mutual Technical Cooperation Program for the Central American Isthmus.
3. Establishment of a Unit for the Preparation and Implementation of Strategic Regional Projects.
4. Cooperative Program for Agricultural Research for Central America, Panamá, and the Dominican Republic.
5. Institutional Strengthening for Improving the Use of Irrigation and Drainage in the Central American Isthmus.
6. Program for Exploitation of Seafood and the Development of Mariculture.
7. Training of Peasant Trainers in the Context of Comprehensive Rural Development Projects.
8. Training of Credit Agents and Extension Workers in the Preparation and Evaluation of Agricultural Projects for Agricultural Enterprises.
9. Development of Agro-industry Making Use of the Flora and Fauna.
10. Strategy for Reconversion of the Sugar Industry in the Central American Isthmus.
11. Institutional Strengthening of the International Agricultural Emergency and Quarantine Systems in the Central American Isthmus.

12. Technological Exchange in Animal Health and Livestock Development among the Central American Countries.
13. Development and Strengthening of the Export Process (Search for Alternatives for the Sanitary Treatment of Tropical Fruits).
14. Strengthening of Public-Sector Institutions and Support for Non-Governmental Organizations for the Development, Use, and Conversion of Renewable Natural Resources.
15. Development of Watersheds in Border Areas.

Summary of Project Profiles

1. Planning of Agricultural Production

Main Objectives:
To support the processes of integration, agricultural modernization, and economic reactivation of the region by improving the competitiveness of export products and planning for each export item, and for each country, in a manner consonant with the buyer markets.

Main Aspects of the Strategy:
Project implementation is conceived of in two stages:
(i) identification of and a wide-ranging and detailed market study for the main agricultural export products;
(ii) establishing priorities among export items and proposing a scheme for institutionalizing an executive group or Executive Commission for the Development of Central American Agricultural Exports.

Goals/Results:
–Planning and studies on competitiveness of all traditional export products and the main nontraditional ones.
–Lay the bases for the establishment of the Executive Group or Committee for the Development of Central American Agricultural Exports.

Implementation Period: 1½ years

Budget (thousands of US dollars): $977

2. Mutual Technical Cooperation Program for the Central American Isthmus

Main Objectives:
To develop mutual cooperation among the member countries in order to eliminate uneven development in scientific and technological knowledge and to accelerate growth in agriculture.

Main Aspects of the Strategy:
Technical cooperation missions will be carried out by specialists in the sector in a wide range of thematic areas to assist in solving the problems identified.

Goals/Results:
–360 Technical Cooperation Missions (TCM) are to be carried out, along with a similar number of specific technical publications. The TCMs will take place as follows:

Year	No. of TCMS
I	60
2	80
3	100
4	120
Total	360

Implementation Period: 4 years

Budget (thousands of US dollars): $1,076

3. Establishment of a Unit for the Preparation and Implementation of Strategic Regional Projects

Main Objectives:
To support socioeconomic development efforts aimed at integration and support for recovery and modernization of agriculture in the Central American countries through the preparation and implementation of strategic regional projects.

Main Aspects of the Strategy:
–Establishing a Unit for the Preparation and Implementation of Regional Projects to achieve the proposed objectives.
–Supporting and complementing the efforts that regional organizations (SIECA, CABIE, ECLAC, IICA, and others) are carrying out for the region.
–Complementing and coordinating efforts with national and regional insti-

tutions and entities specialized in the preparation and evaluation of, and training for, agricultural investment and development projects.

Goals/Results:
Institutionalization and Full Operation of the Unit for Preparation and Implementation of Strategic Regional Projects.

Implementation Period: 4 years

Budget (thousands of US dollars): $8,086

4. Cooperative Program for Agricultural Research for Central America, Panamá, and the Dominican Republic

Main Objectives:
To promote development of agricultural research capabilities subregionally, as a mechanism for resolving or minimizing the impact of the problem of small-scale economies faced by the countries through mechanisms for integration of and cooperation among the national systems of research and transfer of technology.

Main Aspects of the Strategy:
–A high level of coordination and operational integration will be established among the national research systems for participants in the program.
–A clear definition of the priorities and establishment of common policies for action among the institutions is important in the implementation of this strategy.

Goals/Results:
Fulfillment of the goals will be measured based on the extent to which the following activities have been undertaken:
–Training: in-service, in other institutions, short courses, and postgraduate study.
–International consultancies.
–Collaborative research.
–Mutual technical cooperation.

Implementation Period: 4 years

Budget (thousands of US dollars): $5,235

5. Institutional Strengthening for Improving the Use of Irrigation and Drainage in the Central American Isthmus

Main Objectives:
To propose, through the use of irrigation and drainage, development of high-input agriculture adapted to the needs and physical, economic, and social characteristics of Central American agriculture and an increase in the volumes and yields, as well as diversification of crop and livestock production.

Main Aspects of the Strategy:
–Promoting more efficient use of existing irrigation and drainage infrastructure.
–Increasing current capacity and setting priorities among projects for expanding irrigation.
–Training technical personnel and farmers.
–Promoting the participation of small and medium producers in irrigated agriculture.

Goals/Results:
–Training of 30 professionals in agriculture.
–Training of 500 small and medium producers.
–Training of 30 hydraulic civil engineers.
–Training of 18 agricultural economists.
–Preparation of technical manuals; adjusting legislation; establishing information systems; formulating feasibility studies; etc.

Implementation Period: 3 years

Budget (thousands of US dollars): $4,256

6. Program for Exploitation of Seafood and the Development of Mariculture

Main Objectives:
–To support the development of aquaculture with a major emphasis on mariculture;
–To improve the systems for processing and marketing of seafood and mariculture;
–To promote the use of new production techniques and more intensive catch of seafood.

Main Aspects of the Strategy:
–Training of officials and local community workers.
–Technical cooperation to support the pre-investment and investment phases.
–Development of the infrastructure and equipment needed.

Goals/Results:
–Train 54 technical experts.
–Technical cooperation received of the 264 expert/months.
–Install and operate 6 multiple-use mariculture laboratories, 1 regional quality control laboratory, and 2 pilot projects on the use of new techniques of intensive fishing.

Implementation Period: 5 years

Budget (thousands of US dollars): $7,358

7. Training of Peasant Trainers in the Context of Comprehensive Rural Development Projects

Main Objectives:
To contribute to the institutional strengthening of public and private (NGO) organizations working in rural development, specifically in training peasants, in the Central American region.

Main Aspects of the Strategy:
–Development of methodologies that encourage participation of trainers and peasants.
–Design of participatory methods and techniques.
–Production of adequate means.
–Generation of institutional models for organization and administration in accordance with participatory principles.
–Definition of appropriate curricula.

Goals/Results:
The following will be trained:
–280 trainers
–2,800 promoters

Implementation Period: 4 years

Budget (thousands of US dollars): $2,000

8. Training of Credit Agents and Extension Workers in the Preparation and Evaluation of Agricultural Projects for Agricultural Enterprises

Main Objectives:
Institutional strengthening of the development banking sector, ministries of agriculture, and related institutions involved in supporting productive activities in the agricultural sector, by training their professional staff in identification, formulation, and evaluation of projects.

Main Aspects of the Strategy:
The central element of the strategy will be using the training program as an instrument for integrating the agricultural entities providing technical assistance, which will make it possible to prepare and expand the skills of the technical personnel in the project area. They, in turn, will transfer the methodology to the rest of the personnel.

Goals/Results:
–Permanent teams of instructors will be trained in each of the six participating development banks and related institutions.
–Sixty to seventy percent of the credit agents of each bank will be trained (60 per institution), along with 20 agricultural extension workers.
–18 national-level courses, 2 international courses, and 6 advanced seminars in applied microcomputing for the projects.

Implementation Period: 5 years

Budget (thousands of US dollars): $5,299

9. Development of Agro-Industry Making Use of the Flora and Fauna

Main Objectives:
–To transfer to the Central American region technologies for agro-industry that contribute to making better use of natural resources (flora and fauna) and of productive capacity
–To promote the establishment of new enterprises that apply such knowledge.

Main Aspects of the Strategy:

–Training the officials and other local community workers associated with project implementation.

–Technical cooperation from the countries and/or institutions that have the technologies that will be transferred to assist in the development of Central American agro-industry, together with the knowledge and demands of the markets and marketing systems of the agro-industrial countries.

–The infrastructure and equipment of entities specialized in agro-industrial technology in the region will be strengthened.

Goals/Results:

–40 technical experts will be trained in: technologies for agro-industrial diversification; exploitation of nontraditional raw materials; establishment of new enterprises; analysis of markets and marketing systems.

–144 expert/months of technical cooperation will be offered in analysis and identification of technologies, markets, agro-industrial assessment, development, and establishment of new enterprises.

Implementation Period: 5 years

Budget (thousands of US dollars): $3,342

10. Strategy for Reconversion of the Sugar Industry in the Central American Isthmus

Main Objectives:

To identify and analyze relevant experiences in the sugar industry, for selecting thematic studies to be carried out in depth by country and for the region as a whole.

–To define guidelines with the purpose of developing a strategy for reconversion of the sugar industry in the Central American isthmus.

–To identify strategic subregional and country-specific projects.

Main Aspects of the Strategy:

–Channelling of the capacities existing in the countries to the improvement and expansion of knowledge on this matter.

–Negotiation and coordination of efforts among countries and cooperation and financing agencies to strengthen such capabilities.

Goals/Results:

–This first phase, which will last six months, will be for preparing the work program that will lead to the assessment of the status and characteristics of the sugar problem in the Central American isthmus, and the identification of specific studies to be carried out subregionally and by country.

–The second phase, 12 months in duration, will include the activities needed for preparing the studies mentioned, which will form the basis for developing the guidelines of the strategy for the reconversion and diversification of the region's sugar industry.

Implementation Period: 1½ years

Budget (thousands of US dollars): $95

11. Institutional Strengthening of the International Agricultural Emergency and Quarantine Systems in the Central American Isthmus

Main Objectives:

–To reinforce phytosanitary and zoosanitary inspection services at maritime ports, international airports, and overland border posts.

–To implement and strengthen the animal and plant health emergency system for rapid detection, control, and eradication of exotic animal and plant diseases.

Main Aspects of the Strategy:

–Strategy of negotiation for the formulation and signing of agreements with the countries to attain their participation in the project.

–Induction strategy to:

Update the assessment.

Characterize the areas at risk.

Determine the magnitude of the emergency and quarantine systems.

Use existing data banks.

Prepare organizational models.

Goals/Results:

–Establishment of the agricultural emergency systems.

–Formation of an emergency animal health reference center.

–Review and standardization of the inspection services' methodologies and procedures.

–Establishment of an inter-American group for the coordination of actions for animal and plant health emergencies.

–Establishment of permanent regional groups analyzing international agricultural trade regulations.

–Establishment of an Evaluation Committee for the International Agricultural Quarantine systems.

Implementation Period: 4 years

Budget (thousands of US dollars): $3,060

12. Technological Exchange in Animal Health and Livestock Development among the Central American Countries

Main Objectives:

–To maximize the use of resources and infrastructure existing at the institutions of the subsector through personnel training

–To render feasible the alternatives for institutional reorganization of the state organizations geared to improving the supply of comprehensive services

–To increase their capacity for generating and transferring technology appropriate to the producers' socioeconomic profile.

Main Aspects of the Strategy:

–Forming a Coordinating Committee.

–Using the Technological Exchange Centers as bases for operation of the project.

–Establishing a data base on available resources for technological exchange and training.

–Training the human resources required by the countries' Animal Health and Livestock Development programs.

Goals/Results:

–Consolidation of 7 International Regional Centers for Technological Exchange as operational bases of the Project.

–Training of 750 professionals and technical personnel to improve their performance in actions for research, transfer, and extension of technologies, and for delivery of services.

Implementation Period: 3 years

Budget (thousands of US dollars): $2,430

13. Development and Strengthening of the Export Process (Search for Alternatives for the Sanitary Treatment of Tropical Fruits)

Main Objectives:
To strengthen the export processes by developing and adapting technologies that do not require agrochemical inputs.

Main Aspects of the Strategy:
–Extrapolating to the rest of the countries in the region the experiments done in Costa Rica to control the fruit fly using technologies that constitute an alternative to ethyl dibromide with mango and papaya production.
–Expanding experiments on technologies that are alternatives to ethyl dibromide or insecticides toxic to other tropical fruits that can be exported.
–Anticipating the animal health problems that may result from the use of agrochemicals, seeking alternative solutions through the use of biotechnology.

Goals/Results:
Establishment and operation of the sanitary treatment system for export fruits.

Implementation Period: 5 years

Budget (thousands of US dollars): $5,793

14. Strengthening of Public-Sector Institutions and Support for Non-Governmental Organizations for the Development, Use, and Conversion of Renewable Natural Resources

Main Objectives:
To strengthen the countries' institutional capacity to identify, formulate, obtain support for, implement, and evaluate pertinent projects for the development and conservation of renewable natural resources.
–To analyze legal documents relating to renewable natural resources with a view to bringing the laws into line with the need to orient the sector's development policies.
–To promote economic activity with a yield that is sustainable in the long run.
–To promote the establishment and management of native plantations and

forests in rural and semi-urban communities of Central America through non-governmental organizations.

Main Aspects of the Strategy:
–Training of personnel in scientific and technical aspects.
–Strengthening the mechanisms for coordination and exchange of information.
–Training of personnel in logistical and administrative matters.
–Preparation of a compendium of laws, decrees, and regulations.
–Preparation of a policy guide for the natural resources sector.
–Training personnel in legal matters and establishing working groups in this area.
–Associating and strengthening the national and regional NGOs.
–Technical and financial support for the establishment and management of plantations and native forests.

Goals/Results:
–Subproject for preparation of projects in renewable natural resources and personnel training for implementing projects.
–Subproject for analysis and adjustment of laws, decrees, and regulations regarding renewable natural resources.
–Subproject for the Development of Fuelwood and Timber Production.

Implementation Period: 5 years

Budget (thousands of US dollars): $8,020

15. Development of Watersheds in Border Areas

Main Objectives:
The coordinated use of land, water, vegetation, and other physical resources and activities, to achieve recovery and guarantee minimal degradation of the soil, and a minimal environmental impact, to achieve sustained development in the border areas, simultaneously promoting integration and regional cooperation.

Main Aspects of the Strategy:
Central aspect of the strategy is the preparation of management plans for the watersheds of the Paz River (Guatemala-El Salvador), the Lempa River

(Guatemala, El Salvador, and Honduras), the Gulf of Fonseca (El Salvador, Honduras, and Nicaragua), the San Juan River (Nicaragua-Costa Rica), and the Sixaola River (Costa Rica-Panamá).

Goals/Results:
At the end of the project the management plans for five border-area watersheds will have been prepared.

Implementation Period: 5 years

Budget (thousands of US dollars): $1,258

Note

1. CORECA: Regional Council for Agricultural Cooperation in Central America, México, Panamá, and the Dominican Republic. Priority Regional Projects for the recovery and development of Central American agriculture. January 1988.

References

Arcia, G., "Assessment of Rural Development in Central America," (draft). Research Triangle Institute. Prepared for the International Commission for Central American Recovery and Development.

Central American Bank for Economic Integration (CABEI). *Sustentación para un programa de financiamiento de los déficit del comercio intrarregional.* July 1981. Tegucigalpa, Honduras.

Colmenares, J.H., and J.A. Aguirre. "Inversión en regadío y capacitación en preparación de proyectos agrícolas." *Conferencias y Conclusiones del Seminario Iberoamericano de Riego y Drenaje.* Ministry of Agriculture, Fishing, and Food, Madrid. November 1986.

Fletcher, L., D. Green, J. de la Cruz, and R. Hager. "Situación de la Seguridad Alimentaria y opciones políticas en la región de CORECA." Report to the Secretariat for Coordination of the Council for Agricultural Cooperation in Central America, Panama, and the Dominican Republic (CORECA), 1985.

General Treaty for Central American Economic Integration. Meeting of Vice-Presidents with Ministers of Foreign Relations, Ministers in charge of Economic Integration and Regional Development, and Ministers of Planning of Central America. Guatemala, January 22, 1988.

Huang, Y., and P. Nicholas. "The Social Costs of Adjustment." *Finance and Development*, Vol. No. 2, June 1987.

InterAmerican Development Bank. *Economic and Social Progress in Latin America* (1985, 1986, and 1987). Washington, D.C.

Interamerican Institute for Cooperation in Agriculture (IICA). Definición de Acciones Conjuntas del Plan Subregional del Area Central. I. La Crisis Económica Regional y su impacto en el Sector Agropecuario. May 1988. San José, Costa Rica.

Interamerican Institute for Cooperation in Agriculture (IICA). *Hacia un modelo de desarrollo rural integral aplicable al caso de América Central*. SDGACE, September 1980. San José, Costa Rica.

Interamerican Institute for Cooperation in Agriculture (IICA). "Lineamientos estratégicos para la acción en Centroamérica." SDGA/DOAC. October 1987 (revision III-B). San José, Costa Rica.

Interamerican Institute for Cooperation in Agriculture (IICA). "Marco de referencia para la definición de acciones conjuntas del Plan Subregional del Area Central" (preliminary draft). Memorandum OC/ADG-160, May 12, 1988 (photocopy). San José, Costa Rica.

Interamerican Institute for Cooperation in Agriculture (IICA). "Plan de acción para la reactivación de la agricultura en América Latina y el Caribe: lineamientos para su preparación." December 1987, 2nd version. San José, Costa Rica.

Interamerican Institute for Cooperation in Agriculture (IICA). *Tenencia de la tierra y reforma agraria en Centroamérica y Panamá*. September 1983. San José, Costa Rica.

Instituto Centroamericano de Documentación e Investigación Social (ICADIS). Proyecto: Crisis y alternativas en Centroamérica. Working documents. San José, Costa Rica.

Martínez, D., Manlio, et al. *Cambio Tecnológico en la agricultura de Centroamérica*. Editorial Guaymuras, Tegucigalpa, Honduras, First printing, August 1987.

Molina Chocano, Guillermo. *Centroamérica: la crisis del viejo orden*. Editorial Guaymuras. Tegucigalpa, Honduras. First printing, 1981.

Pinstrup-Andersen, P. "Macroeconomic Adjustment and Human Nutrition." In *Food Policy*, February 1988.

PROCCARA-INA. Chonchol, Jacques, et al. *La Reforma Agraria y el Desarrollo*. Honduras. 1975.

Proenza, F. "Investment for Agricultural Development in Latin America and the Caribbean, with special reference to externally assisted projects." FAO, Investment Centre Staff Paper 61/87 IC-LAC 3SP. Rome, March 1988.

Regional Council for Agricultural Cooperation in Central America, Mexico, Panama, and the Dominican Republic (CORECA). Priority Regional Projects for the recovery and development of Central American agriculture. January 1988.

Reutlinger, S. "La seguridad alimentaria y la pobreza en los países menos desarrollados." *Finance and Development*, Vol. 22, No. 4, December.

Rosenthal, G. "Some Guidelines for a Medium and Long Term Development Strategy for Central America" (photocopy). January 26, 1988.

Selowsky, M. "Adjustment in the 1980s: An Overview of Issues." *Finance and Development*, Vol. No. 2, June 1987.

Torres Rivas, Edelberto. *Crisis del poder en Centroamérica*. Editorial Universitaria Centroamericana. 2nd printing, 1983.

United Nations Economic Commission for Latin America and the Caribbean (ECLAC). *Centroamérica: crisis agrícola y perspectivas de un nuevo dinamismo*. February 1986.

United Nations Economic Commission for Latin America and the Caribbean (ECLAC). "Lineamientos Metodológicos de una estrategia de Seguridad Alimentaria" (LC/MEX/L. 49) May 20, 1987.

United Nations Economic Commission for Latin America and the Caribbean (ECLAC). *Istmo Centroamericano: el carácter de la crisis económica actual, los deafíos que plantea y la solidaridad internacional que demanda*. June 1981.

United Nations Economic Commission for Latin America and the Caribbean (ECLAC). "Restricciones al desarrollo sostenido de América Latina y el Caribe y requisitos para la superación: síntesis." Documento LC/G.1504 (SES. 22/13). February 1988. Version for the 22nd Session of United Nations Economic Commission for Latin America and the Caribbean, Rio de Janeiro, Brazil, April 20-27, 1988.

United Nations Food and Agriculture Organization (FAO). "A Framework for Action for Food, Agriculture, and Rural Development, in Latin America and the Caribbean." LA/C Study Team. Rome, September 1987. Unofficial document for discussion in the Expert Consultation, Regional Office of FAO, Santiago, Chile, October 7-9, 1987.

Villasuzo, J. Manuel. "La política agrícola en Centroamérica," April 1988 (mimeograph).

Chapter 4

A Reconnaissance of Conservation and Development
Issues in Central America
Robert G. Healy

With respect to both the natural characteristics of their land endowments and to the human purposes for which land is used, the five Central American countries are "nations of regions." There is generally more variation in the type and degree of environmental problems within countries than between them. Their diversity of landforms, climates, and soils means, for example, that the central valley of Costa Rica is more similar to Guatemala's volcanic uplands than it is to Costa Rica's own Atlantic coastal plain, barely 50 miles away.

The most important national differences among the countries tend to be institutional. For example, with respect to rural land tenure, Costa Rica and Nicaragua have a somewhat more equal distribution of productive farmland than do Guatemala, Honduras, and El Salvador. Honduras has a surfeit of trained foresters, while Guatemala has relatively few. Costa Rica has a system of national parks far more developed than any of its neighbors. Economic development and political life in Nicaragua and El Salvador are stunted by ongoing civil strife.

From a conservation standpoint, one of the most salient features of Central America is the large percentage of total land area occupied by mountains and humid lowland forests. Historically this has meant that most of the region's population has crowded together onto relatively small areas of arable land, generally in mountain valleys, upland plateaus, and fertile slopes and plains near volcanoes. Until quite recently, large proportions of nearly all the Central American nations (densely settled El Salvador is an exception) remained as wildland, able to harbor wildlife populations and protect water supplies. Today, however, a combination of population pressure, improved transportation, control of endemic diseases of humans and livestock, new technologies, and deliberate government policies has brought massive change within formerly wild areas. Central America still has a number of "frontier" regions, but the settlement within the next decade or so of all but strictly protected conservation areas is almost everywhere in sight.

But the "end of the frontier" will be only one of my themes in this essay. Central America is also grappling with problems of the quality of human life. Costa Rica's central valley has seen its series of distinct cities, both capital and provincial, sprawl into an interconnected and congested metropolis. Guatemala City, the most populous city in Central America, is facing critical problems with urban transportation and the provision of public services. Tegucigalpa, Honduras, which has grown from 71,000 people in 1950 to 750,000 today, faces major difficulties in providing these people with potable water. Almost everywhere in the region, once-promising agricultural advances have turned to stagnation, and long-settled rural areas are unable to generate enough employment to support an increasing population. New technologies are producing problems heretofore unknown in the region, including lead pollution from automobile exhausts, industrial accidents, contamination of groundwater with agrochemicals, and frequent poisonings from agricultural pesticides.

This report is the result of a conservation reconnaissance undertaken in mid-1986 and early 1987. It is a follow-up to a similar investigation conducted for the Conservation Foundation nearly twenty-five years ago by senior staff scientist William Vogt. That report was published by the foundation under the title "Comments on a Brief Reconnaissance of Resource Use, Progress and Conservation Needs in Some Latin American Countries" (Washington, D.C., 1963).

The present report, like Vogt's, mixes analysis and interpretation with personal observation in a way that is deliberately informal. I hope that the result will illustrate my points and prove interesting to the reader. The report is an attempt by a resource economist to evaluate the relative severity of environmental and natural resource problems in this important region and to relate them to the economic development process. It is my unabashed view that, at the levels of per capita income characteristic of Central America, conservation and development need not be values in conflict. Many of the developmental advances that reduce what some have called "the pollution of poverty" can equally be seen as environmental improvements—pure water supplies, better health, recreational opportunity, and improved mobility.

Conversely, at current Central American income levels, natural resources and natural environments are a greater factor in gross domestic product than they are in more highly developed countries. For example, in Honduras 63 percent of the total labor force is employed in agriculture.[1] This compares to only 2 percent in the United States and 6 percent in the industrialized countries as a whole. Much of Central America is "living off nature" in direct ways that no longer characterize the industrialized world.

The report is based on visits to Central America, a review of published and unpublished literature, and interviews with people within the region and elsewhere. I have also benefited greatly from extensive contacts with other members of the staff of the Conservation Foundation and the World Wildlife Fund.[2]

Agriculture and the Land

Underlying both environmental quality and economic development is the use of agricultural land. In his 1963 report Vogt painted a bleak picture of land use throughout Latin America, particularly emphasizing rampant soil erosion and the widespread division of peasant landholdings into parcels too small to be cultivated economically. These problems persist today, and they are particularly pronounced in much of Central America. However, the present agricultural situation in Central America is far too complex to be represented adequately by the image of increasingly numerous peasant cultivators pressing ever more tightly against a limited and fragile land base. Distribution of ownership of productive resources and changing technological and market opportunities are also of great importance.

During the last several decades Central America has followed a variant of what economists call a "dualistic" or "unbalanced" path of agricultural development. That is to say, advances in agricultural productivity (and much of the emphasis of government policy) have been concentrated on large, modern, commercial farms, which have been integrated into the international agricultural system by technology and often by the purchase of inputs and the sale of products. Small peasant producers have not participated much in these productivity gains, even during periods such as 1945–70 when overall productivity was increasing greatly. This dualistic development contrasts with the experience of, for example, Taiwan, which managed to increase productivity on large and small farms simultaneously.

Unlike some other countries that have pursued a dualistic agricultural development strategy, the Central American nations have not simply neglected peasant agriculture. Rather, the "modern" agriculture enterprises have competed actively with traditional agriculture—for land, for labor, and for credit.[3] The modern sector has been particularly favored by government policies that have provided producers with financial incentives and technical assistance while imposing price controls on the basic foodstuffs that have reduced production incentives for the peasant sector. Moreover, the foreign exchange earnings from the modern agricultural sector, which is predominately export-oriented, have made it possible for Central American countries to make up domestic food shortfalls by importing foodstuffs from the United States and other developed agricultural exporters. The supply of basic grains in Central America is also augmented by imports from the United States under concessional terms that permit payment in local currency. Through these processes, domestic elites and urban dwellers generally have been supplied with food, even as domestic food production faltered.

In Central America the differential performance of large and small producers has been exacerbated by maldistribution of land—the peasants have the poorest land, or no land at all.[4] Although this inequality has deep historical roots, it was greatly increased by the post-World War II rise of large-scale, export-oriented farming. Williams (1986), Brockett (1988), and others have documented how wealthy landowners and aggressive urban entrepreneurs responded to opportunities for modernizing agriculture by increasing farm size, displacing long-time peasant sharecroppers and non-rentpaying squatters, and by privatizing lands long held as open access "commons" and used by individuals and indigenous communities. Although there have been significant countervailing attempts, particularly in Honduras and El Salvador, to redistribute land to small farmers, land reform has been crippled by poor planning, ponderous bureaucracy, and the dogged and often violent resistance of the landowning class.[5] Since the Sandinista revolution, Nicaragua has undertaken the region's most widespread redistribution of land, distributing properties confiscated by the Somoza family and from landowners who fled the country. Collective farms, cooperatives,and individual peasants have received land. The subsequent Contra war and U.S. trade embargo have severely disrupted Nicaraguan agriculture, making it impossible to evaluate the impact of this significant land reform on agricultural production.

Other government policies have tended to reinforce rather than reduce the disparities created by inequality of land distribution. In Guatemala, for example, where 3 percent of the farms control 66 percent of the land area, peasant producers have received a disproportionately small share of technical and financial assistance from government agencies. The type of education given agronomists and agricultural technicians reinforces this by concentrating on large-scale, market-oriented production.

The complex interaction between the modern and traditional agricultural sectors has had direct impact on conservation as well as on food production. The competition for land among modern and traditional producers has tended to push the peasant producers onto the poorer quality land that is not only less productive but also more prone to erosion. Displaced peasant farmers generally lack clear land title, usually a prerequisite to obtaining technical assistance and agricultural loans. Lacking titles, credit, and technical assistance, they have little incentive to invest in soil conservation or perennial crops. Commercial agriculture has also provided seasonal jobs for peasant farmers and may have had a role in the abandonment of labor-intensive indigenous agricultural practices such as the use of terraces and contour planting on steep slopes.

For a long time the relative success of large-scale agriculture in Central America obscured the lack of progress on peasant farms. But since about 1970, Central America's agricultural sector has showed very poor performance overall. During the period 1975–86 the annual average growth in agricultural output fell well below the growth rate achieved in the 1964–74 decade in all the Central American countries except Honduras. For example, Costa Rica's agricultural growth fell from 5.3 percent per year to only 2.1 percent and Guatemala's from 3.7 percent to 1.4. Growth in Honduras fell slightly, from 4.1 percent to 3.7 percent. El Salvador and Nicaragua, in part because of war, did worst of all—total 1986 agricultural output in those countries was actually below that achieved in 1975.[6]

Even more worrisome, the rate of agricultural growth during the last decade was below the rate of population growth in Guatemala, El Salvador, Nicaragua, and Costa Rica. In Honduras, agricultural growth just barely exceeded population growth. The same is true for per capita food production: since 1975 Honduras has made essentially no progress, while Nicaragua, El Salvador, Costa Rica, and Guatemala have lost ground.

Lack of growth in per capita food output has been compounded by severe inequality in food consumption. In Guatemala, a 1980 sample survey revealed that 2- to 3-year-old children in farm families with access to 3.5 hectares or more had an average 17.5 percent incidence of weight-for-age retardation, while those in families with access to 1.4 hectares or fewer had an incidence of 38 percent.[7] At least three out of four children in Honduras, Guatemala, and El Salvador are malnourished—but malnutrition is not limited to children. Fifty percent of Central Americans do not eat enough food to meet minimum nutritional requirements.[8] The very high levels of infant mortality in Honduras, El Salvador, Nicaragua, and Guatemala are almost certainly due in part to dietary insufficiency.

The Central American countries have responded to their recent poor agricultural performance largely by continuing the dualistic policy of past years, arguing that the first priority should be to develop a modern, export-oriented agricultural sector. Profits from modern agriculture could be used to gradually raise the level of agriculture as a whole; in the meantime needed food could be imported, at least by those who could afford it. Past experience with "modern sector" agriculture had convinced Central Americans that reliance on single products, such as coffee, cattle, and cotton, presented problems of market saturation and cyclical oversupply. Therefore the current watchwords for agricultural development are "agricultural diversification" and "nontraditional exports"—simultaneous expansion of a large number of crops, including fruits, vegetables, and spices.

(The diversification drive is perhaps best illustrated by a homemade sign I saw on the wall of a government agricultural office in Honduras. A series of photographs of fruits and vegetables appeared under the words "These are the products that the United States and Canada import: flowers from Colombia, pineapples from Hawaii, shallots from France, asparagus from Chile. . . . We in Honduras can export them too!")

Much of the rhetoric of agricultural policy in Central America (and in Latin America generally) presents the dichotomy of commercial producer vs. peasant, export-oriented production vs. national self-sufficiency. The neoclassical economists argue that the economic law of comparative advantage decrees that a labor-rich country should produce crops like tomatoes and cardamom and export them in exchange for the corn, wheat, and beans that the United States and other world-class producers can raise so cheaply. The Marxists argue that trade produces inevitable dependency and exploitation as multinational corporations make Latin American agriculture ever more dependent on them for both markets and inputs. Non-Marxist church and development groups point to the fact that even where comparative advantage is working well for the economy as a whole, its benefits generally do not reach the peasantry. A thriving tomato export industry can easily coexist with peasants too poor to afford tortillas.

Improving Resource Use in Agriculture

The fact is, neither peasant agriculture nor modern agriculture is doing a very good job of resource management. Central American peasants, for example, are often forced by circumstance to plant row crops such as corn and beans on steep slopes.[9] But they generally plow them as though they were flatlands, ignoring the fact that terraces would conserve soil and contain nutrients. Modern farmers have grossly mismanaged irrigation water, wasting large quantities through channel seepage or careless application to crops and degrading large areas of land through salinization. They have also overapplied insecticides, leading to pest resistance and the need for ever-greater chemical use. For both the peasant and the modern farmer the problem seems to be not simple stupidity or carelessness but a poor incentive structure. The small farmer with insecure title cannot be expected to invest in long-term conservation practices; the Honduran cotton farmer cannot be expected to keep close watch over the quantity of pesticide used when the prices of chemicals are so heavily subsidized. But even though these practices are economically "rational" for the individual producer, they are extremely detrimental to the long-term welfare of the society as a whole.

El Salvador and Guatemala face the most serious crisis associated with rampant soil erosion, mainly because of the absence of natural vegetative cover, the continuous seasonal burning of pastures, the steeper slopes of the Pacific watersheds, and the highest concentrations of people and livestock. It is estimated that as much as 65 percent of the land mass of Guatemala is highly susceptible to soil erosion.[10] Uncontrolled erosion can lead to significant declines in crop productivity, as well as downstream flooding and sedimentation. The latter can have particularly important economic consequences in countries that depend heavily on hydroelectric power generation. It has been estimated, for example, that because of land clearing in the basin of Guatemala's Chixoy hydroelectric station, some 760 cubic meters of earth per square kilometer are eroded yearly, reducing the reservoir's useful life.[11]

The same is occurring in Costa Rica's Arenal reservoir, the El Cajon hydroelectric project in Honduras, and in many other projects.

I am intrigued by the possibility that a natural resources/conservation approach offers an alternative way to deal with Central America's admittedly serious agricultural dilemmas, simultaneously raising productivity, more equally distributing income increases, and reducing damage to land and other resources. One way to break the agricultural deadlock is to make the peasant sector as technologically dynamic as the modern sector. There seems to be increasing hope for this, for two reasons. First, as noted above, the modern sector has not been performing well in recent years. Dependent on high levels of capital and imported inputs, it has found its production costs rising while the prices of its internationally traded outputs were at best extremely unstable (e.g. coffee) and at worst in a long-term downward trend (e.g. beef and sugar). Second, a number of creative researchers have begun to combine insights from ecology with observation of native farming practices in developing "farming systems" suitable for profitable small-scale production.

One source of inspiration for developing new small farm systems has come from recent discoveries about the ancient Mayans. The great Mayan civilization that reached its height around 900 A.D. inhabited an area in Southern México, Belize, Guatemala, and Honduras whose soils are considered quite poor for agriculture. Yet the Mayans maintained high population densities and produced an annual food surplus large enough to support a considerable number of priests, artisans, and administrators. Researchers have found that the Mayans did this not by practicing the shifting "cut, clear, and burn" agriculture common in the tropics today, but by carefully raising per acre productivity through drainage and irrigation and the piling up of residues on raised "platform gardens."

Recent experiments in "alternative" small-scale agricultural systems tend to have several things in common. First, they are diversified; they maximize returns to land and labor and reduce vulnerability to crop failure and market swings by mixing field crops, fruit trees, wood-producing trees, and animals in the same agricultural enterprise and sometimes within the same field. For example, at the Center for Research and Teaching on Tropical Agronomy (CATIE) in Turrialba, Costa Rica, I inspected a number of agroforestry experiments. In some, different forms of vegetation were mixed so as to promote growth of a single money crop—nitrogen-fixing trees were intermixed with coffee plantings to enrich the soil. In others, more than one crop was produced—row crops and cattle fodder, for example.

Second, such experiments tend to pay considerable attention to maintaining and enhancing soil fertility by limiting erosion and increasing available nutrients. Such systems are the antithesis of traditional shifting cultivation, which is oriented toward taking as much as possible from the soil during a brief period of cultivation. They are also very different from many "modern" farming methods that rely on high levels of purchased fertilizers to make up for the depletion of natural soil fertility.

Third, the alternative farming systems are specific to the site and specific to the perceived needs of the individual family. In this, they contrast sharply with the traditional approach to agricultural modernization, which has concentrated on developing generalized "packages of cultivation practices" that can be widely diffused to farmers.

Fourth, although increased quantities of purchased inputs (that is, inputs not produced by the farmer himself) such as fertilizer, veterinary medicines, or pesticides, may be required, the emphasis is on better use of inputs, not a general increase in input levels. This, too, contrasts with the usual approach to agricultural modernization, which has given great emphasis to raising productivity by increasing purchased inputs.

A report by the U.S. Office of Technology Assessment has provided a list of adjectives that aptly characterizes the agricultural technologies whose development might revitalize agriculture in Central America. They should be "low risk, resource-conserving, small-scale, affordable (not capital-intensive), locally produced and repaired, adapted to local labor availability, and consistent with traditional agricultural methods."[12]

I have considerable enthusiasm about these new directions in agricultural research, although I also have some reservations. On the positive side, the ecologically-based, low-purchased-input approaches recognize an inescapable fact—rural development in Latin America is not simply a matter of increasing total agricultural production but of providing jobs, food, and income for huge numbers of rural people. Labor-intensive, small-scale production methods, therefore, must take precedence over capital-intensive, large-scale methods, even when the latter are more productive. It is interesting to note that "alternative agriculture" (described by its proponents as "low-cost, resource-conserving, and environmentally sound farming methods") is attracting more interest in the United States as a consequence of high production costs and low crop prices. If these approaches make sense in the United States, they should be even more applicable in Central America, where land under cultivation tends to be more fragile and labor is so cheap.

The negative side of the new approaches to agriculture is the temptation to romanticize aboriginal agricultural practices and to regard peasant labor as without any cost at all. Many studies have shown that while there may appear to be surplus labor in Third World agriculture, there can actually be labor shortages at certain times of the year. In particular, many Central American peasants work for wages off the farm during some parts of the year (harvesting cotton or sugar cane, for example) and depend on these wages for a major part of their cash income. Aboriginal peoples did not have this opportunity. Thus, care must be taken to devise agricultural systems that allow the peasant producer to take full advantage of the whole range of income-generating opportunities that are available.

I saw an example of this issue during a visit to a small town in Honduras. A U.S. Peace Corps volunteer showed me the plot of one of his prize pupils, a farmer who had switched from traditional shifting cultivation to creating a high-productivity, permanently terraced, mixed-crop system on little more than one hectare of land. But when we inspected the plot, it was untended. The owner had decided to take a temporary job harvesting wood for cash wages in a place many miles away.

Attention also must be paid to marketing. Although Central American peasants would certainly benefit from greater family food consumption and a more varied diet made possible by diversified production, they are generally well integrated into a cash economy, though a very low-level one. They have a need, or at least a strong taste, for things that only cash money can purchase. Traditional farm products such as corn, beans, and pigs have a reasonably well-organized, well-understood market. Any new farming or agroforestry system must produce at least some products that can be sold for cash—often this means that as much attention needs to be paid to setting up a marketing system as is paid to the production system itself.[13]

There is, I think, some scope for marketing innovation, including the use of relatively sophisticated processing and packaging technologies. Although I did not see them personally, I am informed that small-scale Guatemalan horticultural operations are successfully producing specialized and high-value products for national and international markets. One problem with this type of operation is that it exposes the producer to the risks of international markets. It makes most sense as a second step, after the country's basic food production system has been upgraded.

Finally, it must be recognized that new production systems are only part of the solution to rural poverty. They will work best when combined with readjustment of land tenure and the development of rural, nonagricultural employment. (See the discussion later in this chapter.)

The "Livestocking" of Agriculture

The Spanish word for "livestock" is "el ganado." It comprises "ganado bovino" (beef), "ganado porcino" (swine), "ganado cabrío" (goats), etc. The raising of these meat animals, particularly cattle, has become dramatically more important to Central American agriculture in recent years. The phrase "la ganaderización de la agricultura" (literally "the livestocking of agriculture") has been used to describe the process—and usually precedes a dire description of its effects.[14]

The expansion of the Central American beef cattle industry and its effects have been documented extensively.[15] Much has been made of the "hamburger connection," that is, the impetus given to cattle raising by the U.S. market for low-grade, grass-fed beef, frequently used by fast-food restaurants. As recently as spring 1986, an environmental coalition took out a full-page advertisement in the *New York Times* decrying the hamburger connection and calling for a boycott of fast-food chains using beef imported from the tropics. Although it is true that during the early 1970s beef exports to the United States from Central America increased greatly, there has been a sharp decline since 1979. Yet the number of beef cattle continued to increase.[16] Says Jim Nations of the University of Texas, "exports were for a long time the driving forces behind [Central American] beef production, with the United States importing most of their exports. New figures indicate that this is no longer true. . . . What's happening now is that beef is being eaten by people in the region. The new driving force behind beef production is population growth and a growth in a middle class that can afford [to eat] beef."[17]

One has only to walk around the bus terminal or urban produce market in any Central American capital to get a feel for what surely will be a major problem for the region in the decades to come. Everywhere are small stands selling food to people waiting for the buses. These are certainly not the poorest people in the region, but they are a reasonable cross-section of the urban population. It is obvious from the sights and smells that this is a region of meat-eaters—or at least a region of people who, if they had the money, would like to eat meat.

Given that this demand is unlikely to go away, the alternatives are threefold: (1) increase beef productivity through better animal health, improvement of the genetic stock, and an increase in the per-acre carrying capacity of grazing land, (2) shift meat consumption toward chicken and pork, which are far less land-intensive and are familiar parts of the urban Central American diet, and (3) increase the use of dual-purpose cattle herds, managed for milk as well as for meat.[18] The latter two options are particularly attractive because they do not encourage the further clearing of marginal land for pasture, they provide high quality protein valuable in upgrading diets, and they tend to be suitable to small-scale producers.

Degrading Central America's Forests

The once extensive forests of Central America are being reduced in quantity and degraded in quality, on a scale that is probably unequalled anywhere in the world. Statistics on rates of forest destruction are available from a variety of sources, and I will not repeat them here, though it must be noted that such statistics tend to understate the degree of forest degradation by failing to count areas that are "high-graded" but not cleared.

Three reasons are usually given for the loss of forest in Central America. In order of importance, these are: (1) clearing for cattle pasture, (2) clearing for peasant crop production, commercial farming or agricultural colonization schemes, and (3) harvest for commercial timber and for fuelwood. I see no reason to argue with this order. But I believe that a fourth factor is also at work, and may be as important as any of the others. This is the role that land ownership—in particular the desire of individual Central Americans, rich and poor, to increase the amount of land to which they have secure legal title—plays in promoting forest clearing.

Securing ownership of land is one of the most attractive ways of obtaining wealth in rural Central America. The explanation is to be found not in notions of the cultural importance of land ownership in Latin countries but in the simple economic reality that there are so few alternatives. The poor want to obtain land; the rich want to hold on to what they have. Clearing forest is a good way for both groups to secure their objectives. (Precisely the same process was dominant in the United States during the period before about 1830.) For the poor, clearing forest, which often is owned by the government or by faraway private owners, gives them the possibility of establishing legal title to it.[19] In Costa Rica, for example, a squatter does not establish title simply by occupying the land. Rather, he can "improve" a piece of land by clearing the forest, and then sell the improvements to a third party. The third party can take the quitclaim deed delivered by the squatter to a government office and obtain a clear legal title. "Most of what agrarian reform agencies do here," notes one observer in Costa Rica, "is to legalize invasions. But this can't go on forever," he adds, "because the agrarian frontier is closing."[20]

As a result of this policy, which exists in slightly different form elsewhere in Latin America, there has developed a sizable group of professional peasant "land improvers." The usual target of their activity is a "baldío," a piece of uncultivated land, often government-owned, sometimes even located within a nominally protected area such as a national forest. This sort of land clearing is often attributed to the cattle industry, because the cleared land usually goes into pasture. But the motivating force is land ownership, not cattle production. I suspect, in fact, that most of this activity would continue even if cattle production had a negative profitability.

The rich person, who already owns some rural land, faces a different situation. In most Central American countries, his ownership right is under considerable pressure. Peasant cultivators, or possibly the above-mentioned land clearers, are likely to move onto land that is not obviously being used. Forest land, because it often does not bear visible signs of use, often becomes the target for such entrepreneurial activity. Frequently, government land reform policy encourages this process by making "underutilized" land subject to expropriation. Land used for cattle grazing, even when it is being grazed inefficiently, is generally considered to be in active use.

I believe that the key to stopping forest clearing in Central America lies as much in changing the land tenure situation as it does in changing the economics of either crop or cattle production.

Although the immediate threat to forestry in Central America is loss of its land base, there are also very important problems with forest quality and with the structure of the forest products industry. These two problems are closely related. Virtually everywhere in Central America, the production of forest products is in what might be termed the "mining" phase. That is, wood is extracted with no provision whatever for sustained yield production in the future. Utilization tends to be very poor, partly because of transportation difficulty, partly because of the large number of species on any given tract, partly because there is little incentive to utilize stems of lower quality when there is so much wood of exceptional quality still available.

Mills are often located far from current harvest areas, making it unprofitable to haul any but the most valuable trees. Mills are often old and inefficient; owners operate them but are unwilling to invest in upgrading in the absence of a long-term timber supply. Most mills are also not vertically integrated; small logs and sawmill trimmings that in the United States or Europe would be made into paper or particleboard are discarded or left in the woods in Central America.

As with land settlement, there is a parallel to U.S. developmental history, which also involved tremendous waste of forest material. I am reminded of a statement by former New Hampshire governor Sherman Adams: "Those who condemn the old logging industry do not take into account the environment in which people lived in those times. Cutting the timber was a means of livelihood just like growing wheat in a prairie state. Today, critics of their methods are unsympathetic to the things a pioneer had to do in order to survive. The use of timber was as much his livelihood as transactions in stocks and bonds on Wall Street are to a stock broker."[21]

Instead of bemoaning the waste, we need to devise reasons for better utilization and for reforestation. The few policies now in place are ineffective, even counterproductive. In Guatemala, since 1978, the National Forestry Institute (INAFOR) has managed a reforestation program intended to cover 100,000 hectares by 1982. Up to 1983, however, only 10 percent of that area had been reforested. Ironically, INAFOR does not have jurisdiction in managing the most significant forest reserves in the country, those in the Petén region. The institution responsible for the Petén, Fomento y Desarrollo de Petén (FYDEP) has limited experience with forestry and conservation.[22] In Costa Rica, landowners are offered the astronomical tax subsidy of up to nearly $1,500 per hectare to replant deforested land. Most of the people who have taken advantage of the offer are owners of rural parcels in a part of the country without good forestry prospects; in many cases they are simply making recreational parcels more attractive or planting trees on land that is better suited to crops. In Honduras, a government timber monopoly

(COHDEFOR) controls all timber harvest. The landowner receives only 30 percent of the revenue and has little control over how and when cutting will occur. As a result, timber owners are eager to harvest simply to get their land out of the forest category.

Yet another forest management problem affects the pine forests of Honduras, among the most commercially valuable in the entire region. This is uncontrolled forest fires, some caused accidentally and spread by the extreme desiccation of the vegetation during the dry season; most are set deliberately. In the spring dry season of 1986 a Honduran newspaper observed in an editorial that, "an intense cloud of smoke covers the greater part of the national territory. Everywhere one observes sadly the eruption of forest fires."[23]

There are several things that could be done to improve forest management in Central America. First, inappropriate government policies, such as those mentioned above, could be abandoned. They give the illusion of attacking the problem, when in fact they are ineffective or even counterproductive. Second, forest land tenure could be clarified. I suspect that the best arrangement is for some land to be national, some operated by parastatal enterprises, some by villages or cooperatives, some (generally the majority) private.[24] Encouraging a variety of ownership forms offers the possibility of useful comparisons in styles of forest management, to the benefit of all owners. But whatever the ownership distribution, the ownership of forestland and the purposes and rights of ownership need to be made clear. Third, timber production could be recognized as a legitimate purpose for owning land, and actively managed timberland not be discriminated against when land reforms are considered. Fourth, more research could be done on low-cost timber production systems for the tropics. High-grading of tropical forests is generally condemned by foresters, but they have few profitable alternatives to offer the landowner.

Perhaps the most important single thing that can be done to improve forest management in Central America is to improve timber markets and develop a permanent system of mills and woodyards. This may seem contradictory, because improvement in markets would result in more timber cutting. However, the existence of a stable, permanent market for wood creates a local (and sometimes national) interest group with a long-term stake in forest survival and productivity. It would also give mill owners a reason to upgrade their machinery and develop secondary wood products.

Veblen (1978) found that the surprising persistance of forests in the Totonicapán department of Guatemala was due in part to a longstanding local wood-using industry which "encourage[s] the Indian community to maintain close vigilance over the use of the communal forests and to punish those who cut wood illegally."[25]

Moreover, the history of the timber industry in the developed countries has shown that sustained yield management does not occur until owners come to believe that there will be a continuing market for stumpage in their locality.[26] As a Costa Rican environmentalist puts it, "the [forest management] problem seems to be the identification of forestry activities with something that is not profitable and not worth any attention." Until that belief changes, forests in Central America will continue to be exploited rather than managed.

Urban Concentration and Pollution

William Vogt's 1963 survey of Latin American conservation issues had virtually nothing to say about the environment of the region's cities. But even as he was writing, high rates of rural-to-urban migration were combining with rapid natural increase to produce unprecedented rates of urban growth. Today, Central America's cities are home to more than 40 percent of its population, and they are continuing to expand each year.

None of Central America's cities is comparable in scale or degree of urban problems to Mexico City, an urban agglomeration of 17 million which has been described as "the most heavily contaminated city on the planet."

But all of Central America's capitals, and some provincial cities, exhibit on a small and growing scale some major environmental problems. Perhaps the most obvious of these is the rings of urban shanty towns that spread out from their edges and often occur on small areas of undesirable land within the main part of the city. These areas are characterized by crowding, crime, poor or nonexistent public services, and inadequate transportation. It is difficult to distinguish problems that we are accustomed to characterize as "environmental" (e.g., polluted drinking water, lack of open space, inadequate garbage disposal) from more generalized problems of housing and transportation. For the poor, multiple problems converge into a generally low quality of life.

Consider, for example, Guatemala City, whose 2 million people make it the largest metropolitan area in Central America. The city doubled its population between 1950 and 1964 and did so again from 1965 to 1984. New arrivals to the city, nearly all poor rural people, find that squatting on outlying or otherwise marginal tracts is the only way to find shelter. Their shacks climb precariously up the steep slopes of hills surrounding the city, or encroach on an old, but still used, railway line. Shantytowns, called "limonadas" (an early shantytown was named Limonada or "lemonade" after that sour drink) have become particularly prevalent since the destructive 1976 earthquake.

Life in the shantytowns, whether in Guatemala City, Tegucigalpa, San Salvador, or elsewhere, is hard. The towns lack nearly all public services. Most are illegal, having occupied government land or lots owned by some other private owner. Some border the garbage dump of the richer part of the city and poor children can be seen picking up food, cans, bags, and other salvage to take back to their hovels. The contrast is striking between the squatter settlements and the modern zones of the city only a few minutes away.

A second set of problems consist of a group of urban and environmental ills that affect rich and poor alike. Among them are severe traffic congestion, high noise levels, destruction of green space on the city's periphery, and a general sense of crowding. In the Central American capitals, air pollution is increasing because of the high sulfur content of gasoline used by the increasing automobile fleet and of fuel oil used by industries. Lack of strict traffic regulation, inefficient public transport, and informal markets in the streets provoke a high external cost for automobile drivers, who lose time and fuel waiting for traffic jams to clear.

Given the many urban problems, why do people continue to move to Central America's cities? The answer varies by social class. For the wealthy, professionals, and intellectuals, each country's capital is simply the center of the nation. Guatemala City, for example, is Guatemala's New York and Chicago and Washington and Los Angeles. Like no city in the United States, Guatemala City dominates the nation's commerce, its governance and its arts and media. For the middle-class and the blue-collar worker the city is the source of decent jobs. The same agglomerative forces that attract people also attract firms. Forty percent of Guatemala's manufacturing (75 percent of large scale manufacturing) is located in Guatemala City, which contains 20 percent of Guatemala's population. Despite the problems, industries in the city have access to electricity, water, transportation, industrial workers, and the country's major market.

Moreover, Guatemala and other capitals offer the chance of advancement for the worker's children. Health care and primary education are more easily accessible than in the countryside. National universities are almost invariably found in the capitals. In Guatemala, the National Autonomous University of San Carlos alone enrolls more than 60,000 students, and it is only one of five universities in the capital. Public university tuition, low to begin with and eroded in real value by inflation, is virtually free. It is not at all unusual to find university students whose parents have not completed grade school.

Even the poor who inhabit the vast squatter settlements that ring the city find advantages in the capital. Economic activity is everywhere; the energetic migrant finds many more opportunities than in the villages or towns. In Guatemala City, for example, the area around the main square in the older part of the city looks depressed but is always congested with people selling goods, running errands, providing services to the bureaucrats and business-men, or standing in line for others at government agencies.

Increased urban populations are also having severe effects on the mountain watersheds that surround nearly all the Central American capitals. "Around San José," says one Costa Rican hydrologic researcher, "more and more people are moving to the heads of small watersheds for residential purposes. People dump trash in the rivers. More and more of the upper watersheds are also used for cattle, which compact the soil. Poor people move along the rivers so as to have a water source, but they also wash their clothes there."[27] This of course contaminates the water further downstream. Above Teguci-galpa, capital of Honduras, major watersheds that were formerly forested are now devoted to vegetable growing and cattle and poultry raising. The removal of trees has caused massive erosion, and animal wastes and pesticides run off into watercourses. Human wastes also are deposited in the watershed as squatters build houses in areas without any sewer service.

Twenty-five years ago Central America faced a fundamental choice about the spatial aspect of its development: to allow massive urbanization to occur or to try to keep people in the countryside. Policy measures to stem urbanization were weak or nonexistent, and the people voted with their feet. Today, despite enormous rural-to-urban migration, Central America has rural populations much larger than those of 1963; they make continued demands on soil, forest, and wildlife resources. But it also has an array of cities and a new set of environmental problems whose outlines were just appearing when Vogt did his original reconnaissance of the region.

Any attempt to cope with Central America's urban problems must deal with the countryside as well as the city. Improvements in education, transportation, and health care in rural areas and smaller towns and cities can help offset the exclusive attractiveness of living in the capital. Costa Rica is an example of both the possibilities and the limitations of this approach. In Costa Rica, rural electrification, public schools, public housing, clinics, and good road networks, along with television and telephone lines, reach every corner of the nation. As a result, the influx to the capital has been lower than elsewhere in Central America. However, despite this policy, San José has continued to grow, though less chaotically than most of the other capitals.

Tourism

Tourism tends to be regarded with mixed feelings by both environmentalists and economic development professionals. Tourism is seen by some environmentalists as a destructive force that can result in rows of high-rises on the beaches and the commercialization of picturesque colonial towns. Yet environmentalists are also aware that the promotion of tourism is a powerful argument for the creation of national parks and reserves and the protection of historic and cultural resources.

For economic development professionals, tourism is recognized as one of the largest economic sectors in many Third World countries and a potent generator of foreign exchange. Yet it is often derided for creating mainly low-wage, dead-end jobs and for generating imports of food, equipment, and other items needed to serve the tourists.

Tourism in Central America tends to concentrate in five types of areas: beach and mountain resorts (e.g. Islas de Roatán, Honduras; Lake Atitlán, Guatemala), major cities (Guatemala City, San José, Costa Rica), colonial towns (Antigua, Guatemala), pre-Columbian ruins (Tikal, Copan) and wildlands (the Costa Rican national parks). Given the proximity of Central America to the world's largest tourist source, the United States, the favorable seasonal climatic contrasts, and the relatively low cost of travel and accommodations, it appears that tourism is far from fully developed in the region.

Tourism between the United States and Central America is minuscule compared with United States-Mexico tourism, and the Mexican experience with tourism offers some potential lessons for Central America. In 1984, some 4.2 million tourists, most of them from the United States, visited Mexico, bringing Mexico $1.8 billion in foreign exchange. Tourism is second only to oil among Mexico's sources of foreign currency, and is drawing more government attention now that the oil boom has collapsed. "When I am asked if tourism can replace oil, my answer is no," says Antonio Enriquez Savignac, Mexico's Minister of Tourism. "But tourism can contribute much more than at present if developed properly."

Over the last 15 years tourist development in Mexico has emphasized four new beach resorts developed by the government agency FONATUR (Fondo Nacional de Fomento al Turismo). The largest and most successful of these is Cancún, developed on a barrier island on the Gulf coast. Occupied by 170 impoverished squatters as recently as 1970, Cancún now has 6,333 hotel rooms and receives 725,000 tourists annually. The tourism minister boasts that this is "more than will visit many entire Caribbean countries."

Cancún comes as a pleasant surprise to an environmentally oriented visitor who was prepared for the worst. The hotels are mostly well-designed, widely spaced, and set back a reasonable distance from the beach. (Mexican law prohibits private beaches, making it possible to walk along the shoreline without encountering stern warnings against trespassing.) A great deal of effort has gone into providing infrastructure, not only for the tourists, but also for the 90,000 Mexicans who now live and work in what had been an almost unpopulated region. A commercial and residential center, Cancún City, lies a few miles—and a convenient bus ride—from the waterside hotel zone. Wages are high by Mexican standards, and employment opportunities relatively good. An earlier Conservation Foundation study of Cancún[28] criticized the resort's environmental planning, particularly the destruction of mangroves and incipient water pollution. Both are still problems, but in general and *considered as an essentially urban environment*, Cancún must be regarded as a rather successful example of large-scale land use planning.

Cancún is perhaps best viewed within its larger regional context. Cancún itself provides an expensive, highly packaged tourist experience which depends on nature for location and climate rather than more specific natural attractions. Twenty or so miles along the coast to the south are a series of small tourist towns, small resorts, and campgrounds that offer less expensive accommodations and an orientation that is more to beach and lagoon than (as in Cancún) to bar and swimming pool. About a hundred miles to the south is Sian Ka'an, a newly designated World Biosphere Reserve. Here are nearly a million acres of coastal lagoons and marshes, set aside as a reserve by the Mexican government. At Sian Ka'an the only attraction is nature itself, interpreted and made accessible, but not touristically developed as at Cancún. Lobster fishing communities and some agriculturists, whose presence antedated the reserve, have been allowed to remain and to use a portion of the reserve.

It seems to me that Cancún works very well as a part of this context—it caters to a particular market segment and makes a particular kind of economic contribution to Mexico's economy. The recipe, I believe, works when two conditions are fulfilled. First, each of the diverse components must be present, including the planned tourism of Cancún, the small-scale, lower-priced, entrepreneurial tourism of the southern coast, and the undeveloped nature preserve of Sian Ka'an. Tourists differ greatly in their preference for developed versus natural settings and a country can maximize its tourism revenues if it has something to offer each segment of the market.

Second, each of the components must work on its own terms. Cancún must remain highly planned, with infrastructure and land uses tightly controlled. (This may be problematic in the future as the wide spaces between hotels start to be filled in and as a relative growth of condominiums starts to replace public space with private space.) The somewhat anarchic development to the south works well because, though sprawling, it is still quite spotty. It will work much less well when the total amount of building doubles or triples. And Sian Ka'an must be managed so that it will be accessible to visitors but will not damage natural systems or disturb the abundant wildlife.

FONATUR's approach to tourism development seems to make sense for Central American countries as well, although certainly on a smaller scale and with an appreciation that the danger of overall market saturation is always present. Like Mexico, Central America is only a short flight from the United States and has a favorable climate and attractive coastlines. Moreover, Guatemala and Honduras have archeological attractions of world significance. Unfortunately, in much of Central America, tourism is presently in a severe slump because of political instability in the region. (Peaceful Costa Rica has experienced continued growth in tourism. It is very likely, however, that Costa Rican revenues would be higher still if conflict elsewhere in the region were to be resolved.)

One possibility for future mass tourism development is to work with Mexico on the creation of an "integrated tourist circuit" linking sites in several countries. One idea is the "Mayan Route," a visitation package linking Cancún, important Mayan sites in Mexico, Guatemala's Lake Atitlán, and Tikal, the great Mayan city in northern Guatemala. The Guatemalan government now has an agreement with Mexico to develop such a package. A recent report by the United Nations Development Programme on future economic cooperation in Central America recommends the implementation of integrated tourist circuits and the promotion of a common tourism image for Central America.[29]

In addition to the mass market, sun-and-relaxation tourism offered by Mexico's planned resorts, there is another form of tourism development that offers both economic benefits and environmental benefits. That is "ecotourism," visitation specifically oriented to natural resources. Although it will never be a very large slice of total tourism, it is one of its fastest growing market segments. Ecotourism includes scientific study of ecosystems (often sponsored by scientific associations or universities), birdwatching, mountain climbing, hiking, and whitewater rafting.

Costa Rica has by far the most developed ecotourism industry in Central America. Ecotourists in considerable numbers visit several of Costa Rica's national parks, the Organization for Tropical Studies' jungle research station (La Selva), and the privately-operated Monteverde Cloud Forest Reserve. There are several firms offering organized visits to national parks, birdwatching tours, and river excursions. U.S.-based environmental groups participate increasingly in ecotourism in Latin America—the Sierra Club's 1986–87 travel offerings include a natural history tour of Costa Rica, a jungle and offshore trip to Belize, and diving and kayaking excursions to Baja California, Mexico. Among World Wildlife Fund's 1987 trips was an excursion to Mexico that included several national parks and biosphere reserves.

Guatemala has begun to take advantage of the tourist potential of its forests and wildlife. Visitation to the extensive Mayan ruins at Tikal was until recently oriented entirely to archeological values; recently tourism emphasis has been placed on the surrounding tropical forest as well. The University of San Carlos has established a "biotope" reserve to protect habitat for the quetzal and is encouraging tourism there.

Ecotourism offers several advantages to developing countries. For one thing, it offers countries a tangible economic return to preserving scenic and recreational resources in a natural state. Most of the ecotourists are foreigners, who bring in foreign exchange. Ecotourism also offers a way to expose travelers, some of them wealthy, to conservation issues. Having experienced the tropics at first-hand, these visitors may become ardent supporters of the tropical conservation cause. The presence of upper-income, articulate foreign tourists interested in nature may even have an effect on the tastes of local elite groups, including political decisionmakers. Finally, unlike resort-oriented tourism, ecotourism does not require elaborate developed facilities.

But ecotourism has its drawbacks. The growing numbers of ecotourists may threaten the resource in their desire to experience it closely or intensely. Infrastructure to accommodate visitation and control its impact—including visitor centers, trails, boardwalks, and warning and interpretive signs—does not even exist in many protected areas. And some of the resources are inherently so sensitive that they may not be able to tolerate mass visitation, however organized. For example, one wonders how many tourists can visit the whale-calving grounds in Scammon's Lagoon in Baja California, Mexico, or the turtle nesting areas in Costa Rica, without having an impact on the wildlife. Ecotourism may also have a great deal of financial "leakage"—most of the revenues may go to foreign tour agencies, which often supply expatriate guides, and to foreign airlines and advertising firms. Actual expenditure on-site may be relatively small.

Ecotourism can have a more beneficial impact on the environment if better ways can be found to tap ecotourists for the cost of maintaining the natural resources which draw them. For example, the Organization for Tropical Studies has a multi-level daily tariff for food and lodging at La Selva: Costa Ricans pay $5 per day, U.S. graduate students pay $20, senior researchers pay $35, and ecotourists pay $60. "Bird groups come to La Selva back-to-back during the winter dry season," says one OTS staff member, "at any one time there may be 30 or so tourists there." For the last two years La Selva has organized a special Christmas bird count to raise money for Costa Rican conservation causes.

Some U.S. environmental groups have also used ecotourism as a fundraising device, requiring tour members to make a (tax-deductible) contribution as a condition of taking a nature-oriented trip. Despite these examples, national parks and other reserved areas in Latin America have far from fully exploited the funding potential of ecotourists. For example, Costa Rican national parks charge a flat entrance fee equal to less than fifty cents, whether a visitor is a local day-tripper or an international tourist who has come to Costa Rica specifically to visit the parks.

There is also untapped potential for better integrating reserved area tourism into *local* economies. Perhaps the best example is the Monteverde Cloud Forest Reserve in Costa Rica, which is run by a nonprofit group and visited by both tourists and scientists. In 1987, more than 12,000 people visited the reserve, which charges adults $2.74 for admission and $1.70 for students. A number of small hotels have sprung up to accommodate the visitors, who also provide a market for locally produced cheeses and handicrafts.[30]

Another example, outside Central America but offering a potentially instructive model, is the Monarch Butterfly reserve in central Mexico, where a private group (Monarca, A.C.) is training rural residents to guide tourists and helping them sell souvenirs and handicrafts to visitors. The idea is that this will give local people an economic interest in the butterflies and will encourage their conservation. Another possible model may be found in Panamá, where the Kuna Indians have allowed carefully controlled visitation to their islands, utilizing the tourists as a ready market for locally made embroideries and other handicrafts. Recently, the Kunas have created an enormous forest reserve on Panamá's mainland, to which they hope to attract scientific tourists and persons interested in nature.

There are also significant possibilities for ecotourism by Central American nationals. Some 80 percent of visitors to Costa Rica's national parks are Costa Ricans, a consequence of the government's efforts to make several of the parks accessible to national visitors. Most of the visitors to Guatemala's Quetzal biotope are Guatemalans, while half of all visitors to Copan are Honduran. This local visitation brings economic benefits to small local enterprises; it is more stable than international tourism, and it has the important side benefit of increasing conservation consciousness among the national population.

Crosscutting Issues

In my travels I became convinced that three crosscutting issues lie behind many of Central America's conservation dilemmas. They are (1) the issue of land tenure, both rural and urban, (2) the issue of non-farm rural employment, and (3) the issue of management and implementation.

Land Tenure. The ownership of land in Central America needs to become both *more equally distributed* and *more secure* for the owner. This applies equally to farmland, forestland, and urban housing sites.

Because of *inequality* of land ownership, much of the land with the highest crop production potential is used for lower-intensity uses such as cattle grazing. Peasant farmers are forced to cultivate marginal land, making it much more difficult for them to take advantage of the new, productivity-raising farming systems mentioned earlier in this essay. Cultivation of marginal land also means that environmental problems such as deforestation and soil erosion are more likely. Finally, the inability of peasant farmers to secure good land in existing agricultural areas provides a very strong motivation for the peasants to move into new territories. These new lands are generally places (often in tropical lowlands) that have great natural value but relatively poor agricultural prospects. Peasant migration is usually encouraged or at least condoned by governments as an alternative to taking action with regard to land reform.

The widespread *insecurity* of land tenure found all over Central America compounds the problem of inequality. This insecurity is associated with both insecurity of land title and the practical insecurity engendered by peasant occupations or potential expropriation. Lack of secure land tenure makes forest owners reluctant to invest in silvicultural practices that have only a long-run payoff. Lack of secure land tenure makes farmland owners reluctant to lease land to peasant farmers because the peasants may later occupy it by force or seek government expropriation. Lack of secure tenure makes it difficult for peasants who do have access to land to get credit or even government-provided technical assistance. Lack of secure tenure to land in urban squatter settlements makes residents uneasy about investing in improvements to their houses or communities. Even governments are in a sense affected by insecurity of land tenure. Much of the wildland now being settled and deforested in Central America is actually owned by the national governments. But (much like the western lands in the settlement of the United States) this land is not managed or effectively controlled by government agencies. It is a sort of commons, now in the process of private expropriation.

From the standpoint of both production efficiency and environmental protection, the present situation of unequal and insecure land tenure is inferior either to one with more equal landownership or one in which inequality of ownership is firmly established.

From an equity standpoint a more equal distribution of land is obviously preferable. At this point it would be simple to call for land reform in Central America and move on to other subjects. But anyone familiar with the region knows that land reform is a bloody issue and has been one for generations.[31] (Even in postrevolutionary Nicaragua, privately owned land has not thus far been extensively redistributed—most land given to peasants to date has come from estates abandoned by the Somoza family and its allies.) Because land tenure is not seen to be a very important issue in North America, outsiders are inclined to look on the land tenure conflicts in, say, El Salvador, as quaint examples of the sort of injustice that no longer exists in modern societies.

I believe that one cannot understand the land tenure issue without clearly understanding the position of the landowners.[32] (One can do this without siding with them or condoning their conduct.) They are people who believe that there is a clear chance that their property will be taken away from them, either by the rural landless or by the government.[33] Their land use behavior has a strong element of economic rationality and will change only when economic incentives change.

There may be some hope for such change. The desired change would involve simultaneously strengthening property rights and changing their distribution. This would include three interrelated steps. First, governments should assert their own property rights by creating effective management agencies for the remaining public commons. Some of this land might be permanently retained by government, either for protection or timber production or both. Some might be distributed to the citizens—but in a systematic manner, rather than by random squatting, poaching, and timber theft. Second, private property rights should be defined and protected, even at the expense of initial inequality. These first steps require as a precondition greatly improved land surveys, titling procedures, and permanent title registries. Third, land should be redistributed so as to increase the number of landowners and make the overall distribution more equal. Redistribution need not come about through confiscation but could be done through open market purchase, perhaps with international aid funds. There is already some experience with this in Costa Rica, where the government agrarian institute (IDA), with considerable USAID assistance, is buying out large private landholdings and giving farms to campesinos. Although the costs of significant land purchases would be high, they might be a bargain in terms of obviated military expenditures and the economic loss of continued civil conflict.

In addition to reducing conflict and helping to increase social justice, land redistribution can help the environment by reducing the pressure on marginal lands. In El Salvador and Costa Rica, land reform programs have been used to acquire forested enclaves within large farms, which have later been turned into national parks. Land capability analysis, including the collection of soil data and the study of present and potential land uses, is particularly important to ensure that land given to farmers in redistribution programs is capable of the intended use, both economically and environmentally.

Nonfarm Rural Employment. Even if Central America succeeds in developing sustainable small-scale agricultural systems, farming will never be able to provide enough employment for a fast-growing rural population. The great migration to the cities will continue, even though the resulting environmental and public service problems will be immense. In order to at least reduce this flood of people, ways must be found to retain people in the countryside. Measures to redirect urban population flows away from capital cities and toward secondary centers, have been less than successful around the world. Mexico, for example, has such a policy under its national urban development plan. It has had little impact on migration flows; moreover, it may be environmentally counterproductive because some of the areas where growth is to be encouraged are themselves overcrowded and underserviced. In Guatemala, the Urban Action Plan (HABITAT-SEGEPLAN, 1986) encourages the development of 13 secondary cities through incentives in the countryside and disincentives in the capital. The 1985 Guatemalan constitution mandated the allocation of at least 8 percent of the national budget to the municipalities and created regional development coordination committees.

Creation of more nonfarm rural jobs is surely one of the great future developmental tasks in Central America. I suspect that the best approach is to encourage what in the United States is called "part-time" farming. There is evidence that such part-time farming enterprises are being developed in and around San José, Costa Rica. It would be most profitable for researchers to try to identify whether other pockets of such activity exist in Central America and to explore the economics of the farm and nonfarm enterprises. Ideally, a family would have some income from farming (including livestock raising) and some from a home manufacturing enterprise or from employment in a rural industrial plant. Breaking down barriers to world trade is very important to such enterprises because the low rural labor costs in Central America are attractive to producers only if they can export the resulting production.

It is not easy to define what these rural enterprises might be—and therein lies the heart of the problem. Certainly agricultural processing and aquaculture would be important. There is also a growing interest in Latin America in so-called microenterprises which produce relatively "high-tech" (or in some cases high-style) goods in homes or in extremely small factories for urban domestic markets or for export.

Not all the rural enterprises, of course, need be in the manufacturing sector. In Mexico, as already noted, Monarca, A.C., a nonprofit environmental group, is considering training local peasants to guide domestic and international tourists through the monarch butterfly refuge that has been established on their *ejido* lands. And in Honduras, with UNESCO assistance young people are being trained to serve as guides to the Mayan ruins at Copan. Various sorts of touristic and tourist-related handicraft enterprises could be an important supplement to farmers' incomes in certain amenity-rich areas, particularly if ways can be found to increase the proportion of the tourist dollar that stays in the local community.

In planning for rural jobs particular attention should be paid to employment for women. One close observer of the region calls rural women an incredibly undervalued and poorly stimulated component of rural employment. Finding more productive activities for women will not only help raise family incomes, but is also likely to help reduce rural population growth.

Management and Implementation. Central America has some farsighted administrators and some well-run agencies (Costa Rica's national parks, for example). But the general level of government management and implementation is quite poor. With respect to environment and resource management, this means that high-minded national laws and progressive management programs are developed, announced with great fanfare, then carried out poorly or not at all. A long history of this has severely eroded confidence in the law, both among government employees and among the public. A vicious circle is created, in which lack of confidence in the ability of government to act encourages disregard for the law and contempt for the bureaucracy.

One component of poor implementation is overcentralization. Local governments in Central America lack financial resources and independent political power. Resource management at the local level tends to be performed by several national ministries, which are ill-coordinated at the national level and which cannot be forced into concert at the local level because local government is so weak.

Another component of poor implementation is corruption. Government officials in the resources and environment field have abundant opportunities to make money by favoritism in awarding contracts, concessions, and licenses. This seems to be a problem throughout the Third World. "The Spanish word for 'forest ranger' is 'forestal,' " says one Mexican forester. "But people here refer to them colloquially as 'mordestales,' after 'la mordida,' the slang expression for 'a bribe' " (literally, "the bite"). In Honduras, officials of the national forestry agency have been accused of corruption in awarding of cutting contracts and export permits. Part of the problem may be low salaries. Hoy and Belisle observe that in Guatemala, "A forest manager or game warden who earns but $100 per month is a prime candidate for bribery to allow illegal tree cutting or poaching. In 1980, for example, it was acknowledged by numerous informants that lumber operators, with the knowledge of members of the forestry service, caused the pine-bark beetle infestation of some protected Western Highland tree stands. Since the remedy for this infestation is to cut out the affected trees, the lumber companies were able to get harvesting permits in heretofore protected areas."[34]

Another problem is that civil service requirements and political patronage make it difficult for agencies to hire knowledgeable local people in rural areas. For example, the Costa Rican National Park service requires that park rangers possess a high school diploma and pass a qualifying test. This eliminates the possibility that highly motivated and field-smart park neighbors be hired as rangers, because they often lack educational requirements.

Yet another problem is that bureaucratic inertia and low pay discourage the brightest and most energetic young people from seeking a government career in natural resources. Even though Central America's governments are financially strapped, economizing on bureaucratic talent probably involves losses in waste and corruption many times the cost of adequate salaries and working conditions.

Environmentalism

Central Americans are not unaware of their environmental and resource problems. Costa Rica has recently seen several extensively publicized studies of its environmental problems, emanating from both government agencies and nongovernmental organizations.

During my visit to Honduras in July 1986 that country's largest newspaper devoted a major editorial to the problem of deforestation, arguing that "it depends upon us whether new generations inherit a garden or a desert."[35] An environmental organization in Honduras showed me large books filled with recent newspaper clippings on environmental problems. In Guatemala dozens of environmental groups have been founded in the last ten years. And there is indication of increased government interest—in 1986 a new environmental law created a national council on environmental development. The law mandates a systematic and comprehensive approach to natural resources and is inspired by sustainable development theory. One of the council's responsibilities is to evaluate the environmental consequences of development projects, including those financed by multilateral institutions. A leading Guatemalan development planner said that he saw increasing interest in developing a plan for improving the administration of renewable natural resources and believed that natural resource management would become a major political issue in the future.

Of course, it is difficult to say whether this sort of information reaches very far into the countryside or beyond that part of the urban population with a postprimary education. Several Peace Corps volunteers with whom I spoke indicated that farmers with whom they worked were unconcerned with soil erosion because they were ignorant of its effects on soil productivity. Many others felt that despite increasing press coverage of the environment there was a lack of perception in the general population of the relationship between the environment and socio-economic development. There also seems to be a certain resignation in the face of environmental problems—even if their existence and importance is recognized, it is believed that nothing effective can be done about them, and that individual action is useless.

As has been the case in the United States, it is likely to take decades of environmental propagandizing to change people's values and to affect various behaviors that affect the environment. For example, the setting of wildfires in rural Honduras stems from the same motives ("greening" the pasture, killing ticks, revenge, entertainment) that long motivated rural firebugs in the American South. Acceptance of controls on hunting is also low in Central America, just as it once was in the South. It took decades of education to reduce incendiarism and poaching in the South; it will likely require the same in Central America. In many cases, there will need to be programs that simultaneously change attitudes and provide effective public services (e.g., both anti-littering campaigns and formal systems of rural trash disposal; both hunter education and aggressive game law enforcement).

Environmental groups in Central America appear to be on an upswing. For example, in early 1987, a meeting in Managua (sponsored by the Nicaraguan Association of Ecologists and Biologists) convened delegates from environmental groups from Guatemala, Costa Rica, El Salvador, Honduras and Panamá. A new regional NGO network was created, called the Regional Network of Environmental Nongovernmental Organizations for the Sustained Development of Central America. Altogether about 140–150 people attended the meeting. A similar number attended a regional meeting in late 1987 in Guatemala that resulted in a unified regional action plan for creation and management of a regional protected areas system.

Debt, Military Activities, and Refugees

No analysis of the environmental situation in Central America can be complete without mentioning three unfortunate but unavoidable variables that provide the context for any conservation and development work within the region.

The first is the crushing burden of international debt and the poor performance of most of the national economies. This has led to pressure to exploit resources rapidly and to austerity programs that have cut deeply into government expenditures and personnel budgets, including those for conservation.

The second variable is the military activity related to widespread civil violence in several countries in the region. This has led to the kidnapping or murder of park guards, foresters, and rural development workers, the use of scorched-earth campaigns, massive military maneuvers on unsuitable terrain, roadbuilding in remote areas, and unsustainable resource extraction schemes to finance military spending or to increase the personal wealth of military commanders.

A third variable, related to the second, is the creation of large numbers of refugees. These people, displaced from their normal territory, have settled (or been resettled) on mainly marginal lands. They have no incentive to use these lands sustainably and contribute to deforestation, poaching, and other forms of environmental degradation.

Recommendations

A Time of Opportunity

There is an unusual opportunity at the present time to improve environmental conditions in Central America, while restarting the engines of economic development. The effort needed to do this must involve not only national governments, but also aid agencies, philanthropic foundations, researchers, and voluntary organizations. In many cases they can increase environmental quality while simultaneously improving the economic welfare of the poorest segments of the population. There are several reasons for this belief.

First, environmental improvement, general economic development, and provision for the basic human needs of the poor are increasingly seen as interrelated processes. Environmental improvement may be a rich source of starting points for what sociologist William McCord has called "virtuous cycles"—chains of mutually supporting developmental events. For example, creation of a national park that provides tourism-related jobs for local people can create local capital that can be invested in raising productivity in other enterprises, such as farming, forestry and fishing. This, in turn, can improve local nutrition and even education. The beginnings of a virtuous cycle may be seen in a rural development project in southeastern Costa Rica, where creation of the new Gandoca-Manzanillo National Wildlife Refuge has been linked to land titling for nearby squatters (to encourage permanent agriculture), agroforestry development, research, and ecotourism. Much of the effort is being undertaken by a small nonprofit conservation organization, supported by international foundations, environmental groups, aid agencies, and the Costa Rican government. By supporting environmental improvement, government agencies and private groups can help create virtuous cycles that resonate far beyond the environment.

Second, more and more attention and financial aid for the region is likely to be coming from the U.S. government and other international sources.

After decades of inattention to Central America, U.S. intellectuals and policymakers are perceiving vital national security interests in the area. Part of this is the result of the Nicaraguan revolution and the continuing war in El Salvador; part is the result of concern over the political and economic stability of Mexico. There is talk of a "new Marshall Plan" for postwar reconstruction in Central America, and of innovative ways to convert debt to equity. Foundations, in their traditional role as catalysts and supporter of small-scale, experimental efforts, can leverage much larger governmental resources.

Third, Central America has recently experienced a surge of attention by United States-based nongovernmental organizations (NGOs) as well as the creation of indigenous NGOs. Some of these NGOs are environmental; others are oriented toward improvement of the economic lot of the poor. Many have both goals in mind. It has become increasingly understood in economic development circles that NGOs have an important role in national development strategies. They are able to effectively administer the small-scale grants (sometimes as little as $100) that governmental aid bureaucracies cannot. They are able to work closely with local people and integrate their needs and desires into projects. As a result, NGOs are taking on ever greater importance as "retailers" of development aid—as recipients of relatively large grants which are then reprogrammed as many small, local projects. NGOs have also been associated with such innovations as "debt-for-nature swaps," by which developing country debt, bought at a discount, is traded to governments for parklands or local currency management funds. By supporting environmental and other NGOs in Central America, development agencies and foundations can create a needed mechanism for redirecting development aid from traditional megaprojects, which do not benefit the poor and which too often injure the environment.

I believe that there are three specific areas in which private philanthropy can be of special importance in promoting environmental improvement in Central America. Each of the three is a traditional area for foundation activity, although a given foundation may not have heretofore made grants in that particular part of the world. The subject areas are: (1) increasing the effectiveness of local institutions, particularly government agencies and indigenous NGOs, (2) promoting sustainable rural development, particularly through research related to land use improvement, and (3) environmental education.

Strengthening Local Institutions

A large number of international institutions are now working in both environmental protection and development promotion in Central America. (For example: Peace Corps, U.S. Agency for International Development, World Neighbors, Nature Conservancy International, World Wildlife Fund, Conservation International, Canadian International Development Agency, and several United Nations agencies.) But ultimately these tasks must fall to local institutions. United States-based philanthropies can make a major contribution by strategic interventions that help government agencies become more effective and by promoting strong NGOs as critics and counterweights to government.

Government agencies can be strengthened in three ways. First, government employees can be helped to secure advanced training. Training can be provided both through short courses and longer term education. The subject matter should include not only technical training (e.g., design of wastewater treatment systems) but also training in environmental economics and policy analysis. Second, good performance, by both agencies and individuals, should be recognized internationally. This can take the form of prizes (e.g., the Getty Prize), funding for attendance at international conferences, and simple verbal recognition. International funders and international NGOs tend to have access to high levels of government in developing countries. How satisfying it must be for the hardworking environmental bureaucrat to have his or her work mentioned favorably to the minister or the president. Third, government agencies can be provided with information. The United States and other developed countries now have nearly twenty years of experience in dealing with environmental pollution. As a result of this experience (and some costly mistakes) there is a large body of technical and socioeconomic information that can be shared with other countries just beginning the task. Although none of Central America's economies is comparable in level of industrialization to the United States, there are a number of specific environmental problems (e.g., pesticide pollution) for which information available in developed countries can be relevant. Ways must be found to package this information, digest it, and get it to the people who need it for management decisions.

Unlike government agencies, NGOs can be funded directly. Given the low salaries prevalent in Central America and the favorable exchange of the dollar with respect to domestic currencies, a small dollar investment can mobilize significant human resources. However, I believe that great care must be taken not to overwhelm a promising NGO with international monies. To do so creates inflated expectations and weakens the recipient's need to develop domestic sources of funds. When outside funds are cut off, as they almost certainly will be, an overly dependent NGO will collapse. It is also important to simultaneously strengthen governmental and nongovernmental agencies. Although some programs are clearly best handled by NGOs, the private institutions should not be strengthened at the expense of weaker government agencies. Massive flight of highly qualified government employees to NGOs is now occurring, in large part due to high salaries and better working conditions made possible by international support. Strengthening one institution at the expense of another is not the answer.

Besides funds, NGOs need advice, training (both technical and managerial), and friendly criticism. The nascent movement toward greater cooperation among Third World NGOs is particularly encouraging and is worthy of international support. In fact, there is great promise in the exchange of experience among developing countries. For example, Costa Rica has experience in parks and ecotourism that could be shared with other countries; successful hillside farming projects in Honduras and Guatemala have relevance elsewhere; Nicaragua has experience with community organization for reforestation and soil conservation; El Salvador and Costa Rica have experience in integrating wildlands management with agrarian reform. NGOs are a logical conduit for sharing this kind of experience.

Sustainable Rural Development

Large numbers of Central Americans still live from the land. Among the most important things that could be done to promote sustainable development in Central America would be to improve land use. Perhaps the best way foundations can help is by supporting research on small-scale, low-capital-intensive, low-purchased-input systems for agriculture, forestry and livestock raising. A good bit of such research is already underway, though it is still dwarfed by more conventional lines of agricultural research and has aroused more interest among ecologists than among mainstream agricultural researchers. The necessary task is threefold.

First, ecologically based/farming systems work needs to be made part of the mainstream. Only if it appeals to the conventional research establishment will it be able to command the large amounts of funds needed for real advance. (Funding levels are particularly important because so much of this research is locality-specific, even farm-specific.)

Second, these lines of research must be rescued from the romanticism of many of their proponents. Central American peasants are likely to be no more willing than are U.S. farmers to go through the backbreaking labor of terrace-building, tree planting, or mixed-crop horticultural production unless there is a clear financial return. And much of that return must come in the form of cash, rather than simply in better family nutrition. Many interesting and potentially valuable production systems are based on traditional Indian ideas. Yet the ultimate purpose of developing new systems should not be to create new tribes of noble savages, but to give some new options to people who (whether they are Indian or Latino) almost certainly, for their own reasons, have an ultimate goal of adopting the consumption patterns of the Westernized, cash-based economy.

Third, the new technologies have to be delivered to the farmers. This is perhaps the weakest link at present. The ecologists, agronomists and foresters who have begun to work on small-scale farm systems for Central America have very little capacity to deliver them in the field. For example, CATIE, the international agricultural institute in Costa Rica that is doing much innovative research, does not even have an extension program. In Honduras, the Escuela Agrícola Panamericana, in nearly all ways an admirable institution, recently suffered from peasant-set fires in the school's experimental forest. A staff member told me that the local farmers deeply resented the fact that the school, which occupies some of the best land in the area, never did anything to help them. The need to "plug into" the existing agricultural extension system is a strong argument for making alternative agricultural technologies acceptable to the agricultural establishment.

I mentioned earlier the need for making small-scale production "technologically dynamic." New technologies will not come directly from the peasant producers, though many of their traditional practices can serve as the starting point for new ideas.[36] Rather, the creative energies of first-rate scientists, engineers, and business planners must be harnessed. Interestingly, I think that some of the brightest minds in Central America and in the aid-giving countries are starting to work on these issues, partly because the problems are so interesting intellectually and partly because of social conscience. A real problem here is the intellectual overcentralization so prevalent throughout the developing world: the people who have the most to contribute are concentrated in the capital, far from the peasant producers they could potentially help.

Another area of emphasis that combines environmental and development interests is the maintenance of commercial and sport fisheries. Fish are an inexpensive source of high-quality protein, their harvest is labor-intensive and a source of rural employment, and for some species the export market is good. Fish population levels also are general indicators of environmental quality because they are affected by sedimentation and by some chemicals. Specific geographic areas that may be worth further study are the estuaries and nearshore areas, such as the Gulf of Fonseca and Gulf of Nicoya, as well as the several important inland lakes, including Atitlán and Amatitlán (Guatemala), Ilopango (El Salvador), Yojoa (Honduras) and Lakes Managua and Nicaragua. In some cases these lakes are important tourist destinations as well as major sources of fish products. Another research priority should be to prepare a series of regional studies of land use problems and opportunities. Land use studies tend to be done either at the national level (e.g., the recent AID "environmental profiles" for Central America) or at the project level. The former tend to be too general to guide effective local action; the latter do not reflect economic or environmental linkages that extend beyond what are often arbitrary geographic boundaries. I believe that there is a need for studies that are comprehensive in terms of the land uses considered (agriculture, livestock raising, timber, urbanization, conservation) and that cover large subnational regions. River basin studies are one approach, but suffer from the limitation of covering areas that overlap political jurisdictions and which have "implementability" only in terms of water development projects, which are usually rather narrowly conceived.

Such regional studies should be dynamic rather than static in their consideration of land use. Far more important than a snapshot of current land use is pinpointing types of land use change. This may imply a historical approach, looking at past land use changes, at the economic and technological forces that motivated them, and at impacts on the environment. Many of the changes that will be encountered in Central America are profound— consider the dramatic land use changes since 1950 in Costa Rica's northern region, or the more recent deforestation of Guatemala's Petén, or the tragic deforestation ongoing within the Rio Platano Biosphere Reserve in eastern Honduras.

Environmental Education

A final area in which private philanthropy can make a difference is environmental education. Two very different kinds of education are needed, one targeted and short-range, the other very broad and with a time horizon of generations. The first kind of environmental education should be directed to decisionmakers, both public and private, and to the professionals (economists, engineers, agronomists) who advise them. In Central America this group has become steadily larger and has gained better technical education. These people are probably the last to be moved by the appeals, partly to fear, partly to sentiment, that the environmental movement uses in motivating the urban public. Rather, they must be convinced that environmental conservation makes economic sense. There are many such arguments that can be made: that erosion reduces the life of hydroelectric plants, that pollution raises public health costs, that mangrove destruction reduces fishery production, that pesticide overuse induces resistance in target insects. Very little effort thus far has been made to reach this specific group through education, rather than through attacks in the press and political pressure on the multinational development banks.

There is also a need to educate more professional resource managers in Central America. Given the small size of the individual Central American countries and the usefulness of sharing information among them, there is good reason for training on a regional basis. (In addition to the five Central American countries, a regional training institution should include Panamá and Belize.) One priority is making better use of existing institutional capacity. For example, the regional forestry technician school in Honduras (ESNACIFOR) is operating at a fraction of capacity, while Guatemala has a critical lack of foresters. CATIE, the agricultural and forestry research and training institute in Costa Rica, excludes Panamá, Nicaragua, and Belize from many projects for political or institutional reasons, despite the fact that most of its findings are applicable to this larger region. An unaddressed priority for regional training is preparing a cadre of forest, park and wildlife rangers. Such a facility might be established at a national park and emphasize both training and continuing education. It is important in such a program to emphasize hands-on training and not to impose rigid entry requirements. In many cases a primary school graduate from a rural area near a park may be a better ranger candidate than a secondary school graduate from the city, yet the former is often excluded from employment by civil service requirements.

A more ambitious undertaking would be to create a regional training program in conservation and sustainable development. Such an institution should be truly regional and should from the outset have an independent and apolitical board of directors so as to minimize the political problems that have hindered past regional efforts. The institute's staff should have a strong conservationist orientation, yet should be able to work effectively with agronomists, foresters, and development economists. It should also have a strong outreach program, a traditional problem for regional agricultural and forestry institutions in the region.

Finally, there is also a role in Central America for more environmental education of a traditional sort: in the schools, on television, in press and poster campaigns. There is a great deal going on in this field at present in Central America, though it still does not reach very far into the countryside. The environmental education that does exist speaks very little to the needs and interests of the rural and urban poor. The emotional and romantic appeals that have a positive impact on the educated urban population make little impression on the poor or those directly involved in poaching wildlife, clearing fields, and spraying insecticides. A totally different approach is needed for these groups.

It must be emphasized that environmental education is a very long-term proposition. Some forms of environmental education have been underway in the United States for fifty years or more—through primary schools, Boy Scouts and Girl Scouts, 4-H, Arbor Day, National Parks, etc. I believe that change in social attitudes about such things as wildlife, preferred forms of outdoor recreation, and management of soils and timber resources comes very slowly, if it comes at all. Programs of general environmental education must become institutions, not "projects," and we must be very patient in waiting for them to have results.

Notes

This essay is excerpted (with additions and adaptations) from a longer and geographically more inclusive report published as "A Reconnaissance of Conservation and Development Issues in Mesoamerica" (Washington, D.C.: The Conservation Foundation, 1987). The material is used with the permission of the foundation. The report was prepared with the financial assistance of the David and Lucile Packard Foundation, whose support is gratefully acknowledged.

1. The figures for the remainder of Central America are: Guatemala, 52 percent; El Salvador, 48 percent; Nicaragua, 39 percent; Costa Rica, 32 percent. There is additional resource-based employment in forestry and fisheries, as well as indirect employment in sectors processing agricultural products or providing inputs. Source: *Production Yearbook 1984* (Rome: FAO).

2. The assistance of Edgar Pape and the advice and comments of James Barborak are also gratefully acknowledged.

3. For excellent analyses of agricultural change in Central America, see Brockett (1988) and Williams (1986).

4. For discussion of land tenure inequality and its consequences in El Salvador and Honduras, see Durham (1979).

5. In Honduras and Costa Rica most "land reform" has been through negotiated purchase of private farms, not expropriation. This tends to reduce conflict, but it is an inherently slow process given the availability of funds.

6. United Nations Food and Agriculture Organization (various dates).

7. World Bank (1986).

8. Barry (1987).

9. Coffee, which is often planted on slopes, presents much less erosion danger because it is a perennial bush crop whose canopy affords the soil some protection from the impact of raindrops and because it has traditionally been planted in the shade of cacao, bananas, or small trees. However, there is a trend toward greater use of shadeless coffee varieties that threatens to increase soil erosion. Studies in Guatemala and El Salvador have also shown that faunal diversity is much higher in areas of coffee grown under natural shade than in shadeless coffee monocultures.

10. Leonard (1987).

11. Goodland and Pollard (1974), cited in Hoy and Belisle (1984).

12. U.S. Office of Technology Assessment (1984).

13. I see this as a major problem with aquaculture. There may be little local market for the (relatively inexpensive) products, and no way to transport them to urban markets where effective demand does exist.

14. Also used to describe the process is "potrerización," or the "pasture-izing" of agriculture.

15. See Myers (1981); Shane (1986).

16. There has been considerable instability in the Central American beef industry within the context of general growth over time. Costa Rica's beef exports to the United States, which declined sharply between 1979 and 1983–84, had by 1986 recovered to their earlier level. Even in Costa Rica, however, cattle numbers in 1986 were 11 percent above their 1979–81 level. Sources: U.S. Department of Agriculture (various dates) and *Production Yearbook* (various dates). Another crisis occurred in Costa Rica in 1987–88, with declining cattle prices, many producers defaulting on loans, and a massive reduction in herds.

17. Interview, June 1986.

18. Ironically, a great deal of Central America's export earnings from beef has in the past been spent to import milk products. Local milk production has been discouraged by the availability of cheap imports of powdered milk from the United States and Europe and by domestic price controls intended to reduce the cost of staple foods.

19. The usual target for the peasant is a "baldío," a piece of uncultivated land, often government-owned, sometimes even within a nominally protected area.

20. In 1986, Costa Rica passed legislation eliminating the provision for securing legal land title by "land improvement." It remains to be seen whether this will reduce the practice or will simply result in illegal occupancy. In the history of U.S. settlement, land titling rules were frequently ignored by settlers who often successfully pressured Congress to legalize land settlements retroactively.

21. Shands and Healy (1977), p. 10.

22. In 1988, both INAFOR and FYDEP were dismantled and their functions transferred to other agencies.

23. *La Tribuna* (April 22, 1986).

24. A useful study in this area would involve comparative analysis of the performance of state forest enterprises such as COHDEFOR, private industrial companies, farm and private owners, and collective forestry enterprises such as Mexico's forestry *ejidos* and Nicaragua's land management cooperatives.

25. Veblen (1978).

26. This has been quite evident in the forest history of the southeastern United States, which witnessed a wave of exploitative lumber cutting in the first two decades of the twentieth century but did not see interest in replanting and forest management until pulp mills were established and industries began to worry about future timber supply.

27. Interview, Carlos Querada, CATIE, Turriabla, Costa Rica, May 1986.

28. Bosselman (1979).

29. United Nations Development Programme (1988). Costa Rica and Belize are, not unreason-

ably, opposed to region-wide promotion as long as the other countries in Central America continue to receive so much negative attention in the press.

30. For more details on tourism in Monteverde, see Healy (1988).

31. Even in Mexico, which has had one of the world's most ambitious land redistribution programs, one frequently sees small stories in the newspapers reporting on rural killings as a result of local land disputes.

32. Williams (1986) gives a very enlightening and evenhanded portrayal of the forces motivating landowners and peasants in Central America. I recommend it highly to anyone trying to understand the motivations behind what seems otherwise to be senseless violence within the region.

33. Perhaps a North American analogy will enable one to better understand the emotional content of the issue. Imagine that tenants of apartments and office buildings throughout the United States begin to assert that their years of paying rent entitle them to ownership of the property rented. Further, imagine that the tenants' claim is supported, in a very inconsistent and arbitrary manner, by some government agencies and that it has the political support of significant numbers of politicians and many of the clergy. Finally, assume that both landlords and tenants are able to assert or protect their claims through the use of violence, with little effective control by the police. This hypothetical situation gives just a taste of the present land tenure conflict in much of Mesoamerica.

34. Hoy and Belisle (1984), p. 163.

35. "Loable Iniciativa," *La Prensa* (San Pedro Sula), July 1, 1986.

36. More than twenty years ago, T. W. Schultz (1964), professor of economics at the University of Chicago and later Nobel laureate, argued that peasant producers make more efficient use of available resources than even farmers in developed countries. The reason is simple—peasants have had centuries to develop technologies that "work" given their circumstances. Outsiders, Schultz argued, can do little to make the peasants better traditional farmers; rather they need to bring new ideas and new technologies (or new products) into the system. This has sometimes been used to justify introducing peasants to high-input Green Revolution technologies. But I think it also implies that an outsider can bring in new knowledge, particularly concepts from plant ecology (for example, beneficial plant-soil and plant-plant interactions) and evaluation methodologies (how have other traditional farming economies been transformed by access to new markets or new inputs?).

References

Barry, Tom (1987). *Land and Hunger in Central America*. Boston: South End Press.

Bosselman, Fred (1979). *In the Wake of the Tourist*. Washington: The Conservation Foundation.

Brockett, Charles D. (1988). *Land, Power and Poverty: Agrarian Transformation and Political Conflict in Central America*. Boston: Unwin Hyman.

Durham, William (1979). *Scarcity and Survival in Central America*. Stanford, Calif.: Stanford University Press.

Goodland, R. and R. Pollard (1974). *Chixoy Development Project: Environmental Impact Reconnaissance Report*. Millbrook, N.Y.: Cary Arboretum, New York Botanical Gardens. Cited in Don R. Hoy and Francis J. Beslisle, "Environmental Protection and Economic Development in Guatemala's Western Highlands," *Journal of Developing Areas* 18, 2: 169.

Healy, Robert G. (1988). *Economic Aspects of Nature-Oriented Tourism: Latin American Case Studies*. Research Triangle Park, North Carolina: U.S. Forest Service, Southeastern Forest Experiment Station.

Hoy, Don R. and Francis J. Beslisle (1974). "Environmental Protection and Economic Development in Guatemala's Western Highlands," *Journal of Developing Areas* 18, 2: 169.

La Tribuna. April 22, 1986. Editorial.

Leonard, H. Jeffrey (1987). *Natural Resources and Economic Development in Central America*. New Brunswick, N.J.: Transaction Books.

"Loable Iniciativa." *La Prensa* (San Pedro Sula). July 1, 1989.

Myers, Norman (1981). "The Hamburger Connection: How Central America's Forests Became North America's Hamburgers." *Ambio* X, 1: 3-8.

Nations, Jim. Interview, June 1986.

Querada, Carlos. Interview, CATIE, Turrialba, Costa Rica, May 1986.

Schultz, T. W. (1964). *Transforming Traditional Agriculture*. New Haven: Yale University Press.

Shands, William E. and Robert G. Healy (1977). *The Lands Nobody Wanted*. Washington: The Conservation Foundation.

Shane, Douglas R. (1986). *Hoofprints on the Forest*. Philadelphia: Institute for the Study of Human Issues.

United Nations Development Programme (1988). *Plan of Economic Cooperation for Central America*. New York: UNDP.

United Nations Food and Agricultural Organization (various dates). *Production Yearbook*. Rome: FAO.

United States Department of Agriculture (various dates). *Agricultural Statistics*. Washington: U.S. Government Printing Office.

United States Office of Technology Assessment (1984). *Africa Tomorrow: Issues in Technology, Agriculture and U.S. Foreign Aid*. Washington: U.S. Government Printing Office.

Veblen, Thomas T. (1978). "Forest Preservation in the Western Highlands of Guatemala." *Geographical Review* 68, 4: 417-34.

Williams, Robert (1986). *Export Agriculture and the Crisis in Central America*. Chapel Hill: The University of North Carolina Press.

World Bank (1986). *Guatemala: Population, Nutrition and Health*. Washington: World Bank.

Chapter 5

Industrial Prospects for Central America: A Macroeconomic Policy Approach for Central America and the International Community for the Future (1987–92)

Colin I. Bradford, Jr.

Introduction

In Central America a decade of political turmoil and economic crises has erected seemingly insurmountable hurdles to short-term recovery. Two out of three Central Americans live in poverty. The region's export earnings have fallen sharply. In some countries, the productive infrastructure—roads, factories, power plants, and ports—lies in ruins. The region's external debt has spiralled to $18 billion.

This chapter demonstrates that, despite all the difficulties the Central American economies have experienced in the 1980s, recovery and development are feasible for all five Central American countries in the relatively near future. Through sound planning and fiscal discipline in the region and support and encouragement from the international community, Central America's economies can grow at a rate that will meet two essential and complementary goals. The first is to improve the well-being of the region's people through increased employment at higher wages. The second is to increase the region's export earnings, which will finance the improvements in living conditions, fuel future production, and help reduce the external debt.

Using a scenario of labor-intensive industrialization, this chapter explores the connections between the financial resources and the growth that can be achieved in the region. It does not prescribe particular actions that each government should take; rather, it outlines broad economic goals. Essentially, this exercise answers the question: What actions in providing financial resources could the Central Americans and the international community adopt to implement a development strategy that improves the lives of the least fortunate people of the region while building a strong export-oriented economy? It establishes orders of magnitude for the efforts needed by both the regional and international actors.

Two Goals: Employment and Exports

The central element in an economic recovery and development effort in Central America must be higher employment and income growth for the lower income wage earner in the region. Dynamic economic growth alone cannot be the goal. Dick McCall from the U.S. Senate staff put it eloquently in the first meeting of the Task Force in September 1987: "We are looking for ways to eliminate polarization and alienation in these societies. . . . Long-run economic stability is necessary to keep the cycle of political disintegration from recurring."

This analysis focuses on the labor-intensive scenario in order to determine the *minimum* financial flows needed to generate the targeted sustained growth rate in Central America. Yet a labor-intensive approach is also good policy. A labor-intensive approach makes use of the input that is abundant—labor—to reduce reliance on the inputs that are less plentiful: land and capital. For Central America, a labor-intensive industrialization process is essential not only to take advantage of the oversupply of inexpensive labor, which is a favorable endowment from an economic point of view, but also to absorb the unemployed into the productive economy, which is essential from a social and political point of view.

Another element critical to the success of development strategies in Central America is the development of the capacity to export at sufficiently high rates of growth to service the external debt. This requirement presents Central America with the healthy discipline of allocating resources in a way that will simultaneously satisfy the current need to increase consumption and incomes and the future need to generate foreign exchange through exports which are competitive in world markets. Thus, the development path has to yield immediate tangible results internally while leading to a stronger competitive position externally.

The importance of both employment and exports means that there is a premium on the wise allocation of investment in Central America in the years immediately ahead. Although the private sector is best able to utilize investment efficiently, current circumstances require that government be intimately involved with the private sector in developing future productive capacity, which, in turn, sets the strategic direction of the economy.

No specific sectoral guidance is contained in this study; this is for each of the five governments to establish through its own political processes. Some consultation with each other will be necessary both to avoid competing with each other in external markets and to take fullest advantage of trade possibilities within the region.

The Basis of the Projections

The basic strategy is to stimulate labor-intensive industrialization through increased investment in manufacturing sectors with export potential. This strategy depends on increased capital flows from outside the region to finance the machinery and equipment imports necessary for industrialization. These capital flows are necessary for two reasons: first, the magnitude of the investment effort required, and second, the need for consumption to grow as employment and low-wage incomes increase.

In order to estimate the resource-growth relationships that are consistent with Central America's capacities, we reviewed the recent past to identify an equivalent five-year period of high, steady economic growth which coincided with years of rapid industrialization. The mid- to late 1960s was such a period for all five countries (see table 5.1). The growth rates of the manufacturing sectors in Central American economies ranged from 7.1 percent in Honduras to 10.0 percent in Nicaragua for the period 1960 to 1970, whereas in the 1970s these varied from 2.4 percent in Nicaragua to 7.4 percent in Costa Rica.

From this fairly stable but dynamic period in the late 1960s, it is possible to derive a relationship between incremental investment and incremental growth. This relationship can serve as a guide to the projection period when the goal is to achieve higher economic growth based on investment-led industrialization. During this period, incremental increases in capital yielded significant increases in growth in the Central American economies. Maintaining low ratios of incremental investment to incremental growth is consistent with investing in labor-intensive industries. This is because lower capital input implies a higher labor or land input.

Investment-led industrialization calls for imported capital equipment and machinery. In all five Central American countries, increased imports have

Table 5.1   Growth of Real GDP from previous year

Year	Costa Rica	El Salvador	Guatemala	Honduras	Nicaragua	Non-oil LDC	All LDC	World
1959	n.a.	4.5	4.9	2.3	1.5	2.9	n.a.	n.a.
1960	n.a.	4.1	2.5	−0.1	3.6	5.3	4.2	4.3
1961	−0.8	3.5	4.3	2.8	7.5	4.9	4.6	4.3
1962	8.2	11.9	3.5	5.1	10.9	4.2	4.4	5.0
1963	4.8	4.3	9.6	3.2	10.8	5.4	5.8	4.8
1964	4.1	9.3	4.6	6.0	11.7	5.8	6.0	6.0
1965	9.8	5.4	4.4	10.3	9.5	5.3	5.6	6.0
1966	7.9	7.2	5.5	5.9	3.3	5.4	5.1	5.5
1967	5.7	5.4	4.1	4.6	7.0	4.7	4.2	3.7
1968	8.5	3.2	8.8	7.3	1.4	5.6	5.9	5.3
1969	5.5	3.5	4.5	0.3	6.2	7.1	7.7	5.4
1970	7.5	3.0	5.7	4.7	1.4	5.1	5.9	3.2
1971	6.8	4.8	5.6	5.4	4.9	5.8	5.9	4.0
1972	8.2	5.5	7.3	4.0	3.2	5.1	5.7	5.3
1973	7.7	5.1	6.8	5.6	6.4	6.3	6.3	5.6
1974	5.5	6.4	6.4	−0.1	13.4	4.9	5.8	1.5
1975	2.1	5.6	1.9	−3.0	−0.1	5.4	4.8	0.3
1976	5.5	4.0	7.4	8.0	5.2	3.9	5.5	5.3
1977	8.9	6.1	7.8	11.5	8.4	5.6	6.0	4.5
1978	6.3	6.4	5.0	7.4	−7.8	5.8	4.3	4.0
1979	4.9	−1.7	4.7	6.8	−26.4	4.9	4.7	3.5
1980	0.7	−8.7	3.7	2.7	10.0	4.9	4.4	1.5
1981	−2.3	−8.3	0.7	1.2	5.3	3.1	2.7	1.8
1982	−7.3	−5.6	−3.5	−1.8	−1.2	1.7	1.8	0.2
1983	2.9	0.7	−2.7	−0.4	5.1	0.8	0.1	2.4
1984	7.5	1.5	0.7	2.8	−1.4	3.9	2.8	4.5
1985	1.0	1.6	−1.1	3.0	−2.6	n.a.	n.a.	n.a.

corresponded closely with increased growth (see graphs). Central American imports of machinery and equipment as a percentage of total imports peaked in the mid-1960s at between 25 and 30 percent; this coincides with the period of rapid industrialization.

Industrialization in Central America has progressed from import substitution toward exports, as can be seen by the increase in manufactured goods exports as a percentage of total exports between 1962 and 1980. Manufactured goods accounted for 7 to 9 percent of total exports in Costa Rica, El Salvador, and Guatemala in 1962; that figure rose to 25 to 35 percent in 1980. In Honduras and Nicaragua, manufactured goods accounted for 2 percent of exports in 1962 and 13 percent in 1980. Nonetheless, Central America cannot rely exclusively on manufactured goods exports even though these exports play an important role in the region's development strategies. Primary product exports are still dominant in trade, and agriculture is still the dominant sector internally in the distribution of the labor force.

Four Economic Assumptions

For a recovery and development strategy to be politically attractive it must generate high enough growth in gross domestic product (GDP) and consumption to improve the living standards of the average person. It is important to note that government policies other than those specified here will be necessary to assure that more dynamic growth is distributed more equally.

Bearing in mind the need to generate growth, this approach adopts four macroeconomic policy guidelines which determine the economic results. Using these guidelines, we have developed scenarios that will permit each of the five countries to progress toward the goals of increased employment and exports. (The methodology for this framework is set forth in appendix I.)

First, to provide for growth in consumption, the gross domestic product must grow faster than the labor force. To establish target growth rates for the 1987 to 1992 period, we have set the GDP growth targets at least two percentage points higher than the rates of growth in the labor force projected by the World Bank for the Central American countries for the period from 1990 to 2000. This procedure yields target rates of GDP growth for 1992 of 6 percent for Costa Rica, El Salvador, and Guatemala, and 6.5 percent for

Honduras and Nicaragua. These are fairly ambitious rates of growth against a background of low, unstable, and frequently negative rates of growth in Central America in the 1980s (see table 5.1).

Second, our scenario assumes investment growth rates in excess of import growth rates. This differential implies policies that restrict consumer goods imports and emphasize capital goods imports, which is consistent with the industrialization plan. Experiments with import growth rates identical to investment growth rates have allowed consumption to grow too fast, indebting the countries excessively. In other words, high import growth rates relative to investment growth rates signify that consumer goods constitute a high proportion of all imports. The scenario assumes policies to encourage the import of the machinery and equipment necessary for industrialization. Therefore, import growth rates were set at between 2.5 and 3.5 percentage points below the investment growth rates for Costa Rica, El Salvador, and Guatemala, and at 5 and 6 percentage points less for Honduras and Nicaragua respectively.

Having established target rates of growth, we can derive investment from the ratio of incremental investment to incremental growth. These ratios are lagged by one year so that investment in one year spurs growth in the following year, reflecting the time needed for investment projects to be completed and contribute to GDP. This is consistent with the investment-led industrialization strategy that relies on increases in productive capacity rather than increases in demand to generate GDP growth.

Third, the scenario assumes that Central American governments will undertake the necessary reductions in their fiscal deficits over the medium term by reducing their expenditures, by increasing taxes, or by some combination of the two. This will ensure that scarce foreign exchange will not be used to finance fiscal deficits. We have set targets for reducing the fiscal deficits of Costa Rica, El Salvador, and Guatemala to 1.0 percent of GDP by 1992. This represents a reduction from 3.6 percent in Costa Rica, 1.8 percent in El Salvador, and 1.4 percent in Guatemala in 1986. The fiscal deficit of Honduras is targeted to decline from 5.6 percent of GDP in 1986 to 2.0 percent in 1992; Nicaragua's would drop from 15.8 percent of GDP in 1986 to 8.0 percent in 1992, a reduction of less than 1.5 percentage points per year. These are not draconian cuts, but they do represent significant efforts by governments to improve fiscal performance and conserve foreign exchange for investment consistent with the thrust of the plan.

Finally, export growth rates should increase as investments in productive capacity increase and manufactured goods exports come on stream. Again, this is consistent with the overall development strategy.

Specifying the GDP growth target, fiscal policy, export growth rates, and import policy, given an investment-growth ratio consistent with labor-intensive industrialization, will allow us to derive consumption for each country. Calculating consumption can help ensure a correct growth target. If we set a growth target that is too high, the necessary investment will either crowd out consumption or burden the country with external debt. If the growth target is too low, it will not keep pace with the increased population and labor force, and consumption will not be able to increase.[1]

Financing Recovery and Development

The financing of the projected growth path can be derived from the same set of relationships. If government revenue were equal to government spending, if domestic savings were sufficient to finance the investment required to achieve the growth target, and if exports exceeded imports by enough to make interest payments on the external debt, there would be no financial gap. Normally, however, there will be a fiscal deficit and a savings gap to be financed. The sum of the fiscal deficit and the savings gap is the "current account deficit." In other words, the current account deficit is the trade balance plus "factor payments," which are primarily interest payments on external debt. In this way, the amount of foreign savings or capital inflows that is required to finance the current account deficit can be derived directly from the variables already specified. For simplicity, we have assumed that no country will draw down its international reserves.[2]

Finally, domestic savings can also be derived in a straightforward way from these already determined variables. Domestic savings is what is left when interest payments on external debt, consumption and taxes have been deducted from total national income (GDP).

These calculations allow us to obtain an unfettered view of the interactions of the key economic policy variables and their impact on the national economies of Central America with the external factors that potentially both constrain and facilitate economic development in the region. As always, the maneuvering room for economic policy is tight, but the opportunities for gains become evident as does the importance of collaboration between internal effort and external support.

The Outcome: Growth Scenarios for Central America

To summarize, we adopted four policy guidelines that drive the results: (1) GDP growth rates have been targeted to be at least two percentage points above the rates of growth of the labor force projected by the World Bank for the 1990s, (2) imports are channeled toward investment rather than consumption by emphasizing machinery and equipment imports over consumer goods imports, (3) fiscal deficits are gradually reduced, principally through cuts in government spending as a share of GDP rather than by increases in taxes, which could reduce private capital available for investment, and (4) export growth rates accelerate gradually over the six-year period, reflecting increases in the capacity to export manufactured goods.

The *economic outcomes* from these policies *and* external flows to cover the financial gaps relate to consumption levels, investment as a share of GDP, savings rates, improvements in trade balances, and capital inflows. These outcomes vary from country to country since the problems and economic structures of the five Central American countries are different. (See the tables in appendix IV for details by country.)

Consumption is maintained at a constant share of GDP during this period of relatively fast GDP growth. This creates conditions in which the standard of living of lower-income earners can improve. Governments must follow through on this result with specific policies to assure more equal income distribution. This is an important result. Without it, there is no incentive for the people of Central America or their governments to support this approach in the short-term. A new economic strategy must show palpable, immediate gains to attract the political support that will make it feasible. In this scenario, annual growth in consumption is nearly two percentage points above the projected labor force growth for each of the five countries in the 1990s. In Nicaragua, for example, perhaps the most important country in which to generate tangible benefits, the annual rate of growth of consumption rises from 5.6 percent in 1988 to 6.7 percent in 1992, up from an average annual growth rate of 0.6 percent in the 1970s and *negative* 9.0 percent in the 1980–85 period.

Investment increases as a share of GDP by two to five percentage points of

GDP in four of the five countries between 1987 and 1992: in Costa Rica and Honduras, investment increases from 15 percent of GDP to 19–20 percent; in El Salvador and Guatemala it increases from 10–12 percent to 14 percent. These patterns are consistent with investment-led industrialization.

For Nicaragua the pattern is somewhat different. While the *amount* of investment remains constant over the six-year period, investment as a share of GDP falls gradually from 19 percent to 13 percent. The ratio of incremental investment to incremental growth drops smoothly from 3 to 2 over the same period. This gradual reduction in the investment-output ratio reflects both an improving efficiency of investment and an increase in the labor intensity of investment. Although this pattern is different than that in the other four countries, the goal of maintaining the amount of investment over the period is consistent with the spirit of the patterns in the other countries.

The initial conditions in Nicaragua are dramatically different than in the four other Central American economies. The fiscal deficit was nearly 16 percent of GDP in 1986, compared with less than 6 percent in the rest of the region, and the trade deficit was nearly 20 percent of GDP in 1986, compared with less than 5 percent of the other nations. An increase in the investment as a share of GDP in Nicaragua is impossible when major improvements in the massive fiscal and trade deficits are projected to occur simultaneously. In many Latin American countries, fiscal and trade deficits were reduced in the early 1980s through contraction in the amount of investment. This has been avoided in the scenario for Nicaragua presented here.

It is important that the effort to achieve economic recovery and development in Central America be the result of mutual effort by both the Central American nations and the international community. In this sense it is important to note that *savings* as a percent of GDP increases from 13 to 17 percent in Costa Rica and from 5 to 11 percent in El Salvador while remaining constant at 11 and 13 percent respectively in Guatemala and Honduras. Domestic savings should complement the investment contemplated from the international community. Again, Nicaragua is the exception. Savings as a share of GDP drops from 8 percent in 1986 to 2 percent in 1992. This drop is offset, and to a large extent explained, by the dramatic reduction in the fiscal deficit as a share of GDP from 15.8 percent in 1986 to 8.0 percent in 1992. The reduction of deficit spending by the public sector is "financed" by domestic savings.

These scenarios show substantial improvement in the *trade balance*, as manufactured exports begin to boost export growth rates toward the end of the projection period. The most striking improvement is in Nicaragua, where the massive trade deficit of 20 percent of GDP in 1986 is reduced to 3 percent in 1992. To achieve this, imports as a share of GDP are cut in half while exports are maintained at 15 percent of GDP. This major improvement in Nicaragua's trade balance positions the country well to finance its debt service in the future. El Salvador and Honduras also show an improvement in their trade balances, reducing their trade deficits from 5 to 6 percent of GDP in 1986 to 3 to 4 percent in 1992. Costa Rica begins and ends the projection period with a slight trade surplus.

Guatemala is the one country whose trade balance deteriorates over the period, falling from a surplus of 1.5 percent of GDP to a deficit of the same size. There are several reasons for this. Guatemala is the most closed economy of the five, with trade as a share of GDP of roughly 15 percent, whereas the openness of the other Central American economies ranges from 25 to 30 percent. Guatemala also has the highest consumption-GDP share at 80 percent (compared to 59 percent for Costa Rica) and the lowest investment-GDP share with 10 percent. The result is that by holding the consumption-GDP share constant and increasing the investment-GDP share while keeping fiscal policy under control, the trade balance has to deteriorate. The increase of 4 percent in the investment-GDP share is "financed" by a shift of 4 percent in the trade balance reflecting increased imported capital goods.

Finally, the gaps between domestic savings and investment and between tax revenues and government expenditures are reflected in the current account balance, which is the sum of the trade balance and interest payments. (See the second page of each country table in appendix IV.) When investment is greater than domestic savings and government spending is greater than tax revenues, demand for goods exceeds the supply of domestically produced goods. This results in an increase in imports and usually in a trade deficit. These internal gaps and the external deficits are financed by *capital inflows* (increased foreign borrowing shown as "exceptional financing" in the country tables). To highlight the impact of internal savings-investment and fiscal gaps on external flows, we assume no changes in international reserves.

Financing Requirements

The external savings—or increased foreign lending—needed to finance the economic strategies embodied in these scenarios totals $18.9 billion over the period from 1987 to 1992 for the five Central American countries. The macroeconomic scenario presented here contemplates continuous payment of both interest and principal on all debt obligations. The result is that there is, simultaneous with the increased borrowing, a substantial flow of debt repayments, amounting to a total of $9.4 billion over the projection period. Long-term capital repayments are substantial in all five countries, and short-term and IMF obligations are paid off. (See table 5.2 and capital account in the country tables in appendix IV.)

As a consequence, the net increase in debt obligations over the projection period averages roughly 8 percent per year. While this growth in net debt obligations is higher than the growth in GDP and export rates, the net new borrowing of $10 billion is being channeled toward investment in industries with the potential for exporting at rapid rates in the 1990s. The new borrowing lays the foundations for dynamic economic and export performance in the future.

The $18.9 billion in new lending over the 1986 to 1992 period compares with $20.8 billion in projected external financial requirements for the 1984 to 1990 period contained in the Kissinger Report. Whereas the total is roughly the same, the country composition of the external financing is quite different, with the Kissinger Commission recommending greater external financing for Costa Rica and El Salvador and less for Honduras and Nicaragua.

Conclusion

Although $19 billion in new lending to Central America over the period is a substantial investment by the international community, there is a sound

Table 5.2   External Savings

	Total Debt 1986	Gross New Finance	Reflows	Net Inflow	Total Debt 1992	Kissinger Commission Report
Costa Rica	4.2	3.5	2.5	+1.0	5.2	5.1
El Salvador	1.8	1.5	0.7	+0.8	2.6	5.5
Guatemala	2.7	4.6	1.5	+3.1	5.8	4.5
Honduras	2.9	3.5	1.5	+2.0	4.9	2.3
Nicaragua	6.0	5.8	2.4	+3.4	9.4	3.4
Total	17.6	18.9	8.6	10.0	27.9	20.8

rationale for this level of support. Foreign financing meshes with a macro-economic strategy that achieves several benefits: an increased domestic savings effort, significant corrective measures in fiscal policy, an increased proportion of resources being channeled into investment, a priority on investment in industries with export potential, projected improvement in trade balances in the region, and continuous fulfillment of debt obligations with substantial payment of interest and principal on external debt.

For the Central American nations, this approach has substantial tangible benefits that would be visible to the Central American people. These benefits are: (1) an investment-led industrialization strategy emphasizing labor-intensive industries with high employment generation, (2) faster rates of economic growth, which ease the pressures on governments from the low consumption, high unemployment, high external debt, and large fiscal and trade deficits characteristic of the recent past, (3) growth rates in consumption significantly in excess of labor force growth rates, maintaining the consumption-GDP share even as GDP growth rates rise toward the end of the period, and (4) the realization of these short-run benefits within a long-term framework of structural adjustment which, in turn, strengthens the future capacity of the Central American economies to manage their internal and external requirements with greater independence.

This strategy for economic recovery and development for Central America presents a sense of direction and dimension for a future that seems decidedly better than the patterns of the recent past. It requires the sympathetic support of the international community, demonstrated by its willingness not only to invest substantial amounts of financial resources, but also to accept increased manufactured goods exports from Central America. It is an illustration of the case that can be made for politically and economically open economies facing and interacting with each other for mutual gains—in contrast to the conditions resulting from closed policies and economies back-to-back in conflict in which all sides stand to lose.

Appendix I: The Projection Methodology

The scenarios presented for each of the five countries are generated from a straightforward national income accounting framework in which the ratio of incremental investment to incremental growth is used as a proxy for the variety of inputs necessary to achieve economic growth. The advantage of this framework is that it is derived fundamentally from several identities that must hold in any economy and that link the economic policy variables, clarifying their interrelatedness. The simple adages that supply must equal demand, savings must equal investment, the current account must equal the capital account, and government revenues should bear some relationship to government expenditures provide a closed circuit within which to check the feasibility of alternative development strategies. No behavioral assumptions, fancy econometric relationships, or policy black boxes drive this framework. The national income accounting framework is policy neutral. (See appendix II for the equations.)

Limitations of the Methodology and the Strategy

The approach outlined here implicitly assumes that economic growth is primarily determined by capital investment. In its most formalized growth model, this would require quite a number of highly restrictive and even rigid assumptions that are known to be distant approximations of real world conditions. These assumptions are not involved in the form used here. The accounting relations specified in this approach prevail *ex post* no matter what causal or behavioral relations are hypothesized. Nevertheless, the incremental capital output ratio used in this approach does involve an explicit relationship of investment to growth. Narrowly taken, this could mean that capital investment is the only variable that drives growth. But given the fact that for a given country in a given period an incremental capital output ratio (ICOR) exists *ex post*, and although other variables contribute to economic growth, some capital investment is needed, and the ICOR estimates what those capital requirements would be for given growth goals. Unless there is significant underutilized capacity in those industries in which export growth is possible, it is hard to see how more dynamic industrial export capability can be forthcoming without more investment. To summarize, the methodology employed here relies on additional investment to achieve additional growth, but it does so within an otherwise policy-neutral accounting framework and its reliance on capital investment does not preclude other determinants of growth or rest on a plethora of restrictive assumptions.

The investment-led recovery and export-oriented industrialization strategy presented in this paper is not the only possible strategy. Because of its reliance on investment and on external financing of the gap between required investment and domestic savings, it generates a development path that is relatively dependent on foreign capital. An alternative strategy might explore the potential for growth in an agricultural-led growth and export strategy where the savings and foreign exchange generated by the agriculture sector would finance industrialization rather than relying on foreign borrowing. The problem with this strategy is that the agriculture sector is, on the average, not significantly larger than the industrial sector in Central America and that it is considerably less dynamic and has less potential for high rates of export growth. This strategy, then, appears to result in more limited prospects for economic recovery and less capability of reducing the burden of foreign debt. Nevertheless, it is an alternative worth further exploitation.

A second strategy might be to turn inward and to try to minimize the need for foreign exchange by relying on internal demand growth and on import substitution. This would minimize the accumulation of additional foreign debt and would limit the scope of industrialization. This strategy would reduce the degree of interaction of the Central American economies with the world economy in both the trade and financial dimensions. The problem with this strategy is that it probably implies a decidedly slower rate of economic growth and greater debt-servicing difficulties.

As a consequence, both the continuation of the methodology utilized in this approach and the strategy chosen, relative to at least the two alternatives just discussed, mean that the development path charted in this analysis is one in which investment and foreign borrowing are important instrument variables relative to what they would be in other approaches and strategies. (See appendix III for an illustration of the sensitivity of the results to alternative assumptions.) This seems to be justified by the goals of recovery and external debt management and by the potential for international collaboration possible within this general framework.

Appendix II: The National Income Accounting Framework

(1) $Y = C + I + G + X - M$

National income (GDP) = consumption + investment + government expenditure + exports − imports

(2) $@ = \delta K/\delta Y = I/\delta Y$; therefore, $I = @\delta Y$ which (dividing both sides by Y) yields $I/Y = @\delta Y/Y$, or investment as a share of GDP = the ICOR

times the growth rate, where @ = the ICOR, δK = additions to capital
stock, and δY/Y = the growth rate.

(3) Y + or − R − T − C = S (by definition); saving (S) = income
adjusted for unilateral transfers (R) − taxes (T) − consumption (C),
where R = interest payments on foreign debt, wage, or profit remittances
to or from abroad, etc.

(4) Add + or − R and subtract T from both sides of equation (1).

Y + or − R − T = C + I + G − T + X + or − R − M

(5) Transpose C and I.

Y + R − T − C − I = G − T + X + R − M; therefore, using
(3),

(6) (S − I) = (G − T) + (X + R − M)

Savings gap = fiscal deficit or surplus + current account (CA).

(7) If changes in reserves = 0, then CA = KA (capital account).

Appendix III: Sensitivity Analysis
Doug Gollon

In any quantitative model the target variable is determined by estimated
values of other variables and parameters. The model we have presented here
is no exception. To judge the applicability of the model, it is useful to
examine the sensitivity of its results to changes in some of the independent
variables.

We begin by retracing some of the underlying assumptions we have made
concerning the role of foreign capital in Central American economies. In the
model presented here, the total capital required by a given country reflects
primarily its need for foreign exchange to service existing debt and to pay
for imports of investment goods. Export earnings provide some of the
necessary foreign exchange, but the remainder must be financed; in the
short run, moreover, exports are essentially determined exogenously.

The focus thus shifts to determinants of the demand for imports of
investment goods. There are two important determinants of investment
demand under this model. One is the rate of GDP growth, and the other is
the incremental capital output ratio (ICOR). In fact, investment demand is
hypothesized to be a linear multiple of actual GDP growth; the multiplier is
the ICOR. We can intuitively see from this that a change in the ICOR will
have a significant effect on a country's capital needs. The ICOR represents a

country's efficiency in converting capital into output. The amount of output growth required and the rate of conversion of capital into output represent the two greatest factors determining capital needs.

Other factors also influence the capital requirements of the different countries; these include, for example, interest rates, consumption behavior, and policies concerning reserve holdings.

To illustrate the relative significance of different variables on the financing needs of the different countries in the model, we have calculated a set of different scenarios involving Guatemala. Beginning with a single base scenario for the period 1987–92, we went on to make a series of changes in single variables. Using five different scenarios, we looked at the changes in financing needs under a given alternative condition. The results are summarized below:

Base scenario: Guatemala, 1987–92

Financing required: $4.4 billion
Assumptions:
ICOR = 2.25
GDP growth accelerates from 5 percent in 1987 to 6 percent in 1992, according to the following pattern:
1987, 5 percent; 1988, 5.2 percent; 1989, 5.4 percent; 1990, 5.6 percent; 1991, 5.8 percent; and 1992, 6 percent.
Export growth rates accelerate from 3.5 percent in 1987 to 7 percent in 1992, according to the following pattern:
1987, 3.5 percent; 1988, 4 percent; 1989, 5 percent; 1990, 5 percent; 1991, 6 percent; and 1992, 7 percent.
Government shrinks from 7.0 percent of GDP to 6.8 percent.
Imports grow or shrink by 2.5 percentage points less than investment.
Interest rates are fixed at 8 percent on long-term debt, 10 percent on short-term, 7 percent on IMF debt, and 7.5 percent on "exceptional" debt (which includes new lending and rescheduling under the recovery plan).
  Scenario 1: ICOR of 2.50 instead of 2.25. Financing required rises from $4.4 to $7.1 billion.
  Scenario 2: GDP growth is slower, with growth rates one-half percentage point lower than in the base scenario for each year of the projection period. Financing required falls from $4.4 billion to $2.0 billion.
  Scenario 3: Export growth slows relative to base scenario (accelerating

from 2 percent in 1987 to 4.5 percent in 1992; see table below for exact schedule.) Financing needs increase from $4.4 billion to $5.6 billion.

Export Growth Rates

	1987	1988	1989	1990	1991	1992
Base	3.5	4.0	5.0	5.0	6.0	7.0
Scenario 3	2.0	2.5	3.0	3.5	4.0	4.5
Scenario 4	5.0	6.0	6.0	7.0	8.0	8.0

Scenario 4: Export growth is more rapid than in base scenario, accelerating from 5 percent to 8 percent over the projection period (see table above). Financing needs decrease from $4.4 billion to $3.3 billion.

Scenario 5: Interest rates are cut sharply, to levels of 5 percent on long-term debt, 7 percent on short-term, 1 percent on IMF, and 3 percent on exceptional. Financing needs fall from $4.4 billion to $3.6 billion.

From these different scenarios we can see clearly that GDP growth rates and the ICOR have the most profound effects on financing needs. Relatively small shifts in the ICOR and in GDP growth rates change the overall conclusions markedly. In contrast, even fairly major shifts in export growth rates and in interest rates have relatively minor impact on total capital requirements. The model we have chosen essentially links investment and growth; not surprisingly, these variables prove to have significant influences on our results.

Appendix IV   Country Tables Projections: 1987–92

National Income Accounts: Costa Rica: 1987–92 (million colonnes; ICOR: 3.25)

Assumptions
GDP grows at an accelerating rate shown below
Exports grow at an accelerating rate as imported capital goods become available
Government falls from 23 percent of GDP to 21 percent
Imports grow or shrink by 2.5 percentage points less than investment
Consumption is the residual
ICOR = 3.25
Exchange rate (units/dollar) = 56

	1987	1988	1989	1990	1991	1992
GDP growth rates	4.0	4.5	5.0	5.5	5.75	6.0
Export growth rates	4.0	4.4	4.8	5.2	5.6	6.0

	1986	1987	1988	1989	1990	1991	1992
GDP	238,468	248,007	259,167	272,125	287,092	303,600	321,816
Consumption	141,653	145,261	154,706	165,527	175,978	187,344	199,345
Government	55,184	56,977	58,829	60,741	62,715	64,754	66,858
Investment	39,686	36,271	42,115	48,642	53,650	59,202	64,846
Exports	75,926	78,963	82,437	86,394	90,887	95,977	101,735
Imports	73,982	69,465	78,920	89,180	96,132	103,676	110,968
Trade Balance	1,944	9,498	3,517	− 2,786	− 5,245	− 7,700	− 9,233

Percentages of GDP

	1986	1987	1988	1989	1990	1991	1992
GDP	100	100	100	100	100	100	100
Consumption	59	59	60	61	61	62	62
Government	23	23	23	22	22	21	21
Investment	17	15	16	18	19	19	20
Exports	32	32	32	32	32	32	32
Imports	31	28	30	33	33	34	34
Trade Balance	1	4	1	− 1	− 2	− 3	3

Annual Growth Rates

	1986	1987	1988	1989	1990	1991	1992
GDP	—	4.0	4.5	5.0	5.5	5.8	6.0
Consumption	—	2.5	6.5	7.0	6.3	6.5	6.4
Government	—	3.2	3.3	3.3	3.2	3.3	3.2
Investment	—	− 8.6	16.1	15.5	10.3	10.3	9.5
Exports	—	4.0	4.4	4.8	5.2	5.6	6.0
Imports	—	− 6.1	13.6	13.0	7.8	7.8	7.0
Trade Balance	—	388.6	− 63.0	− 179.2	88.3	46.8	19.9

Current Account ($m)

	1986	1987	1988	1989	1990	1991	1992
Trade Balance	35	170	63	− 50	− 94	− 137	− 165
Interest Payment	− 317	− 333	− 326	− 328	− 338	− 352	− 371
Other R	96	100	100	100	100	100	100
CA Balance	− 186	− 64	− 164	− 277	− 331	− 389	− 436

Capital Account ($m)

	1986	1987	1988	1989	1990	1991	1992
Transfers	46	50	50	50	50	50	50
Direct Investment	61	65	65	65	65	65	65
Long-Term Capital:							
Inflows	9	100	100	100	100	100	100
Principal	− 301	− 713	− 556	− 537	− 508	− 384	− 222
Net	− 292	− 613	− 456	− 437	− 408	− 284	− 122
Short-Term Capital	− 8	− 11	− 11	− 10	0	0	0
IMF	− 39	− 30	− 30	− 30	− 30	− 30	0
Exceptional Finance	436	603	546	639	654	588	443
KA Balance	243	64	164	277	331	389	436
Changes in Reserves,							
Errors and Omissions	− 57	0	0	0	0	0	0

Appendix IV **(Continued)**

	1986	1987	1988	1989	1990	1991	1992
Estimated Debt							
Total	4,206	4,155	4,203	4,366	4,582	4,856	5,177
Long-Term	3,588	2,975	2,519	2,082	1,674	1,390	1,268
Short-Term	32	21	10	0	0	0	0
IMF	150	120	90	60	30	0	0
Exceptional	436	1,039	1,584	2,224	2,878	3,466	3,909
Estimated Interest							
Total	n/a	333	326	328	338	352	371
Long-Term (8%)	n/a	287	238	202	167	134	111
Short-Term (10%)	n/a	3	2	1	0	0	0
IMF (7%)	n/a	11	8	6	4	2	0
Exceptional (7.5%)	n/a	33	78	119	167	216	260
Government Accounts							
Government	55,184	56,977	58,829	60,741	62,715	64,754	66,858
Taxes	53,755	55,889	57,776	59,768	61,911	64,014	66,210
G-T	1,429	1,088	1,053	973	805	740	648
G-T (% of GDP)	3.6	3.0	2.5	2.0	1.5	1.25	1
Domestic Savings							
GDP	238,468	248,007	259,167	272,125	287,092	303,600	321,816
Factor Payments	− 12,376	− 13,073	− 12,679	− 12,749	− 13,303	− 14,105	− 15,186
Consumption	141,653	145,261	154,706	165,527	175,972	187,344	199,345
Taxes	53,755	55,889	57,776	59,768	61,911	64,014	66,210
Savings	30,684	33,784	34,005	34,081	35,907	38,137	41,075
Savings/GDP	12.9	13.6	13.1	12.5	12.5	12.6	12.8

El Salvador: 1987–92 (million colones; ICOR: 2.3)

Assumptions

GDP grows at an accelerating rate shown below
Exports grow at an accelerating rate as imported capital goods become available
Government falls from 13.6 percent of GDP to 12 percent
Imports grow or shrink by 3.5 percentage points less than investment
Consumption is the residual
ICOR = 2.3
Exchange rate (units/dollar) = 6.2

	1987	1988	1989	1990	1991	1992
GDP growth rates	5.0	5.2	5.4	5.6	5.8	6.0
Export growth rates	1.0	1.5	2.0	2.0	2.5	3.0

	1986	1987	1988	1989	1990	1991	1992
GDP	20,041	21,043	22,137	23,333	24,639	26,068	27,633
Consumption	15,495	16,283	17,280	18,349	19,521	20,781	22,140
Government	2,717	2,805	2,896	2,991	3,088	3,188	3,292
Investment	2,798	2,517	2,749	3,005	3,287	3,597	3,940
Exports	4,555	4,601	4,670	4,763	4,858	4,980	5,129
Imports	5,524	5,162	5,459	5,776	6,115	6,478	6,869
Trade Balance	− 969	− 562	− 789	− 1,013	− 1,256	− 1,499	− 1,740

	1986	1987	1988	1989	1990	1991	1992
Percentages of GDP							
GDP	100	100	100	100	100	100	100
Consumption	77.3	77.4	78.1	78.6	79.2	79.7	80.1
Government	13.6	13.3	13.1	12.8	12.5	12.2	11.9
Investment	14.0	12.0	12.4	12.9	13.3	13.8	14.3
Exports	22.7	21.9	21.1	20.4	19.7	19.1	18.6
Imports	27.6	24.5	24.7	24.8	24.8	24.9	24.9
Trade Balance	−4.8	−2.7	−3.6	−4.3	−5.1	−5.7	−6.3
Annual Growth Rates							
GDP	—	5	5.2	5.4	5.6	5.8	6
Consumption	—	5.08	6.13	6.19	6.39	6.46	6.54
Government	—	3.25	3.25	3.25	3.25	3.25	3.25
Investment	—	−10.05	9.25	9.30	9.37	9.45	9.53
Exports	—	1.00	1.50	2.00	2.00	2.50	3.00
Imports	—	−6.55	5.75	5.80	5.87	5.95	6.03
Trade Balance	—	−42.05	40.53	28.31	24.08	12.98	16.11
Current Account ($m)							
Trade Balance	−156	−91	−127	−163	−203	−242	−281
Interest Payment	−86.1	−141	−135	−138	−147	−161	−178
Other R	−121.9	100	100	100	100	100	100
CA Balance	−364	−132	−162	−201	−250	−302	−359
Capital Account ($m)							
Transfers	344	200	100	50	50	50	50
Direct Investment	12.5	12.5	12.5	12.5	12.5	12.5	12.5
Long-Term Capital							
Inflows	50	50	50	50	50	50	50
Principal	−138	−135	−138	−118	−91	−87	−222
Net	−88	−85	−88	−68	−41	−37	−172
Short-Term Capital	−10	−15	−15	−20	−20	−2	0
IMF	−30	−30	−30	0	0	0	0
Exceptional Finance	187	49	183	227	249	278	469
KA Balance	415	132	162	201	250	302	359
Changes in Reserves, Errors and Omissions	51	0	0	0	0	0	0
Estimated Debt							
Total	1,770	1,689	1,738	1,877	2,064	2,304	2,601
Long-Term	1,411	1,326	1,238	1,170	1,129	1,092	920
Short-Term	82	67	52	32	12	10	10
IMF	90	60	30	30	30	30	30
Exceptional	187	236	419	645	894	1,172	1,641

Appendix IV *(Continued)*

	1986	1987	1988	1989	1990	1991	1992
Estimated Interest							
Total	n/a	141	135	138	147	161	178
Long-Term (8%)	n/a	113	106	99	94	90	87
Short-Term (10%)	n/a	8	7	5	3	1	1
IMF (7%)	n/a	6	4	2	2	2	2
Exceptional (7.5%)	n/a	14	18	31	48	67	88
Government Accounts							
Government	2,717	2,805	2,896	2,991	3,088	3,188	3,292
Taxes	2,356	2,490	2,620	2,699	2,841	2,927	3,015
G-T	361	316	277	292	246	261	276
G-T (% of GDP)	1.8	1.5	1.25	1.25	1	1	1
Domestic Savings							
GDP	20,041	21,043	22,137	23,333	24,639	26,068	27,633
Factor Payments	−1,290	−256	−215	−234	−293	−376	−486
Consumption	15,495	16,283	17,280	18,349	19,521	20,781	22,140
Taxes	2,356	2,490	2,620	2,699	2,841	2,927	3,015
Savings	900	2,014	2,022	2,051	1,984	1,984	1,991
Savings/GDP	4.5	9.6	9.1	8.8	8.1	7.6	7.2

National Income Accounts: Guatemala: 1987–92 (million quetzales; ICOR: 2.25)

Assumptions
GDP grows at an accelerating rate shown below
Exports grow at an accelerating rate as imported capital goods become available
Government falls from 7.0 percent of GDP to 6.0 percent
Imports grow or shrink by 2.5 percentage points less than investment
Consumption is the residual
ICOR = 2.25
Exchange rate (units/dollar) = 1

	1987	1988	1989	1990	1991	1992
GDP growth rates	5.0	5.2	5.4	5.6	5.8	6.0
Export growth rates	3.5	3.75	4.0	4.0	4.25	4.5

	1986	1987	1988	1989	1990	1991	1992
GDP	15,785	16,574	17,436	18,378	19,407	20,532	21,764
Consumption	12,837	13,594	14,328	15,126	16,002	16,957	17,998
Government	1,107	1,140	1,174	1,210	1,246	1,283	1,322
Investment	1,600	1,939	2,118	2,316	2,533	2,772	3,036
Exports	2,542	2,631	2,730	2,839	2,952	3,078	3,216
Imports	2,300	2,730	2,914	3,113	3,326	3,558	3,808
Trade Balance	242	−99	−185	−274	−374	−480	−591

	1986	1987	1988	1989	1990	1991	1992
Percentages of GDP							
GDP	100	100	100	100	100	100	100
Consumption	81.3	82.0	82.2	82.3	82.5	82.6	82.7
Government	7.0	6.9	6.7	6.6	6.4	6.3	6.1
Investment	10.1	11.7	12.2	12.6	13.1	13.5	14.0
Exports	16.1	15.9	15.7	15.4	15.2	15.0	14.8
Imports	14.6	16.5	16.7	16.9	17.1	17.3	17.5
Trade Balance	1.5	− 0.6	− 1.5	− 1.5	− 1.9	− 2.3	− 2.7
Annual Growth Rates							
GDP	—	5	5.2	5.4	5.6	5.8	6
Consumption	—	5.9	5.4	5.6	5.8	6.0	6.1
Government	—	3.0	3.0	3.0	3.0	3.0	3.0
Investment	—	− 21.2	9.2	9.3	9.4	9.4	9.5
Exports	—	3.5	3.8	4.0	4.0	4.3	4.5
Imports	—	18.7	6.7	6.8	6.9	6.9	7.0
Trade Balance	—	− 141.0	86.3	48.3	36.7	28.2	23.3
Current Account							
($m)							
Trade Balance	242	− 99	− 185	− 274	− 374	− 480	− 591
Interest Payment	− 154	− 215	− 230	− 251	− 283	− 324	− 377
Other R	− 194	0	0	0	0	0	0
CA Balance	− 107	− 314	− 415	− 525	− 657	− 804	− 968
Capital Account							
($m)							
Transfers	62	75	75	75	75	75	75
Direct Investment	28	13	13	13	13	13	13
Long-Term Capital							
Inflows	50	50	50	50	50	50	50
Repayment	− 199	− 346	− 457	− 152	− 150	− 142	− 222
Net	− 149	− 296	− 407	− 102	− 100	− 92	− 172
Short-Term Capital	− 20	− 40	− 40	− 40	− 40	− 40	0
IMF	− 15	− 20	− 20	− 20	− 20	− 20	− 20
Exceptional Finance	241	583	794	600	729	869	1,072
KA Balance	147	314	415	525	657	804	968
Changes in Reserves,							
Errors and Omissions	40	0	0	0	0	0	0
Estimated Debt							
Total	2,663	2,890	3,217	3,654	4,224	4,940	5,821
Long-Term	2,073	1,777	1,370	1,267	1,167	1,075	903
Short-Term	231	191	151	111	71	31	31
IMF	118	98	78	58	38	18	2
Exceptional	241	824	1,618	2,218	2,947	3,816	4,889

Appendix IV *(Continued)*

	1986	1987	1988	1989	1990	1991	1992
Estimated Interest							
Total	n/a	215	230	251	283	324	377
Long-Term (8%)	n/a	166	142	110	101	93	86
Short-Term (10%)	n/a	23	19	15	11	7	3
IMF (7%)	n/a	8	7	5	4	3	1
Exceptional (7.5%)	n/a	18	62	121	166	221	286
Government Accounts							
Government	1,107	1,140	1,174	1,210	1,246	1,283	1,322
Taxes	886	925	965	1,007	1,052	1,078	1,104
G-T	221	215	209	202	194	205	218
G-T (% of GDP)	1.4	1.3	1.2	1.1	1	1	1
Domestic Savings							
GDP	15,785	16,574	17,436	18,378	19,407	20,532	21,764
Factor Payments	−349	−215	−230	−251	−283	−324	−377
Consumption	12,837	13,594	14,328	15,126	16,002	16,957	17,998
Taxes	886	925	965	1,007	1,052	1,078	1,104
Savings	1,713	1,840	1,913	1,993	2,070	2,173	2,286
Savings/GDP	10.9	11.1	11.0	10.8	10.7	10.6	10.5

Honduras: 1987–92 (million lempiras; ICOR: 3)

Assumptions
GDP grows at an accelerating rate shown below
Exports grow at an accelerating rate as imported capital goods become available
Government falls from 15.3 percent of GDP to 13.5 percent
Imports grow or shrink by 5 percentage points less than investment
Consumption is the residual
ICOR = 3
Exchange rate (units/dollar) = 2

	1987	1988	1989	1990	1991	1992
GDP growth rates	5.5	5.75	6.0	6.0	6.25	6.5
Export growth rates	1.0	1.5	2.0	2.0	2.5	3.0

	1986	1987	1988	1989	1990	1991	1992
GDP	7,477	7,888	8,342	8,842	9,373	9,959	10,606
Consumption	5,376	5,818	6,195	6,651	6,976	7,436	7,892
Government	1,144	1,181	1,220	1,259	1,300	1,342	1,386
Investment	1,144	1,361	1,502	1,592	1,757	1,942	2,068
Exports	1,996	2,016	2,046	2,087	2,129	2,182	2,248
Imports	2,183	2,487	2,620	2,647	2,790	2,943	2,988
Trade Balance	−187	−471	−574	−560	−661	−761	−740

	1986	1987	1988	1989	1990	1991	1992
Percentages of GDP							
GDP	100	100	100	100	100	100	100
Consumption	71.9	73.8	74.3	74.1	74.4	74.7	74.4
Government	15.3	15.0	14.6	14.2	13.9	13.5	13.1
Investment	15.3	17.3	18.0	18.0	18.8	19.5	19.5
Exports	26.7	25.6	24.5	23.6	22.7	21.9	21.2
Imports	29.2	31.5	31.4	29.9	29.8	29.6	28.2
Trade Balance	− 2.5	− 6.0	− 6.9	− 6.3	− 7.1	− 7.6	− 7.0
Annual Growth Rates							
GDP	—	5.50	5.75	6.00	6.00	6.25	6.50
Consumption	—	8.22	6.48	5.75	6.49	6.58	6.13
Government	—	3.25	3.25	3.25	3.25	3.25	3.25
Investment	—	− 18.94	10.35	6.00	10.42	10.50	6.50
Exports	—	1.00	1.50	2.00	2.00	2.50	3.00
Imports	—	13.94	5.35	1.00	5.42	5.50	1.50
Trade Balance	—	152.11	21.80	− 2.56	18.16	15.16	− 2.80
Current Account (\$m)							
Trade Balance	− 94	− 236	− 287	− 280	− 331	− 381	− 370
Interest Payment	− 159	− 235	− 248	− 265	− 285	− 310	− 341
Other R	− 31.3	100	100	100	100	100	100
CA Balance	− 284	− 370	− 435	− 445	− 516	− 591	− 611
Capital Account (\$m)							
Transfers	129	150	150	150	150	150	150
Direct Investment	29	12.5	12.5	12.5	12.5	12.5	12.5
Long-Term Capital							
Inflows	262	50	50	50	50	50	50
Repayment	− 197	− 346	− 457	− 152	− 150	− 142	− 222
Net	65	− 296	− 407	− 102	− 100	− 92	− 172
Short-Term Capital	6	− 40	− 40	− 40	− 40	− 40	0
IMF	10	− 20	− 20	− 20	− 20	− 20	− 20
Exceptional Finance	40	564	739	445	513	581	640
KA Balance	279	370	435	445	516	591	611
Changes in Reserves,							
Errors and Omissions	− 4	0	0	0	0	0	0
Estimated Debt							
Total	2,884	3,092	3,364	3,647	4,000	4,428	4,877
Long-Term	2,432	2,136	1,729	1,626	1,526	1,424	1,262
Short-Term	272	232	192	152	112	72	72
IMF	140	120	100	80	60	40	20
Exceptional	40	604	1,344	1,788	2,301	2,882	3,523

Appendix IV   *(Continued)*

	1986	1987	1988	1989	1990	1991	1992
Estimated Interest							
Total	n/a	235	248	265	285	310	341
Long-Term (8%)	n/a	195	171	138	130	122	115
Short-Term (10%)	n/a	27	23	19	15	11	7
IMF (7%)	n/a	10	8	7	6	4	3
Exceptional (7.5%)	n/a	3	45	101	134	173	216
Government Accounts							
Government	1,144	1,181	1,220	1,259	1,300	1,342	1,386
Taxes	725	866	928	994	1,066	1,118	1,174
G-T	419	316	292	265	234	224	212
G-T (% of GDP)	5.6	4	3.5	3	2.5	2.25	2
Domestic Savings							
GDP	7,477	7,888	8,342	8,842	9,373	9,959	10,606
Factor Payments	− 381	− 269	− 296	− 331	− 370	− 420	− 482
Consumption	5,376	5,818	6,195	6,551	6,976	7,436	7,892
Taxes	725	866	928	994	1,066	1,118	1,174
Savings	995	936	924	967	961	984	1,058
Savings/GDP	13.3	11.9	11.1	10.9	10.2	9.9	10.0

Nicaragua: 1987–92 (million dollars U.S.; ICOR: 2)

Assumptions
GDP grows at an accelerating rate shown below
Exports grow at an accelerating rate as imported capital goods become available
Government falls from 32.3 percent of GDP to 22.8 percent
Imports grow or shrink by 6 percentage points less than investment
Consumption is the residual
ICOR = 2
Accounts in $m (70 cordobas/$) = 1

	1987	1988	1989	1990	1991	1992
GDP growth rates	5.5	5.75	6.0	6.0	6.25	6.5
Export growth rates	2.0	2.0	3.0	3.0	4.0	4.0

	1986	1987	1988	1989	1990	1991	1992
GDP	2,915	3,075	3,252	3,447	3,654	3,883	4,135
Consumption	1,996	1,922	2,079	2,238	2,414	2,604	2,807
Government	943	943	943	943	943	943	943
Investment	556	354	390	414	457	505	538
Exports	430	439	447	461	475	494	513
Imports	1,011	582	608	608	635	663	666
Trade Balance	− 581	− 144	− 160	− 147	− 160	− 170	− 153

	1986	1987	1988	1989	1990	1991	1992
Percentages of GDP							
GDP	100	100	100	100	100	100	100
Consumption	68.5	62.5	63.9	64.9	66.1	67.1	67.9
Government	32.3	30.7	29.0	27.4	25.8	24.3	22.8
Investment	19.1	11.5	12.0	12.0	12.5	13.0	13.0
Exports	14.8	14.3	13.8	13.4	13.0	12.7	12.4
Imports	34.7	18.9	18.7	17.6	17.4	17.1	16.1
Trade Balance	− 19.9	− 4.7	− 4.9	− 4.3	− 4.4	− 4.4	− 3.7
Annual Growth Rates							
GDP	—	5.50	5.75	6.00	6.00	6.25	6.50
Consumption	—	− 3.68	8.16	7.61	7.90	7.87	7.80
Government	—	0.00	0.00	0.00	0.00	0.00	0.00
Investment	—	− 36.39	10.35	6.00	10.42	10.50	6.50
Exports	—	2.00	2.00	3.00	3.00	4.00	4.00
Imports	—	− 42.39	4.35	− 0.00	4.42	4.50	0.50
Trade Balance	—	− 75.25	11.51	− 8.37	8.86	5.98	− 9.69
Current Account							
Trade Balance	− 581	− 144	− 160	− 147	− 160	− 170	− 153
Interest Payment	− 227.3	− 497	− 529	− 563	− 602	− 644	− 690
Other R	28.7	100	100	100	100	100	100
CA Balance	− 780	− 541	− 589	− 610	− 662	− 713	− 743
Capital Account							
Transfers	100	75	75	50	50	50	50
Direct Investment	0	10	10	10	10	10	10
Long-Term Capital							
Inflows	839	100	100	100	100	100	100
Repayment	− 133	− 425	− 479	− 467	− 449	− 434	− 366
Net	706	− 325	− 379	− 367	− 349	− 334	− 266
Short-Term Capital	23	− 50	− 50	− 50	− 50	− 50	− 50
IMF	0	0	0	0	0	0	0
Exceptional Finance	47	831	933	967	1,001	1,037	999
KA Balance	877	541	589	610	662	713	743
Changes in Reserves,							
Errors and Omissions	97	0	0	0	0	0	0
Estimated Debt							
Total	6,000	6,456	6,960	7,510	8,112	8,765	9,448
Long-Term	5,067	4,742	4,363	3,996	3,647	3,313	3,047
Short-Term	885	835	785	735	685	635	585
IMF	0	0	0	0	0	0	0
Exceptional	47	878	1,812	2,779	3,780	4,817	5,816

Appendix IV   (Continued)

	1986	1987	1988	1989	1990	1991	1992
Estimated Interest							
Total	n/a	497	529	563	602	644	690
Long-Term (8%)	n/a	405	379	349	320	292	265
Short-Term (10%)	n/a	89	84	79	74	69	64
IMF (7%)	n/a	0	0	0	0	0	0
Exceptional (7.5%)	n/a	4	66	136	208	283	361
Government Accounts							
Government	943	943	943	943	943	943	943
Taxes	482	559	585	598	578	612	612
G-T	461	384	358	345	365	331	331
G-T (% of GDP)	15.8	12.5	11	10	10	9	8
Domestic Savings							
GDP	2,915	3,075	3,252	3,447	3,654	3,883	4,135
Factor Payments	− 199	− 397	− 429	− 463	− 502	− 544	− 590
Consumption	1,996	1,922	2,079	2,238	2,414	2,604	2,807
Taxes	482	559	585	598	578	594	612
Savings	238	197	159	148	161	141	185
Savings/GDP	8.2	6.4	4.9	4.3	4.4	3.6	3.0

Notes

I wish to thank Doug Gollon of the Yale International Relations Program for excellent research assistance in executing the quantitative work of this chapter.

1. This is only one strategy and one set of economic outcomes. The strategy can be altered, and the macroeconomic policies embodied in it can be fine-tuned. Different results can be generated within minutes using the national income accounting models set up for each of the five countries. The economic scenarios developed here are internally consistent. This is a policy-neutral framework in which the policymaker manipulates the model rather than one in which the model contains its own behavioral dynamics. Alternative projections can be generated to test different policy alternatives and even different strategies in order to evaluate them in relation to each other.

2. By assuming that no country will draw down on its international reserves, the capital account of the balance of payments (which tracks asset transfers) must equal the current account. The capital account, then, details the international lending pattern consistent with the current account magnitudes derived from the internal requirements of the development strategy. The capital account surplus (capital inflow) must equal the current account deficit. From the capital account, the accumulation and composition of external debt can be measured.

This dependence of capital flows and external debt on internal variables provides a desirable analytical focus and follows from the simplifying assumption of zero change in the level of international reserves. In practice, countries can either accumulate or draw down on their international reserves. These are a separate set of policy considerations which this analysis sets aside in order to focus attention on the interaction of domestic policies and international variables other than reserves.

Chapter 6

Central American Financial Development

Claudio Gonzalez-Vega and Jeffrey Poyo

Summary

The efficient operation of Central America's financial systems can play a key role in renewed growth and structural transformation in the region. Through monetization, intermediation, and reserve-management services, the financial system contributes to market integration, the savings-investment process, and economic development. These contributions depend on the size of the financial sector, in real terms, and on the transaction costs incurred by market participants. With the recent crisis, financial flows declined and transactions costs increased. These results reflected a conflict between these functions of finance and its role as a fiscal instrument.

During the 1960s and 1970s Central America experienced a significant process of financial deepening. Financial deepening is a process of accumulation of financial assets at a rate faster than the accumulation of nonfinancial wealth. This process was a consequence of rapid output growth and price and exchange-rate stability, which in turn reflected cautious fiscal and monetary policies. Numerous institutions were created, the network of branches was expanded, and financial magnitudes increased, both in real terms and as a proportion of the GDP. Markets remained fragmented, however, and the Central American economies continued to rely heavily on foreign savings. The urban bias of financial development and high transaction costs excluded large segments of the population from access to deposit and loan services.

Central American financial systems suffered a major blow from the crisis. The financing of fiscal deficits with domestic credit led to inflation, devaluation, the contraction of the real size of the financial system, and the crowding out of the private sector in domestic credit portfolios. This contraction was not uniform; it came at the expense of the private sector, of the mobilization of deposits in domestic currency, of the regulated segment of the market, of the share of productive sectors in loan portfolios, and of the access of smaller, poorer, riskier producers to financial services.

The financial systems of Central America are dominated by the banking sector, which plays a key role in the savings-investment process. Reluctance to let the market allocate resources has led to the nationalization of the banking system in three countries (Costa Rica, El Salvador, and Nicaragua), the creation of public development banks and investment corporations, selective credit controls, confiscatory reserve requirements, restricted entry into financial markets, market segmentation, interest-rate ceilings, and preferential rediscounting programs. Most of these interventions have been unsuccessful and have further increased transaction costs.

The most important challenge for the Central American financial systems will be to provide access to financial services to large segments of the population. This will require policy and procedure reforms in order to create a hospitable regulatory environment. It will also require cost-reducing financial innovations in order to reduce the costs faced by depositors, borrowers, and intermediaries. High transaction costs reduce the net returns on deposits to savers, increase the total costs of the funds for investor borrowers, and jeopardize the financial viability of regulated intermediaries. Efficient institutions have to be designed, their staff and management trained, and appropriate incentives created. Technologies, institution building, and policy reforms will then reinforce each other. This is a difficult and expensive task, which requires external assistance for research, experimentation, training, and financing set-up costs. Excessive inflows of foreign financial assistance, however, may take away incentives to mobilize domestic resources and may transform existing financial institutions into mere conduits for donor-targeted, concessionary funds. This would further increase financial repression and postpone financial market development.

Introduction

This is a critical period for Central America. Recent geopolitical, social, and economic problems far surpass the difficulties experienced in the 1930s when the region's export earnings sharply declined. High social costs have resulted from the present crisis in view of its depth, its duration, and its impact on each country's institutional framework and political and social fabric. Multiple, accelerating, and dramatic changes have been transforming the political and economic structures of the five countries. As a result, the destiny of the region will be molded during the next few years. The ways in which present economic and political problems are solved will determine the type of society and the level of well-being that Central Americans will enjoy during the rest of the century.

Political turmoil, insurrection, and the prospects for peace have attracted most of the substantially increased international attention that has recently focused on Central America. Although less emphasized, economic stagnation and instability have also been a major component of the recent history of the region. In the 1980s all five countries have shown the symptoms: stagnant or contracting output, rapid decline of their intraregional and international trade, growing unemployment and underemployment, huge public-sector deficits and the corresponding public external debt, increased open or repressed inflationary pressures, and the implicit or explicit devaluation of their currencies. These difficulties have been in sharp contrast with a record of rapid economic growth and sustained price and foreign-exchange stability during the previous two decades.

Numerous plans and programs have been proposed to deal with these problems. A common set of responses has been to request, on the one hand, and to offer, on the other, substantially increased amounts of foreign financial assistance. Large inflows of foreign aid, however, may represent a far more complex and difficult exercise than is usually assumed, and the increased availability of external funds may undermine the will to undertake some of the policy reforms that are essential for renewed economic growth. This is not the place, however, to resolve issues about the role and dangers of large inflows of foreign aid. Rather, the purpose of this analysis is to examine the role of the domestic financial system in mobilizing and in more efficiently allocating local resources in order to facilitate stabilization, structural adjustment, and the resumption of rapid output growth.

This chapter discusses the importance of the financial sector for economic development, the process of financial deepening that preceded the crisis in Central America, and the impact of the recent financial repression on the size and performance of the banking sector. When financial deepening takes place, the real value of key financial magnitudes grows while the rates of return of financial assets are high. A process of financial deepening reflects the efficiency with which the services of the financial sector are being provided. The opposite is financial repression, characterized by the slow or even negative growth of the real value of financial magnitudes. Financial repression usually reflects incorrect policy interventions. This chapter also examines the nature of the Central American financial systems and of the policies that influence their performance and it explores opportunities for their improvement.

1. The Importance of Financial Deepening

The role of the financial system and the nature of its contributions to economic growth have received increasing attention. These contributions are associated with the provision of at least four types of service. The most basic is the monetization of the economy; that is, the provision of a medium of exchange. This service reduces the costs of conducting transactions in the markets for commodities and for factors of production, it increases the flow of trade, and it enlarges market size. These effects, in turn, improve the productivity of resources through specialization and division of labor, greater competition, use of modern technologies, and exploitation of economies of scope and economies of scale.

The efficiency of the monetization effort is reduced by inflation and currency substitution ("dollarization"). In order to avoid the negative impact of inflation, economic agents substitute tangible assets (real estate, inventories, jewelry) and foreign currencies for the domestic money. The domestic currency is no longer considered an efficient medium of exchange and store of value. The funds shifted into inflation hedges, however, provide few social returns. Correct macroeconomic management, which avoids inflation, is thus crucial for adequate monetization.

The financial system also provides services of intermediation between savers and investors, thus enhancing the accumulation of capital and improving its allocation. In the absence of financial markets, many producers are condemned to take advantage of their opportunities only to the extent allowed by their own resources. In other cases, when their resources are abundant compared to their productive options, savers are forced to invest those resources at low marginal rates of return. There is no reason to expect that those with the capacity to save at a given moment are necessarily those with the best investment opportunities. By making the division of labor between savers and investors possible, financial intermediaries channel resources from producers and regions with a limited growth potential and poor productive opportunities to those where a more rapid expansion of output is possible.

Through the provision of intermediation services, therefore, the financial system contributes to the elimination of inferior uses of resources and, at the same time, facilitates better alternative uses of these resources. This is accomplished when the financial system offers wealthholders new assets (for example, bank deposits) that are more attractive forms of holding wealth than the unprofitable uses of resources thus eliminated. The intermediary, in turn, transfers these claims on resources to others, who possess better investment opportunities. From this perspective, the financial system offers valuable services and income-increasing opportunities not only to borrowers, but also to depositors. Financial policies must create a balance, therefore, between the incentives offered to depositors to attract their savings and those offered to borrowers to promote investment. Many credit programs and institutions in Central America, however, have relied heavily upon international donor funds and central bank rediscounting, thus ignoring the provision of deposit services, while financial policies have repressed the rewards offered to depositors.

The financial system also facilitates the reduction of risk and the management of liquidity and reserves. Most economic agents accumulate stores of value for emergencies or to take advantage of future investment opportunities. In the absence of attractive domestic financial assets, they are forced to hold foreign currencies, real estate, and other tangible assets (inventories, animals, jewelry) that yield low social returns. The financial system reduces the costs and risks of holding precautionary and speculative reserves when it offers attractive forms of holding wealth. At the same time, it reduces the size of the required reserves if it offers open lines of credit when needed, and thus releases resources for immediately productive uses.

Finally, the financial system provides services of fiscal support for the public sector. This is an important contribution, in view of weak tax systems and the absence of markets for securities. Whereas the first three functions (monetization, intermediation, and reserve management) are complementary, this fiscal function of the financial system may be in conflict with the former three. When abused, this fiscal role may lead to inflation, devaluation, and the crowding out of the private sector from domestic credit portfolios. When this happens, the financial system ceases to be an intermediary between private savers and investors and becomes a fiscal instrument to tax resources away from depositors in order to finance the public sector's current expenditures. Financial policy must attempt to strike a balance in the provision of these alternative services.

In summary, economic development both depends on and contributes to the growth and diversification of the financial system. Financial deepening matters to the extent to which it integrates markets, provides incentives for savings and investment, encourages savers to hold a larger proportion of their wealth in the form of domestic financial assets rather than in unproductive inflation hedges, foreign assets, and other money substitutes, and channels resources away from low-return toward better alternative uses. The extent to which these services are provided depends on the size of the financial system in real terms; that is, on the purchasing power of domestic financial assets. It also depends on the efficiency of its performance, as measured by the magnitude and dispersion of the transaction costs that are imposed on all market participants, actual and potential.

Market fragmentation, the small size of the transactions, the high costs of information, risk, and uncertainty increase the costs of financial transactions in developing countries. As a result, the net returns to depositors are low, the total costs of the funds to borrowers (including their noninterest expenses) are high, the size of financial markets is small, the volume of the funds channeled and the variety of the services provided are limited, and time horizons are short. Financial progress requires a reduction of these risks and transaction costs. This cannot be done by decree, as attempted, for example, by usury laws. Rather, financial progress requires greater competition and market integration, the exploitation of economies of scale and of economies of scope, professional portfolio management and portfolio diversification, the accumulation of information, and the establishment of bank-customer relationships. Financial progress thus requires a hospitable regulatory and macroeconomic policy environment, viable institutions, and innovations in financial technology in order to reduce risks and transaction costs.

2. Financial Deepening in Central America

During the 1960s and most of the 1970s the Central American countries experienced a significant process of financial deepening, and financial markets served as an important mechanism for economic growth. The evolution of Central American financial markets compared favorably with financial progress in other developing countries, in terms of the traditional measures of performance such as the number, diversity, and growth of financial institutions, the ratio of monetary aggregates to national income, and the proportion of national savings captured by the financial system.

During that period, numerous institutions were established and the range of services offered was widened, competition in financial markets increased, the network of bank branches was substantially expanded, the returns to domestic financial assets were, in real terms, positive, and financial magnitudes, measured in constant prices, grew rapidly. Sustained economic growth and price and exchange-rate stability produced this progress, even in the absence of explicit concern for financial development.

In effect, up to the mid-1970s, the Central American economies were characterized by remarkable price stability. During 1950–69, the annual increase of the consumer price index ranged from 0.3 percent for El Salvador to 3.4 percent for Nicaragua, with rates of inflation in Costa Rica, Guatemala, and Honduras at 1–2 percent per year. None of these countries experienced double-digit inflation until 1973.

In these very open economies the domestic price level was essentially determined by stable international prices, given a fixed exchange rate. Exchange-rate stability reflected, in turn, the willingness to adopt the fiscal and credit discipline that is required by a fixed exchange-rate system. The central banks of the region revealed a preference for monetary stability and had the power to maintain it. In effect, during the 1950s and the 1960s, the rate of monetary expansion averaged less than 10 percent per year in each of these countries despite the fact that incomes were growing rapidly and that the demand for money was increasing at an even faster pace. Costa Rica, the only Central American country that had to devalue in the 1960s, experienced a slightly higher rate of monetary growth (12 percent per year). Even during the 1970s, the average rate of monetary expansion for Central America was only 14 percent per year. Domestic credit, in turn, grew 11 percent per year in the 1960s and 18 percent annually in the 1970s when inflationary pressures began to mount. As a consequence of openness and of exchange-rate stability, therefore, inflation was alien to the Central American economies until the mid-1970s.

The resulting significant degree of financial deepening was reflected by the growth of the ratio of the money supply (M2), in the broad sense of currency and demand, savings, and term deposits, to the gross domestic product (GDP). For the region as a whole, this ratio increased from 15 percent in the early 1960s to 30 percent in the late 1970s. Table 6.1 reports, for the whole of Central America, the ratios of the major monetary and domestic-credit aggregates with respect to the GDP. These figures reflect a sustained process of financial deepening through the 1970s.

Table 6.2 presents, for each of the countries, the ratios of the money supply in a broad sense (M2) to the GDP, at the end of selected years. By 1961 this ratio was highest in El Salvador and Costa Rica, intermediate in Guatemala, and lowest in Honduras and Nicaragua. These ratios became comparatively high in the mid-1970s, particularly with respect to other Latin American countries that experienced sustained inflationary pressures and more acute financial repression. Nevertheless, as the process of financial deepening slowed down, this ratio reached a maximum in 1976 in Guatemala (25 percent) and El Salvador (33 percent), in 1978 in Honduras (30 percent), in 1979 in Nicaragua (31 percent), and in 1980 in Costa Rica (35 percent). These figures exclude deposits in foreign currency. The lower ratio in Guatemala possibly reflected the presence of large subsistence sectors, while Honduras was the country that experienced the most rapid improvement since the early 1960s.

Table 6.1   Central America: Ratios of the Major Monetary and Credit Aggregates to the Gross Domestic Product, 1961–81

	1961	1966	1971	1976	1981
Currency	5.9	5.5	5.1	5.8	5.9
Demand Deposits	5.0	5.8	6.4	7.6	6.3
Money (M1)	10.9	11.3	11.5	13.4	12.2
Quasi-money	4.4	7.6	10.9	15.6	16.6
Money Supply (M2)	15.3	18.8	22.4	28.9	27.5
Domestic Credit	19.6	23.9	27.2	32.8	41.3
Private Sector	16.1	19.5	22.4	26.1	25.0
Public Sector	3.5	4.4	4.8	6.6	16.4

Source: Computed from data in the *Boletín Estadístico* (San José, Costa Rica: Central American Monetary Council).

Table 6.2   Central America: Ratios of the Money Supply (M2) to the Gross
Domestic Product, 1961–86

	1961	1966	1971	1976	1981	1986
Costa Rica	18.0	18.3	27.7	31.9	28.8	44.2
El Salvador	19.7	23.0	24.8	32.9	33.7	35.0
Guatemala	13.9	17.7	19.8	25.2	23.1	24.9
Honduras	12.9	16.7	24.7	30.9	28.0	30.6
Nicaragua	11.7	18.0	17.3	28.1	32.2	50.8*

* This figure reflects problems of measurement for Nicaragua, since there is abundant
evidence about disintermediation in real terms in this country.
Source: Computed from data in the *Boletín Estadístico* (San José, Costa Rica: Central
American Monetary Council).

Most of this impressive process of financial deepening resulted from the
growth of quasi-money (that is, savings and term deposits, rather than
currency and demand deposits). For Central America, the ratio of quasi-
money to the GDP increased from 4 percent in 1961 to 16 percent by 1978.
This growth reflected the diversification of financial portfolios in order to
satisfy diverse tastes for returns, risk, and liquidity. Also, as inflationary
pressures increased, transaction balances were kept in new forms, different
from checking accounts. Deposits in U.S. dollars also increased in relative
importance, particularly in recent times. This reflected the process of currency
substitution associated with the crisis. Deposits in dollars accounted for 11
percent of the Costa Rican GDP in 1983, the country where "dollarization"
was most substantial.

This increasing mobilization of financial resources through the banking
system made possible the rapid expansion of credit. For the region as a
whole, the ratio of domestic credit to the GDP grew from 20 percent in the
early 1960s to 35 percent in the late 1970s (see table 6.1). As shown in table
6.3, by 1961 there were already important differences among the Central
American countries in this respect. At that time, these ratios ranged between
12 percent for Honduras and 32 percent for Costa Rica. The sustained
differences observed for the whole period resulted from different degrees of
use of central bank credit (inflation tax) and foreign savings to complement
domestic resource mobilization, particularly during the more recent years.

Table 6.3   Central America: Ratios of Domestic Credit to the Gross
Domestic Product, 1961–85

	1961	1966	1971	1976	1981	1985
Costa Rica	31.9	33.8	36.6	39.1	25.0	40.7
El Salvador	26.6	26.9	30.7	34.8	57.7	54.2
Guatemala	14.5	18.1	17.5	19.7	28.2	38.6
Honduras	11.8	16.2	31.1	43.5	44.7	56.9
Nicaragua	16.8	27.2	30.4	46.3	78.4	99.6*

* The figures for Nicaragua reflect important measurement errors.
Source: Computed from data in the *Boletín Estadístico* (San José, Costa Rica: Central
American Monetary Council).

Despite financial deepening, the Central American economies continued
to rely heavily on foreign savings for the financing of their domestic
investment. Moreover, domestic financial markets remained highly fragmented, in part as a reflection of underdevelopment and in part as a
consequence of financial policies. A significant degree of urban bias has also
characterized the expansion of the banking system. The network of bank
branches and the flow of deposits and loans have been concentrated in the
few major cities. Only a small proportion of the total population has had
access to the financial services offered. Lack of access has been acute in the
rural areas. The proportion of farmers with access to institutional loans has
been less than 15 percent for the region as a whole and has ranged from less
than five percent in Guatemala to over 30 percent in Costa Rica. The loan
portfolios of the financial institutions have also shown much concentration.
Among those privileged enough to have access to loans, a few have captured
the largest proportion of the funds loaned. For example, in the case of
agricultural loan portfolios, about 10 percent of the number of borrowers
have received about 85 percent of the amounts disbursed. This has happened
even in Costa Rica, despite the nationalization of the banking system in
1948. Loan delinquency and default have also been increasing. Unpaid loans
have thus represented additional transfers of resources to relatively wealthy
borrowers.

High transaction costs have been incurred by all financial market participants. In many cases these costs have been so high that they have excluded

large segments of the Central American population from participation in formal credit markets. Government intervention has accentuated market fragmentation and has further increased transaction costs. This intervention has taken the form of interest rate restrictions, selective credit allocations, high and differentiated reserve requirements, preferential rediscounting schemes, and restricted entry into financial activities. The increased financial repression that has resulted from the recent economic and financial crisis has accentuated all of these shortcomings of the Central American financial systems. The number of bank clients has declined, the concentration of credit portfolios has increased, and transaction costs have augmented.

3. Financial Repression: The Impact of the Crisis

The Central American countries have been in the midst of an acute economic crisis. The difficulties have resulted from a combination of long-term trends and unfavorable short-term circumstances, both foreign and domestic. The long-term, structural determinants of the crisis have reflected a contradiction between the region's basic characteristics (small, open economies, abundant in labor and with very specialized natural resources) and the features of the protectionist strategy of development adopted in the late 1950s. The penalization of agriculture and the bias against exports have produced high costs and distortions. The short-term determinants of the crisis, on the other hand, have reflected major external shocks, political turmoil, and the unfortunate domestic policies adopted in response to the shocks. External influences have included sharp swings in the region's international terms of trade and drastic changes in the conditions of its access to international financial markets.

The Central American financial systems have suffered significantly with the crisis, probably more than any other sector in the economy. There has been essentially a fiscal reason for this. When the stagnation and contraction of real incomes in the early 1980s reduced the rate of growth of government revenues (which in some cases became negative even in nominal terms), the Central American governments faced severe political and administrative constraints for an additional mobilization of domestic resources with the use of the conventional tools of taxation. It became difficult to increase taxes in the middle of an economic recession, given pessimistic expectations and intense capital flight. Several attempts at tax reform did not bear the desired revenues. At the same time, public sector expenditures and implicit, nonrecorded subsidies and entitlements continued to grow at rates increasingly faster than those associated with revenues. Moreover, the absence of a significant securities market precluded any substantial placement of government debt with the private sector.

Given the increasing discrepancy between public sector revenues and expenditures, for a time the authorities financed budget deficits by placing their debt abroad. This has been particularly substantial in Costa Rica and Nicaragua and significant in the other countries. When the limit to the stock of public external debt which foreign lenders were willing to accumulate was finally reached and programmed expenditures had not yet been reduced, the Central American governments forced the placement of their debt with the domestic financial system. Table 6.4 reports how the proportion of domestic credit captured by the public sector increased substantially in the five countries.

Domestic financing of public sector deficits had two consequences. Too rapid an expansion of domestic credit led to the loss of international monetary reserves, to accelerating inflation, and eventually to devaluation. The rate of domestic credit expansion was no longer compatible with price and exchange-rate stability. On the other hand, the private sector was crowded out of domestic credit portfolios. Thus, growing fiscal deficits were financed with the loss of international monetary reserves, accelerated borrowing abroad and, finally, with the inflation tax and the financial repression of the private sector.

Table 6.4   Central America: Proportion of Domestic Credit Outstanding Captured by the Public Sector, 1961–85

	1961	1966	1971	1976	1981	1985
Costa Rica	12.9	17.1	16.7	23.0	46.7	52.4
El Salvador	14.9	15.9	17.3	16.7	51.0	44.8
Guatemala	25.2	27.3	27.4	36.9	40.4	49.4
Honduras	23.4	17.5	20.3	19.7	31.9	36.5
Nicaragua	14.3	9.9	4.6	3.8	29.6	50.7

Source: Computed from data in the *Boletín Estadístico* (San José, Costa Rica: Central American Monetary Council), several years.

To avoid the inflation tax the Central Americans revised their wealth portfolios, reduced their holdings of domestic financial assets, and increased their holdings of tangible assets (inflation hedges) and foreign assets (currency substitution). Controls over interest rates and exchange rates, combined with inflation and devaluation expectations, fueled capital flight. Among the consequences was a contraction of the domestic financial systems as inflation eroded the real value of credit portfolios and deposit liabilities and as economic agents moved away from domestic currencies. All previously growing financial magnitudes declined both when measured in real terms and as a proportion of the GDP.

Table 6.5 shows how inflation accelerated in Costa Rica in the early 1980s and in all of the other countries except Honduras in the mid-1980s. Relative price stability in Honduras has reflected substantial inflows of foreign financial assistance. Fiscal control and foreign assistance allowed Costa Rica to reduce the rate of inflation to more moderate levels in the mid-1980s.

Table 6.6 shows how financial deepening proceeded at an exceptionally rapid pace during most of the 1970s. This process was reversed, however, in the late 1970s and in the 1980s. The extent and the timing of the disintermediation differed from country to country. (Due to the use of uniform dates in table 6.6, these differences are not shown in full by this table.)

In Guatemala the real money supply (M2) grew rapidly in the 1970s, reached a maximum in 1978, declined 5 percent in 1979, and continued to grow through 1982. This was mostly due to expanding holdings of quasi-money. Inflation accelerated after 1983 as a consequence of a rapid expansion

Table 6.5   Central America: Inflation Rates (Annual Percentage Changes in the Consumer Price Index), 1981–86

	1981	1982	1983	1984	1985	1986
Costa Rica	37.0	90.1	32.6	12.0	15.1	11.8
El Salvador	14.8	11.7	13.1	11.7	22.3	31.9
Guatemala	11.5	5.0	6.4	3.6	18.0	37.0
Honduras	9.4	9.0	8.3	4.7	3.4	4.4
Nicaragua	23.9	24.8	31.0	35.4	219.5	681.6

Source: *Boletín Estadístico* (San José, Costa Rica: Central American Monetary Council, 1986).

Table 6.6 Central America: Annual Average Rates of Growth of Monetary and Credit Aggregates, in Real Terms, 1970–86

	Guatemala	El Salvador	Honduras	Costa Rica
Money Supply (M1)				
1970–78	7.0	7.0	9.3	11.3
1978–82	−2.4	−6.2	−1.4	−3.7
1982–86	3.1	−3.4	1.8	4.7
Money Supply (M2)				
1970–78	9.0	7.7	9.7	16.7
1978–82	3.8	−6.4	−0.5	−3.6
1982–86	0.1	2.4	6.8	4.3
Domestic Credit				
1970–78	8.2	6.8	10.6	13.4
1978–82	16.5	4.9	2.2	−8.3
1982–86	−6.1	−6.6	8.1	10.2
Domestic Credit for the Private Sector				
1970–78	6.6	6.8	9.8	11.5
1978–82	7.4	−7.9	−1.8	−15.3
1982–86	−3.3	−2.3	8.2	6.1

Source: (Data for Nicaragua are too unreliable, so they are not reported here.) Computed from data in the *Boletín Estadístico* (San José, Costa Rica: Central American Monetary Council).

of domestic credit, particularly for the public sector. In real terms, domestic credit declined during the most recent years. The contraction has been dramatic in El Salvador, where political difficulties have been added to economic problems. The broad money supply (M2) declined rapidly after 1977 and by 1983 it represented only 72 percent of its 1977 level. Money in a narrow sense (M1) represented 59 percent of its 1977 level. In Honduras, where the contraction has been less acute, the dollarization of deposits has been significant. Low levels of inflation in this country have been due to massive inflows of foreign assistance, which have made it possible to divert inflationary pressures toward imports and to finance them with the loss of reserves. The contraction was dramatic in Costa Rica. The money supply (M2) had grown more rapidly than in the other countries, but it then declined. By 1982, the real money supply was only 74 percent of its 1978 value.

As a result of the contraction of the real size of the financial system, the ratio of M2 to the GDP declined in the four countries (data for Nicaragua are not reliable). In Costa Rica, this ratio dropped from 41 percent in 1980 to 29 percent in 1981. If dollar-denominated deposits are excluded, the reduction was from 35 to 21 percent. In El Salvador this ratio diminished from 33 percent in 1976 to 29 percent in 1980.

The rapid expansion of domestic resource mobilization that took place during the 1970s made the increase of domestic credit possible. In Costa Rica real domestic credit increased through 1980, helped by increased borrowing abroad by the banking system, but it declined 30.4 percent in 1981 and 22.4 percent in 1982. By 1982 its real value was only 54 percent of the 1980 level. That is, the inflationary pressures generated by the rapid expansion of domestic credit (in nominal terms) eventually resulted in a contraction of its real value. In the race between growth of domestic credit in nominal colones and inflation, the latter was the easy winner. A similar process took place later in Guatemala and in El Salvador.

The proportion of domestic credit allocated to the public sector was fairly constant during the 1960s and early 1970s, when it ranged between 17 and 20 percent of the total. During the second half of the 1970s, however, it increased rapidly. By 1982 it was 44 percent for Central America. In 1985 the proportion of domestic credit granted to the public sector ranged between 36 percent in Honduras and 52 percent in Costa Rica (see table 6.4).

Domestic credit for the private sector grew exceptionally fast in Costa Rica in the 1970s; after that it declined dramatically. By 1982 domestic credit for the private sector represented only 49 percent of its 1978 value. That is, the private sector was receiving less than one-half of the purchasing power it obtained from the banks a few years earlier. Domestic credit for the public sector continued growing after 1978, but eventually it also declined. By 1982 domestic credit for the public sector represented only 58 percent of its 1980 value. The lesson is clear: too rapid an expansion of domestic credit, in nominal terms, resulted in reduced real credit flows, even for the public sector.

While this contraction of the real flows of domestic credit was taking place, the flows of external credit were also being curtailed, and inflation was severely reducing the real value of the working capital of firms. Therefore, the financial crunch was acute from all sources. Moreover, significant portions of the portfolio of the banking system, particularly in the case of the government-owned banks, became overdue. Since defaulted loans have not been written off, the volumes of credit outstanding reported here overestimate the true availability of loanable funds.

The decline of these financial ratios has also reflected, in part, the loss in relative market share of the regulated, institutionalized market, for which the central banks report statistical information. In recent years there has been a vigorous development of nonregulated financial institutions almost everywhere. Not constrained by central-bank and interest-rate regulations, these intermediaries have been more aggressive than the formal market in the mobilization of domestic resources. In this sense, the reduction in the levels of financial intermediation has been less than reported here.

The contraction of the Central American financial sectors has not been uniform. The private sector has been crowded out from domestic credit portfolios, while the public sector has significantly increased its share. Nonregulated intermediaries have gained at the expense of institutional markets, while dollar-denominated deposits have expanded at the expense of deposits in domestic currencies. The share of "productive" sectors in credit portfolios, particularly that of agriculture, has declined, while the share of more "speculative" activities has increased.

With inflation and devaluation, the opportunity cost of holding domestic financial assets has increased. These assets have become poor stores of value and have forced savers to look for alternative ways to hold wealth. As a result, the financial sector has shrunk. This in turn has reflected an abuse of the fiscal function of financial markets, which has reduced their ability to promote stability and growth. This is unfortunate because financial inter-mediation is critical during periods of structural adjustment and resource reallocation.

4. Financial Market Structure

One of the main features of the financial systems of Central America is the predominance of the banking sector and, within this sector, the dominant role of the commercial banks. As in other developing countries, open markets for common stocks, mortgages, bonds, or even commercial bills are non-existent or insignificant. This simply reflects the low levels of per capita income and the resulting small scale of individual savings and investment transactions. Information is insufficient to have small farmers or merchants issue their own notes or shares to be publicly traded. As a result, private financial savings are largely held in the form of currency and bank deposits. Within the modern sector of the economy, bank loans represent the most important source of funds for firms, both for working capital and for investment. Thus, banks and similar intermediaries play a key role in the savings-investment process and in the allocation of resources.

The financial systems of the Central American countries include commercial banks, mortgage banks, and development banks, as well as near banks such as savings and loan associations (with the exception of Guatemala) and finance corporations (*financieras*), capitalization companies, and insurance companies. There is a wide spectrum of nonregulated intermediaries as well. In Guatemala, bonded warehouses (*almacenes de depósito*) have become very important as a source of short-term working capital for private firms.

In addition, in each of the countries there is a fairly active cooperative movement that also provides financial services, although its relative size within the financial system is still fairly small. Financial institutions other than commercial and development banks and credit unions are completely concentrated in the large urban centers. In Honduras, for example, 91 percent of the value of all deposits, 93 percent of the volume of loans, and 97 percent of all central-bank rediscounts and foreign assistance credit flows have been concentrated in Tegucigalpa, San Pedro de Sula, and La Ceiba.

Table 6.7 presents the number of commercial and development banks and the number of branches in each one of the countries. The financial systems of Guatemala and Honduras have been composed predominantly of private sector institutions. With the crisis, however, the public development banks have maintained a privileged access to central bank rediscounting and to funds from international donors, while the private banks have faced severe constraints on funds mobilization and lending activities. Thus, there have been important changes in market shares.

The Costa Rican banking system was nationalized in 1948, and only the four public commercial banks have been allowed to mobilize demand deposits and savings accounts from the public. Only these banks have enjoyed access to central-bank rediscounting. Recently, however, private banks, which are allowed to offer only long-term certificates of deposit, have gained in market share at the expense of the nationalized banks. This has reflected both the

Table 6.7 Central America: Number of Commercial and Development Banks and Number of Bank Branches, 1986

	Number of Banks			Number of Branches			Population per Office
	Total	Private	Public	Total	Private	Public	
Costa Rica	17	13	4	248	23	235	9,950
El Salvador	9	1	8	104	4	100	50,272
Guatemala	20	17	3	234	147	84	33,775
Honduras	14	13	1	234	203	31	18,106
Nicaragua	5	0	5	203	0	203	15,064

Source: *Guía Bancaria Latinoamericana, 1986* (Bogotá, Colombia: Latin American Federation of Banks).

Table 6.8 Central America: Representative Real Interest Rates on Loans and Deposits (percentages), 1982–86

	1982	1983	1984	1985	1986
Loans					
Costa Rica	−32.0	−5.1	12.4	9.7	10.9
El Salvador	3.4	1.0	2.0	−5.3	−10.4
Guatemala	7.0	8.2	−6.9	−14.0	−16.9
Honduras	10.5	7.6	10.7	9.0	10.0
Nicaragua	−6.5	−11.4	−14.9	−62.3	−82.7
Deposits					
Costa Rica	−34.2	−8.0	9.9	5.0	6.4
El Salvador	−0.9	−2.7	−1.8	−8.6	−15.2
Guatemala	4.1	5.3	−9.4	−16.4	−19.1
Honduras	5.3	1.8	5.0	3.8	4.6
Nicaragua	−11.4	−15.6	−16.5	−62.7	−82.8

Source: *Boletín Estadístico* (San José, Costa Rica: Central American Monetary Council, 1986).

rigidity and the obsolescence of the public banks, which had become used to operating without competition, and the aggressive behavior of the private banks, heavily supported by USAID (the United States Agency for International Development) with loanable funds in the form of long-term lines of credit and quasi-capital contributions. This support has reflected the shift of USAID programs from the public to the private sector in an effort to strengthen private enterprise and the market forces. On the other hand, the banking systems of Nicaragua and El Salvador were also recently nationalized, at a time when there has been an increasing trend toward privatization in Costa Rica. While the recent developments in Costa Rica have been fueled by growing unhappiness with the public banks, these other two countries have placed all of their trust in the ability of the public sector to become an efficient financial intermediary.

Costa Rica possesses not only the lowest ratio of population per bank branch in Central America, but it has also the third lowest ratio in Latin America, after Uruguay and Trinidad-Tobago. In addition, a large portion of this network comprises rural branches (*Juntas Rurales de Crédito Agrícola*) created in 1914, which have allowed a greater penetration of credit into the countryside than in the other countries. Access to banking services, on the other hand, has been most restricted in El Salvador and Guatemala.

Attempts to develop a securities market in El Salvador and Nicaragua have failed. On the other hand, much emphasis has recently been placed on such an objective in Honduras and Guatemala. The creation of a stock market in Honduras, however, is still in the planning stages, and a very small stock exchange is functioning in Guatemala. In the case of Costa Rica, the overwhelming proportion of the stock exchange transactions, both in number and in volume, involve public sector debt instruments. Private sector participation has steadily grown over the past ten years, particularly as financial repression reduced the relative importance of the banking system, but the trading in shares is still insignificant even in Costa Rica. More than a market for shares, Costa Rica's stock exchange has been a market for obligations.

5. Financial Policies and Regulation

Banks have frequently been criticized for contributing little to economic development. Commercial banks have been seen as too averse to risk and too slow to supply credit for new, nontraditional investment opportunities. The ostensible justification for the nationalization of banking in Central America has been the presumed unwillingness of private banks to channel resources to priority sectors. The pool of financial savings has been perceived as a kind of a "public good," whose optimal use can be achieved only if the state intervenes in the process of financial intermediation. The experience of Costa Rica, where banks have been nationalized for four decades, raises serious doubts about the advantages of nationalization in practice. The government banks have been slow, conservative, and vulnerable to political pressures. With their bureaucratic procedures, they have imposed high transaction costs on their customers. Rigid institutional structures, inadequate incentives, and inconsistent objectives have made them increasingly unable to respond to the dynamic demands of a complex economy in transformation. Nationalized banks in El Salvador and Nicaragua have discovered that a simple change of ownership is not enough to improve performance. Similarly, the region's public development banks have exhibited a sad record of portfolio management and financial viability.

In addition to nationalization, several policies and regulations have been used to redirect funds to preferred sectors. With assistance from international donors, several specialized public development banks (particularly agricultural banks) were established throughout the region in the mid-1950s, in order to target loans, at preferential interest rates, to specific sectors. Many of these banks have gone bankrupt several times, but they reemerge, with a new name and under new management. Frequently their portfolio includes a substantial proportion of overdue loans, because collection is not a major concern for these institutions. Rather, they are conduits for central bank, government, and donor funds that need to be rapidly disbursed for political or bureaucratic reasons. Because the interest rates charged seldom cover costs and losses from default, these banks must be periodically recapitalized in order to continue to operate. Similarly, in the mid-1970s several industrial and development investment corporations were created (e.g., CODESA in Costa Rica, CONADI in Honduras) to promote the establishment of new enterprises too big or too risky for the private sector. These agencies failed, too, mostly because they were run with political rather than financial criteria. They are now in a process of dismantling or of privatization, with the assistance of international donors.

Attempts have also been made to redirect the resources mobilized by private commercial banks. These have included confiscatory reserve requirements and selective credit controls. For many years the Central Bank of Costa Rica established *topes de cartera*, administratively set ceilings and floors on the amount of credit to be granted by sector of economic activity, by crop, or by other specific criteria. These quantitative restrictions on credit failed because the authorities could not adequately predict demand. Such controls were futile in the first place, given the fungibility of credit. Loans provide the borrower with generalized purchasing power, and the lender cannot control marginal substitutions of these funds for other funds under the borrower's control. Only a complete account of all of the borrower's sources and uses of funds would allow a determination of the actual use of the borrowed funds. The Central Bank of Costa Rica no longer dictates to the nationalized commercial banks the allocation of their portfolio. Rather, it employs reserve requirements and open-market operations for general monetary management.

In most of Central America high inflation rates combined with interest-rate ceilings resulted in negative interest rates in real terms in the 1980s, as shown in table 6.8. These negative rates have jeopardized the ability of the regulated financial institutions to compete with nonregulated intermediaries and to attract deposits from the public. Negative interest rates on loans have generated an excess demand for credit, which has required nonprice forms of rationing to clear the market. Frequently this rationing has been based on collateral or on bureaucratic considerations, rather than on creditworthiness and the selection of the best investment projects. Loan approval criteria have been vulnerable to the influence of strong pressure groups or to the abuse of political power, particularly in the case of the public development banks. Negative interest rates have also discouraged loans that involve more than a minimal risk and administrative costs. These interest rates have not been sufficient to cover the costs and risks associated with the administration of a credit portfolio that includes more than a traditional clientele, unless the institution has been willing to incur operating losses and to risk decapitalization. Thus, to remain financially viable, many intermediaries have restricted their operations to the largest and safest of their clients, while smaller, poorer, or more innovative producers have been denied access to the subsidized loans. These underpriced loans, however, have transferred a substantial income subsidy to a few privileged borrowers. Although the majority of borrowers has been excluded from access to credit and thus to the transfer, only a few have benefited from the subsidy. At the same time, the institutions created to promote development have been destroyed.

This regressive impact of the subsidy has characterized even the nationalized banking systems. During the 1970s the implicit subsidy was substantial in Costa Rica. The real rate charged on loans during 1974, for example, was a negative 20 percent. Under the conservative assumption that the social opportunity cost of the funds was 10 percent per year in real terms, the implicit rate of subsidy was 30 percent. At that time, agricultural credit represented close to 60 percent of the value of the gross agricultural output and over one-half of the loan portfolio of the nationalized banks. This meant that, in the important case of agriculture, the grant transferred through subsidized credit was equivalent to 20 to 25 percent of the value of the gross agricultural output. On the other hand, only between 30 and 40 percent of the agricultural producers had access to bank credit, while the remaining 60 to 70 percent were excluded from the subsidy.

In addition, there was a high degree of portfolio concentration. In the case of the *Banco Nacional de Costa Rica*, which grants over one-half of all agricultural credit in the country, less than two percent of the borrowers (number of loans) received over 60 percent of the amounts loaned for agriculture. About 10 percent of the number of loans corresponded to over 83 percent of the amount of credit granted. This meant that about 1 percent of the agricultural producers of Costa Rica received over 65 percent of the agricultural credit granted by the banks and over 65 percent of a substantial subsidy. This subsidy was equivalent to almost 25 percent of the value of the agricultural output in 1974.

Due to the decline in inflation rates during the second half of the 1970s, as well as the increase in nominal rates of interest, the magnitude of the subsidy declined but remained important. The subsidy significantly increased again during the early 1980s, while concentration of the loan portfolio became more accentuated. In addition, by the end of the decade it was estimated that about 50 percent of the loan portfolio of the nationalized banks represented defaulted loans. There was a significant transfer on this count, too, to the few privileged very large borrowers who did not repay their loans.

In addition, the banking regulatory structure has severely restricted competition among different intermediaries, via interest-rate controls, market segmentation, and loan targeting. In view of the recent political and economic instability, moreover, the maturity of both assets and liabilities has been severely shortened. Improvements in banking technology and the promotion of new financial products have lagged behind developments in other countries. In fact, some of the most interesting innovations in the Central American financial markets have occurred in institutions which were originally established outside, and in some cases remain outside, the regulated banking system. Higher risks and costs are associated, however, with these markets.

In Costa Rica, particularly in recent years, there has been an improvement in the regulatory environment, as the Central Bank has attempted to inject a greater degree of competition and efficiency into the financial market. Interest rate controls have been significantly loosened and selective credit allocations have virtually disappeared. This has reversed the severe disinter-mediation trend of the early 1980s. In Honduras, attempts to reduce domestic inflation and to maintain a fixed exchange rate with the use of substantial foreign financial assistance have produced positive real interest rates, too. Nevertheless, it is the increasing claim of the public sector on domestic credit that has been mostly responsible for the comparatively high real rates of interest rates observed in Honduras and Costa Rica. Attempts to reduce these interest rates artificially, however, would only lead to greater disinter-mediation and to excess credit demands from the private sector, given the prevailing crowding-out effect. The artificially lower interest rates will not make available to productive firms the funds that are being captured by the government, while the reduced ability to mobilize deposits will make loanable funds even more scarce. Only fiscal austerity would allow a reduction of the real interest rates in these countries.

In Guatemala, on the other hand, there have been no significant attempts to liberalize financial markets, which continue to operate under a rather repressive regulatory framework. Finally, in both El Salvador and Nicaragua, state intervention in financial markets has been expanded, with the complete elimination of competition for and market allocation of funds, and the transformation of this sector into a public monopoly. Unfortunately, the problems that the nationalization of these banking systems has set out to resolve are more intractable than this simplistic solution assumes, while nationalization itself may create distorted incentives for the operation of these institutions, which in turn may lead to unexpected and unintended results.

6. Financial Market Development

The most important challenge for the Central American financial systems is to provide access to a wide set of financial services for the majority of the population, particularly in the rural areas. The provision of financial services, however, is a difficult and expensive task. Success will depend upon many factors. These include key features of the environment, the degree of organization of society, the impact of nonfinancial and of financial policies, the design of financial institutions and instruments, and the choice of appropriate technologies to produce financial services.

The features of underdevelopment explain, in part, the difficulties. Potential depositors and borrowers are very heterogeneous, they are geo-graphically dispersed, their transactions are small, and they face high risks. It is difficult for intermediaries from outside the local communities to acquire and interpret information about their creditworthiness. The result is high transaction costs that increase the total cost of funds for borrowers, reduce the net returns on deposits for savers, and diminish the profitability of potential intermediaries. Lenders perceive that the costs of managing numerous small savings accounts and of determining the creditworthiness of small, diverse producers are too high, given the scarcity of information and the nature of the risks involved.

What matters for production and investment decisions is the total cost of borrowed funds. In addition to interest payments, the total cost of borrowing includes explicit and implicit noninterest costs, such as legal, document, and registration fees, commissions, forced purchases of other financial services, taxes, transportation and lodging expenses, the opportunity cost of the time spent in conducting the loans transactions and in preparing investment plans, the costs of entertaining bank officials, and bribes. Borrowing costs are also increased by compensating balances required from borrowers, delays in the disbursement of funds, and insufficient financing which results in lower yields.

What matters for savings is the net return to depositors, which is reduced by taxes, penalties for early withdrawal, lodging and transportation expenses, and the opportunity cost of the time spent in depositing and withdrawing funds. In turn, intermediation margins must cover mobilization and lending costs to generate a profit for the intermediary. These costs include the administrative expenses associated with deposit accounts, promotion costs, the impact of reserve requirements, loan handling costs (documentation, record-keeping, disbursement), and costs to reduce the risk of default (loan evaluation, monitoring, supervision, and collection) as well as losses due to lack of prompt payment.

All components of these transaction costs are high in Central America. In the case of the nationalized banking system of Costa Rica, the average noninterest costs of borrowing for agricultural loans were 11.5 percent per year, to be added to average interest payments of 13.6 percent per year. Moreover, while interest rates ranged between 8.0 and 26.5 percent, noninterest borrowing costs ranged between 0.2 and 117.5 percent per year. This enormous dispersion of transaction costs across borrowers reflected a negative correlation with loan and farm size. These costs made financial transactions prohibitive for the smaller, poorer, more remote potential borrowers.

Lending costs have also been high, particularly in the rural areas. In Honduras in 1982 lending costs averaged 18.8 percent for an agricultural development bank and 8.4 percent for the agricultural loans of a major private commercial bank. A substantial portion of these lending and borrowing costs has been associated with the rationing mechanisms which are necessary in the presence of excess demands for credit, given under-equilibrium interest rates. These transaction costs have also been related to the loan targeting usually required by international donors and to the screening, documentation, supervision, and extensive reporting requirements that are inevitably associated with a multitude of separate special lines of credit and with selective credit controls.

Insufficient organization also increases the costs and risks of financial transactions. If property rights are not adequately defined and if contracts cannot be specified simply and enforced successfully, only the least risky financial transactions take place. In the absence of proper land titles the offer of adequate collateral is not possible. This institutional deficiency slows down the penetration of the banks in the countryside. When there are no efficient, impartial courts, loan contracts have no meaning and banking is shallow. When information is expensive, unreliable, and not accessible, the most important input in the financial production function is missing. Where there are no roads, people cannot visit bank branches. Where potential customers cannot read or write, they cannot fill out a loan application and communications are more costly. Where there is no adequate supervision of the financial system, depositors will not be protected.

Economic policies that repress growth and incomes in specific sectors of the economy (for example, policies that repress rural incomes) constrain deposit and loan demand and reduce creditworthiness. The strength of financial institutions depends on the solvency and dynamism of their clientele. Producers who receive low prices for their output, pay high prices for their inputs, obtain poor yields, and do not have access to markets and to public services are not good bank clients. For these reasons, the crisis not only shrank the size of financial markets, but it also reduced the quality of loan portfolios, given the deterioration of the economic situation of the banks' clientele.

As pointed out, rigid financial policies also constrain the growth of financial markets. Inflation and devaluation expectations, combined with interest-rate ceilings, reduce the net returns to be earned on domestic financial assets and lead to currency substitution, the accumulation of financial hedges, and the contraction of the financial system. The financing of fiscal deficits with bank credit leads to the crowding out of the private sector in credit portfolios.

In a highly restrictive regulatory environment, with binding interest-rate ceilings and a significant excess demand for credit, where bankers are protected from competition by barriers to entry and exit and by market segmentation, it is not surprising that banks do not go out of their way to venture into risky territory; they simply ration credit to the least risky and costly clientele. The ability to evaluate and take risks, which is the banks' most important function, is never tested or exercised. The internal rate of return or cash flow of a particular project becomes of secondary importance, while the supply of collateral takes the place of project and creditworthiness evaluation. In this environment, financial market regulation provides incentives and government sanction for the oligopolistic behavior of banks. Reforms of the regulatory framework should attempt to reduce the degree of specialization in financial markets (as experience has shown even in the much larger financial markets of the United States), and they should promote the ability to diversify geographically and in terms of maturities and loan uses.

Financial liberalization is not easy, however. Although increased competition will provide incentives for innovation in financial products and technology, it may at the same time increase fragility. There are difficulties in the transition, when the detailed rules under which the banks have become used to operating are modified, and these institutions are given greater degrees of freedom and are forced to formulate strategies and accept responsibility for their decisions. To head off potential negative effects of the reforms, significant improvements must be made in the banking supervision functions of the monetary authorities (superintendency of banks). In addition, training programs would be an important instrument with which to improve the managerial abilities of bank executives and to increase their capacity to flexibly respond to a more competitive environment.

Design contributes to the success or failure of financial institutions. Multiple and inconsistent objectives, frequently found in public development banks, reduce institutional viability. Undue specialization increases risks and the potential for moral hazard. In particular, the absence of deposit mobilization activities seriously weakens financial institutions. Specialized retailers of central bank or donor funds have been particularly unsuccessful. Unless authority for the evaluation of creditworthiness and for the collection of loans is granted and accountability is specified, the intermediary will be crippled. Political intrusion must also be avoided.

The evaluation of risk requires information. Mutual organizations and other base-level institutions, such as credit unions, have a comparative advantage in servicing low-income groups in view of their access to the relevant information and a favorable cost structure. Their financial strength derives from the mobilization of local deposits. Policies directed to linking these intermediaries to the regulated, institutionalized financial markets, by improving their access to funds and providing technical assistance, may significantly improve access to financial services by the marginal populations.

The development of securities markets may help to redistribute risks more efficiently. The ability to attract investors directly, through the sale of shares, would improve access to financial markets on the part of entrepreneurs with relatively risky projects, who at present cannot obtain the necessary resources. Development of the securities market would also reduce the very high levels of credit leverage that characterize Central American firms. An excessive reliance on debt, rather than equity, has been one of the weaknesses of the Central American private sector. Again, a concerted effort to produce the required information is indispensable if such a market is to be developed. Given the small size of the market, uncertainties about the future, and the high costs of information, however, it will take a long time for a securities market to contribute significantly to economic development. Efforts toward improvement of the financial systems of Central America, therefore, should not focus entirely, not even as a priority, on the development of stock exchanges. Financial market development in the region will continue to rest largely upon progress of the banking industry.

For all of these purposes, cost-reducing innovations will be needed in order to increase access to financial services and to improve their quality. Incorrect incentives have stunted financial innovation in the past in Central America. Once the regulatory framework becomes more hospitable and financial prices are allowed to reflect true scarcities, however, institutional experimentation and product development will be needed.

7. Conclusions

Renewed economic growth and structural transformation in Central America will require a substantial reallocation of resources, innovation, the ability to identify and take advantage of new and different productive opportunities, and the capacity to evaluate and take reasonable risks. The efficient performance of the financial system, particularly in its intermediation function, will be a key determinant of the success of these efforts. The contributions of the financial system will depend on the volume of resources mobilized, on the ability of the market participants to identify the investment projects with the highest social marginal rates of return, and on the efficiency of the financial transactions. Such efficiency will be reflected mostly by the magnitude and the dispersion of the transaction costs imposed on all market participants, both actual and potential, and by the divergence of marginal rates of return in the economy.

A sharp reduction in the real value of financial flows has accompanied the recent economic and political crisis in Central America. This reduction has severely constrained the availability of loanable funds for investment and for working capital. The contraction has had a fiscal root. Inflation, devaluation, and the crowding out of the private sector in domestic credit portfolios have been the result of large fiscal deficits financed with bank credit. A reduction of this financial repression will require the reestablishment of fiscal and monetary discipline. Successful macroeconomic management, therefore, is a major precondition for the efficient performance of the Central American financial sector.

High transaction costs, which already reflected the consequences of underdevelopment, have been augmented by unnecessarily detailed regulations and restrictions on the operations of financial intermediaries. Transaction costs have also been increased by the targeting of loans through a multitude of concessionary credit lines (for specific crops, inputs, or investments), each with its own eligibility conditions, lending terms, and reporting requirements. Because of the fungibility of money, however, targeting does not guarantee additionality. In most cases there is little correlation between the proposed use of the funds and the marginal activity actually promoted by the loan. Targeting, on the other hand, increases transaction costs and makes apparently "cheap" credit expensive. These transaction costs have reduced the net returns to saver-depositors, have increased the total effective costs of the funds for investor-borrowers, have endangered the financial viability of banks and of other financial institutions and, in particular, have excluded important segments of the population from access to financial services, specially in the rural areas.

The most important challenge for the Central American financial systems, therefore, is to provide increasing access to financial services for the majority of the population, in ways which contribute to growth and structural transformation. For this, an appropriate policy and regulatory environment has to be established, new cost-reducing financial innovations have to be designed, tested, and adapted to the local circumstances, and viable institutions have to be promoted. This is a difficult and expensive undertaking.

If the policy environment is not hospitable, financial intermediaries will not survive. Positive real rates of interest on deposits and loans, nonpreferential interest rates on central bank rediscounting, low and uniform reserve requirements, and limited targeting are the most basic goals of policy reform. The extent and timing of these reforms must reflect the initial conditions and the political and administrative constraints in each country. An efficient division of labor and increasing competition between formal and informal intermediaries and among different institutional types (public development banks, private commercial banks, credit unions) must be promoted. The ultimate goal should be to create a market in which cost-efficient linkages among different types of participants guarantee the smooth operation of the whole system. The use of urban banks as wholesalers and of rural credit unions as retailers of funds, for example, is an attractive possibility. Increased competition and stronger linkages would make it possible, in turn, to use the power of finance to assist in the integration of other markets.

Appropriate policies and regulation, however, are not a sufficient condition for financial progress. Given the magnitude and dispersion of transaction costs, only lower-cost technologies for deposit and loan activities will increase the access of large segments of the population to financial services and will make the intermediaries which provide these services viable. New financial technologies are needed to take advantage of socially profitable opportunities for expanding financial markets, for reducing uncertainty, and for managing risk. Institutional and technological innovations will have to be adapted to the size of the Central American financial markets. Appropriate financial technologies are essential for the economic use of resources in the operation of financial institutions and in order to reduce transaction costs. Technologies, institution building, and policy reforms must reinforce each other. Substantial efforts will be required, however, to implement the policy reforms, create viable institutions, and accelerate cost-reducing technological progress.

Most of the programs for economic recovery in Central America have assigned no active role to the domestic financial systems. At best, financial intermediaries have been perceived as convenient conduits to channel foreign funds, most likely to targeted beneficiaries in concessionary terms, in order to take advantage of the established network of branches and institutions. Domestic deposit mobilization, the other side of the intermediation process, has been completely ignored. There is not only neglect of the functions of finance, but also potential damage. Too much foreign financial assistance disbursed through the existing financial systems may take the incentives to mobilize domestic resources away and may make it possible to postpone overdue reforms needed for renewed growth, stability, and efficiency. Development of the domestic financial markets, on the other hand, will be a difficult exercise. Policy and procedure reforms, experiments, and learning processes are expensive. External assistance can play a useful role, not only in inducing the changes, but also in helping to finance the set-up costs (including research, training, and technical assistance) and in sharing in the costs associated with changes in institutional structures and procedures. To make these efforts successful, however, a clear understanding of the nature and role of finance and of the preconditions for the efficient performance of the system is essential.

References

Adams, Dale W., Claudio Gonzalez-Vega, and J. D. Von Pischke, eds. *Crédito Agrícola y Desarrollo Rural: La Nueva Visión.* San José: Trejos Hermanos for The Ohio State University, 1987.

Central American Monetary Council. Boletín Estadístico. San José, Costa Rica: CAMC, several years.

Gonzalez-Vega, Claudio. "Crisis y el Sistema Bancario Costarricense." *Revista de Ciencias Económicas*, vol. V, no. 1, 1985, pp. 63–74.

———. "Impacto de la Crisis Económica sobre la Movilización de Recursos Internos en Centroamérica." *Revista de la Integración y el Desarrollo de Centroamérica*, no. 39, December 1986, pp. 129–54.

———. *Mercados Financieros y Desarrollo*. Santo Domingo: Centro de Estudios Monetarios y Bancarios, 1986.

Latin American Federation of Banks. *Guía Bancaria Latinoamericana, 1986*. Bogotá, Colombia: Latin American Federation of Banks.

McKinnon, Ronald I. *Money and Capital in Economic Development*. Washington, D.C.: The Brookings Institution, 1973.

Shaw, Edward S. *Financial Deepening in Economic Development*. New York: Oxford University Press, 1973.

Chapter 7

Health Care in Central America
John J. Freiberger

Health is both an outcome and a determinant of an overall development process, the end of which is the general welfare.—"The Health Situation, Child Health." *Health Conditions in the Americas, 1981–1984,* Pan American Health Organization, 1986.

The people of Central America today suffer and die from conditions that are treated and cured by medicines, practices, and technology available in the developed world. The predominant health care problems of this region conform to those of Latin America as a whole. When infant mortality rates are used as an indicator of the overall state of health care, statistics for Latin America reveal a level of development that is between that of Africa and Asia and that of the United States and Europe.[1] Of Latin America's 270 million people, 135 million live in extreme poverty or in isolated rural areas. They have essentially no access to health care. Of Central America's 27 million people, almost 50 percent have no access to any system of organized health care services. Indeed, 50 percent of Central America's population does not have access to safe drinking water. As a result, diarrheal diseases and malnutrition take a high toll in human lives and resources.

A further complicating factor is that the region's population is predicted to grow by another 15 million people by the year 2000. This growth will place additional demands on the already stressed health care delivery system. As stated by the director of the Pan American Health Organization, ". . . in the next 13 years we must create, organize and set in motion health services that will double the coverage of what we have been able to reach today."[2] That statement certainly applies to Central America. Central America has the highest birth and death rates in Latin America. Women have an average of more than six children, giving Central America the highest annual population growth rate in the hemisphere.[3]

Good health care could work to reverse this trend. Population growth can be shown to be related to survival statistics for children under the age of five. In contrast to what one might expect, a reduction in infant and child mortality has been shown to enhance the acceptance of family planning and result in a decrease in overall population growth. Between 1960 and 1980, when the infant mortality rate dropped from 80 to 16 deaths per thousand live births, the total marital fertility rate of Costa Rica declined from 7.6 to 3.4 births per couple.[4] Apparently confidence that one's offspring will survive allowed parents to risk having fewer children and thus reap the economic benefits that smaller families provide. This side effect of lowered infant mortality has been felt for many years in the United States and Europe, and a glance at birth and child mortality rates for Western industrialized countries forcefully highlights this trend.[5]

In spite of significant improvements over the last two decades, the most common causes of death continue to be diseases easily prevented by standard public health measures such as immunization, health education, and sanitary engineering. Of these treatable afflictions, parasitic diseases, diarrheal diseases, pneumonia, and influenza cause most of the illness and death. Current sociopolitical conditions are the direct causes of a significant number of additional deaths through homicide and war. Malnutrition—from both lack of vitamins and low protein and calorie intake—also results from the ongoing social and economic upheaval.

The major problems with health care delivery in Central America can be summarized as:

(1) lack of adequate resources,
(2) inadequate distribution of available resources, and
(3) inappropriate focus on curative rather than preventive health care.

Each of these topics will be discussed in turn.

Lack of Adequate Resources

The economic crisis that occurred throughout Latin America in 1982–87 severely strained the ability of Central American health care systems to continue their previous pace of improvements. The overall decrease in the standard of living is reflected in the services of the health care sector. Following a 6 percent annual economic growth rate in the 1960s, and a 4 percent growth rate in the 1970s, economic declines in the 1980s have resulted in budgetary constraints that have impeded a further lowering of infant mortality rates. Even when growth rates were high, many people were left in poverty. Archaic economic structures have resulted in skewed patterns of land ownership and income distribution. Two-thirds of the population of Central America live below the poverty line set by the United Nations Economic Commission for Latin America (ECLAC).

Much of the economic expansion seen from 1960 to 1980 was in the area of exports of agricultural commodities such as coffee, sugar, and bananas. Since 1980, falling world prices for these traditional export products have combined with rising expenses for oil and debt service to seriously limit the availability of hard currency for the purchase of expensive imported health care technology. This has resulted in an overall decrease in per-capita health care spending.

Table 7.1   Per Capita Government Health Care Funding (1980)

Country	Amount ($U.S.)
Costa Rica	28.00
El Salvador	9.00
Guatemala	13.00
Honduras	8.00
Nicaragua	36.00
Developing Countries	13.00
Latin America	27.00
World	100.00
Developed Countries	383.00
United States	439.00
Canada	515.00

Sources: "Health and the World Economy," in *Sociology in Medicine* (Oxford University Press, 1985); and "The Health Situation: Health Systems Infrastructure," *Health Conditions in the Americas, 1981–1984*, scientific publication 500 (Washington, D.C.: Pan American Health Organization, 1986), p. 136.

Inadequate Distribution of Available Resources

In spite of the pressing needs of the rural population, a funding bias in favor of urban, hospital-based systems is common. Approximately 40 percent of the entire population of Central America lacks access to any health care services.[6] Adequate provision for the health care needs of rural populations has been made more difficult by lack of logistic support. Even in relatively well-served Costa Rica the infant mortality rate is 50 percent higher in the rural areas than in the cities.

Throughout Central America access to hospitals is limited by poor roads and challenging geography. Transportation of medicines, vaccines, and supplies to rural clinics can be highly irregular and undependable. Military operations have disrupted and in some cases targeted health care vehicles and personnel. Transport of critically ill patients to urban centers is a serious problem. A patient requiring referral from a rural clinic to a regional or metropolitan hospital may have to provide for his own transport either by private vehicle or public transportation. This severely limits the effectiveness of the referral system. The better funded and better staffed urban hospitals usually receive patients who are either well enough to travel on their own or who have had their condition greatly worsened by both delay and the transportation process itself.

Vaccination programs are hampered by budgetary, political, and infra-structure-related problems. As a result, many preventable diseases, including measles, polio, diphtheria, whooping cough, and tetanus, continue to be significant health problems in the region. In 1982 an outbreak of 136 cases of polio was noted in Guatemala. A second epidemic occurred in 1986. (Wild polio virus has not been seen in the United States since 1981.)

There is an imbalance between the number and type of health care workers trained and the positions needed. The number of physicians per capita in Central America is the lowest in Latin America. They are still, however, being trained in excess of the needs of the health care sector as a whole. The most pressing need is for more nonphysician health care workers. Medicine is an extremely labor-intensive endeavor requiring specific degrees of skill for practitioners at each level. There are few trained nurses, technical workers, and auxiliary health care assistants. Laboratory and X-ray workers, anesthesia technicians, and malaria workers are in extremely short supply.

This lack of auxiliary health care professionals results from a lack of adequate training funds and low enrollment in technical and paramedical schools. Even when funds are made available, the low salaries and status of these professionals keep enrollment low. In Costa Rica in 1986 there were only 22 students enrolled in the school of nursing, while over 200 physician candidates were preparing for graduation from the national medical school. The imbalance is similar for nurses, medical technicians, and laboratory workers throughout Central America. Foreign aid programs have provided some assistance in the training of the administrative arm of the health care system and the collective purchasing of expensive imported foreign pharmaceuticals. Programs for the training of maintenance technicians have also been sponsored by AID and other foreign sources.[7]

This relative surplus of physicians is highest in urban areas because most doctors prefer to practice in these better-equipped and more lucrative districts. The physician surplus in urban Costa Rica has forced some doctors to take jobs requiring lower skill levels than that for which they were trained. To some extent, this physician surplus encourages migration of doctors away from the cities to rural areas, but the overall effect is less significant than might be predicted. Rural areas remain understaffed.

*Inappropriate Focus on Curative Rather Than
Preventive Health Care*

The imbalance in the nurse-physician ratio may also contribute to both the emphasis on curative rather than preventive care and the underutilization of simple but highly cost-effective technologies such as vaccinations.[8]

Preventable conditions cause the majority of illnesses in all population groups in Central America. Death from preventable diseases is generally a result of: (1) unsanitary health conditions and practices, and (2) malnutrition, which causes reduced resistance to the challenge of disease.

Unsanitary Health Conditions and Practices. Countries with the highest infant mortality rates show a preponderance of diseases that can be fought effectively with basic measures. In these countries gastroenteritis (inflamed lining of the stomach and intestines) and diarrheal diseases are the first or second leading cause of death. In 1975, Central America reported per capita death rates for infectious, parasitic, and diarrheal diseases that were 50 times greater than the rate for the United States. These maladies represent conditions that respond readily to basic education and sanitary waste disposal programs.

It is estimated that over half of the inhabitants of Central America do not have adequate access to safe drinking water and sanitary waste disposal.[9] A 1980 World Health Organization Survey[10] found that the principal factors hindering the delivery of these essential services were:

(1) insufficient political support,
(2) inadequate infrastructure and legal framework, with responsibilities sector-divided among several entities with no effective coordination,
(3) weak institutional programs, including those for manpower training,
(4) complex policies and slow mechanisms for financing,
(5) frequent use of technologies inappropriate for local conditions,
(6) limited capacity of institutions for operations and maintenance, and
(7) lack of awareness among the population about the importance to their health of water supply and sanitation.

Education and awareness are important in overall health care, but are particularly important to child survival. "Wellness" can also be shown to be associated with educational levels. For the period around 1970 Behm[11] showed a strong negative correlation between a mother's education and child mortality in Latin America. Children of illiterate women had four times the probability of dying as did children whose mothers had a secondary education. This figure is not felt to represent economic or nutritional status, but to reflect mothers' ability to gain access to available health care services and to adequately act on instructions given.

Governments can help to remedy unsanitary health conditions and practices. In Costa Rica, statistical analysis identified *health interventions* as the main determinant of the drop in infant mortality during this same time period. Primary preventive health care programs such as vaccinations, rural/community health programs, and environmental sanitation were shown to be especially important. The death rate from pneumonia and influenza is nine times higher in Central America than in the United States. These conditions can be combatted effectively with vaccination, oral rehydration, and community sanitation efforts. Usually it is the disenfranchised and powerless portion of the population that suffers from the lack of organized public health measures in basic sanitation.

Malnutrition. Chronic malnutrition is considered to be one of the major obstacles to raising the levels of health and welfare of the community in general and of infants and children in particular. "The maintenance of an adequate nutritional status in a population requires a supply of food sufficient to cover nutritional requirements, equitable distribution of the food among different social groups, consumption in proper quantities and qualities, and the assured uptake of nutrients."[12] Although a large percentage of the malnutrition seen in Central America is the direct result of protein/calorie loss from successive infections (especially diarrheal diseases),[13] a significant portion of the population also suffers from inadequate diet.[14] Inadequate diet contributes to vitamin deficiencies and secondary nutritional anemias such as that caused by iron deficiency. Iron absorption is favored by dietary meat and citrus fruit, which are scarce in the diets of poorer populations. Inadequate diet *in utero* and in early life can cause irreversible mental underdevelopment.[15]

Unlike regions with widespread famine, Central America's dietary deficiency is due more to a lack of purchasing power on the part of the indigent population than to an overall unavailability of food. Wide inequalities in food consumption are seen among the different socioeconomic strata. The problem is particularly critical in poverty-stricken rural areas and in underemployed urban populations. Authorities generally show little interest in ascertaining and publicizing unfavorable data on food and nutrition because of the possible political consequences. The return on investment in food and nutrition is considered to be lower than on investments in other aspects of health.

Food aid programs have been conducted by governmental and public institutions, local sources, and international nongovernmental sources from abroad. There is information to suggest that such programs have helped to improve the nutritional status of certain segments of the population at risk.[16]

Children under the age of five and their mothers are those affected most severely by malnutrition. Of the 850,000 children born each year in Central America, 100,000 suffer from low birth weight and the same number will die before their fifth birthday. Two-thirds of those who survive will be malnourished, and approximately 10 percent of those born will have permanent physical or mental limitations as a result of malnutrition.[17]

Table 7.2   Per Capita Calorie and Protein Availability 1975–77 and 1981–82

Country	1975–77 (calories/grams of protein)	1981–82 (calories/grams of protein)
Costa Rica	2,487/58.1	2,637/61.8
El Salvador	2,071/54.4	2,094/53.7
Guatemala	2,023/53.7	2,099/56.6
Honduras	2,084/51.5	2,171/55.6
Nicaragua	2,452/70.1	2,260/56.6
United States	3,539/106.2	3,641/105.6

Source: Same as table 7.1.

Specific Health Care Systems and Problems in the Central American Republics

Health care systems in Central America can be divided into three basic types:

(1) countries with universal coverage and little or no private sector participation, with responsibility primarily in the hands of the health ministry (Nicaragua),

(2) countries with prepaid insurance, with medical services divided among the ministries of health, social security systems, and private insurance companies (Costa Rica), and

(3) countries with some private insurance, a high dependence on the ministry of health, but without universal coverage (Honduras, Guatemala, El Salvador).

Countries employing the first two models claim to provide access to health care services for the entire populations they serve. Countries employing the third model make no such claim and likely provide access to between 8 and 15 percent of their populations.[18] Specifics for each country follow:

Costa Rica

Health care concerns in Costa Rica are those of a developed, rather than a developing, nation. Life expectancy is greater than 70 years and the majority of all adult deaths are caused by cancer, cardiac disease, or trauma. The major urban adult health problems are gynecologic cancers (especially cervical cancer), stomach cancer, and care for the elderly. There is a claimed 100 percent access to health services. This effort requires approximately 50 percent of the national budget. Expenditures are divided between the Ministerio de Salud (for preventive care) and the Seguridad Social (for hospital inpatient acute care). The Social Security system was inaugurated in 1970 and has improved the management of basic health care problems such as environmental hygiene, infectious diseases, and prenatal care at the rural level. This has given Costa Rica the most favorable statistics for infant mortality and overall life expectancy in all of Latin America. Infant mortality is 14/1000 births. In urban areas deaths are largely caused by congenital defects and low birth weight.

The medical system of Costa Rica is structured in four levels:

–primary clinics, staffed by general practitioners (who have no residency training)
–rural hospitals, usually of 50–250 beds, staffed by general practitioners and some specialists (general surgery and ob-gyn), which provide the capability to perform limited surgical procedures such as deliveries and cesarian sections
–regional hospitals, which have a wider selection of available specialists (neurologists, cardiologists). These hospitals may or may not perform major operations, have an intensive care unit, or provide resident training
–metropolitan hospitals, including Hospital Mexico, San Juan de Dios, Calderón Guardia and El Hospital de Niños. They provide referral service, based on geographic division, to patients originating at lower levels in the health care system

Most formal health care training takes place in the four metropolitan hospitals. Medicine is socialized and all patients in the country have access to any level of care available. As in most other countries with socialized medicine, there is a waiting list for non-urgent surgery.

Although medicine is socialized, private practices and clinics do exist. Physicians work eight-hour days for the Social Security system, and many also maintain private practices to supplement their government salaries with work performed on paying patients. Low physician salaries encourage this activity. Monthly pay scales in the Social Security system run from 22,000 colones for a general practitioner to 45,000 colones for a chief of service

($300 to $600). Minimal supplements are given for university lectures and teaching. Additional earnings must be generated by private sector work.

Since a large portion of many physicians' income is provided in the private sector, allegiance to the Social Security system is waning. This is a self-reinforcing process. Because most physicians effectively work two jobs, there is little time or incentive for medical research. When research is undertaken, it is usually funded and performed by individuals and organizations with resources outside of Costa Rica.

In spite of the generally favorable picture just described, the economic crisis of the mid-1980s placed severe strain on the resources of the Costa Rican medical system and has led to an overall deterioration of the physical infrastructure and limited its ability to continue the previous pace of improvements. The overall drop in the standard of living of Costa Rica has been felt in the services of the health care sector. Budgetary constraints have impeded a further lowering of the infant mortality rate. Lack of funds has forced a moratorium on new equipment purchases and forced severe reductions in necessary ongoing maintenance of technical equipment. As a result of this economic stress, a description of the technologically-intensive areas of even the major Costa Rican referral hospitals would appear to have been taken from an American or European model 10 to 15 years in the past. In spite of these limitations (and possibly in condemnation of the effectiveness of the developed world's medical technology), a statistical analysis of the Costa Rican heath care system still compares favorably with that of the United States and Europe. In spite of economic constraints, basic services have continued to be met through the imaginative use of available resources. In one instance, a Costa Rican agricultural product (coffee) was bartered to pay for technologically advanced equipment from international vendors. This avoided the problem posed by the scarcity of foreign capital.

Unfortunately, a reduction in specialized training and research has also been necessary. Lack of funds has also necessitated the application of a small user's fee for access to the system. It has been necessary to restrict the use of newer, unproven medicines and medical and surgical techniques.

In summary, although Costa Rica provides a high level of medical care, continuing economic fragility, combined with the massive influx of refugees, is placing severe strains on the status quo. In the future, logistical, not medical, problems are expected to lead to a deterioration of health care delivery if the economic situation does not improve promptly.

In contrast to Costa Rica, the other four countries of Central America have not yet successfully managed the health care problems that could be alleviated by the application of simple public health measures such as basic hygiene and the rational use of modern pharmaceuticals and vaccinations. Homicide, suicide, and war-related deaths make up a disproportionately large percentage of the overall mortality.

Honduras

The health care system of Honduras is divided between the twenty-five-year-old Social Security system and the hospitals of the Ministry of Public Health. The Social Security system covers approximately 8 percent of the population and the hospitals of the Ministry of Public Health, in theory, cover the rest. Only workers who have jobs allowing them to contribute to Social Security are protected under this system. Overall, the percentage of the population with access to organized health care is small.

Approximately 10 percent of the government's budget goes for health care needs. Fifty percent of that figure is allocated to the Social Security system's hospitals. The system is pyramidal, with five national, six regional, and ten area hospitals supplemented by clinics in the rural regions. There are five distinct health care regions divided according to political, geographic, and population differences. There is one national medical school in Tegucigalpa associated with the Universidad Autónoma and a smaller new private medical school in San Pedro Sula. There are a number of private physicians and some private hospitals in larger cities that are not associated with the national health system; they provide excellent care to those who can afford their cost. The Inter-American Development Bank has approved loans for the construction of five additional hospitals. Construction has begun on several of these projects, but none has been completed or staffed because of the lack of adequate funding.

Medical visits to the Social Security system are not free, yet they are highly subsidized, costing 1 lempira ($0.50) for each rural clinic visit. There is a one-time charge of 20 lempiras for a hospital admission. In the past this charge was waived if either the patient or a family member donated a unit of blood. At present this policy is being reevaluated as a result of the possibility of AIDS transmission.

The major health care problems in Honduras remain those of all underdeveloped nations. Diarrhea and acute respiratory infections cause the bulk of the deaths in children under 5 years old and contribute to the country's high infant mortality rate. Malnutrition contributes to the seriousness of the above diseases but is not usually statistically noted. General and infant mortality are linked to the population's educational level. In 1985 the illiteracy level was estimated at 41.4 percent for men and 49.9 percent for women. There is an increasing incidence of war-related and violent deaths in all sectors of the population.

The Ministry of Health has given its highest priority to addressing the problems of the marginal urban and rural poor populations. Adequate provision for the health care needs of the rural population has been made more difficult by the lack of logistic support for the workers in the rural clinics. As previously mentioned, there are few trained nurses, technical workers, and auxiliary health care assistants. Lab workers, X-ray and anesthesia technicians, and malaria workers are in extremely short supply as a result of the lack of adequate training funds and low enrollment in the schools.[19]

Guatemala

As in Honduras, the major health problems are: infectious diseases, diseases that could be prevented by vaccination, parasitic diseases, malaria, malnutrition, and violence. Rural mortality is 33 percent higher than urban mortality. Indian mortality is 50 percent higher than that of the mestizo population. The leading cause of death among males is homicide or war (17.4 percent of all male deaths). Approximately 12.7 percent of government expenditures are for health. Rural coverage is scarce and there is virtually no inpatient hospital care in some regions. There is a separate health care program for the Guatemalan military. Untreated sewage and agricultural pesticide runoff are creating a critical problem of water pollution.[20]

El Salvador

In 1984 there were 341 health care centers, 46 of which were closed as a result of violent conflict. Homicide was the third leading cause of death for the entire population and the leading cause of death for adult males. The children aged 1–4 were the most vulnerable to poor environmental conditions, infectious diseases, and malnutrition. Between 1981 and 1984 the birth rate fell sharply from 35.6 to 29.5 per 1000 inhabitants. The above, combined with emigration, has slowed the growth of the population. Many physicians, nurses, and dentists are among those who have left the country for political and economic reasons. The remaining human resources are concentrated in urban hospitals, leaving deficiencies in the rural areas, especially those affected by the war. The 8 percent of the national budget assigned to health care in 1981 has declined in more recent years as a result of the unsettled political situation. Health care resources in El Salvador are insufficient for the growing demand.[21]

Nicaragua

Nicaragua is a special case. Improvements in health care made by the present government have significantly improved the lives of many Nicaraguans. In 1982 the World Health Organization named Nicaragua the Third World's "model country" in health care. In August 1979 a single national health care system united the 23 separate institutions present under the prerevolutionary government, and the system as a whole has become both more efficient and extensive. The country's health budget rose by over 50 percent in the first year after the revolution.

In recent years, however, economic instability, natural disaster, and civil strife have combined to damage severely the physical infrastructure (hospital buildings, libraries, trained personnel) of the country's health care system. A number of medical facilities were almost totally destroyed during the earthquakes of the early 1970s and war operations during 1978–79. The Sandinista revolution resulted in a large exodus of trained technical personnel, leaving the remaining system relatively unattended.

Since 1982 the counterrevolution has caused serious damage to the excellent program of rural health inaugurated by the present government. These attacks, documented by international organizations such as Americas Watch, the International Red Cross, and the Pan American Health Organization, have rendered unusable an estimated fifty-five of the nations 388 health centers. The selection of clinics as both military depots and targets has further increased the level of misery of the Nicaraguan poor.

Presently, inflation, lack of foreign exchange, the U.S. trade embargo, and rural-to-urban migration have caused extremely severe shortages of drugs and supplies. Virtually all technical supplies must be imported. Powdered milk and diapers were being rationed in December 1987. The black market is currently the only reliable source of antibiotics. Unsanitary conditions caused by reuse of disposable needles and syringes, lack of appropriate suture material, and the scarcity of antibiotics have led to a high surgical mortality from postoperative septicemia. Private citizens with funds and permission to travel outside of the country return from trips to neighboring El Salvador and Honduras laden with medicines and supplies.

The current water shortage has restricted the running water supply even to critical areas. The children's hospital has recently been without water two or more days per week. Hepatitis from inadequate or nonexistent sewer treatment is endemic. Dengue fever and meningitis epidemics occurred in 1985–86. Lake Managua is highly polluted from both industrial waste and untreated urban sewage. The water level in the lagoons used to supply drinking water to the city is in danger of falling, therefore risking contamination by the entry of polluted water from Lake Managua through underground communications between the lagoons and the lake. Plans have been studied to bring water over the mountains from neighboring Lake Nicaragua, but the promised funding has not yet materialized. Unsanitary conditions caused by the present water shortage place the city at risk for the spread of epidemic diseases.[22]

Problems for the Future

Acquired Immune Deficiency Syndrome (AIDS)

Although AIDS is not presently a major problem in Latin America, social conditions present in the region create the potential for the rapid spread of this uniformly fatal illness. The social epidemiology of AIDS has some similarities to malaria. The eradication of malaria in the 1950s allowed for unprecedented economic growth in many areas of Latin America. New lands were opened, the industrial and agricultural work force became more productive, and food exports from the region were first made possible. Because AIDS, like malaria, infects young men and women in their reproductive and most economically productive years, the consequences of an epidemic for the region's economy are potentially serious. The death of people in this particular age group leaves families without wage earners and leaders.

Economic destitution, exploitation, deterioration in diet, and crowded living conditions may result. By contributing to the continuing spread of the disease, these conditions lock in a desperate cycle.

Unlike malaria, AIDS is a disease that depends on human behavior modification to limit its spread. Although in the developed world AIDS is thought of as a disease primarily affecting homosexual males, statistics from the Caribbean and Africa point out that it can and has become established in the sexually active heterosexual population. In Trinidad, Haiti, and the Dominican Republic approximately 40 percent of all cases occur in heterosexual females. In Honduras that figure is presently at 23 percent. Latin American social traditions (*machismo*) may cause a higher percentage of homosexuals to be less open about their sexual preferences. As a result, it has been estimated that up to one-third of all male homosexuals in Central America are not exclusively homosexual but are in fact bisexual, possibly married men with families. This tendency may increase the likelihood of transmission to the more universal, heterosexual population groups.[23]

Small as the numbers may presently be, the AIDS virus is established in the region. When economic necessity causes crowded living conditions, the reuse of otherwise disposable medical supplies (needles, syringes, invasive catheters), and low levels of public awareness of the mechanisms and danger of AIDS transmission, the disease has epidemic potential. AIDS in Costa Rica is growing at the same rate as in Los Angeles, where 13 percent of the homosexual population is estimated to be infected. Although there is no official data on Latin America, studies in the United States estimate that perhaps 6 percent of the sexually active population is homosexual. The figures for Costa Rica are probably similar. It is also estimated that up to 10 percent of the people who may transmit the disease may remain asymptomatic and unaware of their infective potential.

Interpolating and calculating a 13 percent infection rate in the 30,000 Costa Rica homosexuals, the resulting number of AIDS cases would doubtlessly bankrupt the present medical system and cripple many productive members of the work force by the middle of the next decade. Unless a serious campaign of public awareness and education is undertaken, the potential exists for economic devastation and social paralysis from the presence of large numbers of AIDS patients. Presently, the only way to avoid this calculated eventuality is to promote frank and serious public information campaigns aimed at altering sexual practices to prevent the further transmission of the disease.

These campaigns have begun in Costa Rica and Honduras. Although there is still little information on their effectiveness in Central America, similar efforts in the United States have been shown to decrease the infection rate.[24]

Refugees

In addition to inflation and an overall weakening of the Central American economies, economically and politically motivated displacements have severely burdened the system of health care delivery throughout the region. As of November 1987 there were 30,000 officially recognized refugees and approximately 200,000 undocumented or displaced persons in Costa Rica alone. Massive population dislocations cause otherwise preventable health care problems to recur. When military or economic imperatives force abandonment and resettlement of rural populations, poverty is an immediate consequence. Agricultural practices suffer, and dietary inadequacies are a common result of the subsistence-level life that follows until the first new crop is harvested. New soil environments, altitude, and climates confront the migrants with health care problems with which they have had little contact. A combination of reduced knowledge and, in some cases, inadequate immunity makes the newcomers more susceptible to endemic diseases. When the physiologic stress of a marginal diet is added to the equation, mortality rates soar.

   Displaced people often choose not to register with the government for fear of forced repatriation or expulsion. These unregistered displaced people become the undocumented workers of Central America and are often forced to work for subsistence wages. Economic exploitation is commonplace. Because they avoid registration, these people rarely benefit from the services provided by the existing organizations caring for refugees. In the urban zones they are forced to populate the slum areas of the cities. This economic situation generates extreme conditions that could spawn serious public health risks.[25]

Conclusions and Recommendations

Summary of Regional Problems

The current systems have proven to be inadequate in many areas. Major areas of concern remain:

–political violence[26]
–the bias toward expensive curative measures rather than more cost-effective preventive measures
–the bias towards urban, rather than rural, expenditures in health care (a possible consequence of the item above)
–the relative excess of physicians and a shortage of other health care workers and technicians (a possible consequence of the previous two items)
–the lack of maintenance and growth of the technical infrastructure of modern medicine (a result of both the depressed condition of the region's economy and the politically-motivated embargoes)
–long-term environmental damage from pesticides, pollutants, and deforestation

Suggestions for Change

–Cease outside support for all forms of political violence.
–Work toward repatriating and resettling refugees and displaced persons.
–Reorient existing curative services toward prevention of disease through sanitary and environmental protection, nutrition, vaccination, and health education—including AIDS education—at the household level.
–Shift funding priorities from urban to rural areas, and support community-based health programs.
–Create economic incentives for health professionals to relocate to rural areas.
–Create economic and social incentives for students to seek careers in nursing and other nonphysician health care work.
–Eliminate trade embargoes impeding the flow of health supplies.
–Halt the use of long-lasting, environmentally dangerous chemicals and of short-sighted agricultural practices.

Good health practices raise living standards, enhance economic and political security, and encourage peace. Political, economic, and ecological benefits have been shown to accrue to a system that cares for the well-being of its participants.[27] Adequate health care is essential for practical as well as for humanitarian reasons. The health care needs of Central America are priority issues for the International Commission for Central American Recovery and Development in its efforts to promote economic and social development in the region.

In 1983 the Central American countries and the Pan American Health Organization developed a regional health care initiative, *Priority Health Needs for Central America and Panamá*, also known as *Health as a Bridge for Peace*.[28] This effort has provided a forum for health-related dialogue, cooperation, and understanding among the region's nations and the developed world. It has been supported politically by the Contadora nations and financially by regional and international development agencies and the international community. More than $102 million has been raised and more than $255 million pledged in external funds. Projects have been targeted to address the health care needs of the region's most vulnerable population groups (mothers, children under five, refugees, displaced persons, and the rural and urban poor). Initiatives such as this provide the framework and multidisciplinary skill to effectively address the above-mentioned problems and deserve the commission's support.

Moreover, in the turbulent political climate of Central America the acceptance of health care as a priority provides a consensus issue from which individuals holding otherwise conflicting political and economic viewpoints can begin fruitful discussion concerning the region's common problems. In planning the international effort *Health as a Bridge for Peace*, Dr. Carlyle Guerra de Macedo from the Pan American Health Organization stated, "Health was the one area where everyone could agree, the one goal which overrode the differences, the one field where there was an impressive tradition of Central American cooperation and the one sector where a common long term ideal, Health for All by the year 2000 already was shared."[29]

Notes

1. "The Health Situation, Child Health." *Health Conditions in the Americas, 1981–1984*, scientific publication 500, (1):34. Washington, D.C.: Pan American Health Organization, 1986.

230 John J. Freiberger

2. C. Guerra de Macedo, "The Challenges Ahead," *Magazine of the World Health Organization*, October 1987, p. 27.

3. *Health Conditions in the Americas*, scientific publication 427. Washington, D.C.: Pan American Health Organization, 1982.

4. Louis Rosero-Bixby, "Infant Mortality in Costa Rica: Explaining the Recent Decline." *Studies in Family Planning*, (1986) 17:(2):116–23.

5. C. L. Marshall and C. L. Paul, "Reduced Population Growth as Related to the Urbanization Process," *Clinical Pediatrics*, December 1970; 9(12):736–41.

6. "Necesidades Prioritarias de Salud en Centro América y Panamá," documento básico. Madrid: Publicado por el Instituto de Cooperación Iberoamericana, March 1984.

7. R. M. Garfield and P. F. Rodriguez, "Health and Health Services in Central America," *Journal of the American Medical Association* 1985; 254:(7) 936–94.

8. "Necesidades Prioritarias de Salud en Centro América y Panamá," *Informe de Avance*, August 1987.

9. "The Health Situation: Environmental Health." *Health Conditions in the Americas, 1981–1984*, p. 130.

10. World Health Organization, Offset Publication No. 85, Geneva, 1985.

11. H. Behm, "Socioeconomic Determinants of Mortality in Latin America." *Populations Bulletin of the United Nations 1980*. UN Publication No. ST/ESA/series N/13, pp. 1–16.

12. "The Health Situation: Food and Nutrition." *Health Conditions in the Americas, 1981–1984*, p. 57.

13. L. Mata, *The Children of Santa María Cauque: A Prospective Field Study of Health and Growth*. Cambridge, Mass.: MIT Press, 1978.

14. "Necesidades Prioritarias de Salud en Centro América y Panamá," documento básico. San José, Costa Rica: Pan American Health Organization, March 1984.

15. J. Villar, L. Altobelli, E. Kestler, and J. Belizan, "A Health Priority for Developing Countries: The Prevention of Chronic Fetal Malnutrition." *Bulletin of the World Health Organization* 64, (6):847–51 (1986).

16. "The Health Situation: Food and Nutrition." *Health Conditions in the Americas, 1981–1984*, p. 61.

17. R. M. Garfield and P. F. Rodriguez, "Health and Health Services in Central America." *Journal of the American Medical Association* 1985; 245:(7) 936–43.

18. Ibid., 936–94; and "Health Systems Infrastructure: Development of the Infrastructure," *Health Conditions in the Americas, 1981-1984*, p. 134, and J. Haddad, "Current Status of Public Health Education in Central America," *Educación Medicina y Salud* 1982, 16(1): 69–76.

19. "The Health Situation: Honduras." *Health Conditions in the Americas, 1981–1984*, pp. 143–

48. Also Dr. Yanurio García, Minister of Health, Tegucigalpa, Honduras. Interview, December, 1987.

20. "The Health Situation: Guatemala," *Health Conditions in the Americas, 1981-1984*, pp. 123–29, and G. Chapin and R. Wasserstrom, "Pesticide Use and Malaria Resurgence in Central America and India," *Social Science and Medicine* 1983, 17(5):273–90.

21. "The Health Situation: El Salvador." *Health Conditions in the Americas, 1981–1984*, pp. 112–16.

22. "The Health Situation: Nicaragua." Ibid., pp. 172–76; J. Preston, "Nicaraguan Medical Care Crimped by Shortages," *Washington Post*, January 27, 1987; and F. N. Garfield, T. Frieden, and S. H. Vermund, "Health-related Outcomes of War in Nicaragua," *American Journal of Public Health* 77:615-18; (1987).

23. L. Mata, Interview, December 11, 1987, San José, Costa Rica.

24. G. H. Friedland and R. S. Klein, "Transmission of Human Immunodeficiency Virus," *New England Journal of Medicine* 317, issue 18 (October 1987): 1125–35.

25. The following discussion of the refugee problem evolved directly from an interview with Carlos Muñoz Retana, director of Costa Rica's "Salud Rural," in December, 1987:

In Costa Rica 80 percent of the undocumented people are from Nicaragua. Although self-interest should have led most of the people crossing the border from Nicaragua to Costa Rica to register as refugees (due to excellent international assistance provided to this population by groups such as the UN High Commissioner for Refugees), most of the refugees have chosen not to register with the Costa Rican authorities from unwarranted fear of either forced repatriation or expulsion. As such, these unregistered, displaced people have become the undocumented workers of Costa Rica, working for subsistence wages and benefiting neither from the services provided by the multitude of international organizations caring for refugees nor from the services the Costa Rican government provides for its citizens in the form of its socialized health care system. Paradoxically, the official 30,000 refugees may in fact benefit from better health care than the citizens of their host country. Aggressive programs of disinfection, vaccination, and acute therapy, unimpeded by the bureaucratic inefficiency of the Social Security system, have recently lowered infant mortality among refugees to 0 percent in the period from July–December 1987.

The makeup of the "indocumentados" has changed with the passage of time and the evolution of the political situation in Nicaragua. Prior to the summer of 1987 the majority of the immigrants were either members of the more wealthy Nicaraguan middle (professional) classes from the larger cities or poor, mostly illiterate, peasants from the southeastern region of the country who were directly affected by military activity. During this period the numbers of immigrants was smaller than at present, approximately fifty a day. The more educated group brought both money and professional skills and was easily assimilated into the existing economic structure. Although no one significant event occurred to abruptly change the character of the

Nicaraguan population seeking refuge in Costa Rica, by the end of August 1987 the character of this population changed to people who were leaving Nicaragua for economic rather than political reasons. Instead of a more rural people from relatively unpopulated war zones in the southeast, this new group was urban in origin, from the more heavily populated zones to the northwest where the potential for further migration is much greater. At present approximately 600 people a day are successfully crossing the international border.

This new wave of "indocumentados" poses severe challenges to the established health care delivery system both as a result of their large numbers as well as from the humble socioeconomic character of the people themselves. Either through ignorance of the existence of refugee relief organizations or from fear of exportation, these people slip through the threadbare yet mostly effective safety net provided by international relief organizations such as the UN High Commissioner for Refugees. A large percentage of these new arrivals support themselves with subsistence-level wages, sometimes working only for the most meager diet and shelter. As in countries such as the United States, undocumented workers provide a ready source of cheap, passive labor which is taken advantage of in the urban zones by the construction industry and by agricultural concerns (coffee, sugar) in the country. In the urban zones these are the people who populate the slum areas of the cities, often living in conditions that could spawn serious public health risks both for the slum dwellers themselves as well as the population living in adjacent areas of the cities.

Although the Ministry of Health is presently trying to determine the number of "indocumentados" through house-to-house survey methods, accurate data are presently unavailable and little progress is being made in even determining the scope of the problem, much less addressing specific public health issues in this population. The overall issues are economic. It is lack of work and resources that is forcing these people to live in overcrowded, relatively unsanitary conditions.

26. To reiterate, political violence has caused multiple problems. These problems have been thoroughly discussed by many authors and include:

(a) Direct, acute and chronic injury to the land and people
(b) Destruction of the health care system infrastructure
(c) Diversion of scarce foreign exchange dollars needed for health-related technology
(d) Diversion of the most economically productive segment of the society to nonproductive military affairs
(e) Forced migration of large populations and extremes of poverty, overcrowding, and a high percentage of dependency
(f) Emigration of trained personnel.

27. K. M. Leisinger, "Health Policy for Less Developed Countries." In *Social Strategies: Monographs on Sociology and Social Policy*, ed. Paul Trappe. Basel, Switzerland: Social Strategies Publishers, 1985.

28. *Health: A Bridge for Peace*. Progress Report, second Madrid Conference, April 1988.

Priority Health Needs in Central America and Panamá (PPS/CAP). Pan American Health Organization.

29. M. L. Schneider, "Health as a Bridge for Peace," *Magazine of the World Health Organization,* October 1987, p. 5.

References

Behm, H. "Socioeconomic Determinants of Mortality in Latin America." *Populations Bulletin of the United Nations 1980.* UN Publication No. ST/ESA/series N/13.

Chapin, G. and R. Wasserstrom. "Pesticide Use and Malaria Resurgence in Central America and India." *Social Science and Medicine* 1983, 17(5):273–90.

Friedland, G. H., and R. S. Klein. "Transmission of Human Immunodeficiency Virus." *New England Journal of Medicine,* 1987.

García, Dr. Yanurio. Minister of Health, Tegucigalpa, Honduras. Interview, December, 1987.

Garfield, F. N., T. Frieden, and S. H. Vermund. "Health-related Outcomes of War in Nicaragua." *American Journal of Public Health* 77:615-18; (1987).

Garfield, R. M. and P. F. Rodriguez. "Health and Health Services in Central America." *Journal of the American Medical Association* 1985; 254:(7) 936–94

Haddad, J. "Current Status of Public Health Education in Central America." *Educación Medicina y Salud* 1982, 16(1): 69–76.

Health: A Bridge for Peace. Progress Report, second Madrid Conference, April 1988. Priority Health Needs in Central America and Panamá (PPS/CAP). Pan American Health Organization.

Health Conditions in the Americas. Scientific Publication 427. Washington: Pan American Health Organization, 1982.

"The Health Situation, Child Health." *Health Conditions in the Americas, 1981–1984.* Scientific Publication 500, (1):34. Washington: Pan American Health Organization, 1986.

"The Health Situation: El Salvador." *Health Conditions in the Americas, 1981–1984,* pp. 112–16. Scientific Publication 500, (1):34. Washington: Pan American Health Organization, 1986.

"The Health Situation: Environmental Health." *Health Conditions in the Americas, 1981–1984.* Scientific Publication 500, (1):34. Washington: Pan American Health Organization, 1986.

"The Health Situation: Food and Nutrition." *Health Conditions in the Americas, 1981–1984.* Scientific Publication 500, (1):34. Washington: Pan American Health Organization, 1986.

"The Health Situation: Guatemala," *Health Conditions in the Americas, 1981-1984,* pp. 123–29. Scientific Publication 500, (1):34. Washington: Pan American Health Organization, 1986.

"The Health Situation: Honduras." *Health Conditions in the Americas, 1981–1984,* pp. 143–48. Scientific Publication 500, (1):34. Washington: Pan American Health Organization, 1986.

"The Health Situation: Nicaragua." *Health Conditions in the Americas, 1981–1984*, pp. 172–76. Scientific Publication 500, (1):34. Washington: Pan American Health Organization, 1986.

"Health Systems Infrastructure: Development of the Infrastructure," *Health Conditions in the Americas, 1981-1984*. Scientific Publication 500, (1):34. Washington: Pan American Health Organization, 1986.

Leisinger, K. M. "Health Policy for Less Developed Countries." In *Social Strategies, Monographs on Sociology and Social Policy*, ed. Paul Trappe. Basil 1985.

Macedo, C. Guerra de. "The Challenges Ahead." *Magazine of the World Health Organization*, October 1987.

Marshall, C. L. and C. L. Paul. "Reduced Population Growth as Related to the Urbanization Process." *Clinical Pediatrics*, December 1970; 9(12):736–41.

Mata, L. *The Children of Santa María Cauque: A Prospective Field Study of Health and Growth.* Cambridge, Mass.: MIT Press, 1978.

Mata, L. Interview, December 11, 1987, San José, Costa Rica.

"Necesidades Prioritarias de Salud en Centro América y Panamá," documento básico. Madrid: Instituto de Cooperación Iberoamericana, March 1984.

Preston, J. "Nicaraguan Medical Care Crimped by Shortages." *Washington Post*, January 27, 1987.

Retana, Carlos Muñoz. Interview, December 1987.

Rosero-Bixby, Louis. "Infant Mortality in Costa Rica: Explaining the Recent Decline." *Studies in Family Planning*, (1986) 17:(2):116–23.

Schneider, M. L. "Health as a Bridge for Peace." *Magazine of the World Health Organization*, October 1987, p. 5.

Villar, J., L. Altobelli, E. Kestler, and J. Belizan. "A Health Priority for Developing Countries: The Prevention of Chronic Fetal Malnutrition." *Bulletin of the World Health Organization* 64, (6):847–51 (1986).

World Health Organization. Offset Publication No. 85, Geneva, 1985.

Chapter 8

Access and Opportunity for Women in Central America:
A Challenge for Peace
Sally W. Yudelman

Introduction

Building more democratic societies in Central America requires the active participation of women. If the region is to move from its authoritarian past to a more participatory and equitable future, women must have more equal access to opportunities and resources. Access to opportunity assumes increased participation in the political process, including election to public office and serving in policymaking positions, reduction of discrimination in the terms and conditions of employment, and greater equality before the law. Access to resources assumes increased access to education and training, credit and land, social services and benefits.

Participation, however, is a power-sharing issue. Equal participation of women challenges deeply held convictions of what women's roles are or should be. Cultural constraints limit women's access in all five countries, particularly in rural areas. Equal access to resources, moreover, poses competition to men. Researchers have pointed out that "action for poor women . . . is conditional on the assessment that investments in women will not affect or cut back on development investments in poor men" (Buvinic, 1986). Thus, possible declines in external aid to the region as armed conflicts diminish suggest that unless women are specifically targeted as recipients they will not receive the assistance they need.

Yet lack of access to resources is the critical economic determinant that continues to impoverish women. Women in Central America are disproportionately represented among the poor, the malnourished, the illiterate, the unemployed, and the underemployed. Poor women with limited or no education and skills work as agricultural laborers, domestics, vendors, or prostitutes. Most women in the wage labor force are engaged in low-paying, low-status factory, service, or sales jobs. In addition, women carry primary responsibility for domestic work and child care. Because of the civil wars that have ravaged the region, thousands more are widows and/or refugees in their own or neighboring countries. These women are truly among the "poorest of the poor," and they and their children will require special assistance during the reconstruction period.

The UN Decade for Women (1976–85) represented a global effort to tackle women's lack of access to opportunity and resources. Looking back over the past twelve years, it is clear that some progress has been made. Due in large part to the efforts of women themselves, women's issues have become visible and have gained some legitimacy. But the inability of Central American governments, the private sector, trade unions, cooperative federations, and nongovernmental organizations to recognize women's economic role has resulted in the continuation of a social welfare approach. Programs for women still focus overwhelmingly on their traditional roles in the home and family. Economic projects for women tend to be small and marginal, and new technologies benefit men. Women continue to be trained in sex-segregated skills such as sewing, food processing, and handicrafts. Finally, women are still woefully underrepresented at the policy and decisionmaking levels in both the public and private sectors, as well as in political parties, trade unions, and cooperative federations. For cultural and other reasons, a policy environment responsive to the needs of women has not existed in most Central American countries.

Despite the obstacles, two trends are changing women's lives in all five countries. Gains have been made in education, particularly in urban areas. Enrollment of women, both in absolute terms and in comparison to men's enrollment, has increased at the intermediate and upper levels. Progress has also been made in literacy, and there has been some diversification in technical and vocational training. But literacy rates in rural areas are still abysmally low, and access to secondary education is limited. The belief that it is more important to educate boys than girls, whose destiny is the home and family, prevails in the countryside. Too many Central American women consider themselves fortunate to have had two or three years of schooling. Education and literacy, however, are required to enter the labor market and are essential for securing better jobs in the formal sector.

A second trend is the increasing numbers of women entering the wage labor force, particularly in urban areas. Simultaneously, there has been a significant increase in female participation in the informal sector—those vendors, artisans, and other small-scale entrepreneurs who operate without legal protection or benefits and whose income goes unreported. Between 1950 and 1980 women's participation in the wage labor force grew by 23 percent throughout Latin America (Paolisso et al., 1988). This is due in part to increased rural-urban migration, in part to declining economic standards and real wages due to inflation, recession, austerity measures, and cutbacks in public expenditures. The ravages of civil wars and the rise in the number of women-headed households are also contributing factors.

The employment demand for women in Latin America is predicted to rise in the years ahead (3.5 percent per year between 1985 and 2000) (Paolisso et al., 1988). Unless laws that discriminate against women are changed and programs to broaden women's access to education, training, credit, and land are implemented, women's participation in the economy will continue to be limited to the informal sector, labor-intensive export industries, and seasonal work in commercial and export agriculture. A more equitable Central America will surely require that women have access to better opportunities.

This paper provides a general overview of the major problems that women in Costa Rica, El Salvador, Guatemala, Honduras, and Nicaragua face in workplaces, agriculture, education, health, political participation, and the law, and makes recommendations for consideration by the International Commission for Central American Recovery and Development.

Women in the Workplace

The majority of Central American women work because they have to. Declining economic standards, increasing poverty, and the rise in numbers of women-headed households have pushed women into the labor force in growing numbers. Data from the early 1970s indicate a range from 15 percent (Guatemala) to 22 percent (Honduras) of families in the region that are headed by women (Balakrishnan and Firebaugh, 1987). The instability and economic crises of the 1980s have surely increased those percentages.

Nevertheless, official data continue to underestimate the total number of Central American women who are economically active. There are several explanations for the cloak of invisibility that veils women's work. First, women define themselves as housewives. Second, they move in and out of the labor force, and third, the work they do in agriculture and the informal sector is rarely represented in government labor force statistics. Because women's work is invisible, their economic contributions are ignored by policy planners.

For example, in an experimental population census carried out in May 1983 in the district of San Juan in San Ramón de Alajuela, Costa Rica, there was a special assessment of the extent to which the 1973 population census and national household surveys underestimated women's participation in the economy. Interviewers found that many of the inactive women had worked for pay during the reference week or seasonally during the coffee harvest. Others reported working six months of the year or more. This information increased urban women's labor force participation in the area from the 31 percent recorded in the 1983 national household survey to 48 percent, and the participation rate of rural women from 23 percent to 45 percent (Buvinic and Horenstein, 1986). Similar findings in other Central American countries also reveal the extent to which women participate in the market economy.

With few exceptions, women's gains in education have not resulted in improved economic opportunities in the marketplace. Women, even those with educational backgrounds equivalent to their male counterparts, earn less. Wage discrimination by gender coexists with women's increased participation in the labor force and their educational attainments, and seems to have worsened over time. For example, in Costa Rica in 1978 men received wages 14 percent higher than those of women; by 1980 their wages were 19 percent higher (Buvinic and Horenstein, 1986). In general, hourly wages of women in the manufacturing sector are 75 percent of the wages of men who do similar work (Sivard, 1985).

Employment opportunities in the formal sector for women with little or no education are limited. Some young unmarried women find work as seamstresses in clothing factories or as assemblers in export-processing industries. Although it is generally believed in Costa Rica that *maquilas* (apparel assembly plants) are significantly expanding employment opportunities for women, they have generated employment for only about seven percent of the urban labor force (Buvinic and Horenstein, 1986). Other women do piecework at home, subcontracted by larger companies, often multinationals. These domestic outworkers generally do not earn the minimum wage, nor do they receive health and other benefits. Domestic service continues to be the main occupation for urban women workers (50–70 percent throughout Latin America) (Chaney, 1984).

Women who do find wage labor face an almost insurmountable series of obstacles in addition to home and family responsibilities: lack of child care facilities, employment located far from their homes, inadequate public transportation, expectations that they will work for a lower rate of pay than men, and often no benefits. Since they are usually unaware of their legal rights they do not challenge discrimination (Yudelman, 1987).

The informal sector is an increasingly important source of work for both men and women. In San Salvador, for example, an estimated 85 percent of poor households are engaged in informal sector work that provides approximately 50 percent of household income (Lycette, ___ ___ ___ ___ disproportionately represented in the informal sect___ lack access to education and training that might ___ also because the informal sector provides the flexibil___ household, nurturing, and reproductive responsibili___

The major problem male and female microentrep___ capital. Without working capital they cannot pur___ stocks to last longer than one or two days, nor can ___ quantity discounts or sell when prices are most profitable. Access to credit becomes critical.

Women's growing demand for small amounts of credit suggests that they have had limited access to the formal financial system, but little direct evidence exists due to the lack of sex-desegregated data (Lycette, 1984). As a rule, however, financial institutions are reluctant to make small loans because unit costs are higher. In addition, interest rate policies have often contributed to restrictions on credit by forcing the institutions to bear the opportunity costs of providing "cheap" credit. On the demand side, a number of factors inhibit women in particular from approaching formal financial institutions: high transaction costs, collateral requirements (women are often legally restricted from holding land or other income-generating properties in their own names), and complex application procedures that discriminate against women (who are more likely than men to be illiterate or semiliterate) (Lycette, 1984). There is mounting evidence, however, that when women do receive credit (from nongovernmental organizations, for example), their repayment rates are as good as, if not better than, men's (Lycette, 1984; Yudelman, 1987).

Perhaps the one area where women with education have found greater opportunity is government, particularly in departments that deal with women's traditional concerns—health, education, and welfare. Throughout Central America women can be found in mid-level professional positions in government bureaus and ministries. They are seldom visible at upper levels. Thus cutbacks in public expenditures, especially social services, because of the economic crisis are likely to have diminished women's employment and earning opportunities disproportionately.

Although no empirical analysis has been done because of limited sex-desegregated data, current research suggests that the economic crisis has had a particularly negative impact on women. Since women's earned incomes are generally lower than men's, and a higher proportion is derived from transfers, their incomes are likely to have declined as economic conditions have deteriorated. Devaluation benefits traders rather than those who sell services. Because women are heavily concentrated in the service sector, their levels of employment or wages have most likely fallen. As male incomes decline, women receive less for household expenses, and the nutritional status of the household suffers. As food prices rise, pregnant and nursing women, already at risk, decrease their food intake and the quality of their diet, with serious consequences for their own health and that of their children. Girls' access to education, already limited, may decline further when government expenditures are cut and their labor is needed in the household to care for other children while their mothers go out to work. Finally, as health services shrink from government cutbacks, and fees rise, women's and children's access shrinks (Joekes et al., 1988). In 1984 health workers in a peasant women's primary health care program in Honduras turned to natural medicines when prices for pharmaceuticals rose beyond the ability of their clients to pay (Yudelman, 1987).

Women in Agriculture

Women's participation within family farming systems is critically important to agricultural production in Central America, especially among the poorest small holders and the near landless. (Women grow 40 percent of the food multinationals. These domestic outworkers generally do not earn the minimum wage, nor do they receive health and other benefits. Domestic service continues to be the main occupation for urban women workers (50–70 percent throughout Latin America) (Chaney, 1984).

Women who do find wage labor face an almost insurmountable series of obstacles in addition to home and family responsibilities: lack of child care facilities, employment located far from their homes, inadequate public transportation, expectations that they will work for a lower rate of pay than men, and often no benefits. Since they are usually unaware of their legal rights they do not challenge discrimination (Yudelman, 1987).

The informal sector is an increasingly important source of work for both men and women. In San Salvador, for example, an estimated 85 percent of poor households are engaged in informal sector work that provides approximately 50 percent of household income (Lycette, 1984). Women are disproportionately represented in the informal sector, not only because they lack access to education and training that might provide alternatives, but also because the informal sector provides the flexibility they need to balance household, nurturing, and reproductive responsibilities.

The major problem male and female microentrepreneurs face is lack of capital. Without working capital they cannot purchase raw materials or stocks to last longer than one or two days, nor can they take advantage of quantity discounts or sell when prices are most profitable. Access to credit becomes critical.

Women's growing demand for small amounts of credit suggests that they have had limited access to the formal financial system, but little direct evidence exists due to the lack of sex-desegregated data (Lycette, 1984). As a rule, however, financial institutions are reluctant to make small loans because unit costs are higher. In addition, interest rate policies have often contributed to restrictions on credit by forcing the institutions to bear the opportunity costs of providing "cheap" credit. On the demand side, a number of factors inhibit women in particular from approaching formal financial institutions: high transaction costs, collateral requirements (women are often legally restricted from holding land or other income-generating properties in their own names), and complex application procedures that discriminate against women (who are more likely than men to be illiterate or semiliterate) (Lycette, 1984). There is mounting evidence, however, that when women do receive credit (from nongovernmental organizations, for example), their repayment rates are as good as, if not better than, men's (Lycette, 1984; Yudelman, 1987).

Perhaps the one area where women with education have found greater opportunity is government, particularly in departments that deal with women's traditional concerns—health, education, and welfare. Throughout Central America women can be found in mid-level professional positions in government bureaus and ministries. They are seldom visible at upper levels. Thus cutbacks in public expenditures, especially social services, because of the economic crisis are likely to have diminished women's employment and earning opportunities disproportionately.

Although no empirical analysis has been done because of limited sex-desegregated data, current research suggests that the economic crisis has had a particularly negative impact on women. Since women's earned incomes are generally lower than men's, and a higher proportion is derived from transfers, their incomes are likely to have declined as economic conditions have deteriorated. Devaluation benefits traders rather than those who sell services. Because women are heavily concentrated in the service sector, their levels of employment or wages have most likely fallen. As male incomes decline, women receive less for household expenses, and the nutritional status of the household suffers. As food prices rise, pregnant and nursing women, already at risk, decrease their food intake and the quality of their diet, with serious consequences for their own health and that of their children. Girls' access to education, already limited, may decline further when government expenditures are cut and their labor is needed in the household to care for other children while their mothers go out to work. Finally, as health services shrink from government cutbacks, and fees rise, women's and children's access shrinks (Joekes et al., 1988). In 1984 health workers in a peasant women's primary health care program in Honduras turned to natural medicines when prices for pharmaceuticals rose beyond the ability of their clients to pay (Yudelman, 1987).

Women in Agriculture

Women's participation within family farming systems is critically important to agricultural production in Central America, especially among the poorest small holders and the near landless. (Women grow 40 percent of the food crops in Latin America as a whole.) Throughout Central America women plant and harvest crops, cultivate home vegetable gardens, raise animals, market produce, and work as agricultural wage laborers in addition to performing household tasks and caring for children. Rural women carry a heavier workload than urban women because of the lack of infrastructure: potable water, electricity, roads, and transportation. Their domestic technology also tends to be primitive, resulting in eighteen-hour workdays (Deere and Leon, 1978).

Despite their economic contributions, women's agricultural role is still largely invisible in government labor force statistics. This is because women are often unpaid family workers, work seasonally in cash crops, or engage in informal sector activities off the farm (Buvinic and Horenstein, 1986). For example, Honduran government statistics suggest that only seven percent of rural women are in the labor force (Chaney, 1984). Yet researchers have pointed out that women make up 40 percent of the wage labor force in tobacco and 90 percent in coffee (Lycette et al., 1988). A study of four Honduran agrarian reform settlements and two villages showed that 46 percent of the women did agricultural work: sowing (39 percent), hoeing (41 percent), harvesting (39 percent), and weeding (22 percent) (Safilios Rothschild, 1984). Similarly, the 1983 Costa Rican census revealed that women made up only five percent of the agricultural labor force (Buvinic and Horenstein, 1986). But a 1984 study by the Agrarian Reform Institute on the participation of women in agricultural production concluded that "between 20 percent and 30 percent of the women defined as economically inactive carry out productive activities" (MIDEPLAN/IDA, 1984). Nicaraguan data show that women made up 70 percent of the wage labor force in the coffee and tobacco harvests in 1984–85 (Padilla et al., 1987).

Perhaps the most serious problem faced by women farmers in Central America is lack of access to land. The rights they do have are poorly defined and limited by notions that empower male heads of households (Bossen, 1984). Even when they have rights of inheritance, they often lose their land to male relatives because they are not knowledgeable about those rights.

The four agrarian reforms in Central America (Costa Rica, El Salvador, Honduras, and Nicaragua) have benefited women only minimally. Only 3.8 percent of Honduran beneficiaries are women (Deere, 1985). Although widows and single heads of household in Honduras can hold title under the law, they generally have last priority on land being allocated—after male-headed households and single males aged 16 years and up (Yudelman, 1987). While Costa Rican land and colonization laws do not discriminate against women as beneficiaries, the agrarian reform agency has consistently awarded titles to men (Madden, 1984). Although the Nicaraguan government has passed laws granting women equal rights to land, membership in cooperatives, and equal pay for equal work, women make up only 8 percent of the beneficiaries of the agrarian reform, and only 6 percent of the 82,000 members of 3,213 agrarian reform cooperatives (Padilla et al., 1987). In some cases requests for admission by landless women have been denied, and in others, women have been allowed to join only if they own land that they are willing to pool. Women who are members, however, do have access to credit and have benefited along with men from technical assistance and organizational training courses (Padilla et al., 1987). In the case of El Salvador, two household surveys conducted by Project for Planning and Evaluating Agrarian Reform (PERA) showed that women-headed households in Phase I (the expropriation of agricultural estates of 500 or more hectares and the subsequent organization of workers' production cooperatives) had significantly less access to land (36 percent less), capital goods, and technical assistance than did male-headed households. Only 14 percent of the households had women cooperative members (Lastarria-Cornhiel, 1988).

Because women are seldom beneficiaries of agrarian reforms, they are excluded from membership in the cooperatives or settlements that assure access to credit, technical assistance, and new technologies, and from the decisions about labor allocations, wages, and surplus produced (Deere, 1985). Studies in Costa Rica, Honduras, and Nicaragua have shown that women are interested in participating but are ignored by men, who believe women cannot carry out a sufficient number of agricultural tasks. Case studies of ten cooperatives in Nicaragua, however, revealed that women participated in productive activities equally with men (Deere, 1983). The same has been reported in Costa Rica and Honduras.

It seems clear that cultural norms reflecting what women's role should be—in the home while the man is in the fields—continue to constitute a significant barrier to the incorporation of women into agrarian reforms (Deere, 1985). These norms are reinforced by agricultural extension services and rural cooperative federations that focus on women's domestic roles.

On the other hand, it does not appear that women in Central America have been marginalized by the development of commercial or export crops (Deere and Leon, 1987). Women have been increasingly employed in the coffee, tobacco, and cotton harvests. As numbers of available male workers have declined, the demand for female labor has risen. This has been particularly true in the case of Nicaragua because of the civil war. For the most part, however, the terms of women's incorporation into the agricultural wage labor force have been unfavorable. Women are paid less than men, lack legal protection and benefits, and have less access to permanent positions (Deere and Leon, 1987).

Further, the commercialization of agriculture appears to have increased women's workloads and, in some cases, to have displaced them from traditional productive and income-generating activities such as food crops or handicrafts. In the case of Guatemala, for example, small-farm diversification into nontraditional vegetable exports (cauliflower, broccoli, snowpeas) has led to women's working longer hours caring for export crops at the expense of growing food crops or making handicrafts for sale in local markets. Studies of two agricultural diversification projects showed that women supplied from 22 percent to 44 percent of the additional labor depending on farm size (Paolisso et al., 1988). The consequences to women have been lower incomes and a decline in their status and the nutrition within their families.

The point here is that while the addition of women's labor to the cultivation of commercial or export crops may raise total household income, that income is not necessarily shared. As a rule, men are the primary beneficiaries of agricultural diversification projects. Research has shown that benefits to the male head of household do not necessarily accrue to other household members.

At the same time, commercial and export agriculture have offered women off-farm employment in local agribusinesses and packing plants. Employers prefer to hire women in agro-processing industries where importance is attached to having a docile work force and regular work attendance. As is the case with women who work as seasonal laborers, women in agro-processing industries are seldom paid the minimum wage, even when it is mandated by law. In general, agro-industries that employ women are characterized by shorter training times, lower rates of pay, difficult and often unhealthy working conditions, and seasonal fluctuations resulting in unemployment (Paolisso et al., 1988). Nevertheless, employment in agro-industries does enable women to retain control of their income, contributing to financial independence and a higher status within the family.

Women and Education

Education for women is an equity issue, but education and literacy also exercise important direct and indirect influences on women's family relationships, childbearing, and economic opportunities (Chaney, 1984). Educated women tend to marry later and have fewer children. Their children are more likely to attend school and to be healthier and better nourished.

In Latin America as a whole school enrollment for girls nearly doubled between 1965 and 1977 at primary and secondary levels (IDB, 1982). Even though Central American women's access to education has increased, particularly in urban areas, a higher percentage of women than men are still illiterate. In rural areas of all countries save Costa Rica (17.5 percent in 1973), illiteracy rates for women are high, the highest being 77.6 percent in Guatemala, also in 1973 (Gallardo and López, 1986). A 1981 study of a 5,000-member peasant women's federation in Honduras noted illiteracy rates of the membership to be 33 percent in the department of Occidente, 25 percent in Yoro and 57 percent in Choluteca (de Soriano, 1981). El Salvador, Guatemala, Honduras, and Nicaragua show extreme contrasts between rural and urban literacy rates, suggesting that rural education has been neglected in favor of the cities and towns.

Low literacy rates for women have a common denominator in poverty and cultural mores. Women's low enrollment and high drop-out rates in rural areas result from the continuing belief that it is more important to educate boys than girls. This is especially true in the Indian communities of the Guatemalan highlands, where far fewer women than men speak Spanish.

Cultural mores also influence curriculum. Curricula for boys and girls often differ at the postprimary level. Young men study math, science, and industrial and agricultural arts; young women enroll in home economics or commercial courses. Vocational training programs for women still focus overwhelmingly on traditional skills: handicrafts, food processing and preparation, how to operate industrial sewing machines, and secretarial skills. Nonformal education courses, the highly touted answer for rural women (and men) who have had limited schooling, are also dominated by traditional handicraft and homemaking skills rather than the skills women need to carry out their agricultural or commercial responsibilities. Only Costa Rica has more equitable vocational training policies.

The largest differences in registration between men and women are found at the university level, where far fewer women than men are enrolled in relation to their numbers in the total population. The percentage of women registered at universities in the region ranges from a high of 25 percent in Costa Rica to a low of 6 percent in Guatemala, with the other countries showing 13 percent (Honduras), 11 percent (Nicaragua), and 9 percent (El Salvador) (Sivard, 1985). At universities the majority of women are found in faculties that train them for traditional careers—education, liberal arts, social work, nursing—rather than for scientific, industrial, or commercial careers. There are signs of change, however. The number of women lawyers and economists is increasing, and the Central American Institute for Business Administration (INCAE), the graduate school of business with campuses in Nicaragua and Costa Rica, reports a quantum jump in women students over the past few years. Women are also entering the fields of statistics, computer programming, television, and journalism.

Although more women have entered universities in Central America in the past 20 years, they (and their male counterparts) represent a minuscule number in relation to the total numbers of men and women in the region. Still, these small numbers hold implications for government planning and policy. The growth of the pool of educated women suggests that there is less reason today to exclude qualified women from the top levels of politics and government (Chaney, 1984).

Women's Health

Average life expectancy at birth for women in Central America ranges from a high of 70 in Costa Rica to 61 in El Salvador, and 55 in Honduras, Nicaragua, and Guatemala (IACW, 1985a). Because of environmental conditions such as absence of clean water and scarce food supply, rural women tend to have higher malnutrition and death rates than urban women.

Infant mortality rates have fallen steadily since 1970, but are still high in El Salvador, Guatemala, Honduras, and Nicaragua where they register at, respectively, 71, 81, 84, and 67 for each 1,000 live births (Chaney, 1984). Higher life expectancies and lower infant mortality rates are the result of maternal/child health care and feeding programs, better control of infectious diseases, vaccination campaigns, antibiotics, and the eradication of malaria, at least in some areas.

Public health budgets throughout the region have suffered because of the economic crisis, particularly the provision of primary health care services to rural areas. Health budgets in 1983 as a percentage of the national budget ranged from a high of 11 percent in Honduras to a low of 3 percent in Costa Rica (Gallardo and López, 1987). Modern medical services do not exist in most rural areas, and doctors tend to settle in the larger towns and cities. In general, women's access to government-subsidized health services is less than men's because of the link between social security health programs and employment in the formal sector.

Yet women are the principal users, providers, and promoters of health care. They are responsible for the nutrition of their families, the growth of their children, and for household hygiene, clothing, and first aid. They decide when to seek medical services. As a rule, they put the health of their children and other family members before their own, and often do not seek medical attention for themselves until they are seriously ill.

The burdens of the double day (rural or urban workloads in addition to household responsibilities and child care) place a tremendous physical and mental strain on poor women. As a result, they are predisposed to illnesses that are different in nature from those that affect men. They are more prone to diseases transmitted by water, to accidents and illnesses caused by the use of toxic chemicals in the home, and to a wide range of problems related to their reproductive roles. These include sexually transmitted diseases that cause infertility and infections, the after-effects of clandestinely induced abortions, the physical toll of adolescent and repeated pregnancies, cancers of the reproductive system, contraceptive side effects, and malnutrition and anemia. The unequal distribution of food within the family favors men and male children and takes a heavy nutritional toll on female children and their mothers, who are likely to be pregnant or lactating.

Central America has the highest crude birthrates in Latin America. In El Salvador, Honduras, and Nicaragua, average rates of six or more births per woman are found, while rates almost as high are found in Guatemala. In rural areas of El Salvador and Honduras, total fertility rates (TFR) rise to an average of over eight births per woman, whereas the TFR for women in Costa Rica is 3.5 (Chaney, 1984). Fertility and mortality are inextricably intertwined in that two of the key factors contributing to high mortality rates are high fertility and the close spacing of births, resulting in premature deliveries, weak and underformed infants, and maternal mortality. Rapid population growth in the region has increased pressures on land, labor markets, and the ability of governments to provide services (Diaz Briquets, 1986).

Four countries support family planning, either to reduce fertility for demographic reasons (El Salvador, Guatemala) or to fulfill human rights and health objectives with fertility reduction as an important by-product (Costa Rica, Honduras). Nicaragua has no national family planning policy (Padilla et al., 1987).

Existing family planning service delivery systems are erratic and sorely limited in rural areas. The most recent acceptance rates for the percentage of married women using contraception are: 48 percent in El Salvador, 25 percent in Guatemala, 35 percent in Honduras, and 65 in Costa Rica. The 1977 estimate for Nicaragua was nine percent (IBRD, 1987). These percentages do not reflect the large numbers of women who are cohabiting with men to whom they are not married.

Nor do family planning policies include abortion, despite the fact that it is widely used as a method of birth control. In Central America abortion is either illegal or tolerated only to save the mother's life. Induced abortion, however, probably accounts for the highest proportion of maternal deaths in all five countries, and is the most frequent cause of hospital admissions among women (IACW, 1985a).

Except for a few women doctors, most women in the field of public health are nurses, midwives, and community health workers. Their participation at the policy and decisionmaking levels in ministries of health is restricted and sporadic. In particular, family planning is a male-dominated field.

Women, Politics, and the Law

Women gained the right to vote in all five countries between 1949 (Costa Rica) and 1965 (Guatemala), and are voting in increasing numbers when elections are held (Sivard, 1985). Participation in the political process, however, has not advanced much beyond voting. Women do not hold more than 10 percent of the positions in national legislatures (Sivard, 1985). Data available in 1985, for example, showed that 7 percent of the Costa Rican and Honduran and 10 percent of El Salvadoran legislators were women

(Sivard, 1985). Today five women serve in the Costa Rican legislature, seven in the Guatemalan (including one Indian woman), and 25 in the Honduran (8 permanent deputies and 17 substitutes or *suplentes*). There is also one woman cabinet minister each in Costa Rica, Honduras, and Nicaragua, and two in Guatemala.

Women are not leaders of political parties, nor are they represented among the national leadership of trade unions or cooperative federations. Occasionally women are officers of a cooperative at the community level. Most political parties and organizations with political agendas assign a separate role to women. Women participate in political life through special wings of the parties, unions, and cooperative federations. An exception is Nicaragua, where the official women's organization, AMNLAE, is a separate arm of party policy.

In general, official political support for women's issues has been demonstrated by the establishment of government women's bureaus. As a rule, these offices are underfunded, understaffed, and have limited political clout. Although they have carried out worthwhile projects, their influence on planning and policy has been minimal.

There are reasons why women's political participation has been limited. Multiple roles in the household and in production and reproduction limit their time. Cultural mores limit their incentive to compete politically. Myths about women's roles follow them, in particular the strong tradition that public affairs are exclusively men's domain and that women's participation in public life should be limited to the areas society has identified as "appropriate" for them. Most important, men hold the reins of power and finance (Sivard, 1985). Perhaps because of their exclusion from political participation, women in Central America share a history of collective action. Injustice has brought out "unsuspected capacities for indignation, resistance, and common action" (Hirschman, 1984). Women's actions usually have been spontaneous, directed against the state, and have entailed marches or demonstrations to protest rising prices (Costa Rica), human rights violations (El Salvador, Guatemala, and Honduras), or to make political demands (Honduras and Nicaragua). Nicaraguan women played a critical role in the revolution that overthrew Anastasio Somoza in 1979. Although collective action provides important educational and organizing experiences to women, it is no substitute for participation in political parties and other organizations with political agendas.

All Central American countries except Guatemala have guaranteed equal rights for women in their national constitutions (Sivard, 1985). But the seven international agreements relating to gender equality from the 1950s to the 1980s better illustrate the extent of adherence by Central American governments to the concept of women's equality, as table 8.1 demonstrates. Governments that have ratified conventions agree to be legally bound and to take specific actions to comply with the provisions (Sivard, 1985).

The road is long, however, from the ratification or signing of an international convention to the taking of legislative action and the initiation of legal reforms. Laws that do benefit women, such as the right to be paid the minimum wage (where it exists), are not enforced. Perhaps the most burdensome restrictions on women in Central America derive from laws limiting their access to land and other income-producing property.

Some action has been taken. Costa Rica has revised its family code, and Costa Rica, El Salvador, and Nicaragua recognize mutual parental authority. In 1981 Nicaragua gave both parents equal obligations to children and the sharing of housework. Equal obligations or access, however, do not guarantee a more equal sharing of responsibility. Nor is the implementation of laws that protect women who are separated or divorced, or that protect women from domestic violence, automatic. In Costa Rica, for example, women's organizations have played an important role in bringing child-support and battered wives' cases to court.

Table 8.1   Central American Ratification of Selected International Conventions on the Rights of Women (R—ratified or acceded; S—signed but did not ratify)

	Costa Rica	El Salvador	Honduras	Guatemala	Nicaragua
Elimination of all Discrimination	S	R	R	R	R
Equal Political Rights	R	S	—	R	—
Equal Marriage Rights	—	—	—	R	—
Equality in Education	R	—	—	R	—
Equal Pay for Equal Value	R	—	R	R	R
Maternity Protection	—	R	—	—	—
Equality in Employment	R	—	R	R	R

Summary and Recommendations

Summary

The improvement of women's well-being and status is essential to the establishment of more democratic and equitable societies in Central America. Women in the region are poor and are constrained legally and culturally from full participation in the social, political, and economic lives of their countries. Their considerable gains in education and their increasing entry into the wage labor force have not resulted in improved economic opportunities. Women continue to be paid less than men, and have less access to health and other benefits. They also have less access to credit and technical assistance. Nor have they benefited more than minimally from agrarian reforms. Their right to own land and other income-generating property is restricted.

In rural areas illiteracy rates are much higher for women. Girls who do go beyond primary school are likely to find role stereotyping that results in a narrower range of occupational choices. In general, the small percentage of women who attend universities are concentrated in faculties that train women for traditional careers: nursing, social work, education, and liberal arts.

In addition to participation in the work force, women are responsible for domestic chores and child care, a particularly heavy burden for the growing number of women-headed households. Women have limited access to day-care facilities and to health services, notably reproductive health care, especially in rural areas.

Too few professional women are involved at the policy and decisionmaking levels of public and private entities. Their participation at the managerial level in the private sector is minimal. In government it is confined to mid-level, primarily to those agencies dealing with women's traditional concerns—health, education, and welfare. In labor unions, political parties, and cooperative federations, women are sidelined into special wings. Few women hold elective office in the region and there are only five women cabinet ministers in all five countries.

Central American women have not been passive in the face of these constraints. Increasingly, they are organizing, articulating their demands and developing their own programs with support from external donor agencies. In so doing, they are challenging the status quo. Although women's priorities differ among classes and cultures, women are beginning to come together around issues such as peace, human rights, legal discrimination, access to resources, and quality reproductive health care. One of the most significant outcomes of the UN Decade for Women has been the willingness of women to work together, recognizing that they must organize to pressure for change. Women represent a strong and positive force for change in the region.

Recommendations

Improving women's access to resources and opportunities in Central America is premised on three conditions. First, there must be peace in the region, or at the very least a winding-down of active hostilities. Economic conditions cannot improve or social services expand in countries whose economies are devastated by war and weighed down by heavy debt burdens. Second, there must be a commitment to social change that will produce a policy environment responsive to equity issues in general, and to the needs of the poor in particular, including poor women. Third, women must be specifically targeted as beneficiaries of programs to improve access to resources. There is ample evidence to show that benefits to male heads of households do not automatically "trickle down" within families.

Legal Reforms. A likely place for Central American governments to begin to improve women's access to resources and opportunities will be to ratify the international conventions relating to gender equality that they have not ratified, and to begin to translate the principles into action. This will require the implementation of existing laws that benefit women, such as the right to be paid the minimum legal wage; the reform of others that are discriminatory, in particular restrictions on women's owning land and other income-generating property; and the passing of new laws, such as laws guaranteeing women's right to equal pay for equal work.

Education. Women should be guaranteed at least six years of primary school and increased access to secondary education as well. Primary education and literacy and equivalency programs should be expanded in general, but priority should be given to rural areas because of the higher illiteracy rates and the critical long-term impact of literacy on women's employment options. Girls who do go beyond primary school must be offered the opportunity to choose nontraditional subjects and receive training in technical, managerial, and leadership skills to broaden work options. Nonformal education programs which can be carried out by governments and nongovernmental organizations alike need to be expanded and, more importantly, reconstituted to increase agricultural and commercial skills.

The Workplace. The veil of invisibility must be stripped from women's contributions to the economy. Census and government labor offices should collect data on women's productive activities and desegregate statistics by gender. Women in the informal sector need access to credit—small, short-term loans that offer low transaction costs and no collateral requirements. Financial reforms to open up access to credit should include the development of intermediate credit institutions and programs to leverage women and men into formal sector borrowing. This will entail a commitment at the policy level to improve the financial services available to both sexes. Governments should establish or support financial extension services capable of assisting women to apply for credit, including help with application procedures and negotiations, and technical assistance for business development. Nongovernmental organizations and cooperative federations that have had experience managing revolving loan funds can play an important intermediary role.

Women in the wage labor force should receive equal pay for equal work, the minimum wage where it is mandated by law, and access to health and other benefits. Child care services should be expanded in urban areas, and laws requiring companies with a given number of employees to provide day-care services should be implemented. Finally, women who wish to organize or to join trade unions should have the right to do so without jeopardizing their job security.

Women should qualify as beneficiaries of agrarian reforms with equal access to land and services and the opportunity to become members of agrarian reform cooperatives. They should have access to new technologies, and to credit and technical assistance for their agricultural activities, from extension services, nongovernmental organizations and rural cooperative federations. Programs should be undertaken to bring potable water, electricity, and roads to rural areas.

Health. The nutritional and general health levels of women must be raised. Primary and preventive health care programs should be expanded, particularly in rural areas. These programs should include quality reproductive health care: access to safe contraception, infertility counseling, treatment of sexually transmitted diseases and other gynecological problems, and maternal/child services. The high mortality rate of women as a result of septic abortion should be addressed through the universal expansion of family planning services. Women's organizations can play a critical role in the expansion of such services.

Participation. Qualified women should be brought into decisionmaking positions in government, the private sector, labor unions, cooperative federations, and nongovernmental organizations. Women should be encouraged to run for public office and should be supported financially and politically.

Donor agencies have a role to play in supporting programs that improve women's access and opportunities, both at governmental and nongovernmental levels. In particular, continuing financial support, including technical assistance, should be provided to women's organizations that are working to better the status of poor women in the region.

Finally, in implementing these recommendations priority access to services and productive resources should be given to the most vulnerable female population: women who are heads of households with small children, especially those who have been widowed and/or displaced by civil war.

Conclusion

If peace should come, or if regional hostilities should wind down, the reconstruction period offers an *apertura* for women. New initiatives to raise economic standards and meet basic needs provide an opportunity to assure women more equal access to resources, and to involve qualified women, as well as women's organizations, in policy formulation and decisionmaking. The reconstruction period could bring access and opportunities together in a meaningful way. Whether or not this will happen will depend on many factors, not the least of which will be the willingness of public and private entities to share resources and power more equitably. As noted in the introduction, economic equality for women threatens men's access to already scarce resources. Since greater equality within the family is a power-sharing issue, it is likely to be the most difficult to address. Traditional roles are reinforced by both family and community and are the most resistant to change. But the countries of Central America cannot build more equitable and participatory societies by continuing to exclude the more than 50 percent of the population who are female. And without the participation of women, all development efforts are weakened.

References

Aviel, JoAnn Fagot (n.d.). "Changing the Political Role of Women." San Francisco, Calif.: California State University.

Balakrishnan, Revathi, and Francille Firebaugh (1987). "Profile of Women-Headed Households in El Salvador." Working Paper 87-02. Columbus, Ohio: Ohio State University.

Bossen, Laurel Herbenar (1984). *The Redivision of Labor: Women and Economic Choice in Four Guatemalan Communities*. Albany, N.Y.: State University of New York Press.

Buvinic, Mayra (1984). *Projects for Women in the Third World: Explaining Their Misbehavior.* Washington, D.C.: International Center for Research on Women.

Buvinic, Mayra, Nadia H. Youssef, and Barbara Von Elm (1978). *Women-Headed Households: The Ignored Factor in Development Planning.* Washington, D.C.: International Center for Research on Women.

Buvinic, Mayra, and Nadine R. Horenstein (1986). *Women's Issues in Shelter, Agriculture, Training, and Institutional Development: Assessment for* USAID/*Costa Rica.* Washington, D.C.: International Center for Research on Women.

Cairns, Gail (1984). *Law and the Status of Women in Latin America: A Survey.* New York: Center for Population and Family Health, Columbia University.

Chaney, Elsa (1984). *Women of the World: Latin America and the Caribbean.* Washington, D.C.: Bureau of the Census/U.S. Department of Commerce and Office of Women in Development/ USAID.

Deere, Carmen Diana (1983). "Cooperative Development and Women's Participation in the Nicaragua Agrarian Reform." Paper presented to AWID Conference, Washington, D.C.

——— (1985). "Rural Women and State Policy: The Latin American Agrarian Reform Experience." *World Development* 13, no. 9, 1037–53.

Deere, Carmen Diana, and Magdalena Leon, eds. (1987). *Rural Women and State Policy: Feminist Perspectives on Latin American Agricultural Development.* Boulder, Colo.: Westview Press.

Diaz Briquets, Sergio (1986). *Conflict in Central America: The Demographic Dimension.* Washington, D.C.: The Population Reference Bureau.

Flora, Cornelia B. (n.d.). "Women in Latin America: A Force for Tradition or Change?" Mimeo. Inter-American Commission of Women Library.

Food and Agricultural Organization of the United Nations (1985). *Women in Developing Agriculture.* Rome: FAO.

Fordham, Miriam (1982). "Women's Economic Strategies in Southern Honduras." Paper presented to annual meeting of the American Anthropological Association, Washington, D.C.

Gallardo, María Eugenia, and José Roberto López (1986). *Centroamérica: La Crisis en Cifras.* San José: IICA/FLACSO.

Harrison, Polly (1981). "Women in Development Strategy." Prepared for USAID/Tegucigalpa, Honduras.

Hirschman, Albert O. (1984). *Getting Ahead Collectively: Grassroots Experiences in Latin America.* Elmsford, N.Y.: Pergamon Press.

Inter-American Commission of Women (1985a). *Status of Women in the Americas at the End of the Decade (1976–1985): An Overview and General Strategy for the Year 2000.* Washington, D.C.: General Secretariat/Organization of American States.

———— (1985b). *Situation Pertaining to Women as of 1985: Socio-economic Situation and Status of Women.* Washington, D.C.: General Secretariat/Organization of American States.

———— (1985c). *Situation Pertaining to American Women as of 1985: State of Health and Nutrition of Women.* Washington, D.C.: General Secretariat/Organization of American States.

Inter-American Development Bank (1982). "Women in the Economic Development of Latin America." Chapter 5 in *Economic and Social Progress in Latin America: 1980-1981.* Washington, D.C.: IDB.

International Bank for Reconstruction and Development (1984). *World Development Report 1984.* New York, N.Y.: Oxford University Press.

———— (1987). *Social Indicators of Development.* Washington, D.C.: Social Economic Data Division/IBRD.

Joekes, Susan, Margaret Lycette, Lisa McGowan, and Karen Searle (1988). *Women and Structural Adjustment: Part II: Technical Document.* Washington, D.C.: International Center for Research on Women.

Lastarria-Cornhiel, Susana (1988). "Female Farmers and Agricultural Production in El Salvador." Forthcoming in *Development and Change.*

Leon, Magdalena, and Carmen Diana Deere (1980). "The Study of Rural Women and the Development of Capitalism in Colombian Agriculture." In *Women in Rural Development: Critical Issues,* pp. 21–25. Geneva: International Labor Office.

Leon, Magdalena (1987). "Colombian Agricultural Policies and the Debate on Policies Toward Rural Women." In *Rural Women and State Policy,* pp. 84–104. Boulder, Colo.: Westview Press.

Lycette, Margaret A. (1984). *Improving Women's Access to Credit in the Third World: Policy and Project Recommendations.* Washington, D.C.: International Center for Research on Women.

Madden, Rosemary (1984). "Aspectos Jurídicos Sobre la Incorporación de la Mujer a Programas de Desarrollo Agrario del IDA." San José: Agrarian Reform Institute.

MIDEPLAN and IDA (1984). *Taller Sobre la Participación de la Mujer Campesina en Actividades Productivas del Sector Primario: Síntesis y Recomendaciones Finales.* San José: Agrarian Reform Institute.

Mones, Belkis, and Lydia Grant (1987). "Agricultural Development, the Economic Crisis, and Rural Women in the Dominican Republic." In *Rural Women and State Policy*, pp. 35–50. Boulder, Colo.: Westview Press.

Norem, Rosalie H., and Eric A. Abbot (1983). "The Economic Contribution of Women to Family Household Systems in Central America." Paper presented to AWID Conference, Washington, D.C.

Padilla, Martha Luz, Clara Murguialday, and Ana Criquillon (1987). "Impact of the Sandinista Agrarian Reform on Rural Women's Subordination." In *Rural Women and State Policy*, pp. 24–141. Boulder, Colo.: Westview Press.

Paolisso, Michael, Meg Berger, and Karen Searle (1988). "Guatemalan Women in Development: Opportunities and Constraints." Draft. Washington, D.C.: International Center for Research on Women.

Safilios Rothschild, Constantina (1984). *Women and the Agrarian Reform in Honduras.* New York: Population Council.

Sherman, Nancy (1984). "Costa Rican Women on the Threshold of Change." Prepared for Canadian International Development Agency. San José: Canadian Embassy.

Sivard, Ruth (1985). *Women: A World Survey.* Washington, D.C.: World Priorities.

de Soriano, Flor Osejo (1981). *Estudio Institucional: FEHMUC.* Tegucigalpa: ASEPADE.

Thomas, Sandra T. (1977). *Women of the Americas: Political Participation Emerging in an Era of Change: Ways to Promote Broader Political Participation Among Women.* Washington, D.C.: Inter-American Commission of Women/General Secretariat/Organization of American States.

Von Braun, Joachim, and Eileen Kennedy (1986). *Commercialization of Subsistence Agriculture: Income and Nutritional Effects in Developing Countries.* Washington, D.C.: International Food Policy Research Institute.

Wiarda, Ieda Siquiera, and Judith F. Helzner (1981). *Women, Population and International Development in Latin America: Persistent Legacies and New Perceptions for the 1980s.* Occasional Papers Series no. 13. Amherst, Mass: International Areas Studies Program, University of Massachusetts at Amherst.

Yudelman, Sally W. (1987). *Hopeful Openings: A Study of Five Women's Development Organizations in Latin America and the Caribbean.* West Hartford, Conn.: Kumarian Press.

Part 2

The International Economic Context

Chapter 9

Central American Debt: Genuine Case-by-Case Studies
Richard Feinberg

Introduction

The debt profile of Central America has deteriorated sharply during the 1980s. The region has borrowed heavily, while its ability to service debt has failed to keep pace as annual production and export revenues have stagnated. Two nations—Nicaragua and Costa Rica—have debt burdens that they cannot service while maintaining adequate import levels. However, the three other countries have debts that are still manageable, provided that they cease to acquire new debt obligations without improving their ability to service them. The future of Central America could resemble the discouraging present of many other Latin American nations that have been transferring 3–6 percent of their gross domestic product (GDP) to their creditors.[1] In other words, highly indebted countries make interest and amortization payments well in excess of new credit inflows. These net outflows are depriving the major Latin American debtors of one-quarter to one-third of their savings, and are undermining future growth by depressing investment.

Payments to commercial banks from Brazil, Mexico, and other major debtors account for the lion's share of net financial transfers. Because Central America (except Costa Rica) has not borrowed heavily from commercial banks, it is not suffering from a comparable negative financial transfer.

On the contrary, Central America (again, excluding Costa Rica) continues to receive external finance in excess of its debt payments. The region is benefiting from its relatively low indebtedness to private banks and the special attention it is receiving from foreign assistance agencies in both capitalist and socialist countries. For El Salvador, Honduras, and Guatemala, capital inflows exceed debt service requirements, and for Nicaragua they exceed actual debt payments. In contrast, Costa Rica, with its large proportion of commercial bank debts, is burdened with debt service obligations that if met would fully consume new capital inflows.

If a structural debt crisis is characterized by a chronic negative resource transfer, Central America as a region is an exception to the Latin American condition. But the trends are worrisome and unsustainable. And the region is heavily dependent on massive aid flows. In the absence of these official flows, Central America would find itself facing an overwhelming negative resource transfer problem.

To date, the industrial nations that manage the international debt strategy claim to be operating on a case-by-case basis, but in fact a single basic formula has been applied to all countries across the board. An examination of Central America's debt problems indicates the fallacy of this universalism and argues instead for a more differentiated set of approaches tailored to the particular circumstances of each debtor.

This chapter will divide the region into three categories: the still solvent recipients of official aid (El Salvador, Honduras, and Guatemala), the insolvent recipient of official aid (Nicaragua), and the heavily indebted (Costa Rica). The categories differentiate among nations according to their type of debt (public or private) and their ability to meet debt service obligation.

The chapter will first discuss the processes whereby the various Central American countries accumulated their debts, then describe their current external financial position, and conclude with policy options for external debt management consistent with renewed growth. Appropriate policy responses differ for each category of debtor.

Debt Accumulation

Central America's outstanding, disbursed debt has risen steadily, roughly doubling every five years. From the level of $3.4 billion in 1975 the debt rose to $8.5 billion in 1980, and reached nearly $18 billion by the end of 1986 (table 9.1).

This debt buildup is the result of a complex web of external and internal factors. Over the last decade Central America has suffered severe external shocks. Most notably, the region has been confronted with erratic and often unfavorable international markets for its major commodity exports. The prices of coffee and cotton have fluctuated sharply, while sugar prices have been severely depressed. As a result, the region's terms of trade fell by nearly one-quarter between 1978–84.[2] In addition, the region's export volume (emphasis on "volume") declined during the 1980s; flagging international demand for commodities was compounded by reduced supply capacity in El Salvador and Nicaragua. By 1986, the region's exporters were earning less in foreign exchange than at the start of the decade (table 9.3).

Low commodity earnings meant less import capacity, lower tax revenues, and reduced savings by government and the private sector. Central American governments have sought to compensate for this weak export performance by borrowing. Foreign loans and grants financed badly needed imports, helped reduce government deficits, and partially made up for reduced domestic savings.

Whereas Central American investment declined sharply during the 1980s, domestic savings fell even more drastically. The region's rate of savings as a percentage of GDP fell from 19 percent in 1977 to 10 percent in 1983–84 (table 9.4). The countries turned to tapping external savings to place a floor under investment rates.

Similarly, governments used foreign capital to finance deficits that resulted from shrinking tax bases and increased government spending intended to offset the decline in private-sector activity. The region abandoned its historical commitment to fiscal conservatism, and the ratio of budget deficits to GNP approximately doubled from 1978 to 1983–85 (table 9.5). Political pressures have impeded a return to fiscal discipline, although Costa Rica eventually responded by increasing taxes to reduce its fiscal deficit, and governments in El Salvador and Guatemala had some success in 1986–87 in introducing new tax packages.[3] The Sandinistas raised taxes sharply in Nicaragua, but revenues lagged behind the expenditures for consumer subsidies, security forces, and the defense of a multiple exchange-rate regime.

National investment levels and government spending were higher than they would have been in the absence of external resources. But foreign capital also helped to finance capital flight. The UN Economic Commission for Latin America and the Caribbean (ECLAC) estimates capital flight during the 1980s at over $4.5 billion.[4]

This intimate mesh of external and internal factors produced severe imbalances in the current account of the balance of payments (the difference between exports and imports of goods and services, including interest payments, plus transfers). The region's aggregate current-account deficits surpassed $1.5 billion annually during 1980–85 (table 9.6). These imbalances were financed in part by grants from official donors, which were averaging over $300 million by mid-decade (table 9.6). Most of the deficits, however, were covered by debt finance.

The Debt Burden

The entire region has suffered from adverse commodity prices, high international interest rates, lack of fiscal discipline, and maladjusted exchange rates, while the political strife in El Salvador and Nicaragua affected the economic climate everywhere. However, the relative weight of these factors behind the debt buildup has varied sharply from country to country. Consequently, the size, composition, and relative weight of the debt also differ radically from country to country, dividing the region into three debtor types: the solvent, aid-dependent northern tier states; insolvent, aid-dependent Nicaragua; and Costa Rica, which is heavily indebted to private banks.

The Northern Tier States

The northern tier states (El Salvador, Guatemala, and Honduras) have had substantial deficits in their merchandise and services accounts throughout the 1980s (table 9.6). Reacting negatively to the region's economic and political performance, and as part of their response to the broader Latin American debt crisis, commercial banks not only chose not to finance these current-account deficits but sought to reduce their exposure in Central America. Consequently, the deficits have been covered by official grants and credits. For El Salvador and, to a lesser degree, Honduras, a sizeable portion of the external deficit has been filled by unrequited (non-debt creating) private and official transfers (table 9.6). Despite this generosity, the debts of the three northern tier states have been rising and now equal a significant portion of their stagnating GNP. Since 1980, the debt/GNP ratio for Honduras has risen from about 63 percent to 85 percent; for El Salvador, from 26 percent to 47 percent; and for Guatemala, from 15 percent to 24 percent (table 9.2a).

At first glance the current debt/GNP ratios of El Salvador and Guatemala look alarming. They are in the same league as the other Latin American debtors, whose accumulated debts equal 62 percent of their annual production.[5] Nonetheless, the burden of the northern tier's debts is relatively light.

The northern tier's debt service burden appears high if amortization and interest charges are included. But this is misleading because, under today's implicit rules for the global debt game, most principal is not being repaid. Principal is either formally rescheduled, as in the Paris Club, or is refinanced. A better measure of the debt burden is the interest payments, which generally are made. Because most of the northern tier's debts are owed to official agencies and bear concessional rates (table 9.2), the telling ratios of interest payments to GNP, or interest payments to export earnings, suggest a different story.

The northern tier states have had to turn over considerably less foreign exchange than the big Latin American debtors, whose interest payments have been consuming 3–6 percent of GNP. The ratio of interest payments to GNP for El Salvador and Guatemala has fallen under 2 percent, while Honduras's is 3 percent (table 9.8).

The northern tier's debt service burden appears even lighter when viewed in relation to export earnings. Since foreign trade accounts for a high percentage of these countries' economic activity, debt service consumes a smaller share of export earnings. For these highly open economies, the ratio of interest payments to the export of goods and services does not surpass 15 percent, compared to a Latin American average of 35 percent (table 9.9).

The trend, however, is unfavorable. Export growth has not kept pace with rising debt service requirements. Consequently, since 1980 the ratio of interest payments to export revenues nearly doubled for El Salvador and nearly tripled for Guatemala. At the same time it has risen almost one-third for Honduras between 1980 and 1984–85, but improved in 1986. Larger interest payments reflect the high cost of private debt and the buildup of credit owed to official sources.

Costa Rica

During the late 1970s and early 1980s Costa Rica was hit particularly hard by a deterioration in the terms of trade, while domestic savings dropped by half. The government of the period attempted to maintain living standards by keeping imports flowing, which led to a trade deficit totaling nearly $900 million, or 10 percent of GDP, during 1979–80. The yawning financing gap was closed by borrowing heavily abroad from willing commercial bankers. As rising global interest rates pushed up the cost of the commercial debt, Costa Rica required new credits in order to refinance a portion of debt service.[6]

As a result, Costa Rica is unique in Central America in having a debt profile reminiscent of the larger Latin American nations. Heavily indebted to commercial banks, scheduled interest payments—which are not being made in full—would carve out about one-quarter of export earnings and an astounding 10 percent of GNP (tables 9.8 and 9.9). If fully paid, the interest burden would deprive Costa Rica of over half of its domestic savings. Consequently, Costa Rica has had to balance its trade, since external borrowings are consumed by debt service and no funds remain to finance additional imports. With good reason, successive Costa Rican governments have argued that debt service as currently scheduled is inconsistent with sustained economic recovery.

Costa Rica's problems have not escaped the attention of the international financial community. Costa Rica is the only country in Central America where the International Monetary Fund has been persistently engaged, and where the World Bank has helped to design successive structural adjustment programs. As in the case of other Latin American nations heavily indebted to private banks, loans from the Bretton Woods institutions have combined with small, new credits extracted from commercial banks to support reform programs. These concerted lending packages enable Costa Rica to service old debts. In effect, the commercial banks have been refinancing a modest portion of the interest due them, while loans from official lenders are recycled to cover the remainder.

Recently, Costa Rica decided that since full debt service was inconsistent with adequate rates of growth, it would quietly allow arrears to accumulate against the commercial banks and some official creditors. The government is seeking to restructure its debt service on more favorable terms, so that the level of interest expenditures is consistent with economic recovery.

Nicaragua

Toward the end of the Somoza era Nicaragua took advantage of the boom in international bank lending to increase its liabilities to private creditors to about $750 million (table 9.2).[7] Large-scale borrowing from official sources began in 1979. Initially, foreign assistance was used to finance growth and new investment projects. But as exports plunged and the budget deficit skyrocketed, foreign aid served to narrow these imbalances and finance essential imports.

This massive borrowing, together with an export collapse, has rendered Nicaragua insolvent. Total external debt rose from $1.4 billion in 1979 to an estimated $5.3 billion (excluding arrears) in 1986—more than double the shrinking GNP—while exports dropped from $700 million to $239 million (tables 9.1 and 9.3). Required debt service would consume well over 100 percent of export earnings. Required interest payments alone would eat up over half of export earnings.[8]

Not surprisingly, Nicaragua has fallen deeply into arrears. U.S. regulators have classified commercial bank loans to Nicaragua "value-impaired," requiring banks to set aside reserves against losses. Nicaragua is also far behind in payments to the World Bank, the Inter-American Development Bank, and many bilateral lenders. Actual interest payments during 1983–85 averaged about 11 percent of exports.[9]

De facto default has not prevented Nicaragua from receiving new grants and credits from politically sympathetic sources. Some Western donors remain willing to continue disbursements so long as Nicaragua makes token payments, and Nicaragua has turned increasingly to socialist nations for financial support. As a result of this continued inflow, and its decision to only partially service its debts, Nicaragua continues to benefit from a substantial net transfer of resources.

Differentiated Solutions

The common thread running through the otherwise distinctive stories of the northern tier states, Costa Rica, and Nicaragua is that foreign borrowing has not translated into economic growth. Most importantly, export earnings have failed to expand commensurate with the accumulating debt. Nicaragua and Costa Rica are already in substantial arrears. The northern tier nations began with lower debt service ratios, but they too will eventually slip into nonpayment unless their rates of GNP and export growth accelerate.

What is needed is a new approach to foreign capital inflows that stimulates rather than retards stronger economic performance in Central America. Also needed is a debt strategy that responds to the particular financial conditions and export prospects of each nation.

The ready provision of foreign assistance has at times enabled governments to postpone necessary economic adjustments. U.S. aid in particular has at times placed security objectives over and above economic rationality. Liberal loan availability has enabled countries to delay exchange-rate adjustments, to postpone financial market reform, and to avoid tax increases.[10] Whether such policies actually serve U.S. political interests is debatable, but they have certainly contributed to the worsening debt situation.

Rather than foster economic inefficiency and the evasion of economic responsibility, foreign capital inflows should stimulate sustainable, growth-oriented economic reforms. The multilateral financial institutions have less partisan political interests and more economic expertise than bilateral agencies. If they were given the authority, the multilateral agencies could work with the Central American nations to design mutually agreeable economic reform packages.

As the Central American Peace Agreement ("Arias Plan") requires, the five Central American nations could jointly draw up and present a plan for economic recovery to the donor community. This broad design could include sub-plans for the economies of each nation. The donors, bilateral and multilateral, could organize themselves into a consortium to jointly consider the Central American presentation. Such procedures would be multilateral on both the donor and recipient ends.[11]

Under the leadership of the World Bank and the International Monetary Fund, the donor consortium could estimate the short- and medium-term financing requirements of each nation consistent with an adequate rate of economic growth. The exact mix of new financing and debt relief would vary from country to country, depending on existing debt structure and growth prospects.

To date, the international debt strategy has claimed to be operating on a case-by-case basis, but in fact the same formula has been applied to all countries. Regardless of the weight of their debt obligations or future export prospects, all countries have been told that they should make timely interest payments as part of a strategy aimed at regaining access to private capital markets. Export-led growth has been universally prescribed as the best method for managing debt and for becoming creditworthy. This strategy makes sense for those countries that can meet their interest obligations and that have favorable export prospects. It makes sense for those countries whose accumulated debts are still small in relation to their economic base, and for countries that have a reasonable chance of impressing private markets. But it does not make sense for countries that have no hope of regaining access to private capital markets in the foreseeable future, and can service interest only at the expense of present investment and future growth.

The international debt strategy has recently been modified to include a more flexible "menu" of options that includes traditional balance of payments loans; secured project loans that can be secured by collateral; short-term, self-liquidating trade finance; debt swaps, in which banks either sell their loans for cash or exchange them for an equity investment; and exit bonds, which are bought by creditors who do not wish to participate in future loan packages, and which may bear concessional rates of interest. This "menu" could be extended to include other forms of debt restructuring and relief, including interest-rate capitalization, which permits debtors to avoid immediate payment of a portion of the interest and roll the delayed payments into the loan principal; below-market interest rates, through which the creditors in effect provide concessional finance; debt writedowns, whereby the principal is reduced in value; securitization, which permits the transformation of loans into fixed-rate instruments; payment of debt service in local currency; and contingency clauses, which provide for reductions in debt service when the debtor nation suffers unforeseen external shocks. In light of an assessment by the IMF and World Bank of each country's situation and prospects, creditors could select, in negotiation with the debtor nation, an appropriate choice of menu items.

The international commercial banks have positioned themselves to absorb losses on their Third World loans by bolstering their general loan loss reserves and capital.[12] More specifically, U.S. government regulators have declared loans to Nicaragua and Costa Rica "value-impaired," requiring U.S. banks to set aside specific reserves against these loans. Many non-U.S. banks have also undertaken such cautionary measures. The banks are financially and psychologically prepared to accept losses on Nicaraguan and Costa Rican debts, although they may wish to postpone formal recognition of these losses until the outlines of a solution to the larger Third World debt problem are clarified.

When banks accept reduced debt service, they are absorbing a portion— but only a portion—of the burden of adjusting Central America's external finance. The banks will pass on some of those costs to the U.S. Treasury in the form of reduced tax liabilities, and perhaps to other borrowers in the form of slightly higher interest rates. Industrial-country governments will bear their portion of the adjustment as they continue to provide official finance, which Central American governments will use to service the remaining debts owed to private lenders.

With or without formal debt relief, the international banks are unlikely in the near future to extend substantial new credits to nations they do not consider creditworthy. At best, the banks will offer short-term credits to facilitate an expansion of trade. Even then they may seek to reduce risk through official guarantees. Until their balance of payments is considerably strengthened, Nicaragua and Costa Rica, as well as the rest of Central America, will have to rely primarily on official finance to meet external financing needs.

Debt relief can, however, lay the foundation for renewed creditworthiness by creating the conditions for growth, provided that the developing nation saves and invests wisely. Paradoxically, it is precisely by the reduction of old debt that the debtor nation can eventually regain creditworthiness. By granting partial debt relief, the creditors also make it more likely that the debtor nation will be able to service the remaining debt.

A genuine case-by-case approach would conclude that the northern tier states of Central America may face occasional liquidity problems but are not yet trapped in a severe debt crisis. They can absorb more debt, provided that they use it productively. In contrast, Costa Rica is saddled with scheduled interest payments that are an overwhelming obstacle to sustained economic growth. The interests of the international financial community as a whole, as well as those of Costa Rica, would be best served by granting limited debt relief. Nicaragua, another singular case, is bankrupt, and private as well as some official donors can expect repayment of only a fraction of their loans.

Northern Tier States

For the northern tier nations, debt service ratios are still manageable without debt relief. Principal payments have needed and will sometimes need restructuring, but interest on existing debt can be paid without impairing growth prospects. The ability to absorb new interest-bearing debt will be a function of export growth, tied in turn to productive use of new credits.

None of the northern tier states can expect to receive much new private bank lending. The northern tier states may attract some direct investment that will stimulate exports, but the associated financial inflows are not likely to be great. So the northern tier will remain dependent on official capital inflows for some time.

The bilateral-multilateral aid mix, however, can be made more effective through a shift toward the multilaterals, provided that governments are willing and able to undertake economic reform programs. The Bretton Woods institutions will only provide significant resources if governments themselves commit to policies on exchange rates, trade policies, and fiscal management that hold the promise of generating a self-sustaining and solvent development process.[13]

Costa Rica

Costa Rica's debt situation calls for more innovative measures, since its existing debt service obligations are inconsistent with adequate rates of domestic investment and growth. Therefore it does not fit the official "Baker Plan" strategy. Rather, Costa Rica requires debt relief.

In a ground-breaking precedent, the IMF in October 1987 approved a stand-by arrangement for Costa Rica despite that country's extended arrears to the banks, with no agreement in sight.[14] The World Bank is in the process of approving a trade-reform loan linked to the IMF credit. These actions by the Bretton Woods agencies amount to an implicit acceptance of Costa Rica's request for relief on its private debt.

Official creditors have good reasons for wanting the banks to grant debt relief to Costa Rica. Costa Rica's extraordinarily high debt service ratios mean that it will be many years before it regains creditworthiness on private markets. In the meantime, official creditors face the prospect of indirectly financing Costa Rica's interest payments. This recycling process does not provide Costa Rica with growth capital, and serves neither the interests of Costa Rica nor of its official creditors. Because it fails to strengthen Costa Rica's future ability to service new debts, this recycling game endangers the financial interests of the Bretton Woods agencies.

There are numerous potential "extended menu" items for reducing Costa

Rica's resource transfer to the private markets.[15] Each bank could decide the form of its participation, once the target figures for reducing the net resource drain had been clearly established. Creditor concessions might be made contingent upon Costa Rica's economic fortune—a favorable increase in its terms of trade triggering higher debt payments. Some commercial banks may also wish to extend modest amounts of new credits, which might be granted preferential status.

Nicaragua

So great is Nicaragua's debt burden, and so depressed are its export earnings, that the country will require debt relief from both private and official creditors. And the relief will have to be deep.

Nicaragua's commercial debts are selling for about 5 cents on the dollar on secondary markets (table 9.7). At that rate, Nicaragua could retire its debts at a small cost. In 1987–88, Bolivia negotiated a deal with its commercial creditors that could serve as a precedent. The commercial banks agreed to exchange about half of their outstanding principal claims for cash at 11 cents on the dollar, while interest arrears were forgiven entirely. Several European and Latin American governments provided Bolivia with cash for the transaction, which the IMF helped to administer.

IMF managing director Michel Camdessus has asked donor nations to grant relief to the world's poorest nations, particularly those of sub-Saharan Africa. In addition, foreign assistance agencies are being asked to convert loans into grants, and export credit agencies (who convene in the "Paris Club" framework) to restructure debt at concessional interest rates. Similar preferential treatment should be extended to Nicaragua.

Nicaragua is also in arrears to the World Bank and IDB, but these agencies have strict policies against restructuring debt, no less providing concessional debt relief. A feasible solution is for them to provide enough new credits so that the resource drain is small or even reversed.

All of these solutions, of course, presuppose dramatic reforms in Nicaraguan economic management. The Bolivian debt retirement scheme follows the adoption of a stringent stabilization program that successfully broke the back of a hyperinflation similar to Nicaragua's. The IMF's structural adjustment facility for the poor nations requires that the recipients be on good terms with both of the Bretton Woods agencies. A resumption of lending by the World Bank and IDB would also be contingent on new economic policies in Nicaragua.

A winding-down of the contra war is a precondition for a major improvement in Nicaragua's macroeconomic accounts. Even then, hard bargaining between external creditors and the Nicaraguan authorities lies ahead before order is restored to Nicaragua's external obligations.

Finally, Nicaragua has accumulated substantial arrears against its Central American trading partners. The revitalization of intraregional trade requires that these debts be reorganized. The intraregional creditor nations—Costa Rica and Guatemala—might offer concessional terms to the region's debtor nations—Nicaragua and El Salvador—as part of a new, multilateral approach to Central America's debt problems.

In Nicaragua, and throughout Central America, the adverse trends in debt accumulation as well as in overall economic performance will be rectified only if the political environment improves. Recent political trends give reason for hope. A subtly differentiated debt strategy that responds to the realities of each country can make debt management a tool of economic growth. A successful debt strategy can, in turn, help to reinforce peaceful political processes.

Table 9.1 Central American Foreign Debt (in millions of U.S. dollars)

	1970	1975	1981	1982	1983	1984	1985	1986
Costa Rica	429	1,032	3,360	3,497	3,848	3,955	4,084	4,000
El Salvador	142	502	1,471	1,710	1,891	1,949	2,003	2,120
Guatemala	281	465	1,305	1,560	2,130	2,463	2,644	2,530
Honduras	183	502	1,708	1,986	2,162	2,392	2,615	2,880
Nicaragua	314	889	2,566	3,139	3,788	3,901	4,616	5,260
Central America	1,349	3,390	10,410	11,892	13,819	14,660	15,962	16,790

Note: Figures for 1986 are preliminary.
Source: For 1970 and 1975, CEPAL, "Centroamérica: El Financimiento Externo en la Evolución Económica, 1950–83." For 1981–86, CEPAL, "Central America: Notes on Economic Developments in 1986," March 1987.

Table 9.2 Type of Debt by Creditor (1970–85)

	1970	1975	1980	1981	1982	1983	1984	1985
Costa Rica								
Disbursed Debt	134.3	421.1	1,700.9	2,521.9	2,469.3	3,325.3	3,358.1	3,665.2
Official Credit	95.9	241.5	795.4	938.8	1,105.9	1,436.6	1,459.5	1,745.4
Private Credit	38.3	179.6	905.6	1,313.1	1,363.5	1,888.7	1,898.7	1,919.8
Official/Private	2.5	1.3	0.9	0.7	0.8	0.8	0.8	0.9
El Salvador								
Disbursed Debt	87.7	195.7	527.1	727.1	957.5	1,346.1	1,387.1	1,460.4
Official Credit	70.3	145.1	515.6	716.2	866.4	1,127.3	1,193.1	1,310.0
Private Credit	17.4	50.7	11.6	11.1	91.2	218.8	194.0	150.4
Official/Private	4.0	2.9	44.4	64.5	9.5	5.2	6.2	8.7
Guatemala								
Disbursed Debt	106.3	143.3	548.9	806.6	1,144.0	1,388.6	1,990.7	2,148.1
Official Credit	54.2	128.8	533.8	739.3	997.2	1,095.7	1,194.3	1,355.2
Private Credit	52.1	14.5	15.1	67.3	146.9	292.9	796.4	792.9
Official/Private	1.0	8.9	35.4	11.0	6.8	3.7	1.5	1.7
Honduras								
Disbursed Debt	95.3	267.6	991.2	1,232.9	1,390.5	1,614.3	1,859.9	2,178.4
Official Credit	91.6	247.8	709.2	858.4	1,002.9	1,190.2	1,437.0	1,716.9
Private Credit	3.7	19.9	282.0	374.5	387.6	424.1	423.0	461.5
Official/Private	24.8	12.5	2.5	2.3	2.6	2.8	3.4	3.7
Nicaragua								
Disbursed Debt	146.8	592.7	1,683.3	2,076.3	2,487.5	3,383.0	4,010.2	4,752.8
Official Credit	101.5	246.9	919.4	1,243.6	1,495.3	2,332.4	2,814.8	3,411.2
Private Credit	45.3	345.8	763.9	832.8	992.2	1,050.6	1,195.4	1,341.6
Official/Private	2.2	0.7	1.2	1.5	1.5	2.2	2.4	2.5
Central America								
Disbursed Debt	570.4	1,620.4	5,451.4	7,364.8	8,448.8	11,057.3	12,606.0	14,204.9
Official Credit	413.5	1,010.1	3,473.4	4,496.3	5,467.7	7,182.2	8,098.7	9,538.7
Private Credit	156.8	610.5	1,978.2	2,598.8	2,981.4	3,875.1	4,507.5	4,666.2
Official/Private	6.9	5.3	16.9	14.0	4.2	2.9	2.8	3.5

Source: World Bank, *World Debt Tables, 1986–87*. Includes public and publicly guaranteed long-term debt only; and excludes non-guaranteed private and short-term debt and use of IMF credit.

Table 9.2a   Ratio of Debt to GNP

	1980	1981	1982	1983	1984	1985	1986
Costa Rica	59.7	149.2	159.1	138.2	119.4	126.3	118.7
El Salvador	26.0	33.3	41.3	46.8	43.2	46.8	43.7
Guatemala	14.9	14.9	17.9	20.2	25.8	40.5	35.7
Honduras	62.5	67.0	69.3	74.3	77.7	85.1	84.0
Nicaragua	107.3	112.0	138.0	170.0	188.0	216.0	236.0
Central America	54.1	73.5	85.1	89.9	90.8	102.9	
Latin America	35.3	37.8	47.5	59.7	60.5	62.3	
Highly Indebted	33.2	37.0	45.6	57.3	58.4	60.2	
Ratios:							
CA/LA	1.5	1.9	1.8	1.5	1.5	1.7	
CrNc/Hi	2.5	3.3	3.2	2.6	2.5	2.7	

Source: World Bank, World Debt Tables, 1986–87.

Highly Indebted Countries: Argentina, Bolivia, Brazil, Chile, Colombia, Costa Rica, Ecuador, Ivory Coast, Jamaica, Mexico, Morocco, Nigeria, Peru, the Philippines, Uruguay, Venezuela, Yugoslavia.

Central American average is a mathematical one.

Table 9.3 Merchandise Export Trends (in millions of U.S. dollars)

	1980	1982	1983	1984	1985	1986
Costa Rica						
Value	1,001	873	873	1,008	964	1,070
Volume	100	99	100	119	98	111
(1980 = 100)						
El Salvador						
Value	1,075	700	735	726	679	727
Volume	100	72	84	82	92	82
(1980 = 100)						
Guatemala						
Value	1,520	1,170	1,092	1,132	1,131	1,111
Volume	100	90	84	82	92	82
(1980 = 100)						
Honduras						
Value	850	677	699	746	805	897
Volume	100	86	87	97	106	113
(1980 = 100)						
Nicaragua						
Value	450	383	428	386	302	239
Volume	n/a	n/a	n/a	n/a	n/a	n/a
(1980 = 100)						

Source: ECLAC, *Preliminary Overview of the Latin American Economy, 1986*, table 7, p. 17; World Bank data; Nicaraguan data from IDB: *Economic and Social Progress in Latin America, 1987*, table 43.

Table 9.4 Ratio of Domestic Savings to GDP (in percentages)

	1977	1979	1981	1983	1984
Costa Rica	22	18	12	13	15
El Salvador	25	19	10	9	9
Guatemala	17	13	9	8	8
Honduras	13	20	16	11	12
Nicaragua	18	− 3	6	6	6
Central America	19	15	11	10	10

Source: ECLAC, *CEPAL Review*, no. 28, April 1986, table 11, p. 27.

Table 9.5   Central Government Deficits (as a percentage of GDP)

	1978	1980	1982	1983	1984	1985
Costa Rica	6.0	9.2	3.2	5.2	4.8	4.1
El Salvador	1.7	5.7	7.9	14.6	8.5	6.9
Guatemala	2.3	5.7	6.0	3.9	4.9	3.3
Honduras	8.2	9.5	14.8	13.8	16.6	15.0
Nicaragua	11.7	7.1	14.4	30.0	24.8	22.2
Regional Average	6.0	7.4	9.3	13.5	11.9	10.3

Note: Figures for 1985 are preliminary.
Sources: ECLAC, CEPAL Review, no. 28, April 1986, table 13, p. 30; and ECLAC
communication.

Table 9.7   Secondary Market Value of Central American Debt

Costa Rica	0.22
Guatemala	0.80
Honduras	0.25
Nicaragua	0.05

Source: Salomon Brothers, "Indicative Prices for Less Developed Country Bank Loans,"
November 2, 1987.

Table 9.8   Ratio of Interest Payments to GNP

	1975	1980	1981	1982	1983	1984	1985
Costa Rica	1.2	2.8	4.9	3.7	17.9	7.0	10.1
El Salvador	0.4	0.7	0.9	1.1	1.8	1.8	1.8
Guatemala	0.2	0.4	0.4	0.7	0.8	0.9	1.0
Honduras	0.9	2.5	3.1	3.7	3.0	2.7	3.0
Nicaragua	2.3	1.8	3.6	4.5	1.5	1.3	0.7
Highly Indebted Countries	0.7	1.7	1.8	2.4	2.9	3.1	3.5
Ratios:							
CRNC	1.8	2.3	4.3	4.1	9.7	4.2	5.4
CRNC/Hi	0.00	1.35	2.39	1.71	3.34	1.35	1.54

Highly Indebted Countries: Argentina, Bolivia, Brazil, Chile, Colombia, Costa Rica, Côte
d'Ivoire, Ecuador, Jamaica, Mexico, Morocco, Nigeria, Peru, Philippines, Uruguay,
Venezuela, Yugoslavia.
Note: CRNC is an unweighted average of Costa Rican and Nicaraguan figures. CRNC/Hi is the
ratio of this figure to the interest/GNP for the highly indebted countries.
Source: World Bank, World Debt Tables, 1986–87. Ratio of interest payments to GNP based
on public and publicly owned guaranteed debt.

Table 9.6 Current Account Balances (in millions of U.S. dollars)

	1975	1980	1981	1982	1983	1984	1985	1986
Costa Rica								
Trade Balance	−134.2	−374.3	−88.0	64.1	−45.3	0.8	−65.8	40.7
Net Services	−93.1	−304.1	−348.2	−366.7	−307.6	−297.8	−281.6	−272.5
Official Transfers	0.1	−5.3	−0.1	1.3	13.4	9.0	11.3	11.0
Current Account	−227.2	−683.7	−436.3	−301.3	−339.5	−288.0	−336.1	−220.8
El Salvador								
Trade Balance	−17.7	178.4	−100.3	−121.8	−95.5	−188.6	−216.0	−247.0
Net Services	−102.6	−196.7	−210.4	−201.4	−212.9	−172.5	−156.3	−133.4
Official Transfers	2.3	31.6	21.2	119.0	174.1	189.6	214.2	393.7
Current Account	−11,210.0	13.3	−289.5	−204.2	−134.3	−171.5	−158.1	13.3
Guatemala								
Trade Balance	−31.4	47.2	−248.7	−113.9	35.7	−50.0	−17.0	138.7
Net Services	−112.1	−320.9	−414.9	−347.9	−290.2	−356.1	−249.0	−245.2
Official Transfers	−0.5	1.2	1.4	0.8	0.8	0.7	0.8	73.0
Current Account	−144.0	−272.5	−662.2	−461.0	−253.7	−405.4	−265.2	−33.5
Honduras								
Trade Balance	−62.7	−103.8	−114.8	−4.2	−57.6	−147.8	−74.1	−1.2
Net Services	−67.4	−234.5	−215.4	−254.1	−206.1	−248.6	−260.0	−283.1
Official Transfers	12.6	14.0	18.6	21.0	34.8	69.7	111.1	116.0
Current Account	−117.5	−324.3	−311.6	−237.3	−228.9	−326.7	−223.0	−168.3
Nicaragua								
Trade Balance	−107.2	−352.5	−414.2	−317.5	−349.3	−414.2	−540.0	−581.0
Net Services	−94.5	−182.8	−247.7	−247.9	−292.1	−341.1	−300.2	−304.4
Official Transfers	12.5	122.3	57.1	43.5	75.7	87.9	56.8	100.0
Current Account	−189.2	−413.0	−604.8	−521.9	−565.7	−667.4	−783.4	−785.4

Source: IMF, *International Financial Statistics Yearbook, 1987*; figures for El Salvador, Guatemala, and Nicaragua in 1986 from IDB, *Economic and Social Progress in Latin America, 1987*, tables 6, 41–43, and 48.

Table 9.9 Ratio of Interest Payments to Exports (in percentages)

	1980	1981	1982	1983	1984	1985	1986
Costa Rica	18.0	28.0	36.1	33.0	26.6	27.3	22.7
El Salvador	5.9	7.8	11.9	12.2	12.3	12.6	10.3
Guatemala	5.3	7.6	7.8	8.7	12.3	14.9	14.9
Honduras	10.6	14.4	22.4	16.4	15.8	15.3	12.7
Nicaragua	17.8	21.9	32.1	14.3	12.1	13.0	25.8
Latin America	20.2	28.0	41.0	36.0	35.6	35.2	35.1

Source: ECLAC, *Preliminary Overview of the Latin American Economy, 1986*, p. 22, table 16. Interest payments include those on short-term debt. Figures for 1986 are preliminary.

Notes

1. On the net transfer problem, see Feinberg (1987a).

2. ECLAC (1986), p. 24, table 7.

3. For a review of each nation's monetary and fiscal policies, see Conrow (1987).

4. Cabelleros (n.d.), p. 129, footnote 6. See also Glower (1986).

5. World Bank (1988), p. 265.

6. For a discussion of this period, see Feinberg (1984).

7. Central Bank of Nicaragua (n.d.), pp. 42 and 48 and table 8.

8. Central Bank of Nicaragua (n.d.), tables 8–13.

9. Ibid.

10. See Feinberg and Bagley (1968).

11. An earlier version of this concept appears in Feinberg and Pastor (1984).

12. Williamson (1988).

13. On the roles of the World Bank and the IMF, see Feinberg (1987b).

14. See Feinberg (1987c).

15. For the proposals of one of Costa Rica's debt negotiators, see Charpentier (1987).

References

Cabelleros, Romulo (n.d.). "External Debt in Central America." *CEPAL Review*. No. 32.

Central Bank of Nicaragua (n.d.). In Sevilla, Mario Arana, Richard Stahler-Sholk, and Gerardo

Timossi Bolinsky, "Deuda, Estabilización y Ajuste: La Transformación en Nicaragua, 1979–1986." Mimeographed.

Charpentier, Silvia (1987). "La Deuda Externa: Conflicto de Conflictos." Paper presented at the seminar, "External Debt and Adjustment Programs," San José, Costa Rica, August 5–7.

Conrow, James W. (1987). Testimony before the Subcommittee on International Economic Policy, Committee on Foreign Relations, U.S. Senate, November 12.

Economic Commission for Latin America and the Caribbean (ECLAC) (1986). *CEPAL Review* 28: various tables.

Feinberg, Richard E. (1984). "Costa Rica: End of the Fiesta." In *From Gunboats to Diplomacy*, ed. Richard S. Newfarmer, pp. 102–15. Baltimore: Johns Hopkins University Press.

——— (1987a). "Third World Debt: Toward A More Balanced Adjustment." *Journal of Inter-American Studies and World Affairs* 29(1): 47–55.

——— (1987b). "Multilateral Lending and Latin America." *The World Economy* 10(2): 205–17.

——— (1987c). "A Break for the Third World." *New York Times*, October 9.

Feinberg, Richard E., and Bruce M. Bagley (1986). *Development Postponed: The Political Economy of Central America in the 1980s.* Boulder, Colo.: Westview Press.

Feinberg, Richard E., and Robert A. Pastor (1984). "Far From Hopeless: An Economic Program for Post-War Central America." In *Central America: Anatomy of Conflict*, ed. Robert S. Leiken, pp. 193–218. New York: Pergamon Press.

Glower, Carlos (1986). *La Fuga de Capital en Centroamérica, 1977–84.* Cuadernos de Economía y Finanzas, Banco Centroaméricano de Integración Económica, No. 1, December.

Williamson, Mary L. (1988). "Banking Regulation and Debt: A Policy of Flexible Response." Overseas Development Council *Policy Focus* 1.

World Bank (1988). *World Debt Tables.* 1986–87 edition. Washington, D.C.: World Bank.

Chapter 10

Prospects for Regional Economic Integration
Eduardo Lizano

Introduction

A better future, albeit still a tenuous one, casts its light today upon Central America. It renews our faith in the potential for a better life for the area—a life based on peace, progress, and justice. It is therefore an appropriate moment to consider once again the possibilities that regional economic integration offer as a means to achieve these fundamental aims so dear to the Central American people.

This analysis of regional integration has three sections. First, a review of the main lessons that can be drawn from Central America's experiences with economic integration. Second, an analysis of the internal and external factors that affect present integration prospects. Finally, a reference to the possible role that regional integration could play in the future development of the countries of the region.

I. Reflecting on the Past: Main Lessons From the Process of Central American Economic Integration

From the beginning, economic integration, as a process in itself, posed the problem of defining the best way in which the Central American countries could achieve progress. The thesis of a priori establishing a comprehensive and global program, with long-term goals to be reached gradually, presented a great intellectual challenge. The risk existed, however, of becoming too abstract and grandiose. Instead, the countries chose to establish limited and concrete objectives. Additionally, this mechanism permitted the analysis of the results—costs and benefits—obtained. Thus, success and failure constituted the grounds for taking further steps ahead. In the case of Central America, this topic acquired great importance due to the failed attempts that had historically been made for achieving, by means of military and political imposition, a Central American union—an experience which created suspicions and resentments. Hence, during the 1950s–1970s the integration process was limited exclusively to economic, financial, and commercial aspects. It is evident, however, that the process could not have progressed much more without contemplating certain aspects of a political nature. This experience with regional integration provides several valuable lessons.

Goals

First, we must bear in mind the two principal goals of economic integration: increasing the size of the Central American market by removing barriers to regional trade, and enabling the region to participate more fully in the world economy.

The possibility of achieving a high level of economic development is linked closely to the size of the market. Market size determines the division of labor, specialization, and economies of scale and, thus, the potential for steadily increasing the productivity of the different factors of production and the accumulation of capital and the application of modern technologies. All of these would bring about an increase in wealth, income, and living standards.

The countries of Central America sought, through economic integration, a way to consolidate the five national markets into a single regional one whose size was four to five times that of any national market taken separately. Hence, economic integration offered new opportunities to improve the division of labor and promote specialization among countries and units of production, which, in turn, allowed for higher production volumes and economies of scale.

Eliminating barriers to intraregional trade created a common market for regionally produced goods. This was, perhaps, the most difficult aspect of integration, given the countries' lack of experience on the subject. Progress was achieved gradually and cautiously. First, bilateral trade agreements were signed; then, a multilateral arrangement was reached, which included the goods subject to regional free trade; finally, a general agreement was signed, which addressed only the products excluded from free trade. Subsequently, a special trade protocol for regionally produced basic grains was signed. Only a relatively small group of products was excluded from regional free trade, namely those with no common external tariff or those which represented an important proportion of a member country's exports, such as coffee and bananas.

The success of the common market was overwhelming. Intraregional trade increased rapidly, both in value and in relative importance. The value of intraregional trade reached one billion dollars in 1980 and represented 20 percent of the five Central American countries' total external trade.

Regional integration in Central America was not conceived as a way to isolate the area from the world economy. On the contrary, it was a means to participate more efficiently in it. The Central American Common Market (CACM) was only the first stage in a steady process of increasing the size of the market. It was obvious from the outset that the regional market, even after integration, was too small. Opportunities for new investment would diminish after a certain period, which demanded the search for ways to expand the CACM. Several complementary alternatives were analyzed:

1. the inclusion of other countries as new members, e.g., Panamá and the Dominican Republic,
2. agreements between the CACM and some "big" neighboring countries such as Mexico or Colombia,
3. the interaction (convergence) of the CACM with other Latin American integration schemes such as the Andean Group, CARICOM, or ALADI, and
4. the review and updating of the common external tariff (CET) of the CACM.

All these measures sought to achieve the same purposes: increasing market size, promoting division of labor, increasing investment opportunities, facilitating specialization, and forcing a greater degree of competitiveness. The market would then expand gradually and in an orderly way, a sine qua non for economic development of the five Central American countries.

Many efforts were made to expand the CACM. For instance, agreements for limited membership were signed with Panamá and Mexico. A special commission was appointed to analyze the possible convergence of the CACM with the former Latin American Free Trade Zone (LAFTA).

It is important to note that the process of regional economic integration in Central America has posed no threats to the international economy. There are several reasons for this. The first is the small size of the Central American economy. Second, the CACM was conceived as an initial step within a much larger and far-reaching process for expanding the market. Third, and something which is often overlooked, the CACM does not pose a choice between free trade and regional integration, but rather between regional integration and national protectionism. In fact, before the establishment of the CACM, each of the five countries already had a protectionist tariff. The process of integration, by widening the market, forced intraregional competition in many fields of production. This became evident given the level of "water" contained in the CET. Thus, given the level of intraregional competition, entrepreneurs could not use all the margin offered by the CET. In sum, the protectionism of the CACM could hardly result in a misallocation of factors of production which could harm the international economy.

Proper Tariff Levels

The protectionism of the CACM cannot be seen as a static measure. Tariff protection has to be a dynamic process for improving the competitiveness of the regional economies, and not as a means of permanently protecting inefficient activities. Therefore, the CET must be subject to an ongoing review in order to adjust it to changing circumstances. Only then will the CET allow the five countries in the region to benefit from new opportunities that arise internationally as a consequence of changes in comparative advantages and of modifications in the trade policies of countries outside the integration scheme.

Hence, the CET must experience changes through time, because it is designed not to isolate the Central American economy, but rather to achieve a better integration of these countries with the world economy.

The task of aligning the national tariffs to the CET was an arduous one. Initial negotiations on the CACM were dedicated to this issue. The results were satisfactory, as regional agreement was achieved on the great majority of tariff items. There was difficulty in establishing a common tariff only in the case of a reduced number of products of a particular fiscal significance (automobiles, liquors), or of strategic importance (fuel, wheat).

Efforts to modify the Central American tariff policy culminated in 1986, with the approval of new legislation in each country for the purpose of:

1. shifting to Brussels's customs classification,

2. reducing the existing dispersion of the CET tariffs,
3. creating more efficient legal and institutional mechanisms to allow for modifications in the CET, and
4. establishing safeguard clauses with a view to protecting the Central American region from unfair commercial practices.

Positive Consequences of Regional Integration

The integration process has had major consequences in other areas, as illustrated by the following three examples.

1. The institutional organizations created during the integration process have proven to be valuable. Some of the institutions are of a general nature, such as the Permanent Secretariat of the General Treaty of Economic Integration (SIECA). Others are specialized: the Central American Monetary Council, the Central American Bank for Economic Integration (CABEI), the Central American Institute of Public Administration (ICAP), and the Central American Institute for Research and Industrial Technology (ICAITI). These diverse entities have proven, through time, great flexibility and resilience in adapting to changing circumstances.

2. The evolution of intraregional trade fostered the creation of a network of entrepreneurial interests. Numerous firms were established, mainly to supply the regional market. These national and regional interests have been the most important support to the consolidation of the CACM.

3. The growth of the manufacturing sector, a consequence of the CACM, has had transcendent effects such as the acceleration of the urbanization process and the formation of an industrial proletariat, of crucial social and political importance in the recent evolution of the area.

Formal integration (treaties, agreements, and regulations) was not the only important element in the evolution of the CACM. Two additional aspects should be mentioned.

First, informal integration has also been important in the process. Perhaps the most evident example is the procedures that gradually, and sometimes ad hoc, were established for solving the conflicts of diverse natures within the CACM. In this context, one of the biggest institutional vacuums of the CACM is the absence of a clear-cut way of solving conflicts and disputes among the member states themselves, and among the individuals of the member states and each of the member states. These quarrels were generally derived from violations related to the clauses that regulated free intraregional trade, e.g., the origin of a certain good, or regarding dispositions linked to the CET. The mechanisms utilized to resolve these daily conflicts were not contemplated in formal integration; they belonged, instead, to the informal integration.

Second, the integration process was complemented by regional cooperation programs. Indeed, the integration process had spillover effects that surpassed the strict integration context—free trade, CET, regional payments system— to cover other areas of cooperation, such as education, health, and telecommunications.

Regional integration also rendered positive results regarding the payments system. The creation and operation of the Central American Clearing House (CACH) allowed the countries to increase intraregional trade considerably without using the very scarce convertible foreign exchange. The countries established a mechanism by which only the outstanding net balances were paid, in dollars, at the end of each semester. An extremely high proportion (90 percent) of the value of regional trade was made through the CACH, representing almost 20 percent of total Central American trade, liberating the use of convertible foreign exchange for other needs. The important lesson is that when countries clearly perceived that a certain decision— creating the regional payments system—meant benefits for each of the five nations, regional cooperation was fruitful. This cooperation ceased, however, when the countries altered the nature of the CACH. As a consequence of their domestic policies, the countries transformed the clearinghouse from a payment system into a credit mechanism by allowing outstanding balances to go unpaid.

Obstacles to Regional Integration

1. Distribution of Costs and Benefits. As with all economic integration schemes, differences in the level of development among the CACM member countries have been the subject, and one of the most troublesome subjects, of many discussions. Disparities determine, to a great extent, the distribution of the costs and benefits of integration among member countries. In Central America, countries with a lesser relative development had a smaller ability to obtain benefits and to avoid the costs of the integration process, which called for policies that secured balanced development, thus achieving an equitable distribution of costs and benefits. This would safeguard the interests of the least developed countries within the CACM. Although technical analyses indicate that all five CACM countries have somehow benefited from integration, the political reality shows that Honduras and, to a lesser degree, Nicaragua, have considered that participation is not equitable, and that they could even be harmed. The possible negative effects are related both to consumption (acquisition of regionally produced goods at prices higher than international prices), and to production (geographical concentration of output, particularly industrial). Thus, if market forces were allowed to act without limit, the rate of growth of the integrated area as a whole could be maximized, but it would not guarantee that each individual country would reach a higher rate of growth than if it did not participate in the process.

Several steps were taken within the CACM to counter this problem:

1. the geographic distribution of the Central American integration industries among the five countries,
2. preferential financing through the Central American Bank for Economic Integration (CABEI), and
3. special treatment in the implementation of the agreement for fiscal incentives to new industrial companies.

These measures notwithstanding, the problem was not properly solved, and it remains a topic of disagreement and controversy among the Central American countries.

2. Lack of Coordination of National Economic Policies. In spite of the CACM's success in establishing a free trade zone and creating a common market, the Central American countries could not satisfactorily take further steps in the coordination of economic policies.

The five nations indeed could not properly perceive that their participation in an integration process implied, in many cases, modifications in their national economic policies. In certain circumstances, regional coordination demanded that some duties and responsibilities be passed on to regional organizations, while in other situations it was necessary that each member country consider the domestic economic policies of the other four. The risks of not doing so were undesired internal results of the policies in question or the possibility of harming other members.

Several examples can be mentioned. First, the program for Central American integration industries could not be developed satisfactorily. This program represented an important complement to free regional trade because it sought to avoid the problem of industrial polarization in one or more member countries. It attempted to achieve the integration of the regional market not only through free trade, but also through complementing production. A number of pressures provoked disagreement among the countries, and the program did not yield the expected results.

Second, the regional industrial incentives policy did not fulfill the expectations placed upon it; on the contrary, it provoked an unfortunate dispute. The efforts of each country to attract investment by granting more incentives than the others led to a huge political erosion among the five countries and to the exaggerated concession of fiscal incentives in each country.

Third, agricultural policy was not coordinated as planned in the Special Grains Protocol. This contributed to the ephemeral life of this agreement, which represented a major failure for the CACM. Some countries have comparative advantages in the production of certain agricultural products, as in the case of Honduras. But while this country has to import industrial goods from the other nations of the CACM, it is not allowed to export its agricultural products to the area. This inequality became a source for permanent frictions that harmed the integration process.

Fourth, monetary policies of the five countries were not coordinated satisfactorily. Too little attention was given to the effects of each country's monetary measures on the regional trade flows and the regional payments agreements. Hence, when a country adopted an expansionary monetary policy, the volume of its imports from Central America increased, and the volume of its exports to the region decreased, generating a deficit in its regional trade. Frequently this situation could not be handled through the established payment agreements, creating many serious crises in the integration program. Thus, the absence of regional policies, or the lack of coordination of national policies, was an important obstacle to the smooth operation and progress of the CACM.

Domestic political pressures have also presented obstacles to the integration process. When countries confront very difficult and complex domestic situations—like the present case of Central America, in which survival is at stake—they concentrate on the search for solutions to their internal problems. Countries facing real internal convulsions are seldom disposed to make commitments to other nations when these commitments establish conditions in the use of domestic economic policy instruments. Countries prefer to keep these instruments under control, and to be able to manage them with discretion. Integration, in this context, does not enjoy enough political support to evolve satisfactorily.

II. Assessing the Present Crisis and Its Main Causes

The unfortunate state of the integration process today has several causes. Foremost is the current economic crisis—one of the deepest and most generalized crises of the twentieth century, which finds its internal roots in the evolution of the economic, social, political, and cultural changes in the region. There are also external factors that have played a major role in the present situation. Additionally, the crisis experienced by the Central American integration process itself should also be addressed.

A. Domestic elements

Among these, the following deserve specific mention. First, the Central American countries have substantially modified the mechanisms traditionally used to adjust their economies in the face of fluctuations of the international economy. Before World War II and the Central American integration program, these small agricultural-exporting economies closely followed the procedures established by the gold standard. Upon a weakening of external demand, resulting from the recurring and cyclical crises of the industrial centers, the decrease in the value of exports was automatically transmitted to the rest of the economy, with the consequent contraction in output and, often, deep cuts in wages and employment. Domestic activity and imports were thus reduced, and internal and external balance restored. Many underdeveloped countries, particularly in Latin America, made attempts to withdraw from this mechanism, according to which the economic evolution of the periphery was subject to cyclical fluctuations of the industrial centers. Given the small size and backwardness of Central America, this problem was recognized as such only after World War II. Diversification of output (industrialization) and greater state economic activity were the means by which the five Central American nations attempted to reduce their external vulnerability.

Second, the countries have also implemented modernization programs. To a great extent this has been the result of diversifying productive activities, which has demanded new programs, such as education, and additional public investments to improve infrastructure. Parallel to these modernization programs, economic growth was outstanding in Central America in the 1950s and 1960s. This growth was a consequence of the sustained increase of agro-exporting activities, the unprecedented expansion of the world economy, and the growing industrialization fostered by integration. Both economic growth and the modernization programs had significant effects, as they promoted the emergence of new social groups that have gravitated in the political and social evolution of these countries: the middle class, the state bureaucracy, the incipient industrial urban proletariat, and the managerial groups.

Third, in recent years natural disasters of huge magnitudes have affected several Central American countries. Such is the case of the earthquakes that shook Nicaragua and Guatemala, and the hurricanes that swept northern Honduras and Nicaragua.

Fourth, convulsion and civil turbulence have been additional elements with marked influence in Nicaragua, El Salvador, and Guatemala, and have presented repercussions in the region as a whole.

The consequences of these domestic elements have been varied:

(1) The attempts to reduce external vulnerability have reduced the governments' degrees of freedom, as they limit the possibilities of placing the costs of economic adjustment on certain social groups. From an economic point of view, all of this delayed and complicated the necessary adjustments.

(2) Modernization programs and growth have been coupled with social demands and expectations, many of which could not be satisfied.

(3) Natural disasters have destroyed factors of production and have impaired output capacity, which, in turn, has discouraged investment and economic growth.

(4) Sociopolitical convulsion and turbulence have caused the destruction of factors of production (private and public), lessened output capacity, provoked a reduction in investment, fostered the migration of workers and entrepreneurs due to growing uncertainty, and accentuated capital flight.

All of this has emphasized a marked economic contraction and a noticeable reduction in the standards of living of wide sectors of a population whose situation already left much to be desired.

B. *The crisis of the integration process*

Regional integration suffered from serious problems in the recent past. These problems have impeded the satisfactory operation of the CACM. Several reasons must be mentioned.

As indicated by Rosenthal (1983), the crisis is more one of expectations than of achievements. Far too many hopes were placed in the integration process, which could not solve the problems for which it was not designed. While regional integration can be an important element for promoting the economic development of the five countries, it cannot be considered a synonym of economic development. This will depend much more on the internal efforts made within each country to increase the quantity and quality of the factors of production, and to improve their allocation.

The crisis of the CACM is also related to the prospects it offers to remove long-term obstacles to the development of the Central American countries. How to make integration not only a positive-sum game for the area as a whole, but also for each of the countries? The inability of the five nations to find an acceptable solution to the problems of regional disparities and of countries with lesser relative development is one of the main reasons for the current state of the CACM.

The weakening of the Central American economy in recent years has had an impact on the integration process. On the one hand, the adverse evolution of the international economy badly affected the outlook for growth in Central America; on the other hand, the sociopolitical convulsion and turbulence created economic distress in the region. As national economies contracted, the prospects for new investments and for regional trade naturally decreased. The payment difficulties experienced by several countries contributed even more to reduce regional trade, so aggravating the situation of the CACM.

Political turbulence has also had far reaching implications in the CACM's operation. Indeed, political disturbances in El Salvador, Nicaragua, and Guatemala have undermined national life. Given the profound rupture between diverse social groups, it is valid to question if these countries offer the necessary conditions to create the minimum social consensus, without which life in common is virtually impossible. It is difficult to find basic constituting elements of a social system; one finds, instead, an accentuated fragmentation that does not allow the establishment of tasks, the distribution of resources, or the control of results.

This political situation has serious consequences for the normal functioning and the potential progress of the economic integration program. Member countries are forced to concentrate their efforts on the solution of domestic problems. The countries "close up," and it becomes very difficult for them to accept regional commitments that could somehow limit, even partially, the use of economic policy instruments. In this situation, countries wish to maintain maximum control over all of these instruments. This represents a serious obstacle to the integration program, because integration requires a growing number of commitments from the member countries. These commitments limit their actions, in that many decisions pass from the national field of action to become the "subject of institutionalized procedures." The negotiating will and possibilities of member countries are thus drastically reduced, and consequently, the functioning of the integration process is hampered.

C. External factors

Central American economies are characterized by their openness. The events and the evolution of the international economy influence significantly the economic situation of these countries. The expansion of the world economy in recent decades was a favorable factor for Central America, but, in a similar way, the serious difficulties that affect the international economy today have negative repercussions in the Central American countries. Three facts must be pointed out:

(1) The economic recession of the main industrialized countries has two adverse effects: it weakens the demand for Central American exports, and it increases the resistance of workers and entrepreneurs within the industrialized countries to eliminate trade barriers and to open up their markets to Central American goods.

(2) World inflation also presents harmful consequences, from at least two points of view. First, inflation in rich countries raises the price of their exports. This price increase, in turn, fuels inflation in the importing countries. Second, inflation causes an increase in interest rates, which

means that Central American nations face higher financial costs in foreign exchange.

(3) The increase in oil prices has also been an important factor, since none of these countries except Guatemala is an oil producer. The bill for oil and its by-products has risen substantially in recent years.

Chenery (1981) points out that given these conditions one of four paths can be taken: increasing exports, increasing external indebtedness, reducing the pace of economic growth, or restricting oil consumption. Central American countries chose to increase their foreign debt, and when it reached unmanageable limits they had no choice but to decrease the rate of economic growth. The shifting of a significant proportion of their national income abroad, through deterioration of terms of trade and increase in the external debt interest bill, has been one of the main factors that explains the economic and social evolution of the Central American countries in recent years.

If these three problems do not receive an adequate solution, it will be very difficult to foster the economic integration program and provide it with a significant role in the future economic development of the area.

There are three indispensable conditions for successful regional integration:

(1) A solution to the problem of peace in the region, and the establishment of grounds for a political consensus that will allow for a reasonable understanding among the deeply divided social forces.
(2) A political solution to the problem of countries with lesser relative economic development so that all five countries can obtain clear net benefits from the integration process. Otherwise, it will be very difficult, if not impossible, to assure the participation of all the five countries in the process.
(3) An improvement in the international economy, which will provide more favorable conditions for trade and financial support for Central America, and consequently, for the reactivation of the integration process.

III. Looking Forward: Discussing the Options

Given the complex and difficult situation faced by Central America, it is worthwhile asking what are the outlooks for the economic integration. Several options must be taken into consideration. It is necessary first to examine such options in the light of the circumstances, and second, to determine the topics that demand immediate attention.

A. The options

1. To abandon the integration program. The most obvious possibility would be to abandon the integration scheme. The CACM would be dismantled, both legally and institutionally. The intention would be to return to the situation prior to integration, in which each country established its own external tariff. This option has few prospects, given the economic development process of poor countries like the Central American nations, and some specific causes related to Central America.

With regard to this option, several points must be considered. First, it is frequently forgotten that most underdeveloped countries participating in economic integration schemes had, prior to integration, a protectionist tariff policy designed to protect the domestic market from outside competition and foster domestic productive activities. The real choice, therefore, is not between free trade and economic integration, but between economic integration and national protectionism. Hence, although integration discriminates against nonmembers, it does permit an expansion of the market. This, in turn, allows for a greater specialization than could be accomplished in each separate market. Countries, in general, are not willing to permit complete access to their markets and to participate fully in the international economy, but they have acquiesced to open, partially and gradually, their national markets in the context of an integration program. This explains why integration schemes among underdeveloped countries, instead of increasing discrimination in the international economic relations, offer, on the contrary, the possibility of reducing distortions by decreasing domestic protectionism and substituting a regional one.

Second, we should not forget the vital role played by the size of the market in the economic development process. By forcing the expansion of the market, integration widens the possibilities of reaching economies of scale (derived from production units with greater dimensions, and from an improved utilization of the installed capacity). A strongly marked division of labor would be reached in this manner.

Third, integration allows member countries the time necessary to learn to produce efficiently and to be able to compete successfully in markets outside the integrated area. This is the well-known argument for infant industries. In other words, many productive activities in these countries—agricultural, industrial, and in the service sector—cannot start their operations if, from the beginning, they have to compete openly in the international markets; this points to the need for a certain degree of temporary protection. This protection could indeed be less and shorter when participating in an integration program than when established by individual countries.

In relation to the specific circumstances linked to Central America, there are several points to consider. First, industrial production represents approximately 20 percent of the region's GDP. This sector has grown mainly as a result of the integration program and depends highly on the dynamism of intraregional trade. If it were to diminish, the situation of many firms would become very difficult. Countries, of course, are not willing to jeopardize manufacturing, given its importance in national output, nontraditional exports, and employment. Additionally, entrepreneurs strongly support intraregional trade, which is crucial to their survival.

Second, integration has started the diversification of production from an agro-exporting base into industrialization. This diversification reduces the costs to Central American economies of readjustment to periodic fluctuations imposed by the international economy. Since diversification permits a growing participation in international trade, experience shows that it puts countries in a better position to adjust to these international fluctuations.

Finally, the Central American Common Market is conceived of as a "launching platform" for new stages of economic development in the area. The regional approach was considered only after the countries first tried to promote development within national borders. Entrepreneurial experience, the training of human resources, and the accumulation of capital and of technological know-how were the factors that laid the ground for the launch of a third stage of greater hope: export promotion to markets outside Central America. The regional market, relatively protected, has played a key role, and will have to continue doing so in the immediate future: it covers a high proportion of the fixed costs of production and permits exporting basically at the marginal cost (wages and cost of raw materials). This subsidy, paid for by the Central American consumer (higher prices or higher taxes), is inevitable at the beginning, but it would have to be reduced as soon as possible.

In view of these arguments, it is unlikely that the Central American countries will choose to abandon the integration program. Additionally, proceeding in this fashion seems inconvenient as long as regional integration is conceived of as a program for fully participating in the international economy, far from avoiding international trade, and even less, from fostering autarchy.

2. *To Reestablish the Integration Process.* The aim would be, in this case, to return to the golden age of integration, that is, to the way the CACM operated in the 1960s, prior to the conflict between Honduras and El Salvador. In those days, the integration process made satisfactory progress and was considered the most successful integration scheme among under-developed countries. Free trade and the common external tariff covered by far the great majority of goods, intraregional trade was a growing proportion of the external trade of each of the member countries, the regional payments system performed nicely, and the institutional organization, as well as the legal framework, were gradually consolidated.

Returning to the past is not a realistic option, for a number of reasons. Three are of great importance. First, even without the internal and external events that have harmed the integration process, it was obvious that the program required a substantial revision. This was the main reason for SIECA's preparation of the "Study of the Decade," in which the CACM was evaluated, and the guidelines for its improvement were established. Intraregional free trade has been considered the essence of the program, but it has also been the source of serious difficulties among the member countries. Doubts emerged about the suitability of free trade for fostering an equitable distribution of the costs and benefits of integration. The importance granted to free trade should yield, and much more emphasis should be given to, investment and production programs as basic instruments of the integration process.

Second, the problem posed by the distribution of costs and benefits of integration is not limited to the effects of intraregional free trade; it also refers to other aspects. This difficulty, recognized from the beginning, has represented a substantial obstacle because countries differ in their perception of the costs they incur and the benefits they receive.

Finally, reference should be made to the effects on the integration program of changes which have occurred in Nicaragua. Traditionally, the economies of the five countries, although mixed, have been basically market-oriented. Regional integration in Central America tried to create a common market among market economies. The events that occurred in Nicaragua have modified the panorama, since the trend toward a centrally directed economy is well defined in this country. In it, economic planning replaces the market as the basic decisionmaking instrument. It is important to remember that the problems due to very marked differences between economic systems of the member countries have become insurmountable. This was the situation with the eastern African community, and with Chile's participation in the Andean Group. The central problem lies in the fact that it is very difficult for participating countries to admit in a regional program what they do not admit as national policies. Hence, it is very unlikely that a country that accepts neither central planning nor the unrestricted operation of the market as a basic instrument of the economic organization will be in favor of fostering an integration program based on planning or on the market, respectively. In the case of countries with mixed economies, they would promote an integration process with a similar economic organization. Thus, proposing to create an integration scheme among countries having substantially different economic organizations is illusory. In the specific case of centrally planned economies, two main features must be kept in mind: prices reflect the preferences of the planners, and the state has the monopoly over external trade—thus the decisions on importing and exporting do not depend on international prices but on considerations of another nature. These characteristics pose problems to the operation of the integration process, particularly if other member countries follow a market-oriented economic system.

For one thing, planning determines the composition of imports and exports according to preestablished priorities in such a way that the firms of the other member countries could not freely buy or sell in the context of integration; that would affect free intraregional trade. Moreover, the state trade corporations in the centrally planned economy could discriminate in favor of national production and against the goods produced in other member countries. That would harm the possibilities of specialization.

The state trade corporations could also discriminate in favor of countries that do not participate in the integration process. That would be an attempt against the common external tariff. The possibility of coordinating the economic policies of the member countries is jeopardized to a great extent, due less to the disparity of objectives than to the use of the available instruments to reach these objectives. The most important economic policy instruments of the market economies (monetary and fiscal policies, prices and subsidies of goods, and factors of production) have a very different meaning in centrally directed economies. In turn, the most significant instrument in the latter (planning) does not play the same role in market economies.

Due to the doubts arising from free trade, the difficulties presented by the distribution of costs and benefits, and the foreseeable problems derived from the differences in the economic systems, it is not likely that the Central American countries will try to reestablish the CACM as it operated in 1969 before the war between Honduras and El Salvador.

3. Restructuring the CACM. This option would consist of the drafting of a new agreement that would supersede the existing program, thereby creating a new integration scheme. This was precisely the intention when the High Level Commission for the Betterment and Restructuring of the Common Market (CAN) was created in 1972. CAN set out to fill its mandate, and in 1976 it presented the region's governments with its findings in a project for establishing the Economic and Social Community for Central America (CESCA). This document proposed a significant modification of the CACM and presented a new approach to the integration process. In spite of the findings of these studies, governments gave them little consideration. The exercise was fruitless.

Due to present circumstances in Central America a radical and comprehensive change in the economic integration program does not seem to be feasible, nor does it appear to be appropriate. In fact, it is important to bear in mind that, given the political turbulence that affects various member countries, the economic integration program has been politically relegated to a secondary position. Countries have concentrated their efforts on solving internal problems; it is a struggle for survival. This situation would impede any initiative to compel these countries to participate in long and complex negotiations for the approval of a new economic integration treaty which would come to restrict the use of an important number of instruments of national economic policy.

To be effective, the integration program must be viewed as part of a broader process of social change and economic development. As such, it is advisable to gradually adjust it to the circumstances as accumulated experience and necessities born of the process may indicate. Rather than global and profound modifications developed through time, the process requires the establishment of a procedure to adopt gradual changes in a permanent manner.

4. Establishing a Transitional Program. Having discarded the previous three options (abandoning the integration program, returning to the situation prior to 1969, or creating a new scheme), it is necessary to examine a fourth possibility. This alternative consists in the adoption of an action plan for a transition period that could have a duration of three to five years.

Such an option has the highest probability of being accepted, as it permits the convergence of two objectives pursued by the countries, which are seemingly not compatible. On the one hand, not to totally disregard the economic integration program, and on the other hand, not to enter into commitments that, due to prevailing circumstances, could not be complied with, because they are either excessively burdensome or vauge. A transition program presents advantages and creates problems. Following is a summary of both conditions.

Concerning advantages, it is worth mentioning that:

(1) The countries would know in advance the time frame within which they acquire commitments, from which they could expect a more predictable outcome. This certainty could increase even more if two complementary measures were taken: the establishment of safeguard clauses and the functioning of an expeditious procedure to settle conflicts between member countries. Hence, the economic integration process would then acquire two basic characteristics, as pointed out by Cohen (1983): first, the program would be, for the most part, negotiated permanently, and, second, the process would not require a commitment on behalf of the countries pertaining to a final objective, for example, the creation of a political union or an economic coalition, but would have limited objectives.

(2) The countries would adopt partial and specific commitments, not general and vague ones. By doing this, specific areas of consensus would be sought and concrete coincidences could be taken advantage of, as Tomassini (1977) would say. Integration would be oriented toward promoting and strengthening interdependence between member countries through the definition of areas of mutual and reciprocal benefits. "Overall aims" and "formal commitments" would give way to "integrating actions."

(3) A new door would open whereby, through adequate coordination, national development strategies (definition of objectives and selection of instruments) would complement the integration process. The transition program would enable the countries to postpone for a future date the discussion on how to achieve a regional development strategy that would encompass or substitute national strategies.

(4) To the extent that the transition program is successful, other such schemes would probably follow. In the long term, a succession of programs would gradually expand and strengthen the integration process through a series of concrete but short steps, instead of indefinite decisions. These advances, based on experience and circumstance, allow for the possibility of taking into account the changes in objectives of member countries.

(5) A transition program would ensure the necessary time and opportunity to face the structural problems inherent in the industrialization model based on import-substitution adopted by the CACM, and the circumstantial ones arising from the economic crises (inflation and recession) that affect industrial centers. The combined effect of these two phenomena has been detrimental to the Central American nations, as is reflected by their serious external imbalances, evident internal imbalances, and by the reduction in economic growth. To face these problems, one would essentially seek, in the first place, a better integration of the CACM into the international economy with the purpose of increasing the prospects for growth that a large market offers. This would demand a reorientation of the Central American productive system to the production of goods and services to be exported outside the area; in the second place, to ensure greater internal financing for economic development, thus reducing dependency on external savings.

A transition program does, however, present its problems.

(1) A program of this type might prove insufficient from the perspective of entrepreneurs. The scheme could be very reduced for investors. As Lara (1977) indicates, a program such as this may not generate the adequate incentives to promote the integration process.

(2) The establishment of procedures to negotiate and carry out a transition program between the countries is a complex task. A transition program is, in reality, what Haas (1980) has called a "regimen," that is, a set of

norms, procedures, and regulations agreed to between countries to regulate a subject of mutual interest.

(3) Due to the prevailing circumstances in Central America today, the transition program should fulfill a set of conditions. First, it must be flexible in order to allow for diverse styles of integration (market integration, integrated development, integration by projects). Second, it should take into consideration the task of coordinating the different economic policies of the member countries. Third, it must take into account the preferences of each member country, in such a way that each may propose priority areas according to its own interests and the type and nature of the commitments it is willing to accept. Fourth, it should also deal with the special case of the relatively less developed countries to ensure their active participation in and their firm support of the integration process. Finally, it should attempt to make the national plans compatible so that each country may be motivated by its own interests, while recognizing that it could not achieve its goals without a process of integration.

The transition program still leaves much to be desired. It is perhaps a "second-best," but it is the only viable option. To attempt a more ambitious scheme would be unrealistic and could lead to failure, which would only worsen a complex and difficult situation. The transition program would allow members to maintain the regional program while laying the ground for the new approach to regional interdependence that might permit them to reach higher stages of development in the future.

B. Main Fields of the Transition Program

The transition program would emphasize the following aspects:

1. Intraregional Trade. It is politically impossible, in the short term, to establish free intraregional trade as the basic condition of any new program of economic integration in Central America. Nevertheless, trade among members continues to be essential for Central American integration. For this reason, a revision of the implementation of a free trade zone is indispensable. "Should we not make this a priority task, it would be practically impossible to define integration, cooperation or harmonization of policies, as we would not have an economic realm to refer to" (Sieca, 1981a). Intraregional trade should be governed by several coexisting regimes:

–"Restricted" trade would protect "sensitive" goods, such as textiles, clothing, and shoes that are typical of the first stage of industrialization and so important to the relatively less developed countries of the region. "Restricted" trade would be based on voluntary export and import quota arrangements.

–"Negotiated" trade could be used for goods produced under regional investment programs. This trade would become unrestricted once the countries came to an agreement over the geographic location of production through Central America.

–Agricultural products—basic grains, oilseed, and dairy products, for example—would be governed by "conditional" trade. In this case, preference would be given to supply national markets so that intraregional trade would only take place in the emergence of surpluses and shortages in the countries.

–"Unrestricted" trade would be applied to all other regional products not otherwise contemplated.

Intraregional trade would thus be the outcome of two different integration approaches: the market approach, through the consolidation of national markets, and the production approach, by regional investment programs.

2. The Common External Tariff. The common external tariff and the intraregional free trade regime are the two basic agreements of the CACM. The first protects the market; the second widens it. In spite of the CACM's significant progress toward establishing a common external tariff, the Central American countries have been preparing a new tariff regime in the last years for two reasons: first, the tariff in force had become obsolete because it was not readjusted to reflect the industrialization process of the region; and second, its unity was broken by measures that the countries have adopted throughout the years. These measures are, in fact, significant unilateral modifications of the common external tariff, for example, surcharges, duties, excise taxes, and duty exemptions.

The proposed new tariff policy "has been designed principally as an instrument for development, thus depriving it from fiscal or balance of payments defense functions" (Sieca, 1981b).

3. Safeguard Measures. Safeguard clauses are considered an indispensable requisite for any integration program, and the CACM is no exception. The proposed measures for intraregional trade and the proposed tariff policy require a high degree of flexibility. Therefore, it is necessary to offer the countries the possibility of modifying the initial agreements, that is, to establish safeguard clauses. To be really effective, the safeguard clauses must specify the measures the countries can take, establish the circumstances under which the safeguard clauses can be applied, and present clearly the procedures for application.

With respect to the measures the countries could take, they would primarily contemplate the postponement of the deadlines formally agreed upon for the adoption of these measures; with respect to the second point, the circumstances of application would be of a varied nature, such as disruption of markets, severe shortages, balance of payments difficulties, or natural disasters. Concerning the third point, the procedures adopted should not be based on unilateral decisions, but rather on regional mechanisms previously negotiated.

4. The Regional Payments System. Among the present problems of the CACM, one of the most serious is the inadequate functioning of the regional payments system. It is in a particularly critical state due to the severe economic problems that Central American countries are facing. In effect, the balance of payments crisis is now generalized, leaving member countries unable to pay in a timely manner. The consequence has been a delay in payments and an accumulation of deficits. Thus, the multilateral system of compensation, created to reduce the use of the scarce foreign exchange in intraregional trade, has become, in fact, a credit mechanism for financing the net balance due. As a result, the countries have established obstacles to regional trade and endangered integration. Countries have been prompted to adopt a series of measures to alleviate this situation. In spite of these, accumulated deficits continue to increase, reaching $500 million. This creates an unbearable situation for creditor nations, forcing them to look for new solutions.

Two additional observations are pertinent. First, neither the measures adopted nor those suggested will be sufficient if the disparity of inflation in these countries is not reduced. If the rates of inflation are dissimilar, and exchange rates are not rapidly adjusted, the accumulation of deficits is inevitable. Second, when establishing the rights and obligations of the debtor countries and their creditors, it is indispensable to consider the global balance of payments situation of each country. It may well be that a creditor country in the CACM could have a global deficit in its balance of payments; a country enjoying a global surplus could present a deficit within the CACM.

5. Other Fields of Cooperation. Given the difficult circumstances that surround the CACM, it is urgent to find new fields of cooperation. Although this cooperation may not specifically address the essential aspects of the integration process, it would reinforce and strengthen the network of common interest. These areas of cooperation must satisfy certain conditions. First, they should not involve significant political compromises. Second, they should not require complex negotiations. Third, they should not demand large human, financial, or institutional resources. Fourth, they should generate benefits in a relatively short time. Following are some prospects:

Agriculture. Agricultural activities offer interesting perspectives for cooperation. Animal and crop disease control, improved seed production, grain storage, information on market conditions, technical assistance, and institutional organization are just a few of the possibilities.

Natural resources. Regional studies on soils, hydraulic resources, forests, minerals, marine life, and energy resources could be fruitful.

Formulation of projects. The formulation and evaluation of projects should become a permanent task of the CACM. It is suitable to support the efforts made by CABEI to create a Regional Pre-Investment Fund. This fund would help finance the promotion and preparation of investment projects.

Exchange of information. It would be very helpful for member countries to improve their information- and statistics-gathering systems. This would unify censuses and surveys, but should not be limited to this traditional type of exchange. It should also include other fields such as health, social security, education, and housing, as well as information on economic policies, financial and human resources, and institutional organization.

Research. Two fields are adequate to enhance regional cooperation: first, agrarian and livestock research, and second, studies on the macroeconomic models already begun by ECID. Both areas open up the possibility of participation to the national research institutions (Delgado, 1975).

Prevention of natural disasters. A regional information system would be established, directed mainly toward meteorology and seismology.

These programs could foster integration from the bottom towards the top, as indicated by ECLAC. They would be "joint actions—with the participation of all five countries—to solve common problems, basically through the execution of projects and programs" (ECLAC, 1976). The importance of this strategy lies in the "possibility of establishing, through it, and in an immediate future, agreements and partial programs without necessarily implying the adoption of a global program of restructuring of the common market" (ECLAC, 1976).

C. The Prerequisites

To successfully implement the transition program, it is necessary to meet certain conditions and to fulfill certain minimum prerequisites. Some are of an internal nature, while others refer to the international environment.

1. Internal Aspects. In order to promote development in the Central American countries through the integration process, it is necessary to put the house in order. Two aspects are essential. First, the domestic economic policy of each member country must be consistent with efforts to achieve sustained economic growth. On one hand, countries must seek to increase the quantity and improve the quality of the factors of production, in such a way as to shift the production possibilities curve gradually to the right. On the other hand, they should be concerned about attaining the optimal allocation of factors of production, so that effective production is located in some point of the production possibilities curve. Second, economic policies with respect to foreign investment are very important. In effect, financial resources, technologies and the access to markets abroad may all play a vital role for economic reactivation in the region. Policies that clearly establish rules for foreign investment will help attract this investment.

2. International Environment. It has already been indicated how the development possibilities of countries as small as the Central American nations depend largely on the evolution of the external circumstances. Two topics are of special interest in the case of Central America.

First is the economic policies of the industrialized countries. These policies should promote economic growth through a permanent structural adjustment process and an opening of their markets. This would permit Central American countries, based on comparative advantages, to increase their exports. Industrialized countries should also adopt financial and monetary stability so as to avoid inflation as well as undesirable exchange rate fluctuations. An economic policy for the highly industrialized countries that reaches these objectives would be, undoubtedly, one of the greatest contributions that the Central American countries could receive.

Second, because of the magnitude and complexity of the problems presently afflicting the region, international cooperation to assist Central America is indispensable. International cooperation should cover several aspects. A primary concern is market access through programs such as the Caribbean Basin Initiative of the government of the United States, and a preferential treatment from the European Economic Community and LAFTA countries. Only if Central America rapidly increases its exports will it outgrow its underdevelopment. Moreover, financial assistance from the international financial community (governments, multilateral institutions, and commercial banks) is required. Fresh resources for complementing domestic saving efforts are needed as much as debt rescheduling in conditions that do not represent an obstacle to development. Technical assistance programs are also important in improving the utilization of natural resources and of the factors of production available in the region.

For international cooperation to be truly useful it should avoid paternalism and imposition. It should be founded, instead, on cooperation and the will to complement internal efforts so that developing countries can overcome the serious problems that affect them. It is thus indispensable to establish procedures for active participation by Central American countries in the decisionmaking process in programs relating to international cooperation.

Conclusions

1. Maintaining the economic integration process to encourage a more active participation in the international economy is necessary for the Central American countries. The immediate political and economic problems should not impede the CACM countries clearly from perceiving the scant viability that each of them, individually, has in the contemporary world. At the same time it is necessary to recognize the internal obstacles and the external limitations that are present today. Current circumstances are not favorable. Not much can be expected from integration these days, but the remaining options are even less promising. Thus, even if little can be done, it is urgent to set hands to the task and try to achieve it as soon as possible.

2. The search for a new modus operandi is a task which CACM countries should insist on. External and internal circumstances force the modification of the integration process. It is necessary to assure the coexistence of countries with different types of political organizations and economic systems. This

demands a search for procedures for the convergence of the integration approach by the consolidation of national markets, with integration through regional investment and production programs.

3. The implementation of a transition program seems to be the most viable option in the present circumstances. The political commitments of countries would be significant, but limited and specific. Countries would then know what to expect, and the benefits would be tangible for each of them.

4. The review of the institutional organization of the CACM is an urgent necessity. Should this be done, countries could then come to basic long-term conciliatory agreements (cooperation for survival, integration for progress) taking into consideration the immediate (political and economic) requirements. The degree of equilibrium attained between long- and short-term interests will determine the level of success of the integration policy. Countries would then accept entering into a game whose result, even in the short term, is not a zero sum, and from which appreciable net benefits can be expected for each of the participants in the medium and short terms.

References

Chenery, Hollis (1981). "Restructuring the World Economy: Round II." *Foreign Affairs* 59 1102–20.

Cohen, Isaac (1983). "El concepto de integración." *ECLAC Review*, December, 149–59.

Delgado, Enrique (1975). "La investigación económica como requisito para el avance del programa de integración económica centroamericana." SIECA/75/DES/IE/39.

ECLAC (1976). "Reactivación del Mercado Común Centroamericano, *Cuadernos de la CEPAL*, no. 10, 31.

Haas, Ernst B. (1980). "Why Collaboration? Issue-Linkage and Third World Regimes." *World Policies*, April, 357–405.

Lara, Cristobal (1977). "Comentario sobre el articulo de Cohen y Rosenthal." *ECLAC Review*, 52–58.

Rosenthal, Gert (1983). "Algunas lecciones de la integración económica en América Latina: el caso de Centoamérica." *Comercio Exterior*, December, 1142–49.

SIECA 1981a. "Consideraciones de la Secretaria Permanente sobre aspectos importantes de la restructuración del Mercado Común Centroamericano." Seminar on the process of Central American economic integration, Panama, October, 21.

SIECA 1981b. "Informe final de la reunión de coordinadores encargados de revisar la politica arancelaria centroamericana," Guatemala, 1981, 2.

Tomassini, Luciano (1977). "Elementos para un estudio sobre los procesos de integración y otras formas de cooperación en la América Latina." *Comercio Exterior*, February, 179–84.

Chapter 11

Currency Convertibility, the Central American Clearing House, and the
Revitalization of Intraregional Trade in the
Central American Common Market
Philip L. Brock, assisted by Dennis Melendez

Introduction

There is a unanimous consensus within Central America today that the most urgent task is to establish a payments regime that will permit the normalization of intraregional trade. As a result of the proliferation and instability of exchange rate regulations that have arisen in response to the economic crisis of the region, economic agents who interact within Central America do not know when or how the payments balances resulting from intraregional commercial transactions will be settled. . . . The five countries have become strangers in their own home, a home that had previously seen the free passage of the goods and services produced by all—Dr. Carlos Manuel Castillo, *La Integración Económica de Centroamérica en la Siguiente Etapa: Problemas y Oportunidades.*

Between 1980 and 1986 intraregional trade in Central America fell by over 60 percent. Unresolved payments arrears among the countries in the Central American Common Market caused the imposition of a set of discriminatory trade and exchange controls that magnified the negative economic impact produced by the confluence of unfavorable world economic conditions and prolonged civil strife within the region. The foreign exchange shortages associated with the payments arrears caused the virtual collapse of the Central American Clearing House, the financial institution that had allowed Central America to enjoy the benefits of free regional trade since 1961.

The imposition of exchange controls and the collapse of the Central American Clearing House put an end to the free convertibility of the Central American currencies with each other. As work by McKinnon (1979) has demonstrated, currency convertibility is essential for the monetization of trade. Without currency convertibility, trade exists only at the barter level between pairs of countries, as has been the case among Eastern European countries for much of the postwar period.[1] Currency convertibility allows multilateral trade to take place, thereby enlarging the possibilities of gains from trade.

Currency convertibility requires that the monetary liabilities of a government be convertible into foreign exchange at some determinate, but possibly time-varying, exchange rate. The breakdown of currency convertibility is always caused by fiscal problems related to the ability of a government to honor its monetary liabilities. Historically the breakdown of currency convertibility has often been produced by external shocks that have led governments to impose trade restrictions and exchange controls because of a lack of international reserves. These restrictions have in turn exacerbated the initial negative impact of the external shocks.

The demonetization of trade that has taken place within Central America will need to be reversed if the region is to recover from the economic decline of the 1980s. The second section of this chapter discusses the creation of currency convertibility among the Central American countries in the 1960s and the functioning of the system of convertibility through the end of the 1970s. Section III then traces the breakdown of convertibility in Central America during the 1980s and examines some of the economic consequences of the breakdown for regional trade. Section IV analyzes why external shocks that produce the end of currency convertibility tend also to produce trade restrictions and exchange controls. Sections V and VI of the essay then draw on the successful application of U.S. Marshall Plan aid to the European Payments Union after World War II in order to suggest the manner by which outside aid to the Central American Clearing House could help to reactivate the payments regime within Central America. The appendix contains a chronology of the most important trade restrictions and exchange controls imposed by the Central American governments during the first half of the 1980s.

II. Currency Convertibility and the Central American Clearing House

Prior to the establishment of the Central American Common Market in 1961 the five countries of Costa Rica, El Salvador, Guatemala, Honduras, and Nicaragua had all pursued restrictive trade and exchange rate policies with the rest of the world. As Lizano (1987) has emphasized, the decision to create the Central American Common Market was not a choice between free trade and protectionism; rather, it was an attempt to rationalize trade controls and to establish free trade among the members of the Common Market. Since 1961 the two most important instruments of the Central American Common Market have been the common external tariff and the guarantee of currency convertibility among the five countries.

Currency convertibility has been established via the institutional mechanism of the Central American Clearing House. The clearing house was established in July 1961 by agreement of representatives of the five Central American central banks. The agreement was quickly ratified by Guatemala, Honduras, and El Salvador so that intraregional clearing operations among the three countries began in October 1961. Nicaragua ratified the agreement in 1962 and Costa Rica in the following year so that by 1963 the clearing house was fully operational. In August 1963 Mexico opened a special line of credit with the clearing house for the clearing of payments between the Bank of Mexico and the other Central American central banks. Colombia also established similar arrangements with the clearing house between the Bank of the Republic of Colombia and the Central American central banks.

The Central American Clearing House is physically located in the Central Bank of Honduras in Tegucigalpa and is managed by the Executive Secretary of the Central American Monetary Council. The five central banks act as agents for the clearing house, advancing local currency to national banks in exchange for payments documents denominated in the other four countries' currencies. The central banks in turn pass on each payments document to the central bank of the country of origin of the document. The documents are then presented to the local banks on which the payments documents were originally drawn. The clearing house is notified of all payments transactions and keeps a record of the net position of each central bank within the clearing house. Before 1984 the central bank positions were liquidated once every six months (in June and December) with payments from the debtor to the creditor central banks made in dollars or other convertible currencies.[2]

The success of the Central American Clearing House has depended on the credibility of official guarantees of the regional convertibility of the national currencies and on the repayment of debit positions every six months in internationally convertible currencies (such as dollars). Although the present collapse of currency convertibility within the Central American Common Market has stemmed from foreign exchange shortages that began at the start of the 1980s, the clearing house had previously had to weather less severe foreign exchange problems that began after the mid-1960s. Between 1966 and 1971 Central America faced a number of intraregional payments problems that produced disruptive unilateral trade policies by several of the region's countries. During 1966 and 1967 international prices of coffee, cotton, and bananas fell, producing declines in the foreign exchange reserves of the Central American countries. In response to the foreign exchange crisis, Costa Rica imposed a dual exchange rate system in January 1967 that discriminated against Central American imports. Although Costa Rica was persuaded to rescind the discriminatory measures, commercial relations among the countries continued to deteriorate.

The failure to adopt region-wide fiscal measures to cope with the region's balance of payments problems provoked a trade war between Nicaragua and its neighbors during 1968. Nicaragua blocked rice imports from Guatemala, shirts from Honduras, and beans and maize from Costa Rica. El Salvador restricted the entry of Guatemalan cigarettes and Costa Rica cut off imports of rice from El Salvador. The July 1969 "soccer war" between Honduras and El Salvador further complicated payments problems in the region. By the end of 1970 the trade deficit of Honduras was $51 million, with $37 million accounted for by Guatemala, Costa Rica, and Nicaragua. On December 31, 1970, Honduras withdrew from the Central American Common Market. The withdrawal of Honduras altered trade patterns among the remaining four countries to the disadvantage of Costa Rica and Nicaragua. Costa Rica responded to its regional trade deficit by imposing new exchange controls and quotas on imports in mid-1971.[3]

By the end of 1971 trade patterns among the Central American countries had begun to return to normal. An improving external environment eased the foreign exchange problem within the region. So, too, did the creation in 1970 of the Central American Monetary Stabilization Fund (FOCEM) to ease the short-run balance-of-payments problems of the five countries. FOCEM began operations from its headquarters in Guatemala with an initial contribution of $4 million from each of the five Central America countries plus an additional $5 million from Venezuela and $10 million from USAID.[4]

FOCEM was created with the hope that it could eliminate the monetary factors that had produced trade restrictions among the five Central American countries between 1966 and 1971. At the beginning of the payments crisis of the 1980s, FOCEM was able to lend $104 million in 1980 through the use of $30 million of its own equity (of a total equity of $67.9 million) and $74 million obtained through credit lines established with international banks. Of the $104 million lent in 1980, $54 million went to the Central Bank of El Salvador, $20 million went to the Central Bank of Honduras, and $30 million went to the Central Bank of Costa Rica. At that time FOCEM also administered a $40.5 million interbank assistance fund for Nicaragua. FOCEM's credit lines were with the Central Bank of Venezuela, Wells Fargo Bank, the Bank of the Republic of Colombia, the Bank of Mexico, Deutsche Sudamerikanische Bank, and USAID.[5]

FOCEM was unable to cope with the severity of the regional payments crisis, however, so that the five countries created a second fund, the Central American Common Market Fund, in 1981 specifically to finance the debit balances that had resulted from the operations of the Central American Clearing House. The Central American Common Market Fund was formed with $50 million from the Latin American Export Bank and with additional contributions equivalent to $100 million in the currencies of the Central American countries.[6] The limited funds of FOCEM and the Common Market Fund were not sufficient to cover the intraregional payments arrears that began to accrue in 1981. The following section documents the set of trade restrictions and exchange controls that grew out of the payments crisis within the region.

III. The Breakdown of Intraregional Trade, 1981–87

After 1980 Central America faced a deteriorating external environment that was characterized by higher oil prices, high world real interest rates, and depressed commodity prices for traditional exports such as coffee and bananas. As in much of the rest of Latin America, the combination of adverse external shocks led to an external debt problem and to a sharp decline in per capita output. Table 11.1 provides figures that indicate the severity of the drop in world prices for the region's exports. During most of the 1980s the terms of trade have been depressed for Central America and have only begun to recover since 1986.

Table 11.2 shows the evolution of per capita levels of output in Central America during the 1980s. Even in Honduras and Costa Rica, the two best

Table 11.1   Central America's Terms of Trade* (1980 = 100)

	1980	1981	1982	1983	1984	1985	1986
Costa Rica	100.0	85.6	76.8	86.0	90.0	88.0	107.0
El Salvador	100.0	87.4	86.7	83.0	73.0	69.0	87.0
Guatemala	100.0	91.8	89.1	85.0	88.0	83.0	95.0
Honduras	100.0	87.0	82.6	93.0	96.0	76.0	95.0
Nicaragua	100.0	88.7	79.2	83.0	105.0	97.0	119.0

* The terms of trade are defined as the unit value of exports divided by the unit value of imports.
Source: Inter-American Development Bank, *Economic and Social Progress in Latin America*, 1986 and 1987 Reports.

Table 11.2   Per Capita Output in Central America* (1980 = 100)

	1980	1981	1982	1983	1984	1985	1986
Costa Rica	100.0	95.1	85.7	85.9	90.6	89.1	89.5
El Salvador	100.0	89.6	82.7	81.6	81.8	81.7	80.8
Guatemala	100.0	97.9	91.7	86.8	84.8	81.6	79.3
Honduras	100.0	98.0	92.3	90.4	90.6	90.2	90.0
Nicaragua	100.0	102.0	97.7	98.0	93.9	86.9	83.6

* The figures adjust GDP growth rates for population growth rates of 2.6 percent per year in Costa Rica, 2.1 percent in El Salvador, 2.8 percent in Guatemala, 3.2 percent in Honduras, and 3.4 percent in Nicaragua.
Source: Inter-American Development Bank, *Economic and Social Progress in Latin America*, 1986 and 1987 Reports.

performing economies in Central America during the 1980s, per capita output was 10 percent lower in 1986 than in 1980. In El Salvador, Guatemala, and Nicaragua, per capita output was 20 percent lower in 1986 than in 1980. For those three countries, even a growth rate of real output on the order of 5 percent per year will not raise per capita output to 1980 levels for another decade.

Unlike the rest of Latin America, Central American economic growth in the 1980s suffered from severe internal problems as well as a deteriorating external environment. Civil wars in Nicaragua and El Salvador disrupted intraregional trade as those two countries began to run large and systematic balance-of-trade deficits with the other countries in the Central American Common Market. In addition, each of the five Central American countries responded to the external debt crisis with different and mutually inconsistent exchange rate and foreign trade policies. The combination of problems caused by the civil wars and the external debt crisis spilled over into the Central American Common Market to disrupt the free flow of trade within the region.

Table 11.3 shows the sharp decline in intraregional trade that took place in Central America between 1980 and 1986. Starting from a level of $2.229 billion in 1980, intraregional trade had fallen by over 60 percent to $839 million in 1986. The fall in the level of intraregional trade was partly a reflection of the overall drop in trade that took place with the drop in the region's income after 1980. However, table 11.3 shows that intraregional trade suffered much more than trade with the rest of the world so that between 1980 and 1986 the proportion of intraregional trade in total trade fell by over 50 percent.

The cause of the sharp decline in intraregional trade is directly linked to the breakdown of the ability of the Central American Clearing House to provide regional convertibility of the Central American currencies. The initial problems of currency convertibility centered around the accumulation of debtor balances by Nicaragua in 1980 and 1981. These balances were initially perceived as a troublesome but transitory problem for the ongoing operations of the Central American Clearing House in settling the payments accounts among the member countries. However, the multilateral compensation scheme employed by the clearinghouse enabled Guatemala and El Salvador to use their Nicaraguan debtor balances within the clearing house as partial payment of their debtor balances with Costa Rica. Normally, Nicaragua would then have settled with Costa Rica by using foreign exchange reserves since the five Central American currencies were supposed to be convertible on a regional basis via the operations of the clearinghouse. However, the inability of Nicaragua to settle its payments arrears arising from intraregional trade caused Costa Rica to initiate restrictive trade measures against Nicaragua in 1982, followed by the announcement of a barter system of trade in 1983. Between 1983 and 1985 Costa Rica, Guatemala, and Honduras all initiated trade restrictions against Nicaragua and El Salvador in order to prevent the accumulation of debts by those two countries with

Table 11.3   Central American Regional and International Trade
(millions of U.S. dollars)

	1980	1981	1982	1983	1984	1985	1986
Exports plus Imports							
Within the CACM:							
Costa Rica	490.1	390.3	279.6	318.4	307.8	236.0	185.5
El Salvador	616.1	511.3	435.0	398.0	411.3	312.5	252.1
Guatemala	559.0	572.8	552.3	545.9	479.1	297.8	269.7
Honduras	187.4	184.0	138.7	166.0	146.5	120.5	78.0
Nicaragua	376.0	281.3	169.0	157.1	111.6	81.4	54.0
Total CACM	2,228.6	1,939.7	1,574.6	1,585.4	1,456.3	1,048.2	839.3
Exports plus Imports							
Outside the CACM:							
Costa Rica	2,035.4	1,820.8	1,482.6	1,521.9	1,783.4	1,805.6	2,049.2
El Salvador	1,485.7	1,271.3	1,121.4	1,252.7	1,292.0	1,327.7	1,395.8
Guatemala	2,559.0	2,392.1	2,006.1	1,680.8	1,931.6	1,936.7	1,761.6
Honduras	1,726.2	1,575.3	1,276.5	1,355.4	1,550.0	1,638.1	1,693.3
Nicaragua	1,045.9	1,226.3	1,012.6	1,097.3	1,122.5	1,184.4	1,015.0
Total CACM	8,852.2	8,285.8	6,899.2	6,908.1	7,679.5	7,892.5	7,914.9
Exports plus Imports							
Within the CACM as a Proportion							
of Total Exports plus Imports							
(1980 = 1.00)							
Costa Rica	1.00	0.91	0.82	0.89	0.76	0.60	0.43
El Salvador	1.00	0.98	0.95	0.82	0.82	0.65	0.52
Guatemala	1.00	1.08	1.20	1.37	1.11	0.74	0.74
Honduras	1.00	1.07	1.00	1.11	0.88	0.70	0.45
Nicaragua	1.00	0.71	0.54	0.47	0.34	0.24	0.19
Total CACM	1.00	0.94	0.92	0.93	0.79	0.58	0.48

Source: International Monetary Fund, *International Financial Statistics*, and Central American
Monetary Council.

the rest of the Central American Common Market. During that period over 200 barter transactions were authorized in Central America, with the majority involving trade with Nicaragua and El Salvador.[7]

Although many trade restrictions were initially directed at Nicaragua and El Salvador, intraregional trade imbalances also affected trade within the rest of the Central American Common Market. These trade imbalances became especially important after 1984 and produced an escalation of the use of discriminatory trade practices. For example, on May 31, 1985, Guatemala and El Salvador agreed to a bilateral arrangement in which local exporters could receive payment in each other's currency without using the Central American Clearing House. Costa Rica briefly joined the scheme but then left, closing its frontiers to the inflow of Guatemalan and Salvadoran imports in the process amid claims of discriminatory trade practices by Guatemala and El Salvador. In December 1985 Guatemala agreed to pay $7 million to Costa Rica corresponding to interest payments in arrears, to acknowledge an additional $22 million in debt to Costa Rica, and to incorporate Costa Rican imports in Guatemala's preferential exchange market. As retaliation for the trade agreement between Costa Rica, Guatemala, and El Salvador, Honduras decreed several exchange rate measures against imports from those countries.

In March 1986 Costa Rica decided to use the Central American Clearing House for a system of bilaterally balanced trade with Nicaragua and to conduct all transactions with El Salvador and Honduras outside of the clearinghouse. The latter decision meant that imports from El Salvador and Honduras were to be treated as imports from the rest of the world and therefore would not be eligible for special tariff or exchange treatment. Also, in March 1986 Guatemala decided to withdraw temporarily from the Central American Clearing House. Costa Rica and Honduras responded by also withdrawing. In May 1986 Honduras decided that all transactions with Guatemala would be made entirely in U.S. dollars. In July 1986 Guatemala and El Salvador agreed upon a new system of bilaterally balanced trade. In the same month Costa Rica and Guatemala once again accused each other of discriminatory trade practices, with each blaming the other for damage resulting from their exchange rate policies.

In a July 1986 meeting of the Integration Secretaries of the Central American Common Market, an attempt was made to circumvent the problem posed by the collapse of the Central American Clearing House. A new payments mechanism called the Central American Importation Right (DICA, *Derecho de Importación Centroaméricano*) was agreed upon for the payment of imports originating in Central America, regardless of the country of origin. DICAs were intended to be negotiable certificates of deposit issued by central banks with a market value freely determined in a secondary market. Originally El Salvador, Guatemala, Nicaragua, and Costa Rica agreed to use DICAs, but the system has foundered on the absence of secondary markets to price the DICAs on the related exchange rate risk involved in the use of DICAs as a payments mechanism for intraregional imports.

As can be seen in table 11.4, problems with the multilateral payments mechanism in the Central American Common Market have caused a sharp decline in the use of the Central American Clearing House. In 1980 and 1981 all commercial payments in the region were handled by the clearing-house. Beginning with the initiation of trade restrictions in 1982, the proportion of commercial transactions handled by the clearinghouse fell over a period of five years to only 45 percent of all transactions in 1986. Even the official level of 45 percent overstates the role of the clearinghouse because

Table 11.4   Intraregional Payments for Trade Made Through the Central American Clearing House (millions of U.S. dollars)

Year	Payments Using the Clearing House	Amount of Intraregional Exports	Percentage of Exports Using the Clearing House*	Non-compensated Payments**
1980	1256.3	1099.5	114.3	—
1981	979.5	972.4	100.7	—
1982	644.0	796.9	80.8	152.9
1983	579.4	810.9	71.5	231.5
1984	506.4	727.2	69.6	220.8
1985	395.5	547.6	72.2	152.1
1986	189.8	420.9	45.0	231.1

* The figures for 1980 and 1981 appear to indicate that the Clearing House was used to make payments for services and capital movements.

** These amounts are paid using alternative payments procedures or remain as accumulated debts.

Source: *Análisis Económico*, based on information compiled by SIECA.

the compensation procedure is now primarily confined to bilateral transactions that have been previously balanced by the use of quantitative restrictions on the volume of trade between any two countries.

At present intraregional trade is mired in a set of discriminatory trade and exchange rate policies that have resulted from the inability of the Central American countries to use the Central American Clearing House to settle their intraregional trade balances. By the end of 1986, according to figures published in *Análisis Económico*, Nicaragua owed Costa Rica $220 million, Guatemala $170 million, El Salvador $90 million, and Honduras $45 million. In addition Costa Rica was owed $70 million by Guatemala, $50 million by Honduras, and $44 million by El Salvador. El Salvador also owed Guatemala $50 million. (All figures are in U.S. dollars.)

These unresolved payments arrears have produced the imposition of the current set of discriminatory trade and exchange rate practices within the region that have accompanied a suspension of regional convertibility of Central American currencies. This suspension of convertibility has in turn amplified the decline of intraregional trade relative to the decline in the region's trade with the rest of the world. Table 11.3 shows that even though Central American trade with the rest of the world has been rising since 1983 (from U.S. $6.908 billion to $7.915 billion in 1986), intraregional trade has continued to decline so that the 1986 level of intraregional trade of U.S. $839 million was only half of the 1983 level. In addition, the bottom row of table 11.3 shows that the initial decline in intraregional trade relative to total trade between 1980 and 1983 was mild and primarily reflected the suspension of intraregional trade with Nicaragua. But the more severe drop in intraregional trade that has taken place since 1983 involves the suspension of regional convertibility among all five Central American countries.

IV. Monetary Liabilities of the Government and Restrictions on Convertibility

The evidence of the previous section has shown that the sharp decline in regional trade in Central America relative to trade with the rest of the world was the product of restrictions on the regional convertibility of Central American currencies. These restrictions were not the product of rational decisions to reduce trade within Central America, because free regional trade had been one of the cornerstones of the Central American Common Market since the early 1960s. Rather, the restrictions reflected an inability of the

Central American governments to maintain the convertibility of their currencies for trade with each other. To understand why maintaining currency convertibility proved impossible in Central America in the 1980s this section examines the nature of the governments' monetary liabilities and the interaction of those liabilities with trade and exchange rate policies.

The most direct monetary liabilities of a government are currency and required reserves held by the banking system. These two items form the monetary base (H) and are the direct liability of the central bank. Corresponding to this liability are the central bank's assets which are composed of international reserves (R) and domestic credit (C). The demand for the base can be expressed as a proportion of nominal expenditure (PA), $H^D = kPA$, where the price level is a weighted average of the prices of importable goods (P^m), exportable goods (P^x), and nontraded goods (P^n): $P = (P^m)^a(P^x)^B(P^n)^{1-a-B}$. The supply of the monetary base is composed of domestic credit and international reserves, $H^S = C + ER$, where international reserves are valued in domestic prices by use of the exchange rate (E). Money market equilibrium requires that the demand for the base equal the supply of the base as shown in equation (1):

$$C + ER = k(P^m)^a(P^x)^B(P^n)^{1-a-B}A$$

The price of importables can be written as $P^m = (1 + t)EP^{m*}$, where t is the tariff (or tariff equivalent of a quota) on imported goods and P^{m*} is the international price of importables. The price of exportables can be written as $P^x = EP^{x*}$, where P^{x*} is the international price of exportables. By dividing both sides of equation (1) by the exchange rate, money market equilibrium can be rewritten as follows in equation (2):

$$C/E + R = kP^{m*}(1+t)^a(p^{x*}/P^{m*})^B(P^n/EP^{m*})^{1-a-B}A$$

In equation (2) the ratio P^{x*}/P^{m*} is the economy's terms of trade (TOT) while the ratio P^n/EP^{m*} is the relative price of nontraded goods (RPN) in terms of the world price of importables so that equation (2) can be rewritten more simply as equation (3):

$$C/E + R = kP^{m*}(1+t)^a(TOT)^B(RPN)^{1-a-B}A$$

When a country suffers a decline in its terms of trade, such as the severe decline faced by Central America in the early 1980s, there are direct and indirect factors that lower the demand for the monetary base. Examination of the right side of equation (3) shows that to the extent that the economy consumes the exported good (where B is the share of the exported good in expenditure), the demand for the monetary base will fall. In addition, the decline in export prices will produce a fall in expenditure (A) that will further reduce the demand for the monetary base. Finally, a shock to the terms of trade that lowers expenditure will, in general, also depress the relative price of nontraded goods since part of the fall in expenditure will be reflected in a reduced demand for nontraded goods.

The three channels through which a terms-of-trade decline reduces the demand for the monetary base require an offsetting adjustment in equation (3) in order to maintain money market equilibrium. If a country maintains a fixed exchange rate and maintains the stock of domestic credit constant, the decline in the demand for the monetary base must produce a decline in the central bank's international reserves. If the central bank does not have enough international reserves to cope with the decline in the demand for the monetary base, the central bank has several policy options. One option is to devalue, pegging the exchange rate at a higher level, so that the ratio C/E declines rather than the level of international reserves. If the government is committed to a fixed exchange rate, then the government can raise tariffs or impose quotas. By raising the price of importables $(1+t)$, the right hand side of equation (3) can be manipulated to raise the domestic price level in order to raise the demand for the monetary base and to prevent the outflow of international reserves. In addition, the central bank can raise reserve requirements on the banking system or impose prior import deposits that require importers to hold central bank liabilities. These actions raise the proportionality factor (k) on the right hand side of equation (3) and thereby offset the decline in the demand for the monetary base.[8]

Unlike an exchange rate devaluation, increases in tariffs, quotas, reserve requirements, and prior import deposits all introduce distortions into the operation of an economy's goods market and credit market by altering relative commodity prices and interests rates. Nevertheless, devaluation is often perceived as a sign of weakness and is sometimes expressly prohibited by a country's constitution. When a government with few international reserves is unwilling or unable to devalue its currency in the aftermath of a large terms-of-trade shock, trade and credit restrictions are inevitable.

At the start of the 1980s the maintenance of fixed exchange rates within Central America had become a symbol of economic stability and was considered an important part of intraregional monetary integration. All five countries attempted to avoid devaluations by imposing restrictive commercial policies to prevent the loss of international reserves. For example, as the chronology of exchange-rate restrictions in the appendix documents, the imposition of prior import deposits became an important and universally adopted way of increasing the demand for the monetary base (i.e., increasing the proportionality factor k in equation 3). Prior import deposits required importers to maintain balances with the central banks and effectively increased the demand for the monetary base (and international reserves) to offset the decline in the demand for the base produced by the decreased demand for currency.

In 1979 Nicaragua and El Salvador established prior import deposits of 100 percent for most types of imports. In 1980 Guatemala established a prior import deposit for all imports involving the use of trade credit. In 1983 Honduras imposed prior import deposits on imports from the rest of Central America that exceeded U.S. $25,000, and in 1984 Costa Rica raised prior import deposits to 100 percent. This use of prior import deposits within Central America was part of an attempt to avoid exchange rate adjustment in response to the external and internal shocks faced by the countries in the region.

Trade restrictions also played an important part of the response of the Central American countries in their attempt to avoid devaluations, because trade raises the demand for the monetary base (via a rise in t on the right hand side of equation 3). As shown in the appendix, in 1980 Guatemala, Nicaragua, Costa Rica, and El Salvador all imposed trade restrictions, including prohibitions on the imports of "nonessential" goods in El Salvador and automobiles and capital goods in Costa Rica. By 1981 all five countries had imposed new taxes on imports and had created numerous exchange control restrictions that prevented the convertibility of domestic currencies into foreign currencies. These restrictions on trade became more stringent during the years between 1982 and 1984 and were the proximate cause of the collapse of intraregional trade.

As equation (3) makes clear, the decrease in the demand for the monetary base associated with a terms-of-trade shock can cause adjustment problems for governments that choose not to devalue. In Central America all five countries resisted devaluations and resorted to the use of trade and exchange control restrictions that reduced the convertibility of their currencies both into dollars and into the other regional currencies. The reduction of convertibility in turn imposed losses on the Central American countries by eliminating the bulk of multilateral trade within the Central American Common Market.

Table 11.5 shows the behavior of exchange rates in the five countries during the period of the imposition of prior import deposits, trade restrictions, and exchange controls. In all countries the free or black market exchange rate began to diverge increasingly from the official exchange rate after 1979. Costa Rica was the first country effectively to abandon its fixed exchange rate when the officially tolerated parallel market exchange rate began to diverge increasingly from the official rate. Between 1979 and 1980 the premium on the parallel market rate over the official rate rose from 2 percent to 70 percent. By 1981 increasingly severe foreign exchange difficulties caused the government to float the exchange rate for all goods except for a small number of insignificant imports that remained at the official exchange rate of C8.57 per dollar. During 1982 El Salvador could no longer sustain its exchange rate and created a multiple exchange rate system in which importable categories were progressively moved from one category to another as part of a gradual devaluation process. Guatemala had maintained an exchange rate of one to one with the U.S. dollar for 65 years prior to the 1980s. In defense of that exchange rate Guatemala exhausted its foreign exchange reserves and imposed prior import deposits and trade restrictions. By 1984 even public opposition to devaluation was not enough to prevent the establishment of a multiple exchange rate system that devalued many commercial transactions and all financial transactions. In 1986 Guatemala officially devalued its exchange rate from Q1 to Q2.5. Honduras is the only country that has maintained its official exchange rate, and it has accomplished that with trade and exchange control restrictions. In addition, between 1981 and 1986 Honduras received about U.S. $1 billion in military and economic aid that provided foreign exchange to support the fixed exchange rate.

The discussion in this section has concentrated up to this point on the monetary base as the government's monetary liability in terms of foreign exchange convertibility. However, the convertibility issue in Central America extended beyond the governments' commitment to exchange domestic currency into dollars. As can be seen in table 11.6, currency is only about 5 percent of gross domestic product in the Central American countries. Even adding required reserves to currency in order to obtain the monetary base

Table 11.5 Central America: Nominal Exchange Rates   (Units of Local Currency per U.S. Dollar) Yearly Average

Year	Costa Rica			El Salvador			
	Official	Interbank	Parallel*	Official	Interbank	Parallel	Free**
1979	8.57	8.57	8.72	2.50	—	—	3.26
1980	8.57	8.57	14.50	2.50	2.88	—	3.68
1981	8.57	21.76	37.99	2.50	2.73	—	5.85
1982	8.57	37.40	45.93	2.50	2.67	3.90	4.27
1983	20.25	41.09	43.90	2.50	2.58	4.00	3.70
1984	20.25	44.53	48.10	2.50	2.50	4.05	4.38
1985	20.25	50.45	53.75	2.50	5.88	4.05	5.90
1986	20.25	55.99	59.55	5.00	6.39	4.53	5.75

Year	Guatemala			Honduras		Nicaragua		
	Official	Interbank	Free**	Official	Free**	Official	Interbank	Free**
1979	1.00	—	1.05	2.00	2.17	9.26	—	11.30
1980	1.00	—	1.15	2.00	2.31	10.05	28.00	16.09
1981	1.00	—	1.26	2.00	2.42	10.05	28.00	36.17
1982	1.00	—	1.20	2.00	2.27	10.05	28.00	43.25
1983	1.00	—	1.23	2.00	2.71	10.05	28.00	46.00
1984	1.00	1.50	1.39	2.00	2.63	10.05	28.00	197.09
1985	1.00	2.74	2.93	2.00	2.72	28.00	31.10	708.80
1986	2.50	2.86	2.89	2.00	2.43	70.00	1285.00	2750.00

* The parallel market rate was an officially accepted rate from 1979 to 1982. After 1982 the parallel rate became a black market rate.
** Usually a black market exchange rate or an exchange rate from an illegal but tolerated exchange market.
Source: Central American Monetary Council.

only brings the governments' monetary liabilities to about 10 percent of GDP. Furthermore, the demand for currency is somewhat predictable since currency is used for transactions purposes.

However, in all five Central American countries government backing of the banking system implies that bank deposits are convertible into currency and therefore are potentially convertible into foreign exchange. The existence of a commitment not to suspend the convertibility of bank deposits into domestic currency creates a much larger monetary liability for the Central American governments than the direct monetary liability of the monetary base. Table 11.6 shows that the use of M2 (currency plus demand deposits plus time deposits) as the true monetary liability of the governments indicates that the governments' commitment to exchange rate convertibility involves claims that are from 20 to 37 percent of GDP. Furthermore, most bank deposits are used as a store of wealth rather than as a means of payment so that the potential for a sharp decline in bank deposits is much greater than the potential for a sharp decline in currency.

The expanded convertibility problem that involves bank deposits became a problem in Central America with the external and internal shocks of the 1980s. These shocks reduced asset values and threatened the loan portfolios of the banks. With the governments' commitment toward convertibility of bank deposits, the potential fiscal cost associated with covering the banks' losses created the need to impose exchange controls that prevented depositors from converting their deposits into foreign exchange. With exchange controls in place, devaluation in all countries except Honduras provided a way of generating negative real rates of interest on deposits that transferred the fiscal cost of the bad loans of the banks to the depositors.

For example, after Costa Rica's decision effectively to devalue in 1980, table 11.6 shows that the cumulative negative real deposit rates between 1981 and 1983 wiped out 49 percent of the value of deposits held in the banking system during those years. Similarly, following El Salvador's decision to devalue in 1980 by establishing an interbank market, the cumulative negative real deposit rates between 1980 and 1986 reduced the real value of deposits by 32 percent. In Guatemala, after the decision to devalue in 1984 the real value of deposits was reduced by 39 percent between 1984 and 1986. In Nicaragua a deposit placed in the banking system in 1981 would have lost 97 percent of its value by 1986. Honduras is the only country that has paid positive real rates of interest between 1981 and 1986, and it is the only

Table 11.6 Central American Real Interest Rates and Monetary Aggregates

Year	Costa Rica Deposit	Costa Rica Loan	El Salvador Deposit	El Salvador Loan	Guatemala Deposit	Guatemala Loan	Honduras Deposit	Honduras Loan	Nicaragua Deposit	Nicaragua Loan
Ex-Post Real Interest Rates*										
1980	−4.7	3.0	−5.2	−0.5	−0.2	2.7	−4.7	1.2	−19.4	−14.9
1981	−11.3	−8.8	−2.8	1.6	−0.1	1.7	0.0	6.3	−8.4	−2.3
1982	−34.2	−32.0	−0.9	3.4	4.1	7.0	5.3	10.5	−11.4	−6.5
1983	−8.0	−5.0	−2.7	1.0	5.3	8.2	1.8	7.6	−15.6	−11.4
1984	9.9	12.4	−1.8	2.0	−9.4	−6.9	5.0	10.7	−16.5	−14.9
1985	5.0	9.7	−8.6	−5.3	−16.4	−14.0	3.8	9.0	−62.7	−62.3
1986	6.4	10.9	−15.2	−10.4	−19.1	−16.9	4.6	10.0	−82.8	−82.7
Monetary Aggregates as a Percentage of GDP**										
Currency	3.9		6.5		4.1		4.8		7.5	
Monet. Base	10.8		12.4		7.0		6.9		10.0	
M1	12.8		14.2		8.0		11.3		17.7	
M2	36.6		28.9		20.3		21.7		28.5	

* The real interest rates are a weighted average of reported nominal deposit and loan rates corrected for actual inflation.

** The computed percentages use 1981 monetary and GDP figures.

Sources: Central American Monetary Council for real interest rates. International Monetary Fund, *International Financial Statistics* for monetary aggregates.

country that has not devalued its exchange rate, partly because of the large amounts of American aid that the country received and partly because of the extensive system of import controls imposed by the government.

The revival of intraregional trade in Central America will depend on measures that the Central American countries take individually and in concert to restore intraregional currency convertibility and the efficient functioning of the Central American Clearing House. The history of the Central American Clearing House indicates that the depletion of the region's international reserves has strong effects on the workings of the intraregional payments regime. In particular, during both the 1967–71 period and the post-1980 period the countries have resorted to restrictive trade measures among themselves as a result of monetary problems related to a lack of international reserves, and not as a result of long-term trade strategies. In the post-1980 period, in particular, the monetary causes of exchange rate restrictions were closely tied to solvency problems of the banking systems of the Central American countries.

The countries have recognized the importance of removing the monetary causes of intraregional trade barriers by their establishment of the Central American Monetary Stabilization Fund in 1970 and the Central American Common Market Fund in 1981. However, it appears that a reestablishment of intraregional trade will require the internal revival of the economies to restore the security of funds placed in each country's financial system. The economic revival of Central America can be quickened, though, by measures that allow an early return to intraregional currency convertibility. Given the limited resources of the Central American governments at this time, such a return to convertibility could be facilitated by a major commitment of foreign exchange to the clearing house and to the two balance-of-payments funds in order to restore the unrestricted multilateral clearing of commercial transactions among the five countries. To illustrate the possible way in which the regional payments mechanisms could be revived by outside aid, the next section will examine the role of Marshall Plan aid to the European Payments Union in restoring trade within Western Europe after 1950.

V. Marshall Plan Aid and the European Payments Union

At the end of World War II European governments faced the task of reconstructing their economies with depleted foreign exchange reserves to finance international trade. Many of the European economies' most urgent needs were for commodities from the dollar area (the United States and Canada), so the limited supply of foreign exchange was directed toward the dollar area. Intra-European trade suffered as a result of an inconvertibility of European currencies that produced bilateral trading agreements and a series of quantitative restrictions on trade. In some cases trade stopped altogether: in 1947 France was temporarily forced to stop importing from Belgium and Switzerland and in March 1948 Sweden placed a ban on imports from Belgium.[9] According to one account of this period,

> By 1947 . . . the system was in deadlock. Debtors were not prepared to make payments in gold or dollars, and creditors were not prepared to extend credit beyond existing limits. Thus there was an incentive to discriminate in trade, debtors discriminating against imports from their creditors in favor of imports from those countries with whom they had a bilateral surplus, hoping that this would prevent a drain on reserves and encourage a repayment of previously extended credit. The consequence of such trade restrictions and discrimination was a stagnation in the growth of intra-European trade in 1947. Europe . . . was being choked by the self-imposed collar of bilateralism.[10]

The recognition of the seriousness of the problems handicapping the recovery of Europe led George Marshall to propose a European Recovery Plan that would rely heavily on U.S. aid. The Committee for European Economic Cooperation involved in drawing up the European proposal for the recovery plan recommended that aid be given to Europe in a form whereby European currencies would become convertible with each other for paying off intraregional balance of payments deficits. The proposal was not adopted by Congress in its April 1948 financing of the Marshall Plan (under the Economic Recovery Act of 1948) for two reasons. First, the proposed incentives in the plan of the Committee for European Economic Cooperation did not encourage creditors in Europe to run surpluses with debtors whose currencies were weak and susceptible to devaluation. Second, the State Department had advised the Senate Foreign Relations Committee against the plan on the grounds that the United States would lose control over any aid given as working capital to establish a multilateral payments regime administered by a European clearinghouse.[11]

Marshall Plan aid was therefore organized on a bilateral basis from April

1948 to September 1950. However, recognizing that the recovery of Western Europe required the revival of intra-European trade, Congress initially authorized "offshore purchases" in which European countries could use dollar aid to buy goods from other European countries rather than from the United States. The establishment of the Intra-European Payments Plan in October 1948 provided a more sophisticated form of aid to intra-European trade. Under the Intra-European Payments Plan the United States would give dollar aid to a European country that ran a bilateral trade surplus with another European country on the condition that the surplus country extend drawing rights in its own currency to the deficit country. The goal of the Intra-European Payments Plan was to make the distribution of Marshall Plan aid more straightforward and to bring about a further redistribution of the benefits of aid within Europe. The conditional dollar aid granted through the Intra-European Payments Union amounted to $800 million out of a total of $4.8 billion of Marshall Plan aid between July 1948 and June 1949.[12]

Despite the boost that the aid via offshore purchases and the Intra-European Payments plan gave to intra-European trade, there was concern that the bilateral characteristics of Marshall Plan aid were not leading to a sustained revival of European trade based on intraregionally convertible currencies. Therefore in 1950 the administrator of the Marshall Plan aid proposed a European clearinghouse to help in the attainment of the following four objectives:[13]

1. Expansion of intra-European trade through a relaxation of trade restrictions.
2. Interconvertibility of European currencies through a system of multilateral settlement of trade balances.
3. Creation of an independent institution that would eventually be financed entirely out of European resources.
4. Strengthening of European economic conditions and thereby augmentation of the common defense effort.

Congress agreed to the request of aid for the establishment of a European clearing house, and in September 1950 the European Payments Union (EPU) was established with an initial working capital of $350 million given in the form of a grant by the United States. After an initial payment of $42.7 million to the EPU, the remainder of the working capital was placed in a special trust account of the U.S. Treasury with arrangements made for sight drafts drawn on the account by the Bank for International Settlements as agent for the Payments Union. Between 1951 and 1953 the EPU withdrew $195 million from the trust account. In addition to the $350 million of working capital, the comptroller general of the United States (1959) estimated that the United States gave $660 million in conditional aid to individual countries of the Payments Union. Countries that were apt to run EPU deficits (Austria, Greece, Iceland, the Netherlands, and Norway) were given initial credit balances amounting to about $290 million, while other countries apt to run surpluses (Belgium-Luxembourg, Sweden, and the United Kingdom) were given aid to induce them to accept initial deficit positions in the Payments Union. During the early years of the European Payments Union $370 million was also paid by the United States to the Bank for International Settlements (as agent for the EPU) to allow Austria, France, Greece, Iceland, and Turkey to finance their intra-European trade deficits.

The results of the establishment of the European Payments Union were quite dramatic. According to Randall Hinshaw (1958), at the end of 1949 only 30 percent of intra-European trade was free from quantitative restrictions while much of the "free" trade was only among a small number of countries. By the end of 1950, after only three months of operation of the EPU, 60 percent of intraregional trade was free from quantitative restrictions and free trade was made nondiscriminatory within the Payments Union. During the first six years of operations of the European Payments Union trade was progressively liberalized until, by early 1957, 90 percent of intra-European trade was free of quotas. The volume of intra-European trade responded rapidly to the easing of trade controls. Taking 1949 as 100, intra-European trade rose to 141 by 1950, to 151 by 1951, and to 226 by 1956.

Unlike the Intra-European Payments Plan of 1948 in which bilateral European trade deficits were financed by dollar aid, in the European Payments Union debtors (those running trade deficits) settled 40 percent of their balances in gold or dollars while creditors (those running trade surpluses) settled by granting 60 percent of their balances in domestic currency credits. In case of default by a debtor country, the working capital of the European Payments Union would provide a settlement of accounts. This payments regime economized on the use of foreign exchange (dollars) and provided incentives for each country to maintain reasonable economic and exchange rate policies in order to participate in the growth of intra-European trade.

During the first three years of operations of the EPU the successful recovery of intra-European trade depended on the drawing down of working capital in the Payments Union to finance intra-European trade deficits. However, after 1953 the balance of over $100 million of the initial $350 million of working capital in the Treasury trust account was left untouched as the European countries began to build their own international reserves on the strength of their recovering economies. In May 1953 the European Payments Union began the operation of an intra-European arbitrage system that decentralized most foreign exchange operations to commercial banks so that the central banks were relieved of most clearinghouse activities. The growing strength of the European economies and the decentralization of the intra-European payments mechanism allowed the EPU to be disbanded in December 1958 with the adoption of full currency convertibility by fourteen Western European countries.

VI. The Role of the Central American Clearing House in the Recovery of Central America

After World War II the scarcity of foreign exchange reserves in Europe caused European countries to impose trade restrictions that suffocated intra-European trade. The present set of trade restrictions among Central American countries is similarly caused by a scarcity of foreign exchange reserves in Central America. An important contribution of the European Payments Union was the elimination of the financial motive for trade restrictions by eliminating the risk of default on accumulated payments balances resulting from bilateral trade deficits. A program of aid to the Central American Clearing House and to the two balance-of-payments funds (the Central American Monetary Stabilization Fund and the Central American Common Market Fund) could likewise revitalize intraregional trade in Central America by increasing the regional convertibility of currencies and by reducing the financial risks associated with multilateral trade.

Given the clear historical success of the financial assistance given to the European Payments Union, it is worth exploring how such assistance works in restoring intraregional convertibility and why such assistance should *not* be initially linked to currency convertibility with the rest of the world. For countries that operate under some system of fixed exchange rates, as do all five Central American countries, a loss of international reserves signals either an excess of domestic spending over income that is not being financed by foreign borrowing, *or* a decline in the demand for the monetary liabilities of the government. The first cause of loss of reserves may call for fiscal measures to reduce domestic spending. The second cause is very closely linked to the efficient functioning of the banking systems of the countries.

For banking systems to operate efficiently in any country, the banks must be solvent—a condition that is not entirely met within Central America today. If banks are not solvent, depositors must at least be assured that their funds are safe and that the problems of bank insolvency will be met by other methods, such as fiscal transfers to the banks. If depositors are not assured of the safety of their deposits, the conditions are ripe for a run on the banking system in which depositors exchange bank deposits for currency and currency for foreign exchange. By over-invoicing imports and under-invoicing exports it is very easy to convert bank deposits into foreign exchange unless there are strict exchange controls.

In any country the existence of a deposit insurance fund for a banking system helps to eliminate the conditions that produce runs on banks, although a deposit insurance fund does not guarantee the solvency of the banking system itself. By creating confidence of depositors in the financial system, deposit insurance does contribute to an efficiently functioning economy. With the loss of confidence in the security of bank deposits, even a fundamentally sound economy can be hobbled by the contraction of the size of the banking system.

The working capital fund for the European Payments Union acted in part as an insurance fund that restored individual confidence in the future of the European economies and, hence, reduced the desire to exchange financial assets for foreign exchange. It is clear that the European Payments Union would not have been successful in the absence of other measures to restore the economic health of Europe. On the other hand, earlier attempts at reviving intra-European trade based on bilateral aid had not worked. Those attempts did not work for the same reason that aid within a country to banks on a case-by-case basis following a financial crisis is not enough to restore confidence by depositors in any given bank. Until there is reasonable security that financial exchange within an economy is secure, bank runs still occur. Likewise, aid on a bilateral basis to Europe only promoted bilateral deficits with the United States as dollar aid was converted into dollar assets of the residents of individual countries. The working capital fund to the European Payments Union provided the financial insurance that was needed to eliminate the incentive to convert the monetary liabilities of governments (including bank deposits) into foreign exchange. With the elimination of that incentive, exchange controls quickly fell, as documented by Hinshaw (1958).

Financial aid to the Central American Clearing House and its balance-of-payments institutions can play the same role as the Marshall Plan aid to the European Payments Union. Although other measures to restore the Central American economies and financial systems are a key to the recovery of Central America, bilateral aid to the Central American countries will not, by itself, restore the confidence of Central Americans in the security of financial assets in that region. Provided that other measures—such as the payment of positive real rates of return on bank deposits—are taken, a major infusion of foreign currency reserves into the stabilization funds associated with the Central American Clearing House could have a large impact on the speed of the economic recovery of the region and on the reversal of the exchange controls put in place by the Central American governments during the 1980s.

The European Payments Union established currency convertibility only within the member countries. It was not until 1959 that currency convertibility was reestablished with the rest of the world. Although the working capital fund of the European Payments Fund, in conjunction with other measures to revive the European economies, was enough to limit capital flight between European countries, the incentives to convert the monetary liabilities of the government into dollar assets in the United States by over-invoicing of imports or under-invoicing of exports did not permit full convertibility until the European economies were much stronger.[14] Likewise, although full currency convertibility of Central America with the rest of the world is a worthwhile long-run goal, the reestablishment of regional convertibility is a more attainable goal in the short run.

The history of the Central American Common Market suggests that the region is vulnerable to downturns in commodity prices that create strains on the domestic financial systems and deplete foreign exchange reserves. The depletion of foreign exchange reserves in turn is the financial cause of intraregional trade restrictions. The long-term success of the Central American Clearing House depends on the ability of Central American governments to permit economic adjustment to adverse movements in world commodity prices without resorting to trade and exchange rate restrictions. That success is closely linked to the financial solvency of the domestic financial systems. Given the link between foreign debt and financial solvency, the success of any current attempt to revitalize the clearinghouse depends on a resolution of the international debt problems of the countries in the region. To the extent that the debt burdens of the countries are unmanageable, working capital of foreign exchange reserves provided to finance the recovery of intraregional trade will be quickly depleted. The revitalization of the Central American Clearing House can aid the recovery of the Central American economies, but the success of the clearinghouse as a financial institution will necessarily depend on the success of other real measures related to the fiscal, trade, and international debt problems of the countries of the region.

The history of Marshall Plan aid to Europe after World War II indicates that the initial reaction of Congress and the State Department was to give aid on a bilateral basis to European countries so as to maintain control over the distribution of the aid. The problems associated with that approach led first to the authorization of "offshore purchases" by European recipients of U.S. aid and then to the formation of the Intra-European Payments Plan to promote intra-European trade. Nevertheless, following two years of evidence that U.S. aid was failing to contribute to a growth of multilateral trade in Europe, Congress approved the funds (amounting eventually to $1.1 billion) necessary to establish the European Payments Union. The results of the European Payments Union were, as documented in section V of this chapter, quite dramatic both in terms of the removal of quantitative restrictions on trade between European countries and in terms of the overall expansion of intra-European trade.

External donors who wish to have bilateral control over their aid may be reluctant to commit large amounts of aid to multilateral bodies such as the Central American Clearing House, the Central American Monetary Stabilization Fund, and the Central American Common Market Fund. These donors, however, should think of such aid as a financial lever that will reduce risk for the private sector and provide incentives for the return of private sector flight capital and for the intelligent use of other external aid to the region. In addition, when this kind of aid is appropriately managed, as in the case of the European Payments Union, the reduction of private sector risk will increase the efficiency of market mechanisms that promote private sector economic activity and intraregional trade.

Appendix: Chronology of the Most Important Trade and Exchange Control Restrictions Imposed in Central America During 1979–85

1979

2-19-79, Nicaragua: A 100-percent prior import deposit of 60 days is established for about 50 percent of all imports. Payments for all imports except those from the Central American Common Market are subject to a seven-day waiting period.

4-6-79, Nicaragua: The official exchange rate is devalued from C$7 to C$10 per dollar, and a multiple exchange rate system for the conversion of foreign exchange proceeds from exports and invisibles is established.

8-30-79, Nicaragua: The export of coffee, cotton, meat, and sugar is nationalized. An extensive list of priorities for imports is established. The multiple exchange rate system is abolished and replaced with a unified exchange rate of C$10 per dollar. The private sale of foreign exchange is prohibited.

9-17-79, El Salvador: A prior import deposit requirement is established for all imports exceeding U.S. $2000.

12-26-79, Honduras: Import duties are created on several classes of commodities. An export tax is levied on cattle, meat, and sugar, while a general export duty of one percent is imposed on all export items except bananas, coffee, and minerals.

1980

2-18-80, El Salvador: Prior import deposits are raised from 100 percent to 200 percent on "luxury" and "nonessential" goods (see 9-17-79). In addition, all payments corresponding to foreign credits are made subject to prior authorization of the Central Bank.

4-23-80, Guatemala: Several measures are taken to control international capital movements, including the imposition of export licenses, prior registration of all imports (except those of the Central American Common Market), a 25-percent prior import deposit, and several restrictions on capital movements.

9-8-80, Nicaragua: New import duties are established on certain goods. A new "sales" tax of 8 percent on imported goods is levied with an additional 2 percent surcharge for imports to Managua. Many luxury and industrial commodities, including textiles and electrical appliances, are moved to a parallel exchange market.

9-26-80, Costa Rica: Quantitative restrictions are imposed on selected imports, including a total prohibition on the import of certain vehicles, ad valorem surcharges of 15–20 percent on certain tariffs, and the institution of prior import deposits ranging from 10 to 50 percent. In addition, a multiple exchange market is created.

11-10-80, El Salvador: The list of "luxury" and "nonessential" goods is expanded (see 2-18-80). The import of many of these goods is banned for 90 days. Additional restrictions are established for the sale of foreign exchange for travel, family assistance abroad, and other invisibles.

12-26-80, Costa Rica: Import surcharges for all imports are unified at 1 percent. The Central Bank gives up control of the foreign exchange market and decides to float the exchange rate and abolish the multiple exchange rate system established on 9-26-80.

1981

3-9-81, Costa Rica: A dual exchange rate market is reestablished.

3-14-81, Nicaragua: Some import requirements are tightened.

3-31-81, Costa Rica: As a result of a severe foreign exchange shortage, the Central Bank tries to generate dollar resources by establishing certificates of deposits for Costa Ricans in U.S. dollars with a guaranteed future repayment in dollars.

4-29-81, Honduras: Import taxes are increased by 10 percent for final goods and by 5 percent for all other goods.

8-27-81, Costa Rica: A generalized system of import licenses is decreed. Only priority imports are eligible for official currency from the banking system. The system of certificates of deposit (see 3-31-81) is abolished.

9-14-81, Guatemala: Additional regulations tighten restrictions for the use of foreign exchange for payments for invisibles.

9-18-81, Honduras: Exchange controls are tightened: banks must sell excess foreign exchange to the Central Bank; a system of priorities in the allocation of foreign exchange is established; all exports must have a previous license and all exporters must surrender all export proceeds within 90 days; any external payment over U.S. $500 requires Central Bank authorization; controls and priorities are established for the payment of foreign debt.

9-19-81, Nicaragua: Only authorized dealers are allowed to operate in the parallel exchange markets. Foreign exchange obtained from invisibles can be sold in the parallel market. Advance prior import deposits (see 2-19-79) are abolished and replaced with additional tariffs ranging from 30 to 100 percent on "luxury" and "nonessential" goods.

9-21-81, Costa Rica: The parallel exchange rate is devalued from C18.40 to C30.06 per dollar. The proportion of export proceeds that must be surrendered at the official exchange rate is raised from 1 percent to 4 percent. New selective consumer taxes from 6 to 100 percent are established on 66 categories of imports.

10-20-81, Costa Rica: The import of autos and capital goods is explicitly prohibited.

11-27-81, El Salvador: Import registration requirements are tightened with a reduction from

U.S. $500 to U.S. $200 in the minimum dollar value requiring registration. Use of the official exchange market is further restricted and measures are taken that permit a quasi-legalization of the parallel exchange market.

12-16-81, El Salvador: Withdrawals of foreign currency deposits are limited to $2000 a month.

12-24-81, Costa Rica: The prohibition on imports of autos and capital goods is removed (see 10-20-81).

1982

1-21-82, Honduras: Monthly quotas are established on the maximum amount of lempira notes and coins that can be purchased by the central banks of other countries in the Central American Common Market.

2-15-82, Nicaragua: A tax of C$5 per dollar is levied on purchases of foreign exchange for nonessential goods.

3-5-82, Nicaragua: Exchange controls are modified to permit greater authorized use of the parallel exchange rate.

5-15-82, Honduras: A prior import deposit of 100 percent is established for all imports involving the use of trade credit.

8-9-82, El Salvador: Commercial banks are authorized to purchase or sell foreign exchange in the parallel market (see 11-27-81).

9-18-82, Costa Rica: The authorization of private foreign exchange establishments is cancelled. The reorganized exchange market is operated exclusively by the banking system.

11-10-82, El Salvador: Regulations covering the purchase and sale of external currency in the parallel market are relaxed (see 8-9-82).

11-14-82, Guatemala: Import quotas for most import items are established based on the level of imports in 1981. The major exempt categories are petroleum imports, goods for re-export, and all imports that do not require foreign exchange obtained at the official rate.

11-19-82, The Central American countries agree to accept payment in local currencies for regional trade. The agreement is never followed.

1983

1-3-83, Nicaragua: New regulations are established regarding the sale of foreign exchange to airlines, travel studies, and medical treatments abroad with payments for these activities moved to the parallel exchange market. In addition all tourists are required to pay hotel charges and telephone calls in dollars as well as to exchange at least U.S. $60 into cordobas upon arrival.

2-18-83, El Salvador: The payment of invisibles, some capital payments, and 77 categories of imports are moved from the official to the parallel market.

5-3-83, Nicaragua: All private exchange houses are closed and a single bank is placed in charge of operations in the parallel market.

6-28-83, Costa Rica: A temporary surcharge of 2.5 percent is placed on imports from outside the Central American Common Market (see 12-26-80).

7-7-83, Guatemala: The Bank of Guatemala announces the issue of $400 million of stabilization bonds denominated in U.S. dollars whose purchase is a requirement for obtaining foreign exchange licenses for external payments.

7-25-83, Guatemala: Restrictions are imposed on foreign exchange for trips to Mexico. On September 7 these restrictions are extended to Central America.

8-19-83, Costa Rica: A general stamp tax of 1 percent is placed on all imports, except for imports of inputs used to produce nontraditional export goods.

9-1-83, El Salvador: Imports of automobiles and other vehicles, which had been banned since 1980 (see 11-10-80), are permitted.

11-7-83, Guatemala: Export licenses are imposed on exports to Nicaragua. On December 2 this decree is extended to the other countries in the Central American Common Market.

11-8-83, Honduras: Payments through the Central American Clearing House must have the prior authorization of the Central Bank.

11-10-83, Honduras: A maximum term of five days to obtain an import license for self-financed imports is established. This measure indirectly provides semi-official acceptance of the parallel market.

11-21-83, Honduras: All imports from the Central American Common Market in excess of U.S. $25,000 are subject to a prior import license.

11-28-83, Guatemala: Temporary import licenses are introduced on imports from the Central American Common Market. This measure is eliminated for Costa Rica on December 19.

12-10-83, Costa Rica: Differential exchange rate taxes (5 percent on exports to the Central American Common Market and 10 percent on traditional exports) are eliminated.

1984

1-19-84, Costa Rica: The 1 percent tax on foreign payments (see 12-26-80) is replaced by a general 1 percent import duty.

2-1-84, Nicaragua: All proceeds from sugar exports must be surrendered at the parallel exchange rate. Similar measures are applied on March 8 for export proceeds from cotton, coffee, and bananas.

2-8-84, El Salvador: As part of a negotiation with Guatemala, 27 import categories formerly moved to the parallel market are moved back to the official market. These same measures are taken with respect to Costa Rica on February 28.

3-14-84, El Salvador: A special exchange rate for imports from the Central American Common Market is created (at a rate of about 70 percent of the parallel rate). This special exchange rate is eliminated on November 21.

4-1-84, Nicaragua: Imports of motor vehicles must use the parallel exchange rate. Certain capital goods are authorized for import at a preferential exchange rate.

6-30-84, Costa Rica: Prior import deposits (see 9-26-80) are raised to 100 percent.

9-25-84 Additional restrictions on exports to Nicaragua are imposed. All payments from the Central American Clearing House are required in U.S. dollars. The use of barter arrangements and one-for-one exchanges of letters of credit for commercial transactions is authorized.

9-28-84, Costa Rica: The general 1 percent import duty (see 1-19-84) is raised to 3 percent.

11-14-84, El Salvador: About 50 percent of 357 categories of intermediate goods and all 110 categories of consumer goods are moved to the parallel market.

11-16-84, Guatemala: A multiple foreign exchange rate system is established. An official rate of Q1 per dollar covers most export proceeds and imports of essential goods, some capital remittances, and other invisibles. A banking market is established with a floating exchange rate for most capital transactions including private sector repayment of external debt. An auction market is used for imports of certain products designated by the Bank of Guatemala.

1985

2-8-85, Nicaragua: A multiple exchange rate system is established: C$10 for debt service: C$20 for imports of raw materials, spare parts and essential goods; C$40 for imports of capital goods; C$50 for exports of several strategic goods and services, student expenditures abroad, credit cards, and professional fees. The "free" rate is over C$700.

2-27-85, Costa Rica: A new series of import categories and export proceeds are moved to the parallel market. This procedure is continued progressively throughout the year.

3-19-85, Honduras: A parallel exchange market is introduced for trade transactions with other countries in the Central American Common Market. Exporters to this market are allowed to retain their foreign exchange proceeds in special freely transferable deposit accounts in the corresponding external currencies for use in importing from those countries.

3-29-85, Guatemala: Fifty percent of proceeds from cotton exports must be surrendered in the banking market (see 11-16-84). Similar regulations are passed in May for sugar and in October for coffee.

5-20-85, Nicaragua: A newly redefined "free" exchange rate begins operations. Only one exchange house is authorized to handle all transactions in this market.

6-12-85, El Salvador: The advance prior import deposit is abolished (see 2-18-80).

7-1-85, Guatemala: a tax of 3.5 percent is levied on most foreign exchange operations.

9-17-85, Costa Rica: The multiple exchange rate system is eliminated and replaced by a unified interbanking rate.

11-20-85, Honduras: Exporters of bananas, minerals, meat, and shrimp are authorized to retain up to 25 percent of their foreign exchange proceeds to finance their own import requirements.

Notes

1. See McKinnon (1979), chapter 3 ("Currency Inconvertibility and the Foreign Trade of Centrally Planned Economies") for an insightful discussion of the costs associated with barter trade in Eastern Europe.

2. At present central bank positions are liquidated at least every other week and sometimes more frequently. See Young (1965) and the Inter-American Development Bank (1984) for additional information on the institutional structure of the clearing house. Payments balances with the Bank of México were historically settled every four months rather than every six months.

3. Chapter 5 ("The San José Protocol") of Shaw (1978) contains much detail on the events leading to the trade restrictions employed by the Central American countries against each other.

4. See Holbik and Swan (1972) for additional information related to the creation of FOCEM.

5. This information is taken from the Inter-American Development Bank (1980–81).

6. This information is contained in the Inter-American Development Bank (1984).

7. The information in this section on the series of restrictive trade measures employed in Central America after 1982 is taken from various issues of *Análisis Económico* (formerly *Correo Económico*).

8. See Brock (1984) and Brock and Tower (1987) for a more theoretical treatment of the ways by which governments can alter the demand for the monetary base.

9. See Bean (1948) for an extended discussion of the trade restrictions that were imposed on intra-European trade in 1947.

10. See Coffey and Presley (1971) as quoted by McKinnon (1979, p. 251).

11. See Rees (1963, p. 69) for a discussion of the negotiations leading to the initial form in which Marshall Plan aid was given to Europe.

12. See Rees (1963, p. 75) for these figures and for discussion of the Intra-European Payments Plan.

13. These four points are contained on page 25 of a report by the comptroller general of the

United States (1959) to Congress evaluating the impact of U.S. contributions to the European Payments Union.

14. On July 15, 1947, Britain made an attempt to reestablish currency convertibility both within and outside of the sterling area. In the six weeks between July 15 and the end of convertibility on August 20, Britain lost about $1 billion in foreign exchange reserves. Rees (1963) shows that the large drain on reserves was with the dollar area.

References

Análisis Económico. Guatemala: Fundación para el Análisis y Desarrollo de Centroamérica (FADES), various issues.

Bean, Robert W. (1948). "European Multilateral Clearing." *Journal of Political Economy* 46 (October), pp. 403–15.

Brock, Philip L. (1984). "Inflationary Finance in an Open Economy." *Journal of Monetary Economy* 14 (July), pp. 37–53.

Brock, Philip L., and Edward Tower (1987). "Economic Liberalization in Less Developed Countries: Guidelines from the Empirical Evidence and Clarification of the Theory," in Michael Connolly and Claudio Gonzalez-Vega (eds.), *Economic Reform and Stabilization in Latin America*, pp. 19-43. New York: Praeger Publishers.

Castillo, Carlos Manuel (1986). *La Integración Económica de Centroamérica en la Siguiente Etapa: Problemas y oportunidades*. Report Commissioned by the Inter-American Development Bank and the Institute for Latin American Integration (March).

Coffey, Peter, and John R. Presley (1971). *European Monetary Integration*. London: The Macmillan Press, Ltd.

Comptroller General of the United States (1959). *Examination of United States Contributions to European Payments Union*. Washington, D.C.: U.S. General Accounting Office, November.

Hinshaw, Randall (1958). "Toward European Convertibility." Princeton University Essays in International Finance, no. 31 (November).

Holbik, Karel, and Philip L. Swan (1972). *Trade and Industrialization in the Central American Common Market*. Studies in Latin American Business, no. 13. Austin: The University of Texas at Austin.

Inter-American Development Bank. *Economic and Social Progress in Latin America*. 1980–81, 1984, 1986, and 1987 reports. Washington, D.C.: Inter-American Development Bank.

Lizano, Eduardo (1987). "Prospects for Regional Economic Integration." Unpublished manuscript, Central Bank of Costa Rica, December.

McKinnon, Ronald I. (1979). *Money in International Exchange: The Convertible Currency System*. Oxford: Oxford University Press.

Rees, Graham L. (1963). *Britain and the Postwar European Payments Systems*. Cardiff: University of Wales Press.

Shaw, Royce Q. (1978). *Central America: Regional Integration and National Political Development*. Boulder, Colo.: Westview Press.

Young, John Parke (1965). *Central American Monetary Union*. Washington, D.C.: U.S. Department of State Agency for International Development.

Part 3

The Legacy of Central American Initiatives

Chapter 12

The Alliance for Progress: An Appraisal
Richard L. McCall

Throughout Latin America, a continent rich in resources and in the spiritual and cultural achievements of its people, millions of men and women suffer the daily degradations of poverty, and hunger. They lack decent shelter or protection from diseases. Their children are deprived of the education and the jobs which are the gateway to a better life. And each day the problems grow more urgent. Population growth is outpacing economic growth; low living standards are further endangered; and discontent—the discontent of a people who know that abundance and the tools of progress are at last within reach—that discontent is growing. In the words of José Figueres, "once-dormant peoples are struggling upward toward the sun, toward a better life."

If we are to meet a problem so staggering in its dimensions, our approach must itself be equally bold—an approach consistent with the majestic concept of Operation Pan America. Therefore, I have called on all people of the hemisphere to join in a new Alliance for Progress—*Alianza para Progreso*—a vast cooperative effort, unparalleled in magnitude and nobility of purpose, to satisfy the basic needs of the American people for homes, work, and land, health, and schools—*techo, trabajo y tierra, salud y escuela*.

With these remarks delivered before the Latin American diplomatic corps and a bipartisan representation of the U.S. Congress, President John F. Kennedy launched the Alliance for Progress at a White House reception on March 13, 1961 (Levinson, p. 355).

The president outlined a ten-point, decade-long program designed to "mark the beginning of a new era in the American experience."

The living standards of every American family will be on the rise, basic education will be available to all, hunger will be a forgotten experience,

the need for massive outside help will have passed, most nations will
have entered a period of self-sustained growth, and though there will
be still much to do, every American republic will be the master of its
own revolution and its own hope and progress (p. 335).

The initiation of the Alliance for Progress represented a marked departure
in inter-American relations in the years following the end of World War II.
Largely ignored because of our preoccupation with the economic rebuilding
of Western Europe and Japan, Latin America had been relegated to the
backwaters of U.S. diplomatic and economic considerations.

Before the creation of the alliance, public economic cooperation with Latin
America was limited to financing exports of U.S. manufactures, to long-
term sales of U.S. agricultural commodities, and to a very modest technical
assistance program for demonstration projects and training in health, education and agriculture. Bilateral development assistance flows from the
United States to the region were negligible, as Latin America competed with
the other developing nations for limited resources from the World Bank. If
balance of payments assistance was needed, then the International Monetary
Fund could fulfill that requirement.

Since the advent of the Marshall Plan and its subsequent success, the
leaders of Latin America had been appealing for a regional program of
significant proportions. U.S. officials explained that the assistance supplied
for the reconstruction of Western Europe was required to meet the challenge
of Soviet communism. Latin America did not face such a security threat
and therefore private capital could satisfy its development needs.

By the late 1950s the environment in Latin America had changed
considerably. President Kennedy's bold new plan was based as much upon
his sense of idealism and vision, as it was on his sense of pragmatism. The
massive social reform in the hemisphere to be brought about by the alliance
would result in long-term stability and prosperity for our Latin American
friends through the economic and political integration of millions of disenfranchised workers and peasants. These efforts would be spearheaded by
the instruments of democratic change throughout Latin America—leaders
committed to social reform and political pluralism.

There was also an urgency born of political pragmatism, if not of necessity.
During the last years of the Eisenhower administration, numerous rebellions
swept from power military dictators in Latin America upon whom we had

relied as the bulwarks against communism. The most unnerving of these revolutions was the overthrow of the Cuban dictator Fulgencio Batista by Fidel Castro in 1959. Thus, the alliance was as much a regionwide crash program of development designed to ameliorate the social conditions which serve as fertile ground for communist-inspired insurrections as it was a product of U.S. beneficence.

In preparing for his March 13 speech, President Kennedy asked the Venezuelan ambassador to the United States, José Antonio Mayobre, for his ideas and suggestions. In formulating his reply Mayobre enlisted the assistance of nine Latin American economists connected with international organizations. The group included Felipe Pazos, who had been president of the Central Bank of Cuba in the first year of the Castro regime but had since defected; Felipe Herrera, president of the Inter-American Development Bank; Jorge Sol Castellanos, executive secretary of the Inter-American Economic and Social Council; and Raul Prebish of the Economic Commission for Latin America. Romulo Betancourt of Colombia and José Figueres of Costa Rica were also consulted.

Of the four basic points contained in Mayobre's response to President Kennedy, two are particularly worth noting:

> . . . this program must capture the imagination of the masses. They must be convinced with clear and palpable evidence that the program is not motivated by a desire to create lucrative fields of investment for foreign private capital. . . . There should be cooperation with the countries willing to make structural social and economic transformations; cooperation should be with present ruling groups if they propose to do it or with new groups that arrive in power by democratic means. . . . Above all, it is necessary to change the agrarian land tenure system, to correct the regressivity of the tax system, to avoid restrictive practices and other distortions that impede the functioning of the economic system and favor great inequalities in the distribution of income (p. 57).

The other point stressed the potential difficulties confronting such an ambitious program of social reform. ". . . [F]rom a political point of view it 'would not always be easy to overcome the resistance of the privileged groups without agitation and disturbances.' If the United States was to enter into a program to transform the social and economic structures of Latin American countries, 'it must be prepared to understand this fact' " (p. 58).

The views of these distinguished Latin American economists and political leaders were not lost on President Kennedy, who incorporated the same themes in his speech launching the alliance. There was an obvious meeting of the minds concerning the nature of the challenge and the goals which must be pursued.

The charter codifying the principles and goals of the Alliance for Progress within the inter-American system was drafted and approved at the Conference of the Inter-American Economic and Social Council, meeting in Punta del Este, Uruguay, August 5–17, 1961. It was at that conference that C. Douglas Dillon, President Kennedy's secretary of the treasury, announced that if the countries of Latin America themselves undertook the necessary internal measures, they could expect to receive $20 billion in external resources over the alliance decade. Dillon emphasized that the Latin Americans could expect that the greatest share of this development financing would come from the United States in the form of foreign assistance.

At the conclusion of the conference, Clemente Mariani, Brazil's minister of finance, summed up the prevailing sentiments of the participants in the following statement:

> In a gesture of political vision, the United States has placed at our disposal the resources which, in conjunction with those of other sources and those we can mobilize ourselves, will be the mainspring of our economic and social development...This economic revolution is to be carried forward with equally needed social reforms. . . . Development is not enough. We need development with social justice. A conscience is being forged, at times in a confused manner, in which the poor, the hungry, the illiterate, the sick, and the despairing clamor to have better days, if not for themselves, at least for their children (p. 73).

The concept behind the alliance was, and remains today, one of the most innovative approaches to peaceful change envisioned by development planners. The alliance was predicated upon the belief that democratic reformers were critical to its successful implementation. Its primary thrust was economic and political democratization. The ultimate goal of the alliance was the economic and political integration of millions of Latin Americans, existing on the margins of their societies, into the mainstream of their nations.

The stakes were high, for as President Kennedy warned at the time, "those who make peaceful revolution impossible, make violent revolution inevitable."

Implementation of the Alliance

The original goal of the alliance, that of a major program of democratic development, was short-lived. By the end of 1963, the alliance had lost its social and political content. There were a number of reasons for this turn of events.

The Congress

The alliance was designed to serve a long-term planning effort in which the governments of Latin America would know well in advance what external resources would be available to supplement their own. From the very beginning, however, President Kennedy experienced problems with the United States Congress.

Kennedy originally requested an initial three-year authorization of $3 billion to finance the alliance. Congress balked. First, $600 million was trimmed from the president's request, and then Congress agreed only to an annual appropriation. There would be no long-term commitment to the goals of the alliance.

The president was successful in obtaining congressional approval for Title VI of the Foreign Assistance Act of 1962, which singled out the alliance for a separate appropriation.

The importance of a multi-year commitment of resources for the alliance cannot be overestimated. Effective development planning takes time. It often takes two years just to prepare adequate feasibility studies showing the relative costs and benefits of an investment. The U.S. administrators of the alliance funds were caught in an immediate dilemma. If all the funds appropriated the previous fiscal year were not used, an already reluctant Congress would most certainly reduce the following year's appropriation.

The administration's solution to this "Catch-22" was to commit significant loan funds as the end of the fiscal year approached. These rapid last-minute experiences only heightened congressional suspicions that excessive resources had already been approved for the alliance program. Needless to say, this made Congress even more reluctant to fund fully the administration's annual requests for the alliance.

The Foreign Assistance Act itself is also fraught with contradictory objectives. The act stipulates that it is the intention of the United States to: ". . . assist the people of less developed countries in their effort to acquire the knowledge and resources essential for development, and to build the economic, political and social institutions which will meet their aspirations for a better life, with freedom and peace."

However, this policy statement is offset by at least two other policy guidelines spelled out in the act. One is concern for U.S. balance of payments, and the other has been restrictions that special-interest groups have been successful in adding to the act over the years.

As the United States began to incur balance of payments deficits in the early 1960s, Congress stipulated that purchases financed by appropriated funds must be made in the United States. In addition, a further restriction was placed on the transportation of commodities financed under the foreign assistance programs. Often this meant a doubling of the transportation costs for commodities being used in projects throughout Latin America and elsewhere. It also meant frequent shipping delays if American shipping was not immediately available to transport the goods.

The act also required the extensive use of U.S. private consultants in project formulation, particularly in technical fields such as engineering. Thus, expensive reports by U.S. private consultants became the norm on project loan applications.

The Executive Branch

The executive branch was also a major source of problems plaguing the implementation of alliance programs. Except in the early years, alliance projects became increasingly bogged down by bureaucratic infighting and parochial interests of individual agencies that were frequently at odds with the goals set out by President Kennedy.

The Department of the Treasury has been responsible for managing and protecting the U.S. balance of payments position in the world. Therefore, the department saw the alliance as a major drain on foreign exchange from the United States.

The Commerce Department has been primarily interested in U.S. exports and increasing those exports. Therefore, its goal is to make the Agency for International Development a vehicle for U.S. exports, while protecting numerous domestic producers, such as textile producers, from project funding that could produce additional foreign competition.

The Department of Agriculture has served to promote the interests of the domestic agricultural sector. Therefore, USDA feared that financing alliance agricultural projects to increase food production would result in the production of commodities which could compete with U.S. producers in the international market.

The Export-Import Bank's sole responsibility was to finance U.S. exports.

In the early years of the alliance, the Latin American Bureau of the U.S. Agency for International Development was able to implement its program with a minimum of interference from other U.S. government agencies. However, Congress provided, in the Foreign Assistance Act, for the establishment of a Development Loan Committee (DLC) to advise the AID administrator on possible conflicts with other aspects of U.S. policy. The members of the DLC were the AID administrator, the president of the Export-Import Bank, and the secretaries of agriculture, commerce, and the treasury.

In 1965, with the appointment of Henry Fowler as secretary of the treasury, President Lyndon Johnson initiated a new commitments procedure under which every loan of $10 million or more had to have Fowler's personal approval. Each loan had to be cleared by the secretary of the treasury—in effect giving the government official, whose primary responsibility was to worry about the overall financial position of the United States, veto power over individual alliance loans.

The impact of alliance resources on U.S. balance of payments became the primary consideration of every loan approval. This led not only to more closely tying alliance funds to the procurement of U.S. goods and services, but also to the use of loans that would lead to the additional export of U.S. goods to a recipient country above what could actually be purchased with each loan. This latter criterion became known as the principle of additionality. In other words, to be eligible for AID funding, alliance projects were narrowed to those that would produce additional purchases to the usual import flow from the United States.

The new procedures were very complex—too much so to be explained in any detail in this paper. Suffice it to say, the new procedures not only delayed even further the project approval process, but also narrowed the types of projects that could be financed by AID. The problems created by this bureaucratic maze are best exemplified by the following anecdote:

> In 1968 the President Lleras Restrepo had to intervene personally in the negotiations for a program loan to Colombia. It took him four months to get a realistic list (of goods from the United States eligible for financing) approved. "Colombia has received two program loans under the alliance," he said before the compromise was reached. "I don't know if we can survive a third." (p. 123)

As was noted earlier, in the first years of the alliance AID was freed from bureaucratic constraints that eventually took over the program. As a result, AID was instrumental in pioneering new lending techniques that the more conventional lending agencies shunned.

> For example, AID supplied $200 million for the establishment of privately owned development financing institutions in Latin America, providing long-term, low-interest loans to Latin American entrepreneurs. The other international lending agencies, which had regarded this kind of lending as too risky, began to make funds available for similar purposes when AID's experience proved successful. But as the Castro threat receded, other concerns within the U.S. government gained precedence and stifled this innovative spirit. (p. 113)

The Changing Scene in Latin America

Developments throughout Latin America also began to take their toll on support in the United States for the original goals of the alliance. One problem was technical, the other political. On the technical side, it was essential to the alliance concept of national development that planning play the major role. Yet in the early years of the alliance, national governments did not have planning ministries staffed by technically trained personnel who could formulate operational plans. Therefore, projects were not ready for financing by even the most modest of standards. Even preliminary technical studies were hampered by the lack of statistical data on such basic issues as income distribution, employment, agricultural production, and education.

As a result, in the early years of the alliance a significant part of the U.S.

foreign aid funds channeled to Latin America served primarily to refinance debt payments to bankers, including the Export-Import Bank. This use of U.S. public funds may have prevented some major Latin American countries from suspending foreign debt payments, but it did not add to the visible accomplishments of the alliance.

On the political side a series of military coups provoked a reappraisal in Washington of U.S. alliance policy. Civilian governments in Argentina and Perú fell first to military coups. Democratic elections scheduled for November 1963 in Guatemala were not held. Juan Bosch was ousted by the military in the Dominican Republic that same year, as was the democratically elected president of Ecuador. The president of Honduras was similarly ousted in a coup in October, 1983.

In the face of these reversals, rather than adhering to the original recommendation contained in Ambassador Mayobre's memorandum to direct alliance resources to reform-minded, democratic regimes, President Lyndon Johnson took steps to reverse these original goals. He placed both the State Department and AID functions under Thomas Mann, who in March 1964 reportedly announced at a private meeting with U.S. ambassadors to Latin American countries the following new policy: "(1) to foster economic growth and be neutral in internal social reform, (2) to protect U.S. private investment in the hemisphere, (3) to show no preference, through aid or otherwise for representative democratic institutions, and (4) to oppose communism" (p. 88). The policy of democratic development had been cast aside.

Old Directions in U.S. Foreign Assistance

Beginning in 1964, the traditional U.S. policy toward Latin America was reconstituted. Our primary concerns would be economic stabilization and the maintenance of political neutrality except toward communist or potentially communist regimes. The alliance lost its soul, and with it, its political appeal. It was soon to lose significant resources as well.

By 1966, the U.S. involvement in Vietnam intruded into the considerations about funding for the alliance. The U.S. government, including the central AID bureaucracy, assigned an ever-higher priority to the assistance program in Vietnam. When William Gaud, the new AID administrator, was asked by the Bureau of the Budget where cuts in the aid program should be taken to compensate for the increases being sought for Vietnam, he replied: "Take it out of the alliance" (p. 115). Congress obliged, slashing the alliance appropriation request in 1969 even deeper.

Capital Flows Under the Alliance

In August of 1961, secretary of the treasury C. Douglas Dillon committed the United States to a $20 billion program of economic assistance over ten years to fund the Alliance for Progress.

In their book *The Alliance That Lost Its Way*, Jerome Levinson and Juan de Onis estimated that between 1961 and 1969 the U.S. government, the international financial institutions, the United Nations, the European Common Market, and the Development Assistance Committee members authorized $18 billion in assistance to Latin America. Of that amount, $4.8 billion in net flows was made available through all U.S. government sources.

In the meantime, the terms of trade with the United States deteriorated for the nations of Latin America. Between 1960 and 1968 Latin America's share of United States merchandise imports fell from 27.2 percent to 15.8 percent.

As Levinson and de Onis noted, the Alliance for Progress was handicapped from the beginning by the level of public indebtedness in Latin America. "In 1960, the figure was over $10 billion. In 1966 it was $12.9 billion, and debt service in Latin America amounted to about 90 percent of grant and loan disbursements—both public and private—a proportion higher than that in any other region of the underdeveloped world. It was 32 percent in Africa, 20.4 percent in South Asia, and 33 percent in East Asia" (p. 133).

U.S. private investment was to have played a significant role as a source of capital during the alliance decade. Yet direct investment from the United States between 1961 and 1968 totaled only $1.4 billion, bringing the total U.S. private investment in Latin America to $12 billion. Of the income received from U.S. private investment (profits and earnings), $1.9 billion of the $7.1 billion was reinvested in Latin America during this period. An estimated $5.7 billion was repatriated to the United States.

This provoked William T. Dentzer, Jr., former deputy U.S. ambassador to the Organization of American States, to observe:

> If one further deducts the net flow of capital income payments to U.S. private investors in the United States, that is to say, gross remittances

less new investments and reinvested earnings, that flow is about nil, in terms of bilateral U.S. capital flows. . . . When you look at net capital flows and their economic effect, and after all due credit is given to the U.S. effort to step up support to Latin America, one sees that not that much money has been put into Latin America after all. (p. 140)

In 1967 Hollis Chenery, then director of AID's Office of Programming and Planning, noted the net effect of U.S. bilateral efforts prevented national bankruptcies which would have been accompanied by severe reductions in production.

What Went Wrong

In 1966 David Rockefeller, writing for *Foreign Affairs*, observed that the "new concept of the Alliance for Progress with its emphasis on economic development" was more conducive to confident investment attitude than the "overly ambitious concepts of revolutionary change" in the early (1961–63) years.

In 1967 President Eduardo Frei of Chile, rebutting this claim in an article also appearing in *Foreign Affairs*, noted that the alliance had "lost its way" precisely because it had abandoned its emphasis on revolutionary social change (p. 204).

Levinson and de Onis noted that "the Alliance for Progress, as originally conceived, represented a new theory of development which stressed social reform and democratic political processes as much as economic growth. This emphasis on deliberate policy measures to speed up the process of income redistribution and redress social injustices gave the alliance its revolutionary impact and uniqueness. Without this democratic and reformist orientation it became just another aid program" (pp. 203–204).

By returning to traditional development assistance programs, the United States was able to assist in accelerating the economic growth of the recipient countries in Latin America. However, the economic benefits derived from traditional development programs usually follow the recipient country's existing pattern of income distribution. This means such benefits will go primarily to those who already hold wealth and power.

The alliance principle of distributing the benefits of economic growth through society by means of social and political reforms was new to both development economists and AID officials administering the program in Washington. As a result, it was difficult to overcome frustrations that naturally occurred when obstacles to the implementation of the alliance program developed. Hence, the easier path was chosen. However, by retrenching into the traditional focus on monetary stabilization and economic growth, the effort was turned away from adult literacy and agrarian reform toward technical education and agricultural production.

What the planners and administrators of the alliance program failed to grasp was that an effective agrarian reform program requires that a society commit itself to heavy investment in its peasants. Such a program requires granting the peasants land, capital, education, technical services, equal access to the market and a voice in the political affairs of the nation. This was the peaceful social revolution that the alliance was attempting to promote.

Washington also underestimated the resistance to the implementation of a massive agrarian reform program throughout Latin America. Such efforts were met with political vacillation in some countries, outright desertion in others, and shifting priorities in the United States. In Washington, it was assumed that the ruling class in Latin America would refrain from obstructing the process of democratic development. President Kennedy was convinced that a sense of pragmatic self-interest would rule the day.

When these obstacles to agrarian reform appeared impossible to overcome, the U.S. government and inter-American development agency officials convinced themselves that agriculture was, after all, a farm problem, rather than a peasant problem. The Kennedy administration's political emphasis on changes in land tenure to prevent violent agrarian upheavals gave way to an economic emphasis on expansion of agricultural production to feed a rapidly multiplying population.

One of the primary lessons of the alliance is that the United States, while not forswearing the principle of democratic development, must recognize its own limitations. Targets that cannot be achieved should not be set. Promises that cannot be kept should not be made.

But one of the most important lessons of the alliance experience is that the United States has to make a distinction between development objectives and security considerations. When the security issue loses its urgency, just as the perception of the Cuban threat receded in 1964, the alliance was undermined. One of the primary driving forces behind the alliance was the need to attack the root causes of instability, which provided the foundation for communist insurrection.

In the case of the alliance, other problems eventually arose which demanded a higher priority, particularly in the allocation of U.S. foreign assistance resources. There was the war in Vietnam, the need to defend the dollar, the pressure from protectionist lobbies, and the domestic urban crisis. These concerns took precedence over the decade-long commitment President John F. Kennedy made to millions of Latin Americans.

This latter point is important if the United States is to avoid the same pitfalls upon which the alliance foundered as consideration is given to the development of a similar program for the countries of Central America. Such a program will require presidential leadership to establish clear priorities among conflicting policies within the executive branch itself. Such a program will require presidential leadership to ensure that these priorities are presented forcefully to the Congress and the public. This emphasis on clear choices and explanations cannot help but produce the reasonable, long-term commitments so necessary to the achievement of the goals we establish.

Such a program should also build on the basic cornerstone of the alliance, which was designed to improve the living standards of millions of Latin Americans within the framework of democratic institutions. That principle remains as relevant today as it was in 1961 when the alliance was conceived and launched. In addition, it is important for the United States to acknowledge that our own limitations and our own national interest are directly linked to assisting those nations who are determined to undertake economic and social reforms and who are committed to strengthening their own democratic processes. It is important for us to realize that there is not a foreign aid program that can bring about democratic and modernizing change of significance in the absence of genuine and sustained political support of the recipient national government. No amount of foreign assistance can do for other countries what they are unwilling to do for themselves.

Both Congress and the executive branch also have to understand that constraints or restrictions placed on an agreed-upon program between ourselves and the nations of Central America will doom any major effort to failure. We just cannot have it both ways. We cannot say that we support democratic economic and political development and at the same time undermine this most desirable goal by protectionist trade policies or aid programs driven by parochial considerations.

Finally, a major constraint on the effectiveness of the alliance stemmed from the enormous debt problem in Latin America. The fact that some 90 percent of the grant and loan disbursements went to service public and private debt of Latin American governments insured that actual capital resources available for development, let alone development directed at major and pressing social and economic restructuring, were minimal at best. This is the problem confronting the countries of Central America today. The economic support funds we provide to Costa Rica, El Salvador, Honduras, and Guatemala are used basically to recycle payments to private and public financial institutions. Very few resources are available to deal with pressing development problems.

The purpose of this essay is not to diminish in any way the efforts undertaken during the alliance decade of the 1960s. It is realistic to point out that the alliance did not come close to achieving most of its original objectives and specific targets. However, it did produce some significant results. The decade gave Latin America a new development consciousness, which affected and permeated large segments of the population. As Levinson and de Onis pointed out, economic planning, particularly in Brazil, Colombia, and Chile, did reach an impressive level of sophistication. Throughout the hemisphere, young, technically trained people came to play major roles in the key public-sector institutions. In addition, there developed within the Latin American private sector a significant cadre of successful middle-level entrepreneurs and an increasing number of efficient managers.

Note

Considerable research material was utilized during the preparation of this paper. The reason for the exclusive use of Jerome Levinson and Juan de Onis's *The Alliance That Lost Its Way* (Chicago: Quadrangle Books, 1970) stems from the fact that I found this publication to be the most comprehensive and cogent review of the alliance experience. All page numbers in parentheses refer to this book.

Chapter 13

Trade Unshackled: Assessing the Value of the

Caribbean Basin Initiative

Stuart K. Tucker

In promoting its Caribbean Basin Initiative, the Reagan administration attempted a classic free-trade maneuver to advance the economies of Central America and the Caribbean, while at the same time promoting U.S. security interests in the region.

The hallmark of the Reagan administration has been its emphasis on development of the private sector. Just as the administration has pushed for deregulation in the U.S. economy, it has attempted to spread the faith about laissez-faire economics on the international level. With the Caribbean Basin Initiative it was hoped that, by breaking the chains that restrain commerce, the full economic potential of the region would be realized. Unfortunately, but not surprisingly, the "unshackling" of trade has produced minimal results. Past trade restraints on much of the region's exports have been minor; the most deleterious "chains" remain in place; and the former "slave" has few resources for dealing with its centuries of commodity-dependence. Certainly, the "unshackling" was a correct action—but one of limited value without the appropriate steps to alleviate the economic distortions created by centuries of dependence.

Since its beginning in 1984 the Caribbean Basin Initiative (CBI) has had minimal effect on trade. Although manufactured export growth has been remarkable, it is not attributable to the CBI. The near- and medium-term prospects for Caribbean basin export expansion and growth are modest at best. Primary commodity price trends outweigh the effect of the program's free trade area. Furthermore, investment in nontraditional exports is unlikely to be significant for quite some time.

Another reason for pessimism is that politicization has reduced the economic effectiveness of the U.S. bilateral aid program, as well as that of the multilateral institutions in the area. Already Caribbean leaders have leveled charges of "breach of faith" at the U.S. government's faltering commitment to the Caribbean Basin Initiative. Prime Minister Errol Barrow of Barbados noted, "The Caribbean Basin Initiative has brought no visible benefits to my country. It was a device by the United States to get money into El Salvador."[1] The high expectations fostered by the initial announcement of the program have not been fulfilled. Although it is important that the United States maintain a positive air of confidence in the region's prospects, the United States has oversold the promise of the CBI's trade provisions.

The CBI provides an example of how a program formulated essentially as an expression of U.S. self-interest is not bringing substantial benefits for the developing countries involved, largely because those countries' interests are not the major motivation for the program. A more valuable approach would be the establishment of an interactive system whereby realpolitik power relations are set aside and meaningful multilateral consultation takes place in the formulation and implementation of trade/investment initiatives. Standard bilateral trade preferences will not have a substantial impact. Success will require well-formulated, complementary programs focusing primarily upon aid and investment incentives.

Key CBI Provisions

The Reagan administration's stated goals for the program are enhancing growth in Central America and the Caribbean and increasing the mutual benefits of economic relations between the United States and the basin. This is to be accomplished through export-oriented growth, limited government intervention, and tighter links between the United States and Caribbean private sectors. The CBI's major goal, however, is the protection of American security interests by fostering political stability through economic growth.[2] The island countries of the Caribbean praised the intent of the program, hoping that their manufactured products would be able to bypass the variety of tariff and nontariff barriers protecting the U.S. market. Some businessmen speculated that Asian investment would relocate to the Caribbean to take advantage of the preferences. Furthermore, they expected that the administration would recognize the negative aspects of U.S. agricultural trade policies and come to the rescue of their flagging agricultural sector, which was suffering from the effects of global overproduction and subsidization.

The countries of Central America were suffering from debt burdens, destruction from internal strife, stagnant export markets, and the collapse of regional trade. They saw the CBI as a form of financial relief combined with renewed American commitment to its political ties with the Central American business class. As some Central American countries were being "graduated" from eligibility in some product-areas in the U.S. Generalized System of Preferences (GSP) program, the CBI promised to hold open the American market.

Trade

The central policy instrument of the Caribbean Basin Initiative is the nonreciprocal preferential treatment of goods from the region—a policy aimed at augmenting the region's growth and diversification through enhanced export access to the U.S. market. Although the U.S. government expressed hope that the program would be complemented by similar programs in other industrialized countries, the CBI is markedly a bilateral program.

The Caribbean Basin Economic Recovery Act (CBERA) reflected Reagan administration desires. The trade provisions in the act allow the president to grant duty-free treatment for twelve years to all imports from designated Caribbean basin countries, except for textiles and apparel articles subject to textile agreements under the Multi-Fiber Arrangement; footwear, handbags, luggage, flat goods, work gloves, and leather wearing apparel excluded from GSP eligibility; canned tuna; petroleum and petroleum products; and watches and parts if they contain any materials produced by "communist" countries. In addition, sugar and beef products lose duty-free treatment if the beneficiary country fails to submit a "stable food production" plan. This provision is intended to remove any incentive to shift production away from grain crops in order to take advantage of duty-free access for sugar and beef exports.[3] In any case, sugar and beef products remain limited by quotas.

All countries in Central America, as well as those adjoining the Caribbean Sea, may be designated as CBI beneficiaries, except for Colombia, Cuba, Mexico, Venezuela, and French territories. Some countries, however, have not applied for this designation.[4] For a product to be eligible, at least 35 percent of its direct cost must be attributable to processing in a beneficiary country (U.S.-made components may comprise 15 of these percentage points). Products made of foreign materials must be "substantially transformed" in a beneficiary country.

Investment

To encourage American investment in the region, the administration had requested a 10 percent tax credit for investment in the region. Since this provision would have applied to both existing and new investment, Congress believed that it would be too costly for the likely benefits for the basin. Therefore, the tax credit was replaced by a narrow provision allowing businesses and individuals to deduct convention expenses from their taxes as long as the country involved has signed a Tax Information Exchange Agreement or other similar arrangement with U.S. Department of the Treasury.

Aid

Highlighting U.S. commitment to economic stabilization in the region at the end of the global recession of 1981–83, the administration sought a supplemental aid package of $350 million to meet balance-of-payment shortfalls. Most of the money was aimed at Central America, with El Salvador slated to receive $128 million. Responding to the charge that the program was a cover for extra aid for war-torn El Salvador, Congress altered the country-recipient mix, reducing El Salvador's share to $75 million. The aid distribution that was passed, however, still heavily favored Central America.

Evolution Since Passage

Efforts to promote the CBI have been highly visible. Although some of these efforts can be criticized for reckless use of dubious figures,[5] the U.S. government has considered these activities necessary to overcome business sector inertia in investment and import sourcing decisions. Several officials admit that the promotional efforts elevate expectations far above what the CBI can produce, but this effort, they say, has beneficial effects by attracting the attention of businessmen to the inherent advantages of doing business in the basin.

These promotional efforts are complemented by a variety of programs of value to the countries of the Caribbean basin.[6] In March 1986, in an effort to extend access to the U.S. apparel market, the Section 807 program was modified to provide guaranteed access to Caribbean basin countries. (Imports entering the United States under Section 807 of the U.S. tariff code are products assembled from materials originally made in the United States. Import duties are assessed only on the value added to the product while outside the United States, thus allowing the value of the original materials to reenter the United States duty-free.) These products, however, are often subject to tariffs, and the "guaranteed access" is limited by "surge" provisions to avert unexpected increases. Finally, changes in the U.S. tax code have allowed Puerto Rico to use its Section 936 funds for twin-plant investments in Puerto Rico and the Caribbean Basin. It was not until the spring of 1988 that IRS regulations were issued on the use of Section 936 funds outside of Puerto Rico. By January 1989 six projects had been endorsed and four certified, totaling about $100 million in lending at interest rates slightly below the market rate.

The Caribbean Basin in the 1980s: Before and After the CBI

After nearly four years of existence the record of the CBI has been disappointing. Although the program is not a failure, neither is it likely to fulfill the high expectations created by its announcement. The slow start of the CBI and the restrictive trends of U.S. trade and foreign aid policy fail to fulfill its good intentions. In short, the CBI is largely irrelevant to the economic dilemmas of Central America and the Caribbean.

Region-Wide Economic Record

Economic Growth and Inflation. The 1980s have been an economic disaster for Central America and the Caribbean. While those countries untouched by the ravages of war have performed better than the war-torn countries of Central America, even the "success stories" have been experiencing economic troubles. The average annual growth rate of gross domestic product during 1981–86 has been, at best, anemic. Of the twelve major countries of the Caribbean basin (listed in table 13.1), only in Panamá did economic growth outpace population growth. El Salvador, Guatemala, Haití, and Trinidad

Table 13.1 GDP Growth in Central America and the Caribbean (percentages)

	1980	1981	1982	1983	1984	1985	1986	Average Annual Growth 1980–86
Central America								
Costa Rica	0.6	-2.3	-7.3	2.9	8.0	1.0	3.0	0.8
El Salvador	-9.6	-8.3	-5.6	0.8	2.3	2.0	1.0	-1.4
Guatemala	3.5	0.7	-3.5	-2.5	0.5	-1.0	0.0	-1.0
Honduras	2.6	1.0	-2.6	1.1	3.5	2.7	3.0	1.4
Nicaragua	10.0	5.4	-0.8	4.6	-1.6	-4.1	-0.4	0.5
Panamá	4.9	4.2	5.5	0.4	-0.4	4.1	2.8	2.7
Caribbean								
Bahamas	6.9	1.0	1.0	1.5	3.0	3.5	2.0	2.0
Barbados	2.8	-3.1	-4.6	0.5	2.2	0.3	4.7	0.0
Dominican Republic	5.5	4.1	1.7	3.9	0.4	-2.2	1.3	1.5
Haiti	5.4	-2.7	-3.5	0.8	0.3	1.1	-0.2	-0.7
Jamaica	-5.4	2.7	1.1	2.3	-0.5	-5.0	2.2	0.4
Trinidad and Tobago	7.4	4.6	4.0	-9.2	-10.6	-5.6	-6.4	-4.1

Source: Inter-American Development Bank, *Economic and Social Progress in Latin America*, 1982 and 1987.

and Tobago produce less now than they did in 1980. The rest remain stagnant. Even in the period of the recovery from the 1981–83 world recession, the record remains bleak. Only the Bahamas, Costa Rica, Honduras, and Panamá show some signs of recovery. These signs have been faint, however, as their growth rates during 1984–86 reached only half the rate achieved by developing countries in the 1970s and remained below the average growth rates of developing countries during 1984–86.

The economic difficulties in these countries are also reflected in inflation rates (see table 13.2). El Salvador, Guatemala, and Nicaragua are currently experiencing rapidly increasing consumer price increases, with Nicaragua's economy approaching hyperinflation. Costa Rica, the Dominican Republic, Jamaica, and Trinidad and Tobago have each gone through bouts of inflation during the last five years. In general, those countries that have had lower inflation rates have been the ones with slightly better GDP growth rates.

The period of operation of the CBI, 1984 to the present, has not proven to be a radical departure from the economic record of the pre-CBI period.

Table 13.2   Change in Consumer Prices in Central America and the Caribbean (percentages)

	1980	1981	1982	1983	1984	1985	1986
Central America							
Costa Rica	18.1	37.1	90.1	32.6	11.9	15.1	11.8
El Salvador	17.4	14.8	11.7	13.1	11.7	22.3	31.9
Guatemala	10.7	11.4	0.2	6.2	2.4	18.7	36.9
Honduras	15.6	9.4	9.0	8.3	4.7	3.4	4.4
Nicaragua	35.3	23.9	24.8	31.1	35.4	219.5	681.6
Panamá	13.8	7.3	4.2	2.1	1.6	1.0	−0.1
Caribbean							
Bahamas	12.1	9.0	6.1	4.1	3.9	4.6	5.4
Barbados	14.4	14.6	10.3	5.3	4.6	3.8	2.0
Dominican Republic	16.3	7.5	7.6	6.9	24.5	37.5	9.7
Haiti	17.9	8.2	9.0	8.8	8.0	8.4	8.0
Jamaica	27.1	12.7	6.9	12.5	28.9	23.0	14.4
Trinidad and Tobago	17.5	14.3	11.4	16.8	13.3	7.7	7.7

Source: Inter-American Development Bank, *Economic and Social Progress in Latin America*, 1982, 1984, and 1987.

No country in Central America or the Caribbean has grown faster than the average developing country. In fact, all have performed worse than either developing countries or industrial countries—most of which have had poor recoveries in comparison with typical expansions after recessions.

Total Trade. International trade is a major reason for the poor economic performance in Central America and the Caribbean. These countries are extremely dependent upon a narrow range of primary commodity exports. Except for coffee in the last few years, the world prices of these commodities have dropped dramatically. As it was in the past commodity busts, Central America and the Caribbean are suffering terribly for their general lack of economic diversification.

Central America's global trade balance went from a $3 billion deficit in 1980 to a $3.6 billion deficit in 1983. After falling to $5.3 billion in 1985, the deficit was $4.7 billion in 1986. The region's exports bottomed out in 1982–83. Since 1983 exports have grown $1 billion, but this increase is almost entirely attributable to the rise in coffee prices, a temporary increase due primarily to disasters with Brazilian coffee production. Central American imports have roughly paralleled exports, except that the dip was shallower and the subsequent rise steeper.

For the six major countries of the Caribbean, the story has been worse. Their exports steadily declined from $9.4 billion in 1980 to $4.9 billion in 1986. Imports fluctuated around a declining trend. The global trade balance of these countries has deteriorated from a $0.6 billion surplus in 1980 to a $1.1 billion deficit in 1983 and a $2.1 billion deficit in 1986. The focal point of these trends has been the oil-refining countries, the Bahamas, and Trinidad and Tobago. The drop of oil prices has destroyed the export earnings of these two countries. The other four major Caribbean countries also saw their export earnings erode and trade balance worsen during the same period.

Trade with the United States. U.S. imports from the six major countries of the Caribbean closely parallel the region's worldwide trend. On the other hand, these Caribbean countries have become greatly dependent upon U.S. products for their imports (46 percent in 1986, whereas the percentage was 30 in 1980).

At the same time Central America has decreased its dependence on the United States for its imports. The U.S. share of the region's imports was 25.7 percent in 1980, 23.2 percent in 1983, and 21.2 percent in 1986. This is counterposed to the increase in the U.S. share of exports from Central

America: 32.3 percent in 1980, 35.2 percent in 1983, and 37.9 percent in 1986. On the surface, these data would suggest that the CBI has had at least some success in diverting Central American exports to the U.S. market, if not in creating new exports. In fact, the CBI had little if anything to do with this shift. If coffee is taken out of the balance, the export gain is virtually erased. The rest of the gain can be explained by products not eligible for duty-free access under the CBI.

U.S. imports of goods from the Caribbean basin fell in 1984-86 (see table 13.3). Total U.S. imports increased 26.4 percent in 1984, 6 percent in 1985, and 7 percent in 1986. Yet, U.S. imports of all goods from CBI countries fell 1.2 percent in 1984, 22.1 percent in 1985, and 8.6 percent in 1986. Preliminary estimates of 1987 U.S. imports reveal a similar contrast. Although U.S. imports from Central America have fared better (up 28.1 percent between 1983 and 1986), even this growth was slower than total U.S. imports (43.4 percent).

Total U.S. imports under the CBERA amounted to $578 million in 1984, declined to $498 million in 1985, then grew to $690 million in 1986. Imports under the Generalized System of Preferences (GSP) program declined 14 percent between 1983 and 1986 and the GSP utilization ratio declined, indicating that some of the gains in CBERA imports were due not to trade creation, but to the simple accounting procedure of shifting the mode of access. Of the top twenty products entering under the CBERA (accounting for 72 percent of CBERA imports), only 44 percent were provided new

Table 13.3   U.S. Imports, 1983–1986 (annual percentage change)

	Percentage Change 1983–1984	Percentage Change 1984–1985	Percentage Change 1985–1986	Estimated Percentage Change* 1986–1987
Total Imports	26.4	6.0	7.0	8.2
From Developing Countries	18.0	−2.5	2.4	7.1
From Latin America	14.9	−1.9	−10.2	4.9
From CBI Beneficiaries	−1.2	−22.1	−8.6	−6.2

* By author, based on first six months of 1987.

Note: Imports values used are c.i.f.

Source: U.S. Department of Commerce.

Table 13.4 U.S. Imports from the Caribbean Basin, 1981–86
(millions of dollars)

	Caribbean Basin Growth Rates for Period		Sector Share of Imports from Caribbean Basin		Central America Growth Rates for Period		Sector Share of Imports from Central America	
	1981–83 (%)	1983–86 (%)	1983 (%)	1986 (%)	1981–83 (%)	1983–86 (%)	1983 (%)	1986 (%)
Total U.S. Imports	-8.9	-30.0	100.0	100.0	2.1	28.1	100.0	100.0
Total Non-oil U.S. Imports	-1.8	19.5						
Food	-6.6	22.0	23.0	40.1	-0.4	29.1	76.5	77.1
Beverage and Tobacco	-2.7	-12.8	1.0	1.3	1.6	-32.3	2.1	1.1
Crude Material	-40.0	-36.9	4.5	4.0	-18.6	-17.8	3.2	2.0
Mineral Fuels	-14.1	-71.5	54.3	22.1	71.9	-37.5	2.6	1.3
Oils and Fats	-36.4	42.9	0.0	0.0	—	—	0.0	0.0
Chemicals	47.8	57.0	1.9	4.3	40.9	406.5	0.2	0.7
Manufactured Goods, by Material	2.8	44.1	1.9	4.0	-3.9	133.0	1.5	2.8
Machine and Transport Equipment	83.0	-23.7	4.0	4.3	19.7	-45.8	5.6	2.3
Miscellaneous Manufactures	20.5	94.4	5.8	16.0	20.9	100.9	7.3	11.5
Not Elsewhere Classified	10.6	-23.7	3.6	3.9	-17.5	40.8	1.0	1.1
Agricultural Commodities	-6.6	20.0	20.7	35.5	0.6	27.0	73.6	73.0
Nonagricultural Commodities	-9.5	-43.1	79.3	64.5	6.5	31.0	26.4	27.0
Food, Feed, and Beverages*	-7.2	23.5	20.8	36.7	0.0	32.5	67.4	69.8
Industrial Supplies*	-15.7	-64.5	60.7	30.8	4.3	-5.0	7.9	5.8
Capital Goods*	80.1	-25.6	3.8	4.1	20.3	-50.8	5.6	2.2

Automotive Goods*	40.4	137.5	0.1	0.3	—	666.7	0.0	0.1
Consumer Goods*	21.7	91.6	7.1	19.4	16.1	94.5	8.2	12.4
Electrical Machinery*	45.4	−20.7	2.5	2.8	21.8	−61.6	5.3	1.6
Nonelectrical Machinery*	228.5	−39.7	1.3	1.1	4.5	55.1	0.4	0.5
Petroleum	−14.2	−71.5	54.2	22.1	69.3	−36.5	2.6	1.3
Textiles	16.1	88.2	0.4	1.0	34.5	143.6	0.7	1.3
Steel	−23.4	10.7	0.5	0.8	—	—	0.0	0.0
Power-Generating Machinery	127.3	232.0	0.0	0.1	—	—	0.0	0.1
Office Machines	136.6	−66.1	0.2	0.1	−50.0	−50.0	0.1	0.0
Electronic Computers	NA	NA	0.0	0.0	—	—	0.0	0.0
Telecommunications	73.3	3.8	0.1	0.2	80.0	33.3	0.1	0.1
Transport Equipment	−41.7	457.1	0.0	0.1	—	166.7	0.1	0.1
Autos	NA	NA	0.0	0.0	—	—	0.0	0.0
Aircraft	200.0	100.0	0.0	0.0	−100.0	—	0.0	0.0
Clothing, except Footwear	21.2	105.4	4.2	12.2	15.7	115.8	5.6	9.4

* Note: Imports are c.i.f., except for the categories with an asterisk, which are customs value basis.

Source: U.S. Department of Commerce.

preferences.[7] The other 56 percent would have been duty-free under GSP or Most-Favored-Nation treatment. Assuming conservatively that only 50 percent of total CBERA imports were due to this kind of accounting procedure, then the CBERA provided $345 million of new U.S. imports, or only 5 percent of 1986 U.S. imports from Caribbean basin countries and 2 percent of total Caribbean basin exports to the world. Even this small "addition" includes goods that would have been exported to other countries. In short, overall creation of new trade has been extremely small.

The sectoral breakdown of U.S. imports from Caribbean basin countries shows that in 1983 nearly 80 percent of U.S. imports were agricultural commodities or petroleum and petroleum products (see table 13.4). With the collapse of the price of oil and the downward trend in commodity prices in general, the value of U.S. imports over the three-year period 1983–86 declined 30 percent. Petroleum imports declined 72 percent. Primary commodities far outweigh CBI-eligible products in Caribbean production. In fact, the 11.4-percent share of CBERA imports in 1985 overstates the importance of preferences, since the petroleum import contraction reduced total imports, and thus raised the CBERA share.

If one looks in isolation at nonprimary product trade, growth has been respectable, but not outstanding. Non-oil imports from the Caribbean basin grew 19.5 percent and manufacturing sector imports (Standard International Trade Classifications 5 through 9) from the Caribbean basin countries increased 33 percent during the first three years of CBERA. This included substantial growth of power-generating machinery, transportation equipment and parts, chemicals, textiles, and clothing (see table 13.4). The manufacturing sector share of non-oil imports increased from 37.5 percent in 1983 to 41.7 percent in 1986.

The growth of manufacturing exports, however, comes from a small base and is not apparently attributable to the CBI. Comparing the manufacturing sector's performance in 1983–86 with the two previous years (prior to the enactment of the CBERA and a period of recession in the United States) shows very little impact of the CBI or tariffs in general. During 1981–83, manufacturing imports grew 29 percent—faster than the 33 percent over three years registered after the start of the preferences. Chemical imports grew at similar rates before and after enactment. Capital goods imports grew more slowly in 1984 and 1985 and then dropped sharply in 1986. Textile and clothing imports—not eligible for the preferences and, in fact, nominally under a quota system—actually grew more quickly after the enactment of the CBERA. Textiles and clothing are the most competitive and successful industries in the region, despite ineligibility for the CBI (see table 13.5).

Another telling sign of the limited impact of the CBERA trade provisions is the relative standing of basin producers in relation to other suppliers to the U.S. market. Presumably basin countries should be gaining a larger share of the import market, due to their preferential advantage over other foreign suppliers. Instead, the share of CBI countries in total imports of important sectors has not lived up to this expectation. The basin's share of animal and vegetable products (the largest category of those goods entering under the duty-free provision of the CBERA) actually fell from 9.3 percent in 1983 to 8.5 percent in 1985. Even more dramatic, despite the rapid two-year growth rate of chemical products, CBI countries have not gained on their competitors, who also experienced rapid growth. The share of non-metallic minerals and products grew from 1.2 percent to 1.3 percent, entirely on the strength of 1985 trade, as the 1984 share was down to 0.6 percent. The metals and metal products share fell drastically as the two-year growth rate amounted to only 3.7 percent compared to 51.7 percent for total U.S. imports of these products. The basin did poorly in the nontraditional, higher technology export sectors as well. Imports of CBI office machines declined, while total U.S. imports grew 52.7 percent. Total imports of electrical capacitors grew 16.5 percent, while imports from the basin countries declined 17.3 percent. Similar stories apply to resistors, articles for making and breaking electrical circuits, miscellaneous electrical articles, and baseball equipment. In one of the few early success stories, monolithic integrated circuits grew 7 percent, but the CBERA was not a factor—only 4.1 percent of these goods entered under the CBERA duty-free provisions. In 1986, even this success disappeared, as imports declined by almost two thirds.[8]

Investment. Investment is a central determinant of economic growth and trade performance by Central American and Caribbean countries. Gross domestic investment (GDI) in Central American countries suffered deep declines during the 1980s (see table 13.6). Since 1983, GDI has continued to be weak. GDI as a percentage of GNP was much lower in 1986 than during the 1970s for most Central American countries. By 1986 Costa Rica had regained much of the decline in its investment ratio. Nicaragua's investment has been strong in the 1980s, comparing quite favorably with the 1970s, when investment was quite low due to the revolution.

Table 13.5 U.S. Imports of Clothing, 1983–86
($ millions and percentages)*

Origin	Imports ($ millions)				Percentage Share (percentages)				Growth Rate for period 1983–86 (%)
	1983	1984	1985	1986	1983	1984	1985	1986	
World	10,292	14,513	16,056	18,554	100.0	100.0	100.0	100.0	80.3
Industrial Countries**	1,202	2,091	2,559	2,888	11.7	14.4	15.9	15.6	140.3
Developing Countries	9,090	12,422	13,497	15,666	88.3	85.6	84.1	84.4	72.3
Latin America	729	1,001	1,199	1,419	7.1	6.9	7.5	7.6	94.6
Central America	98	120	149	211	1.0	0.8	0.9	1.1	115.3
Caribbean	303	380	497	612	2.9	2.6	3.1	3.3	102.0
(Caribbean Basin Total)	401	500	646	823	3.9	3.4	4.0	4.4	105.2

* Clothing and accessories, leather and fur articles except footwear.

** Includes centrally planned economies of Eastern Europe.

Source: U.S. Department of Commerce, *Highlights of U.S. Export and Import Trade*, December 1986.

Table 13.6 Gross Domestic Investment in Central America and the Caribbean
(as % of GDP and annual % growth)

		1970s*	1980	1981	1982	1983	1984	1985	1986	GDI Growth for period 1980–86 (%)
Central America										
Costa Rica	% GDP	23.7	28.5	18.2	14.6	18.9	19.8	21.2	22.5	
	Growth	9.3	7.0	–37.7	–25.5	33.1	13.3	7.8	9.2	–17.6
El Salvador	% GDP	16.8	12.5	13.1	12.5	11.3	11.4	10.6	13.0	
	Growth	3.6	–32.0	–3.9	–10.2	–8.5	3.0	–5.6	24.6	–4.3
Guatemala	% GDP	13.8	11.4	13.1	11.0	9.4	9.9	8.0	8.2	
	Growth	5.2	–14.7	15.3	–19.2	–16.9	6.1	–19.7	2.0	–32.7
Honduras	% GDP	21.4	25.0	20.5	12.4	15.0	20.1	18.5	16.3	
	Growth	7.1	–4.7	–17.0	–41.3	22.1	38.7	–5.5	–9.3	–29.3
Nicaragua	% GDP	15.7	16.8	24.4	20.2	21.0	21.6	22.3	23.7	
	Growth	0.2	n/a	52.9	–17.6	8.7	0.9	–0.6	5.5	44.9
Panamá	% GDP	27.9	23.6	25.5	22.4	17.7	15.8	14.0	13.6	
	Growth	3.8	16.9	12.6	–7.1	–20.8	–11.0	–8.1	0.5	–31.9
Caribbean										
Bahamas	% GDP	9.6	10.2	10.2	10.2	10.2	10.1	10.1	n/a	
	Growth	4.3	16.2	0.9	1.0	1.2	2.8	3.4	n/a	n/a

(*Continued*)

Table 13.6 (Continued)

		1970s*	1980	1981	1982	1983	1984	1985	1986	GDI Growth for period 1980–86 (%)
Caribbean										
Barbados	% GDP	24.8	28.4	33.1	29.6	29.5	29.5	n/a	n/a	
	Growth	3.4	6.6	13.0	−14.7	0.3	2.2	n/a	n/a	n/a
Dominican Republic	% GDP	23.6	25.3	21.7	19.8	19.5	19.6	n/a	n/a	
	Growth	10.0	6.9	−10.9	−7.3	2.5	1.1	n/a	n/a	n/a
Haiti	% GDP	14.0	17.5	18.1	17.5	18.3	18.5	17.0	14.6	
	Growth	11.8	1.4	0.7	−6.8	5.4	1.5	−7.1	−14.5	−20.2
Jamaica	% GDP	23.4	12.7	13.7	14.2	14.1	14.2	14.3	n/a	
	Growth	−9.4	−27.2	10.1	4.9	1.8	0.0	−4.0	n/a	n/a
Trinidad and Tobago	% GDP	45.3	64.6	51.5	52.1	51.2	42.3	47.0	n/a	
	Growth	15.4	22.6	−16.6	5.4	−10.9	−26.2	n/a	n/a	n/a

* % GDP = 1970–79; Growth = 1971–80.

Source: Inter-American Development Bank, *Economic and Social Progress in Latin America*, 1987.

Caribbean countries, for the most part, have not sustained dramatic drops in gross domestic investment of the magnitude of Central America. Investment declines have proven to be a major problem, however, in Haiti and Jamaica.

Investment is slower than trade in reacting to changes in incentives such as the CBI offers. Although data on foreign investment are not generally available, some data on U.S. investment in the region are available for 1984–86, and some preliminary trends are emerging.

U.S. direct foreign investment position in the basin countries has not grown appreciably since 1983 (less than one percent). The difference between investment conditions in Central America and those in the Caribbean is significant (see table 13.7). All of the weakness of U.S. investment can be attributed to the decline of investment positions in Central America. Investment in Panamá fell by 10 percent from 1983 to 1986, while investment in the rest of Central America fell by about 30 percent—reducing U.S. investments to below the 1980 level. On the other hand, investment in the small Caribbean island economies continued to rise. Despite this progress, U.S. investment in the Bahamas, the Dominican Republic, Jamaica, and Trinidad and Tobago has fallen. These drops have been more than counter-acted by the doubling of U.S. direct investment in the British Virgin Islands.

U.S. direct investment in manufacturing enterprises in Central America increased in 1984, dipped in 1985, and regained the 1984 level in 1986. Investment in the Caribbean, after increasing in 1984, declined by more than 40 percent during 1985–86. Manufacturing investment in Jamaica and Trinidad and Tobago suffered significantly larger declines. Income from U.S. direct investment in 1984-86 remained sharply below pre-CBERA rates—not surprisingly, given the poor trade performance of the region.

These data, covering only the first three years of the program, are not very indicative of investment plans for the region. The Department of Commerce and the Department of State conducted a survey of U.S. investment in the region to discern trends. The survey data released in August 1985 show that since the enactment of the CBI, there has been $208 million in new U.S. investment, creating nearly 36,000 jobs and representing no more than 2 percent of current U.S. investment in the region. Although the data indicate a shift of investor interest toward nontraditional exports, the figures do not take into account major planned disinvestments—such as Reynolds Aluminum in Jamaica, United Brands in Costa Rica, and Exxon in the Netherlands Antilles. Given the size of these planned disinvestments

Table 13.7 U.S. Direct Foreign Investment in the Caribbean Basin, 1982–86 ($ millions)

Position

	1982	1983	1984	1985	1986	Annual Growth Rate (percentages)			
						1982–83	1983–84	1984–85	1985–86
Total	11,534	12,896	12,952	12,609	13,033	11.8	0.4	-2.6	3.4
Caribbean	6,134	7,190	7,528	7,849	8,022	17.2	4.7	4.3	2.2
Central America	5,151	5,568	5,293	4,617	4,853	8.1	-4.9	-12.8	5.1
Source Not Disclosed	249	138	131	143	158				

Income

	1982	1983	1984	1985	1986	Annual Growth Rate (percentages)			
						1982–83	1983–84	1984–85	1985–86
Total	3,212	3,107	2,025	2,593	2,271	-3.3	-34.8	28.0	-12.4
Caribbean	2,665	2,302	1,613	2,101	1,375	-13.6	-29.9	30.3	-34.6
Central America	552	850	382	491	900	54.0	-55.1	28.5	83.3
Source Not Disclosed	-5	-45	30	1	-4				

Source: U.S. Dept. of Commerce, *Survey of Current Business*, various issues.

it will be difficult for new investment to offset the economic effects of the plant closings. Furthermore, these data have been greatly criticized by the General Accounting Office (GAO) for inaccuracies and misrepresentations. A GAO report notes that only a few of these reported investments can be even remotely attributed to the CBERA trade or investment provisions.[9] A new report on investment, using revised methods, is not yet available.

Other figures confirming the weak investment activity in the Caribbean basin are U.S. Department of Commerce data on capital expenditures planned by majority-owned foreign affiliates of U.S. companies. In 1986 these expenditures amounted to $116 million in Central America and $282 million in the Caribbean. Company plans for 1987 and 1988 call for $128 million and $118 million in Central America and $207 million and $151 million for the Caribbean respectively. A dramatic drop is also evident in capital expenditure plans in the Caribbean manufacturing sector. Hence, while the near-term investment picture appears to be better in Central America, investment activity does not encourage the hope for an increase in investment in the near future.

Furthermore, a large part of the investment that is taking place in the Caribbean basin is not related to the CBI. Preliminary results of a Department of Commerce investment survey show that of 132 new projects, 55 can be identified as ineligible for duty-free access to the U.S. market (and some of the duty-free related investment is not CBERA-related). In two industries eligible for CBERA duty-free treatment, electrical and electronic components and cut flowers, investment declined in 1986. In the case of the latter, antidumping and countervailing duty cases undermined investor confidence in open access to the U.S. market.[10]

With the CBERA expiring in a little over seven years, there is little reason to expect the trade preferences to generate much more investment than has already been seen. Most investments require roughly five years to reach the point at which the initial outlays have been recouped and the enterprise is profitable. Given these profitability lags, it is highly likely that an investor would see the first several years as the only viable time to invest to take advantage of the CBI, given the current twelve-year time limit.[11] Hence, unless and until the preferences are extended, no significant future investment can be expected to be related to the existence of the CBI.

Development Aid. Since the passage of the CBERA, the U.S. government has continued to transfer large sums of aid to the region (see table 13.8).

Table 13.8   U.S. Economic Assistance to CBI Countries, FY1981–86
(millions of U.S. dollars)

	1981	1982	1983	1984	1985	1986
Costa Rica	13	51	212	175	195	154
El Salvador	114	182	246	323	314	309
Guatemala	17	14	28	32	80	101
Honduras	34	78	106	170	131	123
Panamá	11	13	7	46	35	23
Regional Programs	11	13	19	53	122	101
Central America	200	351	618	799	877	811
Belize	0	0	17	15	10	8
Dominican Republic	36	79	60	143	117	96
Haiti	34	34	46	45	53	50
Jamaica	71	137	102	108	155	109
Eastern Caribbean	27	87	58	106	54	55
Caribbean	168	337	283	417	389	318
Basin Total	368	688	901	1216	1266	1129

Source: U.S. Department of State, *The Caribbean Basin Initiative (CBI): Progress to Date* (May 1986).

Much of this money is in the form of balance-of-payment support and is justified primarily on the grounds of security interests in Central America. The vast majority of the increase in U.S. bilateral aid to the basin has been for Central America. Between fiscal years 1981 and 1986, aid to Central America increased 305 percent, while aid to the Caribbean grew only 89 percent.

The U.S. government hoped that this large influx of U.S. aid would give it more leverage to accomplish the policy reforms necessary to put Central America on a path to stability. However, as AID has admitted, some governments are not moving quickly on reforms and the stabilization phase has taken longer than planned by the Kissinger Commission, largely due to the continued political/military climate. Hence, AID asked and has received from Congress an extension of the implementation period and the monetary commitment related to the recommendations of the Kissinger Commission.[12]

U.S. aid strategy has not found willing collaborators among the multilateral development institutions. The World Bank's International Finance Corporation (IFC), which is designed to aid private sector investment, has opted to stay away from the politicized arena of Central America. IFC activities through its Caribbean Project Development Facility have been limited to the Caribbean islands and have been operated at a steady low-profile level since the 1970s. Relatively unknown, the project has the advantage of longevity, providing the predictability that investors often require. On the other hand, the Inter-American Development Bank (IDB), governed largely by borrowers, has not shied away from the turmoil in Central America; this has caused disputes between the Latin Americans and the United States, which is strongly opposed to lending to Nicaragua and has threatened to discontinue funding the IDB if such loans are approved. Efforts to move the IDB in the direction of private sector promotion have produced a new facility, called the Inter-American Investment Corporation (IIC). The IIC began operation in the spring of 1986. The probable impact of this new initiative is unknown and its prospects are clouded by the continuing dispute over Nicaragua. Thus, in both cases, the effectiveness of the multilateral institution has been reduced by the overriding political goals of the United States.

Prospects for the Future. The stormy global economic climate that has generated the external shocks currently buffeting Central America and the Caribbean bodes an ill future. Except for recent U.S. growth, global income growth has been disappointing in this recovery. As the prospect of another U.S. recession nears, the Caribbean basin is unlikely to find dynamic, alternative markets for its goods. The failure of commodity prices to rebound significantly during this recovery raises fears that there may be a long-term downward trend for the prices of key basin products. This may be due in part to technology shifts and substitutes, but the high level of agricultural market intervention by industrial countries also plays an important role.

The U.S. market itself is subject to CBI beneficiary criticism that its trade and agricultural subsidy policies dampen the willingness of U.S. businessmen to invest in the region. The sugar quota system represents the largest, but by no means the only, countervailing policy working against development prospects in the Caribbean and Central America.[13] Textile protectionism in the form of stricter quantitative restrictions was narrowly averted in August 1986. This is one product area for which the basin countries have high hopes. If their most dynamic economic sectors are going to be under constant political pressure within the U.S. Congress, basin countries are justified in their fear that the CBI is an empty promise—that as soon as there are signs of success, the market access will be shut down. Textiles are not an exception either: tariffs on the order of 60 percent on ethanol were proposed in 1986 and the Tax Reform Act of 1986 places restrictions on the eligibility of ethanol for duty-free treatment; U.S. concerns about its steel industry always garner congressional support; and an expansion of U.S. countervailing duties and antidumping laws was passed on August 23, 1988.[14]

Country Experiences with Exports to the United States

Central America. As can be seen in table 13.9, the coffee export boom played a dominant role in the 1983–86 export success of all Central American countries except Costa Rica. In fact, without Costa Rica or coffee, Central American exports to the United States fell during the first three years of the CBERA.

Costa Rica has been a major participant in those export successes in the Caribbean basin since 1983. Eleven of the top thirty exports of CBI countries have grown faster than total U.S. imports taken as a whole. Costa Rica is a major supplier of five of those 11 categories. The success of Costa Rica has been twofold. A large part of it has been attributable to apparel exports, which are generally not eligible for duty-free access. There has, however, also been a significant expansion of export earnings from nontraditional

Table 13.9   Central American Coffee Exports to the United States, 1983–86
($ millions)

	Coffee			Total	
	1983	1986		1983	1986
Costa Rica	38.8	97.7		451.8	726.4
El Salvador	212.6	271.5		373.6	386.3
Guatemala	151.7	393.5		407.2	660.6
Honduras	42.8	98.7		418.8	485.3
Panamá	10.4	35.2		377.4	397.5
Central America	456.2	896.5		2,028.7	2,656.2
Change			440.3		627.5

Source: U.S. Department of Commerce.

agricultural and aquacultural exports. Of the thirteen product categories (using three-digit numbers of the Tariff Schedule of the United States) which account for more than 1 percent of Costa Rican exports to the United States, 9 showed growth over the last two years. These included coffee, beef, three categories of textiles and apparel, tuna, shellfish, pineapples, and live plants. Two of the categories of apparel exports were not exported prior to 1985, springing into existence and jumping to the rank of fourth and fifth in Costa Rica's exports to the United States within just two years. The four categories that declined in the last two years include bananas, sugar, electrical resistors, and garters and suspenders. Bananas remain the number one export earner in Costa Rican trade with the United States and are twice as large as coffee exports, which rank second.

El Salvador has been the major disappointment in Central America for the CBI program. It is the only country, other than the ineligible and embargoed Nicaragua, to have its exports to the United States decline since 1984. A major cause of this has been the collapse of a variety of electrical machinery exports, which caused an earnings drop larger than the rise from coffee. Two other top earners, sugar and shellfish, have also declined. Significant success has taken place in three categories of apparel and textiles, now ranked fifth, sixth, and seventh among the seven export categories accounting for more than one percent of Salvadoran exports to the United States.

Guatemala has been the biggest beneficiary of the coffee boom, with earnings from coffee exports to the United States rising $242 million since 1983, while total exports to the United States rose $253 million. With the Guatemalan dependence upon primary commodities the most concentrated (coffee, bananas, and sugar account for more than three quarters of its earnings), the CBI is not expected to have a significant influence on its trade patterns.

Honduras has shown only weak export growth under the CBI. Honduran shellfish exports, however, have been strong. Due to Honduras and Panamá, shellfish imports to the U.S. are growing faster than overall imports. Honduran successes in the area of textiles and apparel have modestly followed those of Costa Rica. Honduras is unique in its success in the area of wood and wood furniture exports. Yet this success has been insignificant compared with the dramatic increase in its coffee earnings and the decrease in its sugar earnings.

Panamá's export growth has been even weaker than that of Honduras. Primary commodity exports have fallen, as they have throughout the region. At the same time, successes in nontraditional exports have been only modest. The one departure is the introduction of analgesic production. Formerly produced by only one other Caribbean country—the Bahamas—analgesics now account for about one percent of Panamanian exports to the United States. Analgesics and two categories of wearing apparel were not produced prior to 1985 and now number in the top thirteen exports of Panamá.

Selected Other Countries. Once expected to be the showcase of the CBI, Jamaica has met with success only in its textile and clothing industries. The fall of the price of bauxite eliminated a major chunk of Jamaican export earnings. Sugar, another former key industry, is being phased out, to be diverted in some measure into ethanol. The U.S. ethanol industry, however, has managed to put a pall on Caribbean investment in this industry.

Barbados is a case that argues for wariness about the value of trade preferences for the Caribbean. Successes elsewhere in the region have brought about a decline in light manufacturing, especially its garment industries. In many product areas Caribbean countries find themselves competing as much with each other as with the rest of the world. Barbados is losing because of high wages, even though it has a well-educated work force. Although Barbados is an attractive place for skilled services such as data processing, the departure of INTEL, Inc., from Barbados has done much to damage its economy. The success of Barbados in the area of electronics has not been due to the CBI, since the value added at Barbadan factories is insufficient to qualify its products for duty-free access under the CBERA.

The Dominican Republic is now considered the true showcase of the CBI. Its strong growth in noncoffee exports, however, (27.9 percent in three years) is by no means stronger than Costa Rica's (52.3 percent) and is entirely due to dutiable clothing exports. Thus, little of the Dominican Republic's export expansion has been generated by CBERA-related access.

Strengths and Weaknesses of the CBI

Successful Features

Without question, the CBI has engendered an awareness of the benefits of locating nontraditional export-oriented industries in the Caribbean. The success of these industries has been extremely small relative to the economies in Central America and the Caribbean, but the growth rates have been encouraging. Whether due to the trade preferences or to increased public awareness, these successes are valuable to the region. It will be a long time, however, before the prosperity of Caribbean basin countries relies upon nontraditional exports.

The introduction of the CBI has required a new mentality within the U.S. trade bureaucracy—one directed toward *encouraging* imports into the United States. While most of the U.S. trade bureaucracy is devoted to restricting imports or promoting exports, the U.S. has reoriented itself to promote imports from Central America and the Caribbean. This means helping U.S. businessmen find suppliers abroad as well as looking for opportunities for direct U.S. investment for export to the U.S. market. The U.S. bureaucracy is still looking for ways to improve its understanding of how best to help the region (and the GAO report on the inadequate level of information on investments seems to indicate that there are weaknesses). The U.S. government has created a vast array of investment promotion efforts. If the CBI is starting slowly, the blame does not rest with the U.S. bureaucracy. The administration has successfully drummed up publicity about the CBI through trade fairs, investment missions, data networks, and government-private sector linkages. These efforts have far outweighed the trade incentives of tariff elimination in the minds of some business analysts.

Awareness among U.S. businessmen, combined with the inherent advantages of the Caribbean, can have a positive impact. The economic problems and limitations of the CBI can seem quite daunting at first. Yet the Caribbean basin has several advantages that will serve it well in the coming years. Liberal investment codes give the region an advantage over most Latin American and Asian countries. Proximity to the United States is already boosting service sector trade such as data processing. Well-educated populations make the labor forces highly attractive and adaptable to the changing nature of employment. Good will between the region and American businessmen may overcome the initial problems related to marketing and distribution in the large U.S. market.[15]

Correctable Failures

Those sectors with the most immediate potential for export expansion—textiles and apparel and leather goods—were excluded from the program and remain severely restricted by U.S. trade barriers. Even the revised access provisions for apparel under Section 807 deal only with quantitative restrictions, leaving the products subject to tariffs. Other significant regional exports, such as oil and tuna, were also ineligible. Further, sugar and beef exports face quota limits that have become more restrictive since the start of the CBI. U.S. steel imports remain under the constant cloud of protectionism—a kind of protectionism that especially hurts the newer, lower-cost producers that could develop in the Caribbean. Although some of these products may not be the glamorous nontraditional exports that the CBI is intended to encourage, they provide the bulk of employment and income generation for several countries. Until these countries boost their income from traditional exports, they will not be able to gather the necessary domestic capital to diversify into nontraditional exports. Recent data indicate that significant amounts of foreign capital are not forthcoming.

De facto country limitations also limit the value of the CBI. Although no countries have been formally discouraged from applying, the countries of Nicaragua, Guyana, and Suriname have been discouraged informally and could face being branded "communist" if they applied. This treatment disrupts efforts to formulate integration plans and to coordinate investment region-wide. The outright U.S. trade embargo against Nicaragua sows dissension among the Central American countries and leaves little hope of reactivating the Central American Common Market, once an engine of growth for the region. The lack of regional integration has a high cost: intra-regional trade in Central America (excluding Panamá) fell nearly 25 percent in 1986. The 1986 level is but one third of that achieved in 1980 and is equal to the nominal value of intra-regional trade 15 years ago.[16]

CBI investment incentives are minimal. The act provides only a business convention tax incentive. The utility of this incentive has been limited because, as one U.S. congressman has noted, there are more convention facilities on cruise ships than in most beneficiary nations. Furthermore, CBI countries are reluctant to enter into the required tax information exchange agreements. Only Barbados, Costa Rica, Grenada, and St. Lucia have signed such agreements, and the Costa Rican legislature has resisted ratifying theirs. Jamaica's prior agreements are considered sufficient. The Dominican Republic has initiated discussions toward an agreement now that section 936 funds are available for twin plants with Puerto Rico. The basic problem is that these countries see little need for such information from the United

States and fear that providing information to the United States is a deterrent to investment by U.S. businessmen. This fear may be overcome in time as countries begin to realize how little information is sought by the United States (and only when in conjunction with grand jury indictments). Investment promotion in the Caribbean has inherent problems, as demonstrated by the effort to raise investment for Seaga's bold economic efforts to privatize Jamaica. Most businessmen came away from their visits disillusioned by the state of Jamaica's economy. They were discouraged by bureaucratic tape, excessive centralization, labor unrest, and the structural problems of inadequate infrastructure and a small domestic market. To some degree, many of these characteristics plague the other Caribbean and Central American countries.

One of the most contentious issues affecting the CBI is the distribution of U.S. aid among the beneficiary countries. Outcries have managed to alter slightly the original supplemental package included in the CBERA, but the U.S. bilateral aid program is still skewed toward Central America and the larger Caribbean islands. As long as civil strife continues in Central America, this money has little chance of having a lasting developmental impact. The aid to the larger Caribbean islands has bred hostility and jealousy within the Caribbean Economic Community (Caricom). During oversight hearings conducted in February 1986 the smallest Caribbean islands asked the U.S. Congress for "special treatment" to compensate for the unequal advantages they believe the larger countries receive in the CBI. With the Department of Commerce choosing first Jamaica and now the Dominican Republic as its showcase examples of the potential of the CBI, AID is not the sole agency to blame for this emphasis.

The twelve-year limit to the CBERA has already been shortened in the minds of some Caribbean leaders as U.S. domestic political pressures are producing protectionist rumblings. With a record U.S. trade deficit, pressures may actually culminate in actions that undermine CBI benefits in the future. Already sugar quotas have been tightened during the life of the CBERA. Caribbean leaders wonder what will happen next.

Structural Limitations

The CBI trade preferences are largely irrelevant to the present trade structure of the region. Only about 5 percent of 1986 imports from the basin were not previously covered under other programs. This limited change in access cannot compensate for the larger changes in the world and U.S. economies. Highly dependent upon primary commodities, the region has been damaged severely by the recent depression in commodity prices. The sharp fall of the price of oil, for example, has severely depressed the incomes of the Netherlands Antilles and Trinidad and Tobago. Although the free access provisions may yield some progress in the area of nontraditional, light manufactured exports, these gains will remain largely invisible due to the very small size of this sector.

The advantages of CBI's preferential access are minimal. The average duty on dutiable imports from the CBI countries is already quite low (4.8 percent in 1986). Eliminating these duties will affect few investment decisions. Nor does excluding petroleum imports change this conclusion. Furthermore, figures show that the products with the lower tariffs are the ones taking advantage of the preference treatment. Moreover, the CBI's preferential access does not provide a significant advantage over the GSP program which is afforded to most developing-country competitors.

The lack of infrastructure—telecommunications and transportation in particular—is probably the single biggest obstacle to investment in the region. Like Africa, the Caribbean has few well-developed cities. Power outages are common, even in countries untouched by civil strife. Despite the Caribbean's proximity to the United States, businessmen find it easier to telephone or visit branch offices in East Asia and South America. Thus the Caribbean basin is caught in a vicious circle—with little infrastructure, few export-oriented businesses will take interest; and with export-oriented investments unlikely, few businesses will take an interest in investing in infrastructure. Only direct government aid to expand the infrastructure will break this vicious cycle of underdevelopment.

Unfortunately, little of the massive U.S. aid infusion has gone toward alleviating the region's infrastructure problems. In this sense, the aid budget illustrates the contradiction of U.S. political objectives with economic objectives for the CBI countries. Most U.S. aid is for balance of payments and consumption expenditures in those countries most necessary to the administration's military strategy in Central America (Honduras, El Salvador, and Costa Rica). Perhaps more problematic for U.S. business, the countries receiving the biggest pieces of the aid are precisely those countries with highest political risk—risks which are behind the capital flight from the region.[17] With the austerity of the U.S. budget, increased aid to projects in the Caribbean islands is unlikely. Only 26 percent of the $1,892 million of aid to the CBI countries in fiscal year 1985 actually went to the Caribbean islands. In fiscal year 1986 this percentage remained the same but the pie became smaller—$1,382 million. Of the massive aid to Central America, a sizeable chunk went to military aid or to meeting balance of payments obligations. In short, the days of massive aid to Central America and the Caribbean may be drawing to a close, with little of it having gone for the infrastructure projects that would most help the region economically.

In addition to the above problems, the Caribbean basin countries, each in its own ways, suffer from economic policies that need reforming, from war damage, oligarchical political structures, oligopolistic economic structures, "brain drain," and capital flight. Unless these problems are addressed in conjunction with the trade incentives of the CBI, economic development will not happen. Unfortunately, the reforms necessary to alter these conditions face many obstacles. The most dramatic attempt to deal with such problems, the Nicaraguan revolution, is widely considered a failure. Although the political and economic circumstances in Nicaragua today were caused as much by external factors as by the Nicaraguans themselves, the events in Nicaragua discourage future visionaries from pursuing a similar path.

Recommendations for Improving the CBI

House Ways and Means Committee Proposals

The Oversight Subcommittee of the House Ways and Means Committee is charged with overseeing the implementation of the CBI trade provisions. After reviewing a variety of complaints from the beneficiary countries, hearing expert testimony, and visiting several countries in the region, this subcommittee released its recommendations in May 1987. In March 1989 Representative Gibbons said that his Trade Subcommittee would soon draft legislation for Congress to widen the benefits of the CBI, and U.S. Trade Representative Carla A. Hills testified that the Bush administration was favorably disposed to strengthening the CBI.

The main recommendations of the Oversight Subcommittee include extension of the CBI beyond the 1995 expiration date; eliminating duties on the value-added portion of Section 807/806.30 imports from the Caribbean;

widening the product coverage of the CBERA duty-free list, including some textiles and apparel; allowing entrance of dutiable goods under a quota system, whereby tariffs would be imposed only on imports that exceed 5 percent of total U.S. imports of the goods; establishing a separate injury determination for CBI beneficiary countries in countervailing duty and antidumping unfair trade practice cases; and relaxing "rule-of-origin" requirements for the imports of Eastern Caribbean states. The subcommittee also urged an investigation of the effects of the ethanol provisions of the Tax Reform Act of 1986, the equitability of U.S. Customs Service handling of CBI imports, and the use of Section 936 funds by Puerto Rico. The subcommittee further suggested that high priority be given to continued balance-of-payments support for the CBI countries, especially the Dominican Republic. It urged more assistance for infrastructural development, marketing assistance, mid-level management training, and tourism.

The Gibbons-Pickle legislation embodies the above trade-related recommendations of the subcommittee, and calls for rolling back sugar quotas for the region to 1983 levels. Because these quotas are fundamentally at odds with the laws governing the U.S. sugar program, it is doubtful that they will be enacted. It should also be noted that the Gibbons-Pickle bill provides only a limited amount of increased access for textiles and apparel imports.

Except for the continuing limitations on textiles, apparel, and sugar, these proposals, if enacted, would provide the fullest possible trade benefits to the countries of the Caribbean basin. They even express the sense of Congress that omnibus trade legislation should not adversely affect CBI beneficiaries.

However, as argued earlier in this paper, trade preferences and access can have only a limited effect on the region.

Other Aspects. To bolster the Gibbons-Pickle initiatives, Congressman George Crockett (chairman of the House Foreign Affairs Committee's Western Hemisphere Subcommittee) is formulating proposals to enhance aid and investment. These include measures to address the needs of the rural poor, particularly women; measures to develop infrastructure; aid to small entrepreneurs; scholarships and management training; aid to tourism; cooperation between the U.S. Agency for International Development and the Caribbean Development Bank to make credit available; a reduction of military aid; eased restrictions on use of Section 936 twin plant funds; and decoupling of Section 936 funds and the convention tax exemption from Tax Information Exchange Agreements. Action on these initiatives will take a low priority compared to peace negotiations in Central America, elections in Haiti, and the political disturbances in Panamá.

This list of proposals has its merits, but it fails to accomplish a comprehensive overhaul of the premises of the CBI and its related aid strategy. The Gibbons-Pickle-Crockett approach yields changes on the margin, albeit positive ones, but does nothing to affect the process of economic and political interaction taking place in the region today. Without executive branch leadership on this issue, this may be the best that can be expected.

Going Beyond the CBI: Toward Socioeconomic Progress in Central America

The success of the CBI in assisting development in the next decade will depend on the economic environment in the basin countries, reform of both the private and public sectors, the commitment of the U.S. aid and trade bureaucracy, the willingness of foreign firms to invest, the availability of finance, the openness of the U.S. economy, the dynamism of the U.S. economy, and the nature of political strife in the region. Given these diverse variables, it is clear that the CBI addresses only a small facet of the problems in Central America. The short-term trends and the limited tools of the program provide good reasons for beginning to rethink the strategy and mechanics of the initiative. Unshackling trade is not sufficient. As Swinburne Lestrade, director of economic affairs for the Organization of Eastern Caribbean States argues, "to predicate an entire initiative on the notion that there is a latent private sector waiting in shackles to be freed and to burst forth as the engine of economic growth is false. The CBI must therefore fail."[18]

An effective development strategy requires a broader vision. Such a vision would include the trade expansion being considered by Congress, but more importantly, it would be based on a cooperative, multilateral consultation process designed to produce measures that respond to the region's economic needs, rather than U.S. strategic considerations. There is a strong case that such an approach would yield a better strategic outcome for the United States in the end. Instead of asking what the United States can afford to give, the United States, other donor countries and trade partners, multilateral institutions, and the countries in the region have to assess what the region needs.

Economic Measures

The first and foremost need of a majority of these countries is infrastructural development. Peace is a necessary precondition to investment in basin infrastructure. Infrastructure investments are unproductive, however, in war-torn countries such as Nicaragua and El Salvador. Meanwhile, Costa Rica and the Dominican Republic have made progress in peaceful environments. Until peace is achieved, aid to these countries is best directed at the emergency relief of human suffering.

A review of the recent two years of lending by the World Bank and the Inter-American Development Bank reveals that these institutions recognize these priorities. Aid to El Salvador has been limited to earthquake relief. Aid to Guatemala and Honduras has emphasized development of utilities and promotion of education and health. Aid to Costa Rica has gone into agricultural diversification.[19] This record of well-placed lending argues for shifting donor resources out of bilateral channels and into these multilateral channels.

Of course, the balance-of-payments funding provided by AID is vital to the economic stabilization efforts of Central America. This money, however, continues to be absorbed by the growing debt problems of these countries. Counterbalancing the net transfer of resources from Central American countries to commercial banks is hardly the best use of the talents of AID officials. This is particularly true considering the agency's relative failure to achieve policy reform with the leverage of this money.

Improved economic relations can be achieved by financing regional interchange and coordination through the Central American Bank for Economic Integration (CABEI) and the Central American Common Market (CACM). The first step to achieve this is the end of U.S. efforts to isolate the Nicaraguan economy from its neighbors. The next step is an infusion of funds to CABEI to rectify the payments imbalances that linger from the time when the CACM collapsed. This should be followed by new funds to assist the region in manufacturing specialization. This will move the region away from the current syndrome in which each Central American country is in competition with its neighbors for limited world markets.

In the interim period in which these countries remain largely dependent upon agricultural commodities, efforts to bolster their commodity export earnings would help provide the capital necessary to diversify into nontraditional exports. While global commodity stabilization schemes are largely ineffectual in their current form, some sort of commodity earnings support is necessary. This can be achieved through direct intervention in commodity markets or through compensatory financing during the troughs of commodity price swings. Unfortunately, the Compensatory Financing Facility of the IMF is both underfinanced and poorly managed, requiring repayments from many countries amidst continuing commodity depression. At minimum, action should be taken to change this fact. Additionally, with coffee providing the bulk of Central American earnings, the consuming nations should more actively push for changes in the coffee quotas that would stabilize prices at a higher level.

On the bilateral front, the United States could provide a great deal of relief for the region by rationalizing its own agricultural policies, which have been a major cause of the world's agricultural glut. Altering the sugar quota system is especially important to Central America and the Caribbean.

Political Aspects

The first element of a political strategy to support development in Central America is the achievement of peace and the end of destabilizing actions by the United States. The Administration's policies have fomented rather than diminished civil strife in Central America, thereby chilling the business climate.

The political goals underlying the CBI are in contradiction with the economic ones. The Reagan administration defines U.S. security goals in the basin within the context of the east-west ideological struggle and has placed a heavy emphasis within the program on securing Central American friends from the "threats" posed by Nicaragua and Cuba—considered to be pawns of the Soviet Union. This emphasis has pervaded the economic aid package (which has been skewed toward winning the allegiance of and propping up the countries bordering Nicaragua) and has been reinforced through a variety of other means.[20]

Thus, the CBI's political goals have reinforced a policy aimed at isolating the Sandinista regime in Nicaragua. This goal has tended to run contrary to the stated economic goals of enhancing growth prospects in the region. The isolation of Nicaragua undermines any attempts to revive the Central American Common Market. The attention of the United States to these political divisions in Central America and the protracted military conflicts and tensions scare away foreign and domestic investors. The World Bank has also hesitated to risk its capital amidst Central America's turmoil.

An important complementary element to the above economic efforts is the establishment of a multilateral framework whereby the beneficiary countries can enter into a dialogue with donors on aid, investment, and trade measures. This would not only help avoid contradictory or overlapping efforts, it would also tend to diminish the problem of donors giving for the sake of the donor instead of the recipient.

With technological change proceeding more quickly in the next few years, the level of "human capital" in a society will be an important determinant of its economic success. Central America is woefully backward in this regard and requires urgent attention. The impressive strides achieved by Nicaragua in the areas of health and education during the first few years after the overthrow of Somoza, compared to progress in the rest of Central America, warrant a reassessment by the United States concerning whether its current aid strategies are truly effective in supporting the improvement of the Central American work force and their living conditions. A changed aid strategy in this area would require an openness to political change hitherto not exhibited.

Notes

1. James (1986).

2. For a fuller analysis of the original goals of the CBI, see Feinberg and Newfarmer (1980).

3. Countries that have suspended duty-free treatment for sugar and beef products include Antigua, Aruba, Bahamas, Barbuda, Montserrat, the Netherlands Antilles, St. Lucia, and St. Vincent and the Grenadines.

4. Designated beneficiary countries as of September 1987 include: Antigua and Barbuda, Aruba, Bahamas, Barbados, Belize, the British Virgin Islands, Costa Rica, Dominica, Dominican Republic, El Salvador, Grenada, Guatemala, Haití, Honduras, Jamaica, Montserrat, Netherlands Antilles, Panamá, Saint-Christopher Nevis, Saint Lucia, Saint Vincent and the Grenadines, and Trinidad and Tobago. Nondesignated countries eligible to apply for designated status include: Anguilla, Cayman Islands, Guyana, Nicaragua, Suriname, and the Turks and Caicos Islands.

5. See U.S. General Accounting Office (1986) and the Subcommittee on Oversight of the House Committee on Ways and Means (1986).

6. For an explanation of these complementary programs as well as Section 807 and Section 939, see Tucker (1986).

7. U.S. International Trade Commission (1987), table 14.

8. U.S. International Trade Commission (1986). The ITC's recently released, abbreviated second report does not provide updated data on the products mentioned in this paragraph for 1986. Additional trade data may be found in U.S. Department of Labor (1986) and (1987).

9. U.S. GAO (1986).

10. U.S. ITC (1987), pp. 20–21.

11. The ITC estimates that the investments would have to take place within the first two years to insure profitability over the twelve-year time span. U.S. International Trade Commision (1986), p. 4-1.

12. Testimony by Dwight A. Ink (1987), assistant administrator of the Bureau for Latin America and the Caribbean of the Agency for International Development.

13. See Newfarmer (1985), for an analysis of the impact of sugar quotas.

14. For a brief review of recent actions that threaten to limit the effectiveness of the CBI, see U.S. General Accounting Office (1986).

15. Marketing inexperience is one of the three major problems for the Caribbean basin countries (along with inadequate infrastructure and reluctance to invest while new U.S. trade measures are under consideration). U.S. International Trade Commission (1987), p. 20.

16. Economic Commission for Latin America and the Caribbean (1987).

17. Despite some progress in reversing the capital flight in the recent year, the balance for the recent decade is deeply negative.

18. James (1987).

19. Testimony of Conrow (1987).

20. For an analysis of the political and ideological constraints on development in Central America, see Feinberg and Bagley (1986).

References

Conrow, James W. (1987). Testimony before the Subcommittee on International Economic Policy of the Senate Foreign Relations Committee. November 12.

Economic Commission for Latin America and the Caribbean (1987). *Central America: Notes on Economic Development in 1986.*

Feinberg, Richard E., and Bruce M. Bagley (1986). *Development Postponed: The Political Economy of Central America in the 1980s.* Boulder, Colo.: Westview Press.

Feinberg, Richard E., and Richard Newfarmer (1980). "Caribbean Basin Initiative: Bold Plan or Empty Promise?" In Richard Newfarmer, ed., *From Gunboats to Diplomacy: New U.S. Policies for Latin America*. Baltimore: Johns Hopkins University Press.

Ink, Dwight A. (1987). Testimony before the Subcommittee on International Economic Policy of the Senate Foreign Relations Committee. November 12.

James, Canute (1986). "Trade Preferences Scheme Under Fire." *Journal of Commerce*. October 1.

────── (1987). "Leaders in Caribbean Warm to U.S. Initiative." *Journal of Commerce*. July 7.

Newfarmer, Richard S. (1985). "Economic Policy Toward the Caribbean Basin: The Balance Sheet." *Journal of Interamerican Studies* 27, no. 1:63–89.

Tucker, Stuart K. (1986). "The Caribbean Basin Initiative: Elevated Expectations and Limited Means." Paper presented at the symposium on "Selective Preferential Arrangements Between Developed and Developing Countries (Mini-NIEO)" held by the Institute of Development Studies, Helsinki University. 28–30 November.

United States Department of Labor (1986). *Trade and Employment Effects of the Caribbean Basin Economic Recovery Act: Second Annual Report to the Congress*. Washington, D.C.: U.S. Government Printing Office.

United States Department of Labor (1987). *Trade and Employment Effects of the Caribbean Basin Economic Recovery Act: Third Annual Report to the Congress*. Washington, D.C.: U.S. Government Printing Office.

United States General Accounting Office (1986a). *Caribbean Basin Initiative: Need for More Reliable Data on Business Activity Resulting From the Initiative*. Washington, D.C.: U.S Government Printing Office.

United States General Accounting Office (1986b). *Caribbean Basin Initiative: Legislative and Agency Actions Relating to the* CBI. Washington, D.C.: U.S. Government Printing Office.

United States House of Representatives. Ways and Means Committee. Subcommittee on Oversight (1986). Various testimonies. February 25 and 27.

United States International Trade Commission (1986). *Annual Report on the Impact of the Caribbean Basin Economic Recovery Act on U.S. Industries and Consumers, First Report, 1984–85*. Washington, D.C.: U.S. Government Printing Office.

United States International Trade Commission (1987). *Annual Report on the Impact of the Caribbean Basin Economic Recovery Act on U.S. Industries and Consumers, Second Report 1984–85*. Washington, D.C.: U.S. Government Printing Office.

Chapter 14

Four Years Later: President Reagan's National Bipartisan Commission on Central America

Alan J. Stoga

In 1983 President Reagan established a commission, headed by Henry Kissinger, to analyze developments in Central America and to propose elements of a long term U.S. strategy for the region. The commission delivered its report early in 1984, triggering a frenetic congressional and bureaucratic effort to implement the commission's recommendations, especially in what was assumed to be the less controversial area of economic and social development.

But the commission had devoted considerable effort to designing a development assistance program which challenged, in fundamental ways, the existing U.S. approach to the region. When confronted with this—despite congressional endorsement of the commission's vision—the bureaucracy rejected new approaches and channelled significantly increased U.S. aid (a major legacy of the commission) through existing structures. The result was inadequate to provoke improvements as great as needed in regional economic, social, and political conditions.

This paper examines the Kissinger Commission report, its economic and social program, and the consequences of its efforts. Unfortunately, it is not possible to conclude that the commission's efforts—as implemented—met the challenges which its work identified.

I. The Kissinger Commission: Success or Failure?

The Commission shall study the nature of United States interests in the Central American region and the threats now posed to those interests. Based on its findings, the Commission shall provide advice . . . on elements of a long term United States policy that will best respond to the challenges of social, economic, and democratic development in the region, and to internal and external threats to its security and stability. The Commission shall also provide advice on means of building a national consensus on a comprehensive U.S. policy for the region (Ronald Reagan, July 19, 1983).

With this executive order, President Reagan established the National Bipartisan Commission on Central America (the NBCCA or Kissinger Commission) with the goal of designing a long-term U.S. policy for Central America. The commission's main product was a report that attempted to create a framework for understanding the interrelated political, economic and social crises of Central America, to identify long-term U.S. policy goals, to propose specific policy actions, and to urge emergency economic and military support for democratic forces in the region. The report (which has the unusual distinction, for the product of a government commission, of being well-written and quite readable) easily fulfilled the president's mandate, producing bipartisan, consensus advice which itself was a model of how a national policy consensus might be built.

However, in a more fundamental way, the commission failed on two counts. First, although many of the ideas which the commission advocated were subsequently implemented—and probably would not have been in the absence of the commission—these policies did not add up to a strategic change in the U.S. approach to the region. Second, the commission's program, to the extent that it was implemented, did not accomplish the political and economic goals identified by the commissioners themselves.

In all fairness, both of these were largely beyond the competence of the NBCCA. The commission was in existence for only six months; it quickly disbanded after delivering its report to the President. The commission neither sought nor was asked to "sell" its recommendations to the administration, the Congress, or the public, nor to oversee their implementation. However, individual commissioners, counselors, and head consultants[1] did testify before congressional committees, advised the State Department and the Agency for International Development (AID), and met with many public groups. These efforts were ad hoc, uncoordinated, and—measured by the recent results—largely ineffective: neither U.S. policy nor conditions in the region itself were much improved as a result of the work of the Kissinger Commission, although both Congress and the State Department have gone to great lengths to "demonstrate" that the commission's proposals were implemented.[2]

In my judgment, the explanation for this lies primarily in the nature of presidential commissions and in the particular circumstances of recent years, rather than in flaws in the Kissinger Commission's effort. The commission's analysis, policy framework, and program recommendations have aged well. Indeed, if the commission were reconvened today it would probably produce a similar report.

In the past U.S. presidents have used "blue ribbon" commissions, like the Kissinger Commission, to generate new thinking on public policy problems, to deflect political criticism from ongoing policy initiatives, to gain public support for preferred policy directions, to overcome bureaucratic resistance to their own proposals, or to defuse politically sensitive issues. They rarely use them for all of these, and the NBCCA was no exception. In mid-1983, Central America loomed as a particularly divisive issue in the forthcoming presidential election. Criticism of U.S. policy was increasingly partisan, the administration's policies seemed to be failing,and there was public unease over the basic U.S. approach to Central America, particularly military support for the Contras. The creation of a bipartisan, congressionally endorsed commission in this context served an immediate purpose: to remove the Central American issue from the political debate during the first half of 1983 and prospectively—if the commission were successful—from the election campaign itself. At the same time, it demonstrated a willingness on the part of the administration to expose its policies to criticism in an effort to achieve some measure of bipartisan support. In practice, this proved to be a powerful, if temporary, antidote to what had been growing criticism of the Reagan administration's approach to Central America.

Thus, the NBCCA *was* successful in a short-run political context. Indeed, the economic and social recommendations of the commission, which in sum represented a significant increase in U.S. financial expenditures in the region, were generously funded by the Congress. In itself this was evidence of a bipartisan willingness, which had not existed before the commission's efforts, to accept the administration's basic approach to Central America during an election year. In short, there are several different criteria against which to measure the Kissinger Commission:

–the extent to which it reoriented U.S. Central American policy,

–the extent to which political and economic objectives laid out by the commission were realized,

–the extent to which the commission's analysis and program appear relevant in today's somewhat changed circumstances,

–the extent to which the commission process itself was successful, i.e., that a group of prominent Americans from both political parties, with little knowledge of the region, could agree to a single analysis and draft a more or less consensus program for U.S. policy in the region, and

–the extent to which the commission at least temporarily defused Central America as an issue in the U.S. domestic political debate.

These criteria are listed in order of declining scope or ambition. Unfortunately, in retrospect the National Bipartisan Commission appears to have been most successful when measured against the less demanding criteria: the commission did not result in the creation of a comprehensive long-term U.S. regional strategy. It is not surprising that today U.S. policy in Central America is once again severely being criticized as ineffective at best and counterproductive at worst.

II. What Did the Kissinger Commission Report Say?

The commission defined its work in three stages: to educate itself, to describe the situation in Central America from the U.S. point of view, and to prescribe a strategy for U.S. policy—including both goals and programs.

The process of self-education was an important starting point because few of the twelve commissioners undertook their efforts with detailed knowledge of the region. Indeed, the NBCCA seems to have been conceived in part to demonstrate that a group of prominent nonexperts *could* reach informed conclusions about U.S. interests in the region, overcoming partisan political differences as well as their lack of specific knowledge. In effect, the commissioners took a six-month course in the politics, economics, history, and sociology of Central America.

Throughout the course two ideas were constantly replayed. First, the purpose of the study was to understand Central America as a U.S. policy problem. Criticism of the commission (and its report) as being "inexpert" or excessively "U.S.-oriented" failed to understand this essential element of the nature of the exercise. Second, the "final exam" would be the effort to produce a consensus analysis and, perhaps more importantly, a consensus program. Although none of the commissioners was asked to sacrifice his intellectual integrity, it was clearly understood that success or failure would partly be measured by the number of dissents that commissioners would eventually attach to their report.

Several themes run through the commission's analytic conclusions and, consequently, inform its recommendations.

The first of these is that the military, political, economic, and social elements of the Central American situation are intertwined: "Unless rapid progress can be made on the political, economic and social fronts, peace on the military front will be elusive and would be fragile. But unless the externally supported insurgencies are checked and the violence curbed, progress on those other fronts will be elusive and would be fragile."[3] Nevertheless, in choosing its economic and social objectives and designing its program the commission had to cut into this circular argument and "assume" peace. Although the commissioners recognized that economic and social assistance would be wasted to the extent that fighting continued, since they wanted to make specific policy recommendations—including the identification of broad financial aid magnitudes—they eventually had to contradict, to some extent, their own recognition that the problems were a "seamless web."[4] This allowed the commission to generate economic goals (the achievement of 1980 levels of per capita income at least by 1990), order of magnitude financial assistance needs (global financing requirements of $24 billion for seven Central American countries from 1984 through 1990 of which $8 billion during 1985–90 would come from the United States), and a raft of specific economic and social programs and policies.

The commission attempted to remain true to its "seamless web" theme by emphasizing that the means by which increased U.S. aid would be distributed was almost as important as the amount of aid. There is an extensive discussion of the structure and form of the development effort, and a detailed proposal for a new institution, the Central American Development Organization.[5] CADO was in part a recognition that whereas the numbers would inevitably be wrong, the concept of integrating economic, social, and political development was right. The organization would have several characteristics: regional and multilateral (to dilute the unequal bilateral relationships between a huge donor and small recipients), conditional (to link aid to economic as well as political progress), and tripartite (to open the decisionmaking process especially to entrepreneurs and organized labor). Many of the participants in the commission process almost certainly saw CADO as a more important legacy than the massive expansion of financial aid which would follow from their recommendations.

CADO was also an integral part of a second theme of the commission's analysis and conclusions: that solutions to the Central American crisis would have to be "home-grown." The commission recognized, "We cannot provide what is most vitally needed: a positive Central American vision of the future, and a process for translating that vision into reality."[6] Yet, especially in the discussion of economic and social issues, the commissioners generated a considerable number of detailed program ideas: e.g., a venture capital company, support for small businesses and cooperatives, government-sponsored scholarships for study in the U.S., and establishment of a Literacy Corps. Indeed, there seems to be a traditional "Uncle Sam knows best" approach in the seemingly endless litany of program proposals.

CADO was supposed to be an antidote to this; that the commission report includes both the litany and CADO reflects the underlying drive for consensus, and the commission's inability (or unwillingness) to choose between two fundamentally different approaches to Central American development. One approach emphasized using traditional means of identifying and implementing appropriate programs and policies for U.S. economic support, relying heavily on U.S. decisionmakers and U.S. bureaucrats, especially in AID. The other emphasized the need to shift the bulk of the decisionmaking to Central American participants in the process. Indeed, the commissioners debated whether to include any detailed description of CADO in the report; the eventual decision to provide several pages of explanation reflects the importance which most of the commission placed on the need to change a basic element of the U.S. approach to Central America.

The third theme which recurs throughout the analysis is the contribution of outside forces to the Central American crisis. The report emphasizes the "increasingly dangerous configuration of historic poverty, social injustice, frustrated expectations, and closed political systems"[7] which produced the crisis of the 1970s and 1980s. But it also details the involvement of foreign powers in supporting regional insurrections and the impact of global economic forces—world recession, oil shocks, falling commodity prices, high interest rates, and the debt crisis—on regional economies.

The implication of this analytic perspective is the commission's insistence that sustained domestic political and economic reforms would be necessary, but not sufficient, to overcome the Central American crisis. Outside support is justified in part by the need (as well as the perceived obligation) to offset these external influences, although at the same time the commissioners recognized that the U.S. could not solve any part of the crisis by itself.

The analysis, however, gave rise to a dilemma which the commissioners did not resolve: in both the economic and security portions of the report there is a continual tension between bilateral and multilateral policy recommendations. To the extent that the causes of the crisis are external, there is a tendency in the report to prescribe bilateral (or even unilateral) solutions; to the extent that they are indigenous, the emphasis is on domestic change and self-help efforts. On the one hand, this led to an endorsement of a potentially groundbreaking, multilateral approach to economic assistance (CADO). On the other, it produced only a lukewarm endorsement of the Contradora process. This lack of consistency greatly complicated the program proposed by the commission, reducing its value as a blueprint for government action—even if the government had been inclined to follow its dictates.

A fourth theme of the commission report, reflecting the president's request for "long term" policy advice is the attempt to look at Central America in an historical perspective and to define policy responses that could be sustained over time. The commissioners were acutely aware that their own lack of regional knowledge reflected a broad U.S. ignorance about conditions in Central America. They were also aware that it took a crisis of immense proportion for a president (and the Congress) to seek special counsel on the region and that successor presidents (and Congresses) were unlikely to seek such advice again.

This had several implications:

(1) It led the commission to examine, in surprising detail for a group of Americans, the historic roots of the crisis.
(2) It produced a recognition that U.S. attention to Central America has been sporadic and, further, that this has produced inconsistent U.S. policies toward the region as well as a profound lack of expert knowledge about Central America in the United States.
(3) It convinced the commissioners to seek multi-year funding of an enlarged U.S. financial assistance commitment and to endorse a new institutional arrangement (CADO) which would tend to insulate both the quantity and

purposes of U.S. financial assistance from political fluctuations or, more likely, waning American interest in the region if the intensity of the crisis (and of the immediacy of the threat to U.S. interest) was reduced.

For many of the commissioners, the NBCCA was a unique effort to reorient U.S. policy and to devise a strategy that would be viable and supported in the long run. They realized that high-level political attention was likely to be a temporary phenomenon—even if the crisis continued—and that, if their efforts to develop a new strategy failed, the United States was unlikely to give itself a second such opportunity.

A final theme of the commissioners was conditionality. The report argues repeatedly that the United States has moral as well as self-interest reasons to help the Central Americans address their crisis with large-scale material aid. But it also argues that the United States has definable interests in the region and clear preferences as to how conditions change. Thus, the commissioners strongly endorsed making such U.S. assistance conditional on economic, political, and social performance.

For example, in discussing political conditions in El Salvador, the commission recommended "conditioning military assistance to the government of El Salvador on progress in the effort to bring death squads under control."[8] More broadly, the massive foreign aid proposals were meant to be conditioned in part on sustained economic reform as monitored by IMF and the World Bank.

The proposed new multilateral organization (CADO) was partly a vehicle to condition ongoing disbursement of development aid on measurable progress in political and social as well as economic areas, broadening the sources "for information and . . . analysis including, for example, the deliberations of the Economic Consultative Group, now being organized by the IDB; AID; . . . the Inter-American Court of Human Rights; the ILO; the Inter-American Human Rights Commission of the Organization of American States; and nationally monitoring bodies and appropriate private parties."[9] All of this advice was supposed to flow through an assembly of delegations representing each country (two thirds drawn from the private sector) which, in effect, would certify progress toward agreed developmental goals. These assessments, in the commission's vision, would affect the disbursement of a substantial volume of financial aid. In the case of Nicaragua, CADO was intended to provide positive incentives to demonstrate the same commitment to democracy as other Central American countries.

To some extent, of course, this theme of conditionality runs counter to the report's repeated assertions that Central American problems could ultimately only be solved by Central Americans. Conditionality means not only reserving a veto to donors, but also proactively inserting foreign experts in the decisionmaking process. Conscious of the potential contradiction, the commissioners designed CADO to leave this advice and to emphasize that at least political and social conditionality could best be implemented through a mechanism which was heavily Central American in composition.

These themes came together in the commission's economic and social program, designed to arrest the deterioration in the Central American economies in the short run and to lay the basis for sustained, long-run growth. The commission identified five medium-term development objectives[10] that reflected the report's basic themes of intertwined economic, social, and political elements; the primacy of Central Americans' solving their own problems; the mixed local and foreign origins of the crisis; and the need for long-term, conditional solutions:

–peace,

–development of democratic institutions,

–rapidly growing economies—at per capita annual rates of at least 3 percent in real terms during the 1985–90 period,

–improvements in the health, education, and welfare of Central Americans, and

–substantial improvement in the distribution of income and wealth, with an emphasis on agricultural and land reform.

To achieve these objectives, the commission recommended massive, multi-year foreign economic assistance, dramatic and sustained economic reform, ready access to the U.S. commercial market, broadened land reform programs, and a new, multilateral development approach, embodied in an organizational structure like CADO.

The economic model implicitly endorsed by the commission was one which emphasized extraregional exports as the driving force. This implied a significant reorientation of the region's economies, predicated on several assumptions (although they were not made explicit). The first of these was that the rapid growth of earlier decades, which was built largely on regional economic cooperation, (i.e., the Central American Common Market), could not be replicated at least as long as sharp political differences existed among the Central American countries. Second, the commission believed that simple reinvigoration of existing economic structures would reinforce the power of elites who had contributed to the equal distribution of income and to political repression. And third, the commission assumed, somewhat reluctantly, that in a world characterized by economic stagnation throughout Latin America and growing international trade tensions, the most likely path to economic revival was one predicated on increased exports to the United States.

In economic terms, the commission hoped that this strategy would reinvigorate regional growth over the course of the 1980s at least to the extent that Central America would recapture its 1980 level of per capita income by 1990. To some commissioners this seemed like too modest a goal; in fact, it was a measure of the extent of the depression into which the region had fallen.

III. Why Did It Not Work?

Although the 1985–90 period is not yet over, it is an easy judgment that the commission's economic, social, and political objectives are not likely to be met:

–although economic conditions in the region are somewhat improved, regional growth has been well below the 3 percent per capita level,
–peace remains an elusive goal in Nicaragua and El Salvador,
–although democratic governments are more firmly established in several of the countries of the region, there has been little progress in Nicaragua and democratic forces in El Salvador are again under pressure,
–improvements in social conditions seem to be limited, and
–there is no evidence that income or wealth distribution is improving, although this judgment may be premature.

Yet, the Kissinger Commission stimulated a dramatic increase in U.S. financial assistance to the region and gave birth to a plethora of new U.S.-supported development programs. A Congressional Research Service report in 1987 indicated that, according to the administration accounting, appropriated funds for Central America during fiscal years 1985–87 totaled $2.8

billion, compared to an assumed $3.6 billion Kissinger Commission target.[11] In fiscal 1988 the administration recommended that Central America get $1.1 billion in overall aid; in March 1988 the Congressional Research Service estimated that Congress obligated about $935 million for the fiscal year. The administration's request for fiscal 1989 was reduced to $918 million because of budgetary constraints. These falling spending levels reflected an agreement between the administration and Congress to extend the original post-Kissinger Commission fiscal commitment to the region by three years while maintaining the original total request of $6.5 billion for direct assistance (along with $1.5 billion in guarantee authority). Nevertheless, this spending represented a significant increase in funding, even though it was less than had been recommended by the commission. Similarly, AID followed through on most of the specific programmatic recommendations, such as financial support of the Central American Bank for Economic Integration, a broad program of scholarships for Central American students for study in the United States, and increased public health spending.

Thus, four years after the Kissinger Commission delivered its report to President Reagan, the region is not obviously on the path described by the commission as essential to overcoming the crisis—despite the significant increase in U.S. development assistance efforts. Was the fault in the design of the program or in the implementation of the program proposed by the commission?

The answer, inevitably, is "both." The Kissinger Commission program was both complicated and extensive in its economic and social dimensions— in retrospect, probably too complicated and too extensive. The "laundry list" approach adopted by the commission—reflecting not lack of concept, but lack of discipline among the commissioners—ultimately made it too easy for U.S. development bureaucracy to pick and choose among the recommendations, ignoring the conceptual framework.

The commission recognized the need to channel financial assistance on an emergency basis and urged the U.S. government to work with regional governments in an effort to stabilize economic conditions which, as the commission met in 1983–84, were still deteriorating. To a significant extent this program was realized and contributed importantly to the stabilization of the regional economy. In may ways this was the easiest part of the task.

The medium-term "Reconstruction and Development Program" was another story, however. Its objectives were more aggressive and the proposed design represented a deliberate break with past development efforts. Privately several commissioners were skeptical that AID could manage such an enlarged program or would understand the political and social importance of involving new political groups in the decisionmaking process. In short, there was considerable doubt among the commissioners and drafters of the development program that the bureaucracy *could* implement it as conceived.

More important, perhaps, should have been the question of whether the bureaucracy *would* implement the proposed program. In part because it was consciously designed to circumvent them and in part because they failed to understand or disagreed with the concepts underlying the commission's proposals—as embodied in CADO—the U.S. aid bureaucracy was, from the start, hostile to the commission's efforts to introduce a new development model: even before the public release of the report, AID officials privately indicated their deep-seated opposition to CADO.

Despite this opposition, there have been efforts to develop CADO. In August 1985 the U.S. Congress directed the president to enter into negotiations to establish an organization "to help provide a continuous and coherent approach to the development of the Central American region."[12] The "sense of the Congress" was that the organization should look much like the one suggested by the Kissinger Commission. Its principal function, as embodied in the 1985 legislation, was to make recommendations on political, economic, and social development objectives, the mobilization of external resources and identification of external assistance needs, and the reform of economic policies. In addition, the organization should monitor the performance of member countries against the identified objectives. The Congress urged that at least one quarter of U.S. assistance be disbursed consistent with CADO recommendations.

After Congress acted, the administration followed—one and one-half years after the commission issued its report. The State Department and AID held a series of meetings during late 1985 and early 1986 and sponsored the establishment of the Washington Working Group (including representatives of the State Department, AID, the American Institute for Free Labor Development (AIFLD), the Association of American Chambers of Commerce in Latin America, and the Council of the Americas) to define the structure and purpose of CADO.

In the fall and winter of 1986 a series of meetings was held involving U.S. and Central American representatives of government, business and labor.

Considerable progress was made in developing the CADO concept, in large part because of the enthusiastic support of the AFL-CIO as expressed through AIFLD. (Lane Kirkland, president of the AFL-CIO and of AIFLD, was a member of the Kissinger Commission and a strong supporter of the CADO concept).

According to Congressional testimony in April 1988 by John Joyce, president of the International Union of Bricklayers and Allied Craftsmen, the "last formal meeting to attempt to form CADO was held in Tegucigalpa, Honduras, one year ago. A quick reading of the draft statutes which emerged from that meeting will give . . . an understanding of the areas of agreement, which are substantial, and of the area of disagreement, which boils down to basically one issue—the issue of labor representation."[13] (Joyce's reference to a dispute over labor representation refers to a conflict over who should represent labor in Costa Rica).

The areas of agreement *were* substantial, although they were somewhat different from the original Kissinger Commission concept. In particular, the commission had urged that one quarter of increased U.S. economic assistance be channeled through CADO; the modified CADO retained only an advisory role with respect to financial disbursements. In addition, the evolved version of CADO incorporated "national CADO's" that would play a role in each member country's development efforts with the regional CADO, providing a multilateral forum and injecting a regional perspective into development decisions. Nevertheless, CADO retained its key elements of multilateralism, conditionality, and tripartisanism.

However, in 1989 CADO still does not exist and seems unlikely to appear soon. Why?

Given the original bureaucratic hostility and the reluctant efforts to implement CADO, my judgment is that the fault lies firmly with the administration. Joyce echoed this judgment in his 1987 testimony: "In the view of the AFL-CIO, the negotiations of CADO by representatives of the administration, entrusted to them by law, has been less than energetically pursued."[14] Joyce cited a considerable amount of evidence including his view that "U.S. Ambassadors and (AID) Mission Directors in Central America responsible for representing U.S. policy to Central American governments have shown little knowledge of CADO. In some cases, they have been themselves negative to the concept of CADO. In other cases, they seem to have been simply inadequately informed. . . ."[15]

A contrary view was recently presented by retired ambassador William

Stedman, who in spring 1988 undertook, on behalf of the Department of State, a study on the advisability of CADO. He concluded that the efforts made by U.S. government officials to negotiate the establishment of CADO had been completely satisfactory. What was hindering its establishment, in his view, was the lack of interest, the skepticism, and even outright opposition to it amongst Central Americans.

Stedman argued that many Central Americans believe that CADO is tainted because it is a U.S. initiative; that it is strongly supported by the AFL-CIO; that in light of the Arias Peace Plan and the Central American Parliament its time had passed; that it would adversely complicate individual governmental relations with AID; and that tripartite dialogue on economic and social issues should first be developed on the national rather than regional level.

Curiously, in light of some of these objections, he also concluded that there would be substantial demand in Central America for the United States to support the development of tripartite dialogue at the national level, forming an organization in the spirit of the commission's vision.

Stedman—and members of the administration hostile to CADO—misunderstood the essence of CADO. The commission's analysis, based heavily on testimony from Central Americans, was that too many of the region's governments were not representative of their peoples and that U.S. aid should be used to help open up and democratize national decisionmaking processes in Central America. It is not surprising that those governments would resist pressure to share power with entrepreneurial and labor groups in the key areas of economic and social policies. Further, the regional element of the concept was not designed to force multinational solutions, but to involve the various member governments in setting and administering "home-grown" standards of behavior, rather than relying exclusively on U.S. definitions of appropriate economic, social, and political behavior. Indeed, the key idea underlying CADO was to dilute U.S. influence in the region, even as there was an inevitable rise in dependence on U.S. financial aid. The commission's hope in proposing CADO (or something like it) was to substitute multilateralism for the otherwise inexorable rise in bilateralism.

Not surprisingly, CADO does not exist today; the dramatic increase in development assistance has been channelled through traditional structures. There was no break with the past. (It would be a separate, but worthwhile, research effort to determine how effectively AID has administered the dramatic increase in U.S. financial assistance.)

Part of the fault for this lies with the commission itself. During the fact-finding and drafting stages of its work there was very limited contact with the bureaucrats who would ultimately be charged with implementing the commission's recommendations. And the commission, by design and by its own preference, ceased to exist almost immediately after the delivery of its report.

The last point is important. The bureaucracy might have been hostile to adventurous proposals drafted by outside experts and nonexpert commissioners in any event; it is the nature of bureaucracies. But if the commission had participated in some systematic way in explaining its proposals to the Congress and to the public, perhaps political pressure could have bent the bureaucracy's will to endorse and implement the commission's proposals.

In the best bureaucratic form Congress continues to insist that CADO should be implemented and the administration continues to insist that it is working toward implementation. But the objective reality is that the key concept of the Kissinger Commission in the economic and social area remains today a largely unknown abstraction.

IV. Conclusions

More than four years have passed since Dr. Kissinger and his colleagues delivered their commission's report to President Reagan. Their legacy is a readable and still accurate description of Central American realities, at least as viewed from a North American perspective. And it is a much-enlarged bilateral assistance program which undoubtedly has had something to do with the improvement of economic conditions in most of the Central American countries. (Although beyond the scope of this paper, the commission's legacy also included an extension of support for the Contras.)

These are noteworthy accomplishments, although they fall far short of what could have been done. In the final analysis, the commission failed to change U.S. strategic thinking about Central America or, put differently, to convince U.S. policymakers to adopt as their own the strategic framework developed by the commission. Admittedly, there is little evidence that the Reagan administration was seeking such help, or that there was any receptivity to it. But it was a task that would have been worth doing.

The president had formally asked for advice on "building a national consensus on a comprehensive United States policy." The commission's response, in the words of Henry Kissinger, was that "the best route to consensus on U.S. policy toward Central America is by exposure to the realities of Central America."[16] Although undoubtedly true, this is an opportunity few policymakers and fewer of the public were likely to have. A more effective response would have been for the commissioners to undertake an aggressive effort to educate their fellow citizens about those Central American realities they found so persuasive. The result of not having done so was that U.S. policy in the region has remained unaltered—and has remained unsuccessful.

Notes

1. The commission consisted of twelve commissioners whose work was supplemented by a group of senior counselors (including congressmen and senators), head consultants on economics, politics and other issues, and an executive director, seconded from the State Department. I served as lead consultant on economics, helped to design the economic program, and drafted the section of the commission report dealing with economic issues.

2. See U.S. Department of State (1985) and (1987), and Congressional Research Service (1987).

3. *The Report of the President's National Bipartisan Commission on Central America* (1984), p. 5.

4. Ibid., p. 48.

5. Ibid., p. 72.

6. Ibid., p. 70.

7. Ibid., p. 33.

8. Ibid., p. 102.

9. Ibid., p. 73.

10. Ibid., pp. 60–61.

11. The commission did not attempt to convert its broad financial recommendations into specific program proposals. In fact, the failure to do so caused considerable consternation among bureaucrats who were asked to translate the commission's report into budgetary proposals. Eventually the conventional wisdom in Washington became that the commission sought $1.2 billion in annual U.S. government economic support to the region.

12. "International Security and Development Cooperation Act of 1985," Public Law 99-83, August 8, 1985.

13. Testimony of John T. Joyce (1988).

14. Ibid.

15. Ibid.

16. *The Report of the President's National Bipartisan Commission on Central America* (1984), prologue.

References

Congressional Research Service (1987). *Kissinger Commission Implementation: Action by the Congress Through 1986 on the Recommendations of the National Bipartisan Commission on Central America*. Report no. 87-291 F. Washington, D.C.: U.S. Government Printing Office.

"International Security and Development Cooperation Act of 1985." Public Law 99-83. August 8, 1985.

Joyce, John T. (1988). Testimony before the Subcommittee on International Economic Policy and Trade of the Committee on Foreign Affairs, U.S. House of Representatives. April 13.

The Report of the President's National Bipartisan Commission on Central America (1984). New York: Macmillan Publishing Co.

U.S. Department of State (1985). *Sustaining a Consistent Policy in Central America: One Year After the National Bipartisan Commission Report*. Special report no. 124. Washington, D.C.: U.S. Government Printing Office.

U.S. Department of State (1987). *A Plan for Fully Funding the Recommendation of the National Bipartisan Commission on Central America*. Special report no. 162. Washington, D.C.: U.S. Government Printing Office.

Chapter 15

The Responsiveness of Policy and Institutional
Reform to Aid Conditionality
Lars Schoultz

The Ethics of Conditionality

Aid conditionality is an extraordinarily difficult issue to discuss dispassionately, for many observers reject as unethical and perhaps immoral the notion of establishing conditions upon aid disbursements. These observers often argue that economic aid should be distributed without regard to the policy goals of the donor—that food aid, for example, should be distributed to those who are hungry without regard to the relationships that exist between donors and the governments of hungry recipients. Discussions of conditionality often degenerate into indignant posturing about who "really cares" about the poor or who retains an outmoded "hegemonic vision" of U.S.-Latin American relations.

This is unfortunate, for indignation tends to distract attention from the truly crucial (and highly controversial) distributional issues surrounding aid conditionality. It also creates unnecessary barriers to understanding among individuals who, upon reflection, probably would not differ significantly in their views about conditionality.

The analysis in this chapter proceeds from the assumption that every reader is concerned about the plight of the poor in Central America and elsewhere, and that every reader opposes any donor's use of aid to create or maintain a hegemonic position. But this paper also is based upon the assumption that *it is impossible to distribute aid without establishing conditions to govern its distribution.* As David Baldwin has observed, "the concept of aid without strings implies both that aid would be distributed randomly and that aid would continue to be so allocated regardless of the behavior of the recipient states."[1] This, of course, is a completely irrational expectation; the distribution of aid *must* be based on some set of conditions. Otherwise, it could not be allocated. Some of these conditions are implicit; it goes without saying that aid would be terminated if a recipient were to seize the donor's embassy and hold captive its diplomatic personnel. Other forms of "biting the hand that feeds you" are less obvious, and often they are mentioned explicitly as conditions for continuing an aid relationship. This is particularly true in the case of the U.S. aid program, where each Congress and each administration redefines at least slightly the term "biting the hand that feeds you."

Moreover, whenever donors establish a condition for granting aid, they automatically establish the obverse; i.e., a condition under which aid will be denied. To require that U.S. aid focus upon "the poorest of the poor," as Congress mandated in the mid-1970s, means that one condition of U.S. aid is that it not focus upon the not-quite-desperately needy. To require that U.S. aid be used to assist "the people of less developed *friendly* countries," as the Foreign Assistance Act of 1961 did, or that in disbursing aid "great attention and consideration should be given to those nations which share the view of the United States on the world crisis" (PL 87-329, Section 112) meant that one condition of U.S. aid was that a recipient be allied with the United States in the Cold War. Another condition of U.S. aid is that recipients agree to ignore such basic market forces as prices; the Foreign Assistance Act (Section 604) currently stipulates that "funds made available under this [Foreign Assistance] Act may be used for procurement outside the United States only if the President determines that such procurement will not result in adverse effects upon the economy of the United States or the industrial mobilization base, with special reference to any areas of labor surplus or to the net position of the United States in its balance of payments with the rest of the world." To require that "no assistance may be provided . . . to the government of any country which engages in a consistent pattern of gross violations of internationally recognized human rights" (the Harkin Amendment) means that one condition of U.S. aid is that recipient governments respect their citizens' right to life, liberty, and the security of person.

In brief, conditions are an inevitable aspect of economic assistance programs. Thus a more positive, mutually beneficial relationship between the United States and Central America must proceed from an understanding that there is no such thing as unconditional aid—that all aid is tied aid— and that, as Baldwin recently observed, "strings versus no strings is an intellectual dead end."[2] The *real* questions surrounding conditionality are not related to its existence or its desirability, but rather to determining *what* conditions should be attached to economic assistance and *who* should participate in determining what they are. These are core questions on the U.S.-Central American policymaking agenda.

What is Economic Aid?

Given its name, it is understandable why foreign aid is usually considered a form of international welfare—rich nations helping poor nations with a direct transfer of resources. This conception of aid is incorrect. Economic aid is most appropriately conceptualized as a social exchange in which the government of one country provides resources to the government of another country in the expectation that, sooner or later, the recipient will reciprocate by providing the original donor with some benefit. In social exchange theory, there is no such thing as a "gift" in the pure sense of the word; each gift, rather, is part of a contract. Each exchange (in our case, each transfer of resources called foreign aid) contains an implicit obligation by the recipient to behave in some expected fashion.

Where there is no clear set of expectations (i.e., while the kinks in the exchange are being ironed out), the obligations may be explicit—the Foreign Assistance Act of 1961 is, in large measure, a listing of explicit obligations. So are the contracts the U.S. Agency for International Development signs with each recipient. Over time, as the obligations become understood by both sides, some can be made implicit. Thus in 1967 and 1973 the Foreign Assistance Act was amended to remove the adjective "friendly" from the descriptions of countries that are eligible to receive U.S. aid. The term was obviously not removed in order to permit the Johnson and Nixon administrations to aid unfriendly governments; rather, it simply was no longer necessary to include them because everyone understood the obligation implicit in the exchange. As this obligation (to be friendly) was being moved into the implicit category, another obligation (not to become a gross violator of human rights) was being made explicit. And so it goes, year after year, as the United States exchanges resources called "foreign aid" for immediate or future resources from recipient countries.

Viewed in this exchange context the cost of aid is much easier to justify. Aid is not welfare; it is a direct purchase or, perhaps, a wise investment for the not-so-distant future. In November 1983, the most recent of numerous public commissions to study the U.S. aid program (The Commission on Security and Economic Assistance, often called the Carlucci Commission after its chairman) listed four "objectives" of economic assistance:

Political—"The United States seeks international political relationships that promote U.S. national interests."

Humanitarian—"We cannot promote peace with other nations unless we are fully engaged in the task of ending the scourge of world poverty."

Economic—"The domestic economic success of developing countries is important to our own well-being, which is inextricably bound to the world economy."

Security—"Security interests clearly demand a defense posture . . . that serves as a deterrent to conflict, particularly in view of Soviet efforts to extend their growing power and influence in developing countries. The NATO, Japan, and ANZUS alliances are no longer the only front lines of defense against Soviet threats. Today there are many countries in all regions of the world that face Soviet exploitation in one form or another."

These are the four benefits the United States expects to purchase from the governments of Central America with economic assistance.

Of the four, security is by far the most important. An example of how the United States exchanges economic aid for increased national security in Central America is seen in the Carter administration's request in 1979–80 to Congress for a special authorization of $75 million in aid for the new revolutionary government in Nicaragua. The administration argued that aid was needed in order to ensure the friendship of the Sandinistas. The Carter approach was echoed by the U.S. private sector. A representative of the Council of the Americas, a business lobby, told the members of one House committee, "I am not necessarily bullish on the fact that it [the $75 million] isn't going to go down the drain. I believe, though, . . . in making errors of commission rather than omission, and I think it could guarantee [Nicaragua] going down the drain if it wasn't passed." With that kind of faint praise, the aid bill faced such an uncertain future that the House leadership had to agree to a secret session on February 28, 1980—at the time, only the third such session in history—during which reluctant members were scared just enough to vote "yes" by a State Department/CIA briefing on the extent of Soviet and Cuban influence in Nicaragua. Majority leader Jim Wright emerged from the session convinced of the need to "make a fight for Nicaragua" rather than leave the country "to Cuba's voracious appetite." The policy tool selected for the fight was economic aid.

What is obvious from these quotations is the cost/benefit calculus that governed the disbursement of U.S. aid to revolutionary Nicaragua. As with any economic exchange in a fairly free market, Washington calculated that the cost of aid (in this case, $75 million) was justified by the potential benefit (a decline in Cuban influence and/or a boost in U.S. influence). Because the Sandinistas represented a new, untested relationship for the United States, the reciprocal obligations were made uncommonly explicit—a series of restrictive provisions and reporting requirements unprecedented in the history of the U.S. aid program, including a requirement that one percent of the aid money be used to publicize the fact that the United States was providing aid (PL 96-257).

The reason for emphasizing the "social exchange" nature of economic aid is that it strongly influences our thinking about the effectiveness of aid conditionality. If aid is conceived as welfare, then a donor's threat to cut aid is highly credible—the donor has nothing to lose and, indeed, can save some money. But if aid is conceived as one part of an exchange, then a donor's threat to cut aid is only credible if the other part of the exchange (what the aid recipient provides the donor) is judged to be of modest value. Thus the first important point to recognize in any discussion of conditionality is that *the effectiveness of conditionality depends upon the ability of the donor to make a credible threat*, that is, to establish conditions that a recipient will consider realistic and will therefore respect. To conceive of foreign aid as a welfare program in which poor recipients receive charity from wealthy donors is to conceive of a world of strong donors and weak recipients. In this concept, recipients fulfill conditions whenever possible; failure brings the sanction of an aid cutoff. But to conceive of aid as a social exchange is to alter dramatically the assessment of this power relationship. Viewed as social exchange, aid provides benefits for *both* donors and recipients, and it is far from certain that the failure to live up to conditions will occasion a halt in aid.

Take, for example, the case of El Salvador under the Duarte government. In return for hundreds of millions of dollars of aid in the period 1980-85, the Duarte government has provided the United States with a sizeable number of benefits: a civilian administration at a time when civilian administrations were imperative for the administration's credibility with Congress; a staunch desire to thwart the rise to power of the far right, the moderate left, and the far left; and a moderate reformism that, with time and luck, might have eliminated some of the stark deprivation that breeds unrest. In the context of contemporary Central America in the early and mid-1980s, the Reagan administration perceived these to be extraordinarily valuable benefits. Indeed, many U.S. policymakers believed that the United States simply had to have them. So, although the Salvadoran president may have kissed the U.S. flag during a visit to the White House in 1987, in a broader sense Mr. Duarte certainly knew that U.S. policy required the embrace of Mr. Duarte (or someone very much like Mr. Duarte) in El Salvador. Aid is one way the United States cultivated his affection.

It is also true, of course, that President Duarte understood his own need for continued U.S. aid. Nonetheless, I suspect that he worried very little about fulfilling the conditions attached to the assistance, for any U.S. threat to cut off aid would simply not be credible. In remarks to the House Committee on Foreign Affairs on February 16, 1983, Secretary of State George Shultz asserted that "our security and economic assistance programs are essential instruments of our foreign policy and are directly linked to the national security and economic well-being of the United States." To have cut off aid to El Salvador, then, would have been to threaten U.S. economic and security interests. Given the significant benefits the United States derived from the aid relationship, in the early and mid-1980s no reasonable Salvadoran would have believed U.S. threats to cut aid.

The point to be made is obvious: when properly conceived as an exchange relationship, foreign aid does not confer great power upon the donor, nor does it require dependency on the part of the recipient. Indeed, as the case of El Salvador suggests, at times the donor is more dependent upon the recipient than vice versa. This is not to argue that conditions that donors attach to economic aid are meaningless gestures; indeed, under certain circumstances aid conditionality has been successful in encouraging recipients to act as donors wish. But these circumstances are far more restricted and much less frequent than might be expected by those who conceive of aid as a welfare program.

How Is U.S. Economic Aid Administered?

To understand how conditionality is applied, it is first necessary to understand how U.S. economic aid is administered. By the late 1970s the U.S. economic aid program had become extremely complex and therefore difficult to understand. Each year the complexity increases. The Food for Peace law (PL 83-480), for example, has been amended by no fewer than forty subsequent laws, including such oddities as the Congressional Reports Elimination Act of 1980 (PL 96-470). Once, in 1966, President Lyndon Johnson either thought he was being innovative or made a verbal slip, and Food for Peace became Food for Freedom; it took years before the indexes were straightened out. Even the titles of the laws are unwieldy: there was a time when Congress produced a "Foreign Assistance Act" each year; now, on the increasingly rare occasions when Congress manages to pass an aid authorization bill, we now have titles such as the "International Security and Development Assistance Authorizations Act of 1983." More frequently, the U.S. aid program operates on a continuing resolution,[3] itself an indication of the complexity of the legislative process.

It is useful to think of U.S. economic assistance as falling into four broad categories: development assistance, food assistance, economic support, and trade concessions.

Development Assistance

This category is often considered the core of the U.S. economic aid program, although in the case of Central America in recent years it has not been the largest program in terms of funding. Development assistance is designed to encourage economic growth and to attack the causes of poverty. Program foci are agricultural development, nutrition, health, population growth, education, and alternative energy development. A host of additional programs are also included in this category: the American Institute for Free Labor Development (AIFLD), for example, receives its U.S. government funding as development assistance. In recent years, special efforts to support the development of private enterprise in Latin America have also been funded as development assistance, as have efforts to support Latin American institutions that focus upon the protection of human rights. The work of Peace Corps volunteers is also properly classified as development assistance.

Most development assistance is managed by the U.S. Agency for International Development (AID), a semi-autonomous part of the Department of State.

Most development assistance is authorized by the Foreign Assistance Act of 1961, a formidable document that currently reaches 188 pages in length. Many of these pages stipulate the conditions under which aid will or will not be provided.

Food Assistance

The U.S. food assistance program is called Food for Peace or, quite commonly, PL 480, a shortened title of the program's original authorizing legislation, Public Law 83-480 of 1954. As originally conceived, the goals of Food for Peace were to dispose of the enormous post-Korean War U.S. farm surpluses that were bankrupting many U.S. farmers and, in the process, to promote United States foreign policy. Over time, the self-serving language in a law that is considered part of the U.S. foreign aid program became something of an embarrassment to many citizens, including the program's principal original sponsor, the late Senator Hubert Humphrey. In 1966 he obtained congressional approval to broaden the stated goals of PL 480 to include combating hunger and malnutrition.

Food for Peace is provided in two forms: free and inexpensive. The free food (Title II) consists of U.S. contributions for famine or emergency relief and of U.S. government donations to private voluntary organizations (CARE, Catholic Welfare Conference, Lutheran World Relief, etc.) for distribution overseas. Title II food shipments are among the most unselfish forms of U.S. economic assistance; they are distributed with a relatively small number of conditions. The inexpensive food is often called Title I, and consists of below-market financing for the open-market purchase of food from U.S. commercial vendors. Title I is funded by the U.S. Department of Agriculture, which provides a purchasing government with low-interest, long-term credit through the Commodity Credit Corporation (CCC). The recipient government then purchases the food in the United States through commercial suppliers. Because CCC funds for Title I fluctuate directly with the availability of surplus supplies in the United States, it is probably most appropriate to conceive of Title I as a form of farm subsidy. Nonetheless, Title I does provide for food to flow from the United States to Latin America at less-than-market prices.

Economic Support

This is by far the most controversial category of U.S. economic assistance. The U.S. Economic Support Fund (ESF) is a dollar cash transfer that recipients use to pay for foreign purchases. ESF is probably best described as an interstate subsidy. Sometimes it is a loan with generous repayment terms, but most frequently it is a gift of cash. The typical procedure is, first, for the Agency for International Development and the recipient government to agree upon the use to which ESF money will be put. Then AID writes a check for the appropriate amount of dollars to the recipient government's central bank. Once the money has been transferred, private and public importers in the recipient country apply for the dollars, paying for them with local currency, which the central bank uses for domestic operating expenses.

In virtually every case involving Latin America, the purpose of ESF is to keep troubled economies afloat. In fiscal year 1983, for example, the Reagan administration requested $326 million in ESF "in support of the immediate U.S. objective of assisting stabilization and recovery programs in the Caribbean Basin." Of that amount, the United States gave El Salvador $120 million. The government of El Salvador then sold these dollars to private Salvadoran citizens for 300 million *colones*, which were used, in turn, to cover about 16 percent of the government's operating budget.

Today's ESF began as a form of military aid. When first created in the 1950s, ESF was called Defense Support, and it was designed specifically to pay for the import bills of recipients who, for one reason or another, were devoting their own resources to the purchase of arms. Israel was (and remains) the principal recipient of ESF, with $1.9 billion (or 39 percent) of the $4.9 billion appropriation for fiscal year 1986. During the Kennedy administration, the program's name was changed from Defense Support to the less-bellicose title of Security Supporting Assistance. In 1971, Security Supporting Assistance was specifically moved by Congress from part I of the Foreign Assistance Act of 1961 (the part that governs development assistance) to part II of the same act (the part that governs military aid). In 1978, Security Supporting Assistance was renamed today's Economic Support Fund.

If we remove from consideration the ESF provided to Israel and Egypt ($2.9 billion, or 60 percent of the total ESF budget), then it is possible to reach the following generalization about the politics of ESF: policymakers who focus upon economic aid primarily as a means of alleviating poverty tend to view ESF unfavorably, while those who focus upon economic aid primarily as a means of supporting allies who are involved in struggles to contain the spread of communism tend to like ESF. The critics contend that economic aid should not be a cash transfer; rather, it should be used to finance specific development projects such as health clinics, schools, water purification plants, and market roads. The supporters contend that although these development projects are important, U.S. security interests require the existence of a fund that will underwrite increased defense expenditures by Third World allies.

And, as with most disputes of this type, ESF has become entangled in domestic U.S. politics. Conservatives have become the principal supporters of ESF, while liberals have become the principal critics. Looking over recent debates concerning ESF, it seems clear that the dispute over a *form* of granting aid—ESF—has become part of the broader issue of the *wisdom* of granting aid to specific countries. That is unfortunate, for ESF may well be the most appropriate form of U.S. economic assistance in a broad variety of circumstances that have little to do with anticommunism. In particular, U.S. liberals might want to reconsider their generic opposition to this form of aid, for *it is by far the least intrusive form of U.S. economic assistance.* Any Central American who has been obliged to deal with the U.S. aid bureaucracy would tend to value quite highly a form of economic assistance that can be administered without the constant oversight of a host of U.S. officials.

Trade Concessions

Although not normally considered a part of the U.S. economic assistance program because they do not involve the direct transfer of resources, trade concessions constitute one of the most useful forms of assistance that a donor government can offer to less-developed countries. In recent years, and especially since the inauguration of President Reagan's Caribbean Basin Initiative (CBI), increasing numbers of analysts of all political persuasions have come to consider trade as an alternative to other types of economic aid, just as, about two decades ago, Latin Americans were frequently quoted as asking Washington for "trade, not aid." It appears that the message has finally been heard in Washington.

It is useful to think of trade concessions as being of two types: those that help recipients sell in the U.S. market, and those that help the U.S. private sector to do business in less-developed countries.

Historically, the former type of concession has been associated with the export of the products of tropical agriculture. Beginning with the Cuban Reciprocal Treaty of 1902, the United States has been part (and often a principal part) of a host of schemes that have given preferential tariff treatment to agricultural products from Latin America. In the Cuban case, tariffs on Cuban exports were placed 20 percent below the tariff charged other producers, and the result was a dramatic expansion of the production of sugar, tobacco, and citrus products, which fueled a fairly broad expansion of the Cuban economy in general.

Much of this expansion came at the expense of other Latin American producers, who found that they could not compete in the U.S. market against favored Cuba. Quite obviously, the United States today cannot provide individual Latin American countries with special trade concessions that disadvantage the rest of the nations of the region, but that is not the point to be made here. The point is that one principal lesson of the Cuban experience (and the ensuing experience with sugar quotas)—is that there is considerable value in having preferential access to the U.S. market.

Latin Americans learned this lesson first. Beginning with the initial UN Conference on Trade and Development in 1964, Latin American and other Third World nations began to present concrete proposals that would facilitate their ability to penetrate the markets of industrialized countries. One specific proposal was the Generalized System of Preferences (GSP), which the United States eventually joined in 1976 for an initial period of nine years; in 1984, Congress extended U.S. participation until 1993.

By eliminating import duties on goods exported by less-developed countries, GSP is designed to make LDC products more competitive in developed-country markets. By increasing export opportunities, the program is designed to stimulate employment and economic growth, as well as to provide U.S. consumers with lower-priced products. In the case of the United States, GSP designation has been granted to 114 Third World countries for about 3,000 product categories. Unfortunately, Congress has decided that several groups of products should be excluded in order to avoid a negative impact on domestic producers. These ineligible products include many produced in

Latin America: textile and apparel articles, certain kinds of footwear, and leather goods.

A significant part of the Reagan administration's Caribbean Basin Initiative (CBI) is a special form of GSP for the countries of the Caribbean region. Chapter 13, "Assessment of the Caribbean Basin Initiative," analyzes the CBI in some detail.

The second type of trade concession—those that help U.S. producers conduct business in less-developed countries—has been a part of U.S.-Latin American relations since 1934, when Congress created the Export-Import Bank to assist in overcoming the depression by expanding U.S. exports. The Eximbank is a government corporation that finances the transactions of U.S. exporters when borrowers cannot meet normal commercial repayment terms or, frequently, when a foreign competitor for a given sale is being assisted by its export-promotion bank. Like the Eximbank, the Overseas Private Investment Corporation (OPIC) is a government corporation involved primarily in facilitating U.S. corporations' transactions with the Third World. Unlike the Eximbank, which finances the export of goods, OPIC insures the overseas investments of U.S.-based corporations from losses due to inconvertibility of foreign currency, to expropriation, and to damage by war, revolution, and insurrection. Created in 1969, OPIC is only the latest in a series of government programs to insure corporate investments abroad. OPIC's activities are complemented by a Trade and Development Program (TDP) sponsored by the departments of state and commerce.

Because trade concessions represent resource transfers (or the encouragement of private-sector resource transfers) by the U.S. government to countries in Latin America, they are properly considered part of the foreign assistance program. Indeed, over the course of the past two decades, increasing numbers of analysts and policymakers have come to consider trade concessions as a promising alternative to the other three types of foreign aid. This is particularly true of trade concessions like GSP and the Caribbean Basin Initiative that open the U.S. market to Latin American producers.

Evolution of the U.S. Economic Aid Program

The United States does not have a lengthy experience with foreign aid. Prior to World War II the only U.S. aid to Latin America was an occasional technical mission to provide expertise on such projects as port construction or public health instruction. This modest aid effort did not increase significantly in the years immediately after the war. The first major U.S. aid program, the Marshall Plan, specifically excluded Latin America.

But in the presidential campaign of 1952, candidate Dwight Eisenhower accused the Democratic administration of ignoring Latin America, and he promised to correct the oversight. In mid-1953 he sent his highly respected brother on a month-long fact-finding tour of South America. Milton Eisenhower returned home convinced that the region's grinding poverty and stunted economic development were the principal issues the United States needed to address, for if left to fester these problems would foster instability. His fundamental message was that "a tremendous social ferment exists today throughout Latin America."

> Leaders of the nations to the South, recognizing that too many of their people are desperately poor, that widespread illiteracy is a handicap to progress, that educational and health facilities are woefully inadequate, and that improvement calls for capital for machinery, tools, highways, schools, hospitals, and other facilities, look to the United States for help. . . . They want greater production and higher standards of living, and they want them *now*.[4]

Eisenhower's message was reinforced by two prominent Republican senators, Homer Capehart and Bourke Hickenlooper, who made separate fact-finding trips to Latin America in the early 1950s. Both were impressed by the poverty of the region; both noted what soon came to be known as "the revolution of rising expectations." Both worried about the consequences of this revolution for U.S. security. Both believed that the United States should exchange some aid today for greater stability and security tomorrow.

As a result, in the 1950s the United States began to create an economic aid program for Latin America. This was the Mutual Security Act period (1953–61) and, as the title suggests, aid went primarily to governments that were thought to be threatened by communist subversion. The post-Arbenz governments of Carlos Castillo Armas and Miguel Ydígoras Fuentes in Guatemala were major recipients, for example. Most of Latin America received very little aid, and nearly all of it was in the form of technical assistance. In the eight-year period from 1953 to 1961, U.S. economic aid to Latin America averaged $149 million per year—not much by the standards set by the Marshall Plan and Point Four programs in Europe, but five times greater than the average annual U.S. aid to Latin America in the years immediately after World War II. In the area of trade concessions, it was during this period that Senator Capehart used his position on the Banking Committee to sponsor legislation permitting the Eximbank to finance exports purchased by Latin American governments for development projects.

The Cuban revolution changed forever the somnolent U.S. aid program in Latin America. Among President Kennedy's first legislative initiatives were to request the creation of the Agency for International Development and to propose the creation of an Alliance for Progress. As a consequence of these initiatives, the early and mid-1960s became the heyday of the U.S. economic aid program in Latin America, an era in which entire nations were targeted to be "showcases" for U.S.-directed economic development. As Congress discovered, creating such exhibits was not an inexpensive activity, particularly when a foreign war and a domestic war on poverty broke out and began to compete for scarce financial resources. Bilateral economic aid to Latin America peaked at $888 million in 1966, and then declined dramatically through the end of the Carter administration. AID's $190 million obligation to Latin America in fiscal year 1977 was the lowest in the history of the Agency.

The decline in aid was caused by many factors. One was opposition to the war in Vietnam, which was generalized by many policymakers into an antipathy toward all foreign involvement.[5] This particularly influenced liberal policymakers, the officials who traditionally constitute the core support for foreign aid. Another cause of the decline in aid was the widespread perception in Washington that the Alliance for Progress had failed to meet even its most modest goals. For whatever cause, by the late 1960s Congress had grown increasingly reluctant to fund a large economic aid program, and it was particularly opposed to a continuation of the large-scale "program" loans that had characterized alliance aid to Latin America. As AID turned slowly to more modest "project" loans, it also began to focus more directly on providing aid to needy people rather than on funding large-scale infrastructure projects (airports, roads, etc.). The "New Directions" legislation of the early 1970s made this focus mandatory. Since 1978, aid officials have been required to "emphasize . . . the alleviation of the worst physical manifestations of poverty among the world's poor majority" (Foreign Assistance Act of 1961, PL 87-195, Section 101), and since 1985 AID has been required "to assure that a substantial percentage of development assistance. . . directly improves the lives of the poor majority, with special emphasis on those individuals living in absolute poverty" (Foreign Assistance Act of 1961, PL 87-195, Section 128).

The period from about 1965 (the year of the U.S. invasion of the Dominican Republic, which is often accepted as the end of the Alliance for Progress) until 1977 (the year Jimmy Carter was inaugurated as president) was a period of contraction and malaise in the U.S. economic aid program. During the Johnson and Nixon/Kissinger eras, many of the most competent aid officials left to find more rewarding work, and those who were left spent most of their time in Southeast Asia or in efforts to deflect the Congressional attacks upon the aid budget. It was not an auspicious period. Although the aid budget declined in the Carter years, the aid bureaucracy was revitalized by the heated debates over the proper role of aid in advancing the administration's human rights policy. This new vigor continued into the early Reagan years, when a focus upon U.S. national security concerns in Central America sparked a major growth in economic assistance and signalled a new importance for aid officials. Specifically, in early 1984 the report of the National Bipartisan Commission on Central America (the Kissinger Commission) recommended $8 billion in economic aid for Central America in the five-year period beginning in 1985. This represented a rough doubling of U.S. economic assistance from 1983 levels, which had already risen dramatically from the low levels of the late 1970s.

Conditionality in United States Aid to Latin America

There is no way to determine with certainty the impact of aid conditionality and trade concessions upon recipients. If a recipient is engaged in some action that a donor opposes, and if the donor threatens to terminate aid or trade concessions if the action continues, and if the recipient then discontinues the action, can we correctly conclude that conditionality successfully altered the recipient's behavior? Is it not possible that the recipient would have terminated the action anyway? Similarly, if a recipient does *not* engage in some action, and if a prohibition on that action is a condition a donor attaches to economic aid or trade concessions, can we conclude that the recipient is acting in response to the law of anticipated reactions? Or is it not possible that the recipient would have behaved the same regardless of the donor's conditionality? If the United States makes respect for human rights a condition for receiving U.S. aid, and if a repressive government moderates its repression, how are we to determine that the conditionality (as opposed to a host of other possible causal factors) brought about the decline in repression? Conversely, if the United States makes respect for human rights a condition for receiving U.S. aid, and if a repressive government continues to be repressive, is it reasonable to conclude that the conditionality has failed? Is it not possible that the repressive government would have been much more repressive without the threat of an aid cutoff?

In short, given the large number of potential causal factors behind any government decision, particularly complex decisions to enact significant reforms, we can never be certain whether or to what extent aid conditionality contributed to the decision. On the other hand, the literature on conditionality does clearly indicate that the specific goals and the specific context of conditionality seem to affect the outcome of any effort to use aid to influence the behavior of recipient governments. To study conditionality, then, is to focus upon goals and contexts.

In the history of United States economic assistance to Latin America, there have been four major clusters of goals that have been sought with aid conditionality: to protect U.S. private investments, to promote hemispheric solidarity, to promote human rights (including democracy), and to promote structural economic reforms. Each of these goals provides important insights into the use of conditionality.

Protect U.S. Private Investments

There are many U.S. aid conditions designed to protect U.S. private investments. Most of these methods are specified in Section 620 of the Foreign Assistance Act, which is over eight pages long. Restrictions include prohibitions on economic aid to any government that:

1. refuses to pay legitimate debts to any United States citizen or person,
2. will use the aid "for construction or operation of any productive enterprise in any country where such enterprise will compete with United States enterprise unless the country has agreed that it will" limit the export to the United States of goods from the enterprise to 20 percent of the enterprise's production,
3. "has failed to enter into an agreement with the U.S. president to

institute the investment guaranty program . . . providing protection against the specific risks of inconvertibility . . . and expropriation or confiscation," or

4. "seizes, or imposes any penalty or sanction against, any United States fishing vessel on account of its fishing activities in international waters."

The Hickenlooper Amendment (Section 620e) is by far the best-known example of aid conditionality to protect the U.S. private sector. This amendment requires the president to

suspend assistance to the government of any country . . . when the government of such country . . . has nationalized or expropriated or seized ownership or control of property owned by any United States citizen or by any corporation, . . . has taken steps to repudiate or nullify existing contracts or agreements with any United States citizen or any corporation, . . . or has imposed or enforced discriminatory taxes or other exactions, or restrictive maintenance or operational conditions, or has taken other actions, which have the effect of nationalizing, expropriating, or otherwise seizing ownership or control of property so owned,

unless the country takes "appropriate steps" to provide compensation in convertible foreign exchange or takes steps to provide relief from discriminatory taxation.

The original Hickenlooper Amendment further specified that the aid suspension would continue until appropriate correctional steps had been taken, and that the amendment could not be waived by the president.

Senator Hickenlooper's amendment was a refinement of the Johnston-Bridges amendment to the Mutual Security Act of 1959. When the Foreign Assistance Act of 1961 was created to replace the Mutual Security Act, legislators apparently forgot to include the Johnston-Bridges language. This was corrected in 1962 by Senator Bourke Hickenlooper, who was provided with a draft amendment by the lawyers for the United Fruit Company, which feared that the government of Honduras was about to expropriate its landholdings. This was a propitious time to propose such an amendment, for the government of Cuba had recently sensitized policymakers to the issue by seizing virtually all U.S. assets on the island.

There is considerable controversy over the efficacy of the Hickenlooper

Amendment and, indeed, over the efficacy of all the aid conditions that are designed to protect U.S. private interests in recipient countries. Evaluating the Hickenlooper Amendment is particularly difficult because it has been applied only once—in 1962, when the government of Ceylon expropriated without compensation the refineries of two U.S. oil companies. The United States promptly cut off aid and did not resume it until 1965, when a more conservative government was elected and negotiated a settlement with the oil companies.

As Klaus Knorr observed, "the outcome seems to indicate a successful attempt to exert economic pressure"—that is, the conditionality worked. "But," Knorr continued,

> the causal links are unclear, as they usually are when a change of government intervenes. It cannot be demonstrated that Madame Bandaranaike lost the election as a result of the damage inflicted on the Ceylonese economy by the suspension of a modest amount of American aid, or that this suspension prompted the new prime minister to comply with United States requests. It is at least equally possible that the latter's decision resulted from his general preferences.[6]

On the other hand, Hufbauer and Schott conclude that the effort by the U.S. was highly successful; on a sixteen-point scale, they give U.S. aid conditionality in the case of Ceylon a score of sixteen.[7] Baldwin is less certain, but he concludes that "there is reason to suspect that this may have been a rather cost-effective undertaking from the American point of view."[8]

On the other hand, Lillich argues that the Amendment's "effects actually have been so counterproductive that, in the case of IPC's dispute with Perú in 1969, President Nixon stretched the statute to its limits—and perhaps beyond—to avoid having to apply it."[9] Indeed, the Nixon decision to forgo an aid cutoff when Perú expropriated without compensation the holdings of Standard Oil of New Jersey took all of the teeth out of the amendment. By the end of the 1960s U.S. business interests were urging greater flexibility in the Amendment's application, and in the Foreign Assistance Act of 1973, the president was granted discretion in its application. Since then, the president has been permitted a waiver if he determines that continuing aid "is important to the national interests of the United States."

The details of this evolution should not be allowed to obscure the principal point, which is that there is no clear lesson to be learned about the effects of this type of conditionality upon aid recipients. It is possible, for example, that the weak U.S. reaction to the International Petroleum Company expropriation in Perú encouraged the Allende government in Chile to expropriate U.S. investments there. On the other hand, it is particularly difficult to determine the deterrent effect of the Hickenlooper Amendment; until we are able to estimate how many expropriations did *not* occur because of the Amendment, we will be unable to assess its effectiveness.

The inspection of other instances of aid cutoffs to protect U.S. private investments in Latin America yields similarly inconclusive findings. The fisheries dispute that erupted in 1969 between the United States, on the one hand, and Perú and Ecuador, on the other, led to a suspension of U.S. military aid, but it is not clear that the U.S. decision was based on an effort to protect U.S. fishing rights. Much of the dispute can be attributed to military considerations surrounding Perú and Ecuador's attempt to extend their territorial waters to 200 miles offshore, to Washington's negotiating position at the upcoming Law of the Sea conference, and to general indignation among many U.S. officials that two tiny countries would take such an audacious step and exert jurisdiction over territory that the United States considered international waters. In this case, private U.S. interests may have been protected, but probably only incidentally.

Similarly, although nationalization without compensation was one major reason offered in the case of the U.S. decision to eliminate economic assistance to Chile during the Allende years (1970–73), the decision to halt aid was taken long before any nationalization had occurred and, indeed, before Allende entered office. On September 15, 1970, after Allende had been elected but nearly three months before his inauguration, President Nixon met with National Security Advisor Henry Kissinger, Attorney General John Mitchell, and CIA director Richard Helms to determine U.S. policy toward the Popular Unity victory. According to the now-famous notes Mr. Helms took during the meeting, one decision was to "make the economy scream," a decision implemented in part by an aid embargo.[10] Thus, whereas uncompensated expropriations did occur in Chile, and the United States did halt economic aid, there was no significant causal relationship between the two events.

To this point, our discussion of the conditionality associated with the protection of U.S. private interests has focused upon punitive measures— upon halting aid in response to attacks upon U.S. interests. But there is another way we should approach this issue, and that is to examine the use of aid as a positive reinforcement—as a carrot rather than a stick—to protect U.S. private interests. Here the record may not be much clearer, but it is quite different.

The U.S. economic aid program is based upon the assumption that private enterprise is the most important motor force for economic development. Section 601 of the Foreign Assistance Act declares:

> The Congress of the United States recognizes the vital role of free enterprise in achieving rising levels of production and standards of living essential to economic progress and development. Accordingly, it is declared to be the policy of the United States to encourage the efforts of other countries to increase the flow of international trade, to foster private initiative and competition, to . . . encourage the contribution of United States enterprise toward economic strength of less developed friendly countries, through private trade and investment abroad, private participation in programs carried out under this Act (including the use of private trade channels to the maximum extent practicable in carrying out such programs), and exchange of ideas and technical information on the matters covered by this subsection.

Section 601, which is three pages long, also establishes an International Private Investment Advisory Council on Foreign Aid, whose duties are to make recommendations to the AID administrator "with respect to particular aspects of programs and activities under this Act where private enterprise can play a contributing role and to act as liaison for the Administrator to involve specific private enterprises in such program and activities."

One major condition attached to the U.S. economic aid program, then, is the existence in recipient countries of a social, political, and economic environment that is propitious to the development of private enterprise and, specifically, U.S. private enterprise. Thus in 1983 Congress created a $20 million Private Sector Revolving Fund (with a maximum capital of $100 million) to assist private enterprise, because it was "in the best interests of the United States to assist the development of the private sector in developing countries and to engage the United States private sector in that process." In practice, the most fundamental condition for eligibility to draw upon the revolving fund is a commitment to private sector development and, to a lesser extent, to the involvement of the U.S. private sector.

How important have these "conditionality carrots" been to promote the interests of U.S. private investors and suppliers? To look for specific examples of success is, in my view, to miss the point. These inducements are designed to create a propitious global environment for the U.S. private sector. The basic goal is not to sell U.S. goods and services or to identify investment opportunities (although these things happen), but rather to help create in Latin America and elsewhere the "atmosphere" that facilitates the presence of U.S. investments. Although we have no data at present to assess the effectiveness of these inducements, I suspect that they have been quite effective.

Promote Hemispheric Solidarity

"Since the early 19th century, the primary interest of the United States in Latin America has been to have a peaceful, secure southern flank." Thus begins the brief discussion of Latin America in the most widely adopted U.S. national security textbook of our time.[11] At first, the United States pursued this interest by unilateral measures that were designed to keep foreign powers from seizing territory in Latin America and using it to threaten the security of the United States. The No-Transfer Resolution of 1811, the Monroe Doctrine of 1823, the Roosevelt Corollary of 1904, and the Magdalena Bay Resolution of 1912 are all examples of these unilateral efforts. Other efforts required the cooperation of European powers: the Clayton-Bulwer Treaty of 1850, for example, ensured that Great Britain would not build a canal (and establish a larger foothold) in Central America, and the Hay-Pauncefote Treaty of 1901 formally excluded the British from construction or operation of an isthmian canal. The most interesting aspect of all these declarations and treaties designed to protect U.S. security in Latin America is that they never involved any participation by Latin Americans.

In fairness, it should be noted that the United States sponsored the first Pan American Conference in 1889, and Washington encouraged through the creation of the Pan American Union a sense of hemispheric unity. But the unity was at best superficial, as the United States discovered in World War II, when some Latin American governments, particularly Argentina, were reluctant to declare war on the Axis powers.

Anxious to prevent future neutrality or, worse yet, defections in the event

of a third world war, in 1947 the United States invited the twenty Latin
American republics to a meeting in Rio de Janeiro, where we all signed the
Inter-American Treaty of Reciprocal Assistance. The Rio Treaty was an
attempt to formalize what everyone in the United States presumed: that in
the rapidly emerging, rigid bipolar world, Latin America was going to be
on Washington's side.

The presumption was correct. After the United States had straightened
out a few kinks in the inter-American system—persuading Argentina's
Perónist government to accept U.S. leadership, and helping to overthrow
Guatemala's Arbenz government in 1954—then Latin America played its
proper role. A number of indicators (perhaps voting patterns in the United
Nations is the best) suggest that for a number of years Latin Americans
were extraordinarily responsive to U.S. concerns in international politics.

In this sense, the Cuban revolution and the subsequent U.S. failure to
overthrow the Castro government were major watersheds. They signaled the
breakdown in hemispheric solidarity. U.S. policymakers began to recognize
that some Latin American nations (Argentina and Mexico in particular) had
never accepted their assigned role with any enthusiasm, and they also noted
that other Latin American governments upon whom the United States had
always relied for staunch support (the Dominican Republic, for example)
were acting as if they were nonaligned.

With its aid program and trade concessions, the United States sought to
maintain the commitment of its Latin American allies to hemispheric
solidarity. The conditions attached to the economic aid program were
obvious. For example, Representative Otto Passman, chair of the powerful
House Appropriations Subcommittee on Foreign Operations, added the
amendment noted above that required AID officials to give "great attention
and consideration . . . to those nations which share the view of the United
States on the world crisis" (PL 87-329, Section 112). Other conditions
prohibited (and still today prohibit) aid to any country that is "controlled
by the international communist conspiracy" (Section 620f of the Foreign
Assistance Act), to any country that "severs diplomatic relations with the
United States" (Section 620t), or to "the present government of Cuba"
(Section 620a). All of these conditions are designed to promote hemispheric
solidarity by deterring defections or, in the case of Cuba, to demonstrate
the consequences of defection.

Trade concessions have been perhaps the most important method used by the United States to maintain hemispheric solidarity. Unlike the U.S. economic aid program, the conditions attached to trade concessions are rarely explicit, but they are nonetheless real. One excellent example is the U.S. sugar program, under which the United States has for decades purchased sugar at prices substantially above the world market price. Since all foreign producers want to take advantage of this preferential pricing policy (which has its roots in the Cuban Reciprocal Treaty of 1902 and over time has been expanded to include most sugar producers), the United States assigns import quotas to individual countries. In many Latin American countries, these quotas spell the difference between prosperity and depression; they thereby provide Washington with considerable political leverage.

But the power of this type of conditionality has distinct limits, as the case of Cuba demonstrates. In March, 1960, as Cuban-U.S. relations were deteriorating rapidly, a bill was introduced in the House of Representatives to authorize the president to reduce the Cuban sugar quota. Representative Harris McDowell, Jr., expressed the thinking of many of his colleagues when he remarked that "if Cuba's splendid people understand that they must sell their sugar or their economy will be destroyed, they will themselves find a way to deal with the present misleaders and fomenters of hatred." The bill passed the House by a vote of 396 to 0, and in July President Eisenhower slashed the Cuban quota from 779,000 tons for the second half of 1960 to 40,000 tons. In December the Cuban quota was eliminated entirely for the first quarter of 1961, and the United States has imported no Cuban sugar since that time. Since 1963 the Foreign Assistance Act has stipulated that Cuba shall not "be entitled to receive any quota authorizing the importation of Cuban sugar into the United States or to receive any other benefit under any law of the United States."

In response, in 1961 Cuba arranged to sell 2.7 million tons of sugar to the Soviet Union, 1.0 million tons to the People's Republic of China, and 300,000 tons to the Eastern bloc countries of Europe. These purchases of four million tons exceeded both the U.S. quota and the amount of sugar Cuba had available for sale. If the conditionality attached to the U.S. sugar quota is designed to maintain hemispheric solidarity, then in the case of Cuba the purpose was not realized. Indeed, it is possible to argue that the exercise of conditionality pushed Cuba into the arms of the Soviet Union; conditionality was more than unproductive, it was counterproductive. Wayne Smith, a retired career official and a critic of the Reagan administration's policy toward Latin America, remarked in 1985 that the U.S. embargo "did not change Cuban attitudes, did not resolve any problems, did not cause the government to change course."[12]

There are other explanations for both the breach in hemispheric solidarity and the apparent inability of the United States to use sanctions to reverse the course of the Cuban revolution. The most prominent of these alternative explanations is that Fidel Castro was a communist anyway and would have led Cuba into an alliance with the Soviet Union with or without the U.S. exercise of conditionality. This is a debate we cannot resolve. All that seems certain is that Representative McDowell was both correct and naïve. He was correct in noting that Cuba had to sell sugar in order to survive. He was naïve in thinking that the United States was the only available purchaser.

Nicaragua provides a more recent example of an attempt by the United States to use trade concessions to promote hemispheric solidarity. In May, 1983, the United States reduced its purchases of Nicaraguan sugar by 90 percent; Nicaragua subsequently reported (but provided no data to demonstrate) that increased sugar exports to Iran, Algeria, and Libya had compensated for the loss of the U.S. market. Then on May 1, 1985, President Reagan exercised his power under the 1977 International Emergency Economic Powers Act, declared a national emergency, and placed three major sanctions upon the government of Nicaragua: an embargo on U.S.-Nicaraguan trade, a suspension of the right of Nicaraguan airplanes and ships to use U.S. ports, and (after a required one-year notification) an abrogation of the 1956 Treaty of Friendship, Commerce, and Navigation between the two countries.

By the time the embargo was announced, U.S. imports from Nicaragua had already dropped substantially—from $214 million in 1980 to $58 million in 1984, and not even administration officials thought that the actions would constitute a major economic blow to the Sandinista government. Many analysts concluded that the goal was to indicate U.S. resolve; just weeks earlier, Congress had defeated an administration request for $14 million in funding for the Nicaraguan contras, and it appeared as though the administration was looking for another weapon with which to fight to maintain hemispheric solidarity. How effective has this exercise in conditionality been? Any answer in 1989 is premature. We know that when asked about the strategic implications of the embargo, Nicaraguan vice-president Sergio Ramirez responded that "we will become closer to all countries that support this revolution. This includes the Soviet Union." Taken at face value, this statement indicates that, as in the case of Cuba, the effort to maintain hemispheric solidarity by withdrawing trade concessions has been counter-productive. But we do not know whether this response is an accurate one, nor in 1989 are we able to judge the long-term effects of the U.S. pressure. We do not know, for example, the amount of disaffection that the embargo has produced among Nicaraguans who might normally support the Sandinistas. Nor, for that matter, do we know how much domestic support the Sandinistas gained as nationalistic Nicaraguans decided that they were more willing to tolerate the Sandinistas than to endure further pressure from the Colossus of the North. In the end, I doubt that we will ever be able to determine the influence of the U.S. withdrawal of trade concessions from revolutionary Nicaragua.

Nevertheless, I would like to hazard a guess that is informed not only by the U.S. experiences in Cuba and Nicaragua, but also by the general literature on trade concessions. I doubt the pressure would ever have worked in the case of Cuba, and I doubt it will work in Nicaragua. As one examines the experience of the postwar era, it is difficult to conclude otherwise. Klaus Knorr summarized this experience best:

> . . . [C]oercively wielding economic power by means of trade reprisals or special trade advantages is rarely successful, because even states of great economic strength do not command a compelling degree of monopolist or monopsonist control in their foreign trade, and because the punishment that can be imposed by these means does not inflict enough pain, on the one hand, and tends to arouse the will to resist, on the other. That is not to say, of course, that no power whatever inheres in this sort of commercial strength. There is just ordinarily not very much.[13]

This seems to capture perfectly the experience to date of the United States in attempting to use trade concessions to maintain hemispheric solidarity.

But if the stick does not seem to work, what about using the carrot to maintain hemispheric solidarity? This is the equivalent of asking whether one can buy friends and allies. History indicates that the answer is "yes," but that the friendships so purchased are not particularly valuable except in the very short term. In May 1965, for example, the United States needed fourteen votes in the OAS in order to obtain approval of the creation of an

Inter-American Peacekeeping Force to replace the U.S. armed forces that had invaded the Dominican Republic in late April. One of the fourteen votes came from Duvalier's Haití, which gained in return a modern airport capable of handling jet aircraft.

These types of bargains are struck every day—donors dangle carrots, recipients nibble, and a deal is struck. But when the "deal" involves macro-concepts like maintaining the balance of world power or hemispheric solidarity, then something more is needed than a bunch of carrots, however large. A set of common interests and values is an obvious prerequisite. If that is lacking, then no amount of economic aid and no trade concessions will be sufficient. In a genuine crunch—when allies are *really* needed—a bribed ally is likely to be found sitting on the sideline.

Promote Human Rights and Democracy

The Carter administration's efforts to promote human rights and the Reagan administration's more modest efforts to encourage liberal democracy are remarkably interesting examples of the use of aid conditionality to influence Latin American governments.

It was Congress that placed the issue of human rights on the U.S. foreign policy agenda in the mid-1970s, reacting to the debacles of Vietnam, Watergate, and U.S. complicity in the downfall of the Allende government in Chile. An amendment prohibiting assistance to governments that engaged in the consistent and gross violations of fundamental human rights was added to virtually every piece of U.S. foreign aid legislation. The two most important parts of this legislation were the 1975 Harkin Amendment (Section 116 of the Foreign Assistance Act), which prohibited economic aid, and Section 502B (added in 1974; revised in 1976), which prohibited military aid to human rights violators.

When Jimmy Carter embraced Congress's concern, he raised the issue of human rights to prominence in inter-American relations. The most quoted passage from his otherwise unremarkable inaugural address contained the marching orders for U.S. diplomats: "Because we are free, we can never be indifferent to the fate of freedom elsewhere. Our moral sense dictates a clearcut preference for those societies which share with us an abiding respect for individual human rights." Soon thereafter—on February 24, 1977—Secretary of State Cyrus Vance told a Senate subcommittee that the administration planned to reduce aid to Argentina, Ethiopia, and Uruguay because of their gross violations of human rights. The message was clear: during the Carter administration, aid would be conditioned upon recipient governments' respect for human rights.

Over the course of the next four years, six Latin American governments became particular targets of the administration's human rights policy: Argentina, Chile, El Salvador, Guatemala, Nicaragua, and Uruguay. The governments of each of these countries were pressured to improve their respect for human rights; the withdrawal of aid was one means used to encourage improvement.

Not one of the governments reacted as the Carter administration would have wished. Each became increasingly intransigent, and each continued to violate its citizens' human rights. But the Carter policy nonetheless had a quite noticeable effect, particularly in the three targeted Central American republics: a domestic opposition was emboldened, and in the case of Nicaragua it rose up to overthrow the repressive Somoza dynasty. In nearby El Salvador and Guatemala, large-scale insurgencies developed during the Carter years. As Mr. Carter left office in early 1981, the rebel FMLN was engaged in its ill-fated Final Offensive, and Guatemalan rebels controlled significant parts of the country's heavily populated northwest Indian highlands. In short, *the effect of the Carter human rights policy was to destabilize repressive governments in Latin America.* That was not necessarily the goal of aid conditionality, but for many Carter officials it was a not-unwelcome, unintended consequence.

With the notable exception of Pinochet's Chile, Latin America also began the slow transition to democracy during the Carter years. Mr. Carter was clearly responsible for using the threat to withdraw aid to encourage this transition in the Dominican Republic in 1978. When Dominicans selected opposition candidate Antonio Guzman, they prompted the military supporters of the government's candidate to threaten a coup. The Carter administration then sent the commander of the U.S. Southern Command to inform the Dominican general staff that a coup would do irreparable damage to U.S.-Dominican relations, including a halt in military aid. The preference of the Dominican electorate was honored. To underscore his support for the transition to democracy in Ecuador, President Carter sent his wife and Secretary of State Vance to the inauguration of Jaime Roldós in 1979. By the beginning of the 1980s other Latin American nations were in the final stages of selecting new governments. The opening in Brazil initiated by

President Geisel (1974-79) was given new impetus; in Perú the military handed power over to an elected civilian, Fernando Belaunde Terry, in July 1980; and in 1979 both Argentina and Uruguay announced the beginning of a vaguely defined process to return to democracy.

In short, two important Latin American phenomena seemed to coincide with the Carter human rights policy: the destabilization of repressive governments and the beginning of a transition to democracy. Did aid conditionality contribute to the existence of these two phenomena? In the view of many analysts, including Jeane Kirkpatrick, the Carter policy unquestionably helped destabilize the Somoza government in Nicaragua, the Romero government in El Salvador, and the Lucas García government in Guatemala. I agree. The aid cutoffs and other forms of pressure passed a message to the domestic opponents of these three regimes that the United States was about to stand aside and watch the cookies crumble. In Nicaragua, in particular, no more was necessary in order to seal the fate of Anastasio Somoza.

It is far less certain that the Carter administration's use of aid conditionality contributed to the transition to democracy. This is particularly true of the bureaucratic-authoritarian governments of the Southern Cone—Argentina, Chile, Paraguay, and Uruguay. In my view, the repression exhibited by these regimes reflected the perceived survival needs of the regime's political leaders; unlike Ecuador or the Dominican Republic, leaders of repressive governments in the Southern Cone engaged in the gross violation of human rights in order to maintain their hold upon power. Faced with the choice of, on the one hand, ceasing repression to please the Carter administration and thereby risking being overthrown, and, on the other, forgoing aid but continuing as much repression as needed to retain power, the leaders of the Southern Cone nations selected the latter option.

The Reagan administration's efforts to use economic aid to encourage democracy in Central America are more difficult to assess. Not only are we very close to our data, but also the administration's policy toward Central America is so controversial that dispassionate analyses are almost impossible.

Take, for example, the case of Guatemala, which had been a target of the Carter human rights policy. On May 5, 1981, the Reagan State Department announced that "the Administration would like to establish a more constructive relationship with the Guatemalan Government. Our previous policy clearly failed to contribute to an improvement of the situation inside

Guatemala, while Cuban-supported Marxist guerrillas have gained in strength. We hope changes in the situation in Guatemala will soon permit a closer cooperative relationship. We want to help the Guatemalans to defend themselves against the guerrillas." Within days, the Secretary of State's special emissary, Vernon Walters, visited Guatemala. After meeting with officials of the Lucas government, he told reporters that the United States would help to defend "peace and liberty" and "the constitutional institutions of this country against the ideologies that want to finish off those institutions." This promise was converted into concrete action in early June, when the Department of Commerce approved a $3.1 million cash sale of military vehicles and spare parts to Guatemala.

Soon thereafter the Guatemalan military went into the countryside and, with violence as its tool, stopped the insurgency that had developed during the Carter administration. Once the insurgency was reduced to modest levels, the military called an election, and in 1985 it turned the government administration over to Vinicio Cerezo, a moderate Christian Democrat.

Does the Reagan administration deserve credit for using aid to create an environment which permitted the Guatemalan military to hold an election and pass the presidential office (and some power) to a civilian? To begin to answer this question is to become embroiled in the controversies that have surrounded the administration's views of the causes and consequences of insurgency in Central America. These extremely divisive controversies are far from the central concern of the commission, and I suspect it would be wise to leave them for historians to consider.

Promote Economic Reforms

Since the days of John Kennedy and the Alliance for Progress, the United States has conditioned its economic aid upon economic reforms by Latin American recipients. As originally conceived in early 1961, the Alliance was to be a ten-year cooperative effort to promote economic growth and both political and economic reforms. U.S. aid—$20 billion from both the public and private sectors—was to promote industrialization, agricultural modernization, and socioeconomic infrastructure (schools, health clinics, roads, housing). Latin Americans, in turn, were expected to reform outmoded social structures that were understood to inhibit growth and exacerbate social tensions. Primary among these reforms were changes in tax systems and agrarian landowning patterns. At the August, 1961, meeting at Punta del Este, the receipt of alliance assistance was explicitly conditioned upon the enactment of these socioeconomic reforms.

If the standard of judgment is the extent to which U.S. aid in the 1960s encouraged (or was accompanied by) socioeconomic reforms, then the Alliance for Progress must be judged a failure. Although the 1960s was a period of significant economic growth in Latin America, and although at least some of this growth must be attributed to programs initiated or encouraged by the Alliance for Progress, the basic socioeconomic reforms were not enacted. There was little land reform. There was virtually no tax reform. In Central America in particular, the gap between social classes increased considerably. The rich got much richer, and the poor got only a very little less poor.

Nicaragua is a good example. Between 1961 and 1967 the United States provided the Somoza government with nineteen loans totaling $50 million, the Inter-American Development Bank provided another $50 million, and the U.S. private sector increased its direct investment from $18 million in 1960 to $75 million in 1970. During that decade, Nicaragua's gross national product rose at the annual rate of 6.2 percent. Yet, as Walter LaFeber notes, "Alliance dollars disappeared into agricultural projects that almost solely benefited the oligarchy."[14] Growth occurred primarily in the agricultural export sector, especially cotton and, later, beef, which was dominated by the wealthy. Foreign earnings were used to import luxury goods. Wealth became increasingly ostentatious, and the "revolution of rising expectations" took on a new meaning among the Nicaraguan poor who watched the arrival of automobiles, electronic equipment, and every conceivable North American fad and fashion. LaFeber's conclusion is that "the Alliance accelerated Nicaragua's revolution. The program raised hopes, but it did little or nothing for peasants and laborers who were displaced by machines, forced to subsist as squatters, or searched for survival in the cities."

The crucial lesson to be learned from the Alliance for Progress is that *Latin American governments interested in receiving U.S. economic aid but uninterested in socioeconomic reforms will find a way to obtain the aid without implementing the required reforms.* In the specific case of the alliance, Latin American governments passed model reform legislation, created the appropriate government bureaucracies to oversee the reforms, and then balked at implementation.

The reform program instituted by the Salvadoran government in early

1980 provides additional insight into the use of conditionality to encourage structural reforms by aid recipients. Here, too, the United States attempted to use its aid program to encourage structural reform.

The cornerstone of the 1980 reform effort was a comprehensive agrarian reform. It consisted of three phases. Phase I was to nationalize all large landholdings (over 500 hectares) and convert them into cooperatives owned and operated by landless peasants. Phase II was to divide and redistribute moderately large landholdings (100 to 500 hectares). These parcels constituted the dominant pattern of ownership in the major coffee-producing regions and therefore were the very heart of the oligarchy's economic structure. The third phase, announced somewhat later, was known as the "land-to-the-tiller" program. Its purpose was to provide tenant farmers with titles to the land they were already working. If fully implemented, the agrarian reform would have altered substantially the existing structure of land ownership in El Salvador. To many U.S. policymakers, comprehensive agrarian reform was perceived as an absolutely essential step toward the alleviation of structural poverty and therefore instability in El Salvador.

Two additional reforms were designed to complement the agrarian reform. Commercial banks were to be nationalized, as was the export of El Salvador's three major agricultural products: coffee, cotton, and sugar. Both reforms reflected the view that continued private control of these industries would give the economic elites sufficient power to block the agrarian reform. For the agrarian reform to be effective, money was needed to provide credit and other support services to new landowners, particularly in the initial years of the reform. As in the United States, El Salvador's commercial banks had traditionally been the source of agricultural operating capital, and there was little faith in Washington that El Salvador's private bankers would loan peasants money to plant crops on land that until recently had belonged to the shareholders of the banks.

The nationalization of agricultural exports was designed primarily to "rationalize" the use of export earnings. Under the reformed system, the hard currencies earned by exporting coffee, cotton, and sugar would no longer pass directly into the producers' hands; rather, they would flow first into the nation's central bank. Dollars, pounds, and marks would be retained by the bank, and the producers would be paid in *colones*. In this way, the government would accumulate foreign currencies, which could be purchases with *colones* by importers if the products they wished to import were determined by the government to meet the development needs of the country. The goal was to end the tendency for export earnings to be used for luxury consumption and foreign real estate investments. A secondary motivation was to disable one major vehicle for capital flight, the under-invoicing of exports.

Although it is still early to assess the results of the agrarian reform, some obvious benchmarks can be cited. In January 1981 the head of the Salvadoran agrarian reform institute and two U.S. agrarian reform advisers were shot dead in the coffee shop of the Sheraton Hotel in San Salvador. The act served to highlight the difficult conditions under which El Salvador's agrarian reform bureaucracy was forced to operate. On April 27, 1982, the Salvadoran Constituent Assembly repealed the law permitting the government to expropriate property for the purpose of reform, thereby ending permanently the reform effort. By July 1982 the U.S. assistant secretary of state, Thomas Enders, was telling Congress that phase II was only "a proposal which was drafted by the Duarte government" that "was not backed by the United States at any point. It has now been explicitly set aside by the constituent assembly, but this is not the setting aside of a reform that was underway. This was a reform that was never born."[15] At about the same time, Roy Prosterman, a conservative land reform specialist who acted as an advisor to the Salvadoran agrarian reform institute, asserted that other action by the Constituent Assembly "raises virtually insuperable impediments to the continued viability and implementation of the vital Phase II of the land reform program."[16]

While these events were occurring in El Salvador, U.S. policymakers in Washington were deeply divided over the wisdom of encouraging reform. Although the Reagan administration gave early verbal support for the reforms, many analysts who moved into the administration were already on record as outspoken critics. For example, Roger Fontaine, the first Latin Americanist on Mr. Reagan's National Security Council staff, had written soon after the reforms were announced that the "pro-U.S. military government in El Salvador has been replaced by a center-left government supported by the U.S. embassy" and was bringing "the country to near economic ruin by desperate and sweeping reforms."[17] At the same time, the Heritage Foundation published a study calling for cancellation of phase II. The author, former CIA official Cleto DiGiovanni, wrote that in El Salvador "it is impossible to measure how happy the campesinos are, but in conversations this observer had privately and individually with about a dozen of them in late August, not one felt as much job and personal security under the cooperative system as under the previously private management."[18] The American Legion was especially blunt in its criticism: "The United States should not promote economic reforms for other countries, such as agrarian reform, nationalization of banks, and governmental control over exports, which are inimical to our own free enterprise and capitalist marketing system. . . . At best they are socialist and at worst they are Communist."[19]

These attacks by private citizens upon the reforms were repeated by many senior policymakers. Senator Jesse Helms, chair until 1987 of the Senate Foreign Relations Subcommittee on Western Hemisphere Affairs, noted that "the confiscation of a productive economic system, and its dismemberment or collectivization, is an integral part of every Marxist regime."[20] Representative Clarence Long, chair until 1985 of the powerful House Appropriations Subcommittee on Foreign Operations, held that the agrarian reform was ideologically flawed: "The part which just converts these huge estates into huge cooperatives is exactly what the Russians are doing. The Communists love that big cooperative deal."[21]

It is perhaps premature to reach many firm conclusions about the Salvadoran agrarian reform, but it is not premature to suggest that there is at least one lesson to be drawn from the Salvadoran experience: *efforts to use economic aid to promote structural reforms in Latin America are doomed if both the donor and the recipient are divided as to their wisdom.* Without a clear agreement on the desirability of using aid for this purpose, disaffected U.S. policymakers will hamstring the aid effort. In the case of economic aid to assist with agrarian reform, in 1962 Congress wrote into the Foreign Assistance Act a stipulation (Section 620g) prohibiting the use of U.S. economic aid to compensate owners for expropriated property. The executive branch was thereby denied use of the most significant carrot available to encourage agrarian reform.

Conditionality in Comparative Perspective

The United States is not the world's only aid provider, of course, nor did Washington policymakers invent the concept of conditionality. The fact that the United States has operated the largest foreign assistance program in the postwar era should not permit us to forget that interstate subsidies have been common since the time of the Roman Empire, and today many European providers maintain vigorous aid programs from which we can draw a lesson about the responsiveness of policy and institutional reform to aid conditionality.

France has a fairly large aid program that focuses upon a limited number of countries with which the country has historical ties of one type or another. About 80 percent of French aid is directed toward French-speaking Africa and to France's overseas departments and territories. French assistance heavily focuses upon education (about 40 percent of total aid), and the form of French aid is primarily technical assistance.[22] The nature of this program is closely related to French goals, one of which is what is often called *le besoin de rayonnement*—roughly, the desire to spread one's values to others. While this goal may have declined in post-Gaullist France, it remains a fact that the French aid program places significant stress upon extending French culture, and the focus upon education is hardly incidental to this goal. It can be argued, then, that France's aid program has established as a condition a receptiveness to what Latin Americans would call "cultural imperialism."

Beyond this, however, aid conditionality has never been a prominent issue in the French aid program. This program is widely recognized for its stability—a fairly constant flow of funds, a nearly unchanging set of recipients, and a lack of innovation in approaches. With an uncommonly complex bureaucratic structure and a set of recipients that are largely former colonies, French aid today is highly resistant to the frequent changes that an active policy of conditionality requires.

Germany lacks a colonial experience to match that of France, and its large aid program (third among DAC countries to the United States and France) stretches around the globe to over 120 recipients. At one time, the German government was regularly accused of using its aid too heavily for commercial purposes. For example, from data collected primarily in the late 1970s, Arnold concludes that

the German program has the image of providing products rather than development, tending towards high technology projects requiring a minimum of follow-up. Although it is true that assistance is largely untied, Germans make no secret of the fact that at least 80 percent of German bilateral assistance returns to purchase German goods, providing a significant number of jobs, and it is quite likely that policy-makers would worry should procurement drop significantly. Moreover, German economic sectors defined as in "structural difficulties" (most notably shipbuilding and railways) have special programs, which in fact tie assistance to German products.[23]

Today, this image of the German aid program as an export subsidy for German commercial interests is clearly overblown. The emphasis now is primarily upon alleviating absolute poverty. In determining the countries in which to distribute its aid, the German government is not unaware of the policies of recipients, and it generally conditions its aid to focus upon recipient governments with policies that encourage structural economic reforms. Moreover, gross violators of human rights are not considered appropriate recipients. The effectiveness of this conditionality has never been assessed, but it probably is quite low. With a major portion of the German aid budget dedicated to multilateral aid, and with bilateral assistance spread around a large number of recipients, it is difficult to imagine a situation where a recipient would either embark upon a major reform effort or not violate human rights in order to attract German aid.

The Netherlands has created one of the world's largest (on a per-capita basis, about one percent of GNP), most interesting, and progressive foreign assistance programs. Conditionality is a prominent feature of program administration. Since the late 1970s, three explicit criteria for recipients have guided Dutch aid distributions: appropriate sociopolitical structures (defined as domestic policies encouraging equitable distribution), high levels of poverty and need for assistance, and respect for human rights. Recipients must meet all three criteria. There are other conditions as well. As with most of the rest of Europe, some aid is designed to promote Dutch exports. The purchase of Dutch goods is not a major condition of aid, however, and in 1980 the government explicitly stated that "the use of development funds for the main purpose of subsidizing exports does not conform with the principles behind the Netherlands' policy on development cooperation."[24]

In addition to major aid programs in Suriname and the Netherland Antilles (which together receive about one sixth of all aid), the Dutch have identified about fifteen "target countries" that fit the three criteria. The major recipients have been India, Indonesia, Tanzania, Bangladesh, and Pakistan. As in the case of Germany, there are no data to indicate whether the Dutch program has been effective in influencing the sociopolitical structures or the human rights behavior of the recipient governments. It is more probable that the Dutch government has selected recipients on the basis of their sociopolitical structures and their reasonably good human rights behavior, and that the aid program did not "cause" the reforms or the behavior.

Sweden has developed a foreign assistance program that is widely viewed as being altruistic. In 1968 the government committed the country to spend one percent of GNP on development assistance, a goal that was reached in 1975 and has been maintained since then. Arnold observes that "the Swedish program consistently leads other DAC donors on such criteria as aid volume, favorable terms, and flexible procedures, and has been characterized by a willingness to include more radical regimes and liberation movements among its recipients."[25] The Swedish government has long had a policy of aiding the four front-line southern African states of Botswana, Lesotho, Swaziland, and Zambia, for example. The analysis of Swedish aid allocations has often noted that the primary criterion for significant aid is the Swedish government's assessment of a potential recipient's development strategy. Thus North Vietnam, Cuba,[26] and Allende-era Chile have been Swedish aid recipients, and in the case of Chile aid was stopped when the Allende government was deposed by the Pinochet coup.

The Swedish aid bureaucracy, the Swedish International Development Authority (which has the unfortunate acronym of SIDA, the Spanish word for AIDS), has passed through periods of differing levels of conditionality. The mid-1970s is often referred to as SIDA's "flower power" period, when aid was distributed almost without any conditions whatever. Critics claimed that the lack of conditionality led the government to invest in projects that had little chance of being adequately implemented by the recipient. The result has been increased oversight, bordering on extremely high levels of conditionality. One senior career Swedish aid official, Gus Edgren, cites as an example Sweden's participation in the Chilalo Agricultural Development Unit in Ethiopia, where "it soon became obvious that the benefits of the project would go to the big landlords and that the small tenants would be evicted. The SIDA probably came close to a world record in project conditionality by requesting the Ethiopian Government to undertake a nationwide land reform as a condition of continuing Swedish aid for the project."[27] Edgren continued, "the land reform came about after many years, not so much because of the SIDA's pressure as because a revolution took place. In the process of trying to push the reforms through before the revolution, a

number of leading officials on the Swedish side became quite disenchanted
with the idea of trying to change the country to suit the project, rather than
the other way around." This is another way of saying that Swedish aid
officials became disillusioned with the concept of conditionality. Rather than
use aid as a tool to extract a desired type of behavior from a recipient—in
this case, an agrarian reform from the Ethiopian government—Sweden today
uses its conditions to identify appropriate recipients.

Thus the Swedes, like the Dutch, do not seem to be interested so much
in altering behavior among recipients as in selecting recipients on the basis
of their existing behavior. They are not attempting to extract commitments
to policy or institutional reforms, but rather to identify governments that
are already engaged (or preparing to engage) in these reforms. Here, then,
we are not discussing "conditions" so much as "criteria."

The United Kingdom began a severe reorientation of its aid program in
1979, when the Conservative electoral victory initiated the government of
Margaret Thatcher. Given the new government's commitment to "living
within our means," a decline in bilateral aid was almost inevitable. Britain's
multilateral commitments have been such as to make the overall aid budget
appear fairly stable, but bilateral commitments have declined considerably.

Along with the decline in aid resources has come a shift in the conditions
used to allocate assistance. In a 1980 review for the House of Commons, the
Minister for Overseas Development, Neil Marten, announced that "we
believe that it is right at the present time to give greater weight in the
allocation of our aid to political, industrial, and commercial considerations
alongside our basic developmental objectives."[28] In practice, this has meant
that in the 1980s an increasing amount of British aid has been tied to the
purchase of British goods and services. Other than that, the declining aid
resources have not permitted Britain to pursue a policy of actively attempting
to change recipients' behavior by conditioning aid on policy or institutional
reforms.

If we compare the conditionality of major European aid providers with
the four major goals of U.S. aid conditionality—protect investments, promote
hemispheric solidarity, promote human rights, promote structural economic
reforms—no single, clear conclusion is possible.

No major European donor has predicated its aid program on the condition
that the recipients provide "appropriate" treatment for its private investors;
there is no European equivalent of the Hickenlooper Amendment. On the

other hand, in the 1960s (when the Hickenlooper Amendment and other measures signaled the height of this type of U.S. conditionality), European investors were generally much less prominent in the recipient countries. They seemed to be less involved in recipients' domestic politics and less dominant actors in recipients' economies. From what we know about the German and the British governments' interest in assisting their banks by demanding private debt servicing by Latin American governments at the turn of the century, we know that Europeans are not exempt from the U.S. tendency to use public power to protect private interests abroad. What we do not know is whether aid conditionality would have been one of the tools used for this protection had circumstances permitted the possibility.

Not surprisingly, no major European provider has used aid conditionality to promote Cold War solidarity, although the French use of aid to keep alive the specter of French civilization in non-French areas comes close in intent. As in the case of the United States, European providers operate on the unspoken condition that recipients be "friendly," but it is much easier for a potential recipient to be friendly with most of the European nations discussed in this section, for most Europeans do not define the world in the bipolar terms that make "friendship" a black/white term.

As with the United States, European governments regularly condition their aid programs on respect for human rights. But to date no European government has embarked upon a policy similar to that of the Carter administration, which sought to *alter* human rights behavior by conditioning aid. Europeans tend to select aid recipients on the basis of their existing human rights behavior (which means that appropriate behavior is a condition of aid), but they tend not to use aid to encourage policy reform in the area of human rights. Arnold observes that "Sweden in particular sees its role as that of an international 'conscience,' modeling what it considers to be an ideal behavior for an improved international politics."[29] Respect for human rights is an integral component of that ideal behavior, but Swedish attempts to encourage that behavior by aid recipients differ dramatically to the approach to human rights that characterized both the Carter and Reagan administrations.

The area of conditionality in which the United States and European nations seem most similar is in encouraging structural economic reforms. On balance, however, the Europeans seem to have a more realistic understanding of how effective external assistance can be in this area. Unlike the

U.S. approach that has been illustrated best by the Alliance for Progress and most recently by the sponsorship of structural reforms in El Salvador, no European government provides aid in the belief that the recipient government will respond by altering dramatically the existing structure of socioeconomic privilege.

In sum, while the major European aid providers have established conditions that govern the distribution of their foreign economic assistance, the "conditions" often seem more like "criteria" for identifying desirable aid partners. As noted in the initial pages of this paper, it is not possible to avoid this type of conditionality. The U.S. approach to conditionality contrasts dramatically with that of most European donors because the United States attempts to condition its aid upon the adoption of policy and institutional reforms.

Summary

The utility of aid conditionality and trade concessions to encourage policy and institutional reform by aid recipients is extremely limited.

First, economic aid is a reciprocal exchange, and in most circumstances donors expect to receive as much benefit from the exchange as do recipients. This means that donors' threats to cut aid lack credibility; to reduce aid is to cut off one's nose to spite one's face. Rational policymakers do not act in this fashion, as every sophisticated aid recipient knows.

Second, the larger a donor's aid to a recipient, the less leverage the donor possesses. A large aid program is a clear and unambiguous indicator that the recipient is genuinely important to the donor, and there is little chance of a significant cut. Conversely, a small aid program is a clear indicator that the recipient is relatively unimportant to the donor, and therefore threats to reduce or cut aid are highly credible. But, ironically, since the aid program is small, who cares? As President Carter discovered during his efforts on behalf of human rights, a small aid program grants a donor almost no leverage whatsoever.

Third, the U.S. record with aid conditionality in Latin America cannot be assessed with confidence. There are too many imponderables, the most important of which is the principle of anticipated reactions. For example, did this principle work to make the Hickenlooper Amendment effective; i.e., did recipient governments who were otherwise inclined to expropriate

U.S. property without compensation decide to forgo expropriation because an aid cutoff would have ensued? Did governments who would otherwise have tortured their citizens decide not to torture because they feared implementation of the Harkin Amendment? Nobody knows the answers to these questions.

Fourth, the U.S. record with respect to conditionality suggests that the use of carrots is more effective than the use of sticks. In Latin America in particular, the United States must accept a new reality: threats to withdraw aid are almost certain to arouse extreme animosity across the entire political spectrum. Even the most complaisant governments in the region are likely to tell Washington to take its money and go home. More independent governments will use the threat to bolster domestic support and reaffirm their identity. Finally, carrots don't always work. Sometimes they do not work because, as in the case of the Alliance for Progress, the recipients accept the aid but lack the motivation to take the steps upon which the aid is conditioned. Sometimes they do not work because, as in the more recent case of agrarian reform in El Salvador, the donor is not entirely certain what conditions it wants to see fulfilled. Sometimes they do not work because, as in the case of the more grandiose aspect of the Alliance for Progress, they are simply not realistic.

The overall conclusion is this: conditions are inevitable, but in the history of conditions attached to U.S. aid programs and trade concessions in Latin America, conditions have not worked very well. Perhaps that is because the conditions have been stipulated unilaterally. If the United States could sit down with Latin Americans and design a set of conditions that is acceptable to both donors and recipients (including a set of criteria and mechanisms for evaluating performance by both donors and recipients), perhaps then the record would be different. So long as policymakers in Washington continue to stipulate unilaterally the conditions under which aid will be provided, however, then the record indicates that they should expect to find that policymakers in Latin America will continue to decide unilaterally the conditions under which aid will be accepted.

Notes

1. Baldwin (1985), p. 299.

2. Ibid.

3. A continuing resolution is a congressional authorization or appropriation to continue spending money for purposes specified in the previous authorization or appropriation law. A continuing resolution is the legal mechanism that Congress uses to keep the government functioning when legislators cannot agree on a new law prior to the beginning of a new fiscal year.

4. Eisenhower (1953), pp. 7–8. The report is reprinted in the *Department of State Bulletin*, November 23, 1953.

5. On the post-Vietnam era neoisolationism, see Holsti and Rosenau (1984); Kegley and Wittkopf (1982), pp. 77–106.

6. Knorr (1975), p. 181.

7. Hufbauer and Schott (1983), p. 49.

8. Baldwin (1985), p. 313.

9. Lillich (1975), p. 98.

10. A photocopy of Mr. Helms's handwritten notes is included in U.S. Senate, Select Committee to Study Governmental Operations with Respect to Intelligence Activities, (1975), p. 96.

11. Jordan and Taylor (1981), p. 436.

12. *New York Times*, May 2, 1985, p. A10.

13. Knorr (1975), p. 165.

14. LaFeber (1983), p. 162.

15. U.S. Congress, Senate, Committee on Appropriations (1982), pt. 1, pp. 1,678, 1,664.

16. U.S. Congress, Senate, Committee on Foreign Relations (1982), p. 216.

17. Fontaine, DiGiovanni, and Kruger (1980), p. 26.

18. DiGiovanni (1980), pp. 8, 11.

19. U.S. Congress, House, Committee on Foreign Affairs, Subcommittee on Inter-American Affairs (1981), pp. 224, 211.

20. Office of Senator Jesse Helms, Press release, February 7, 1984.

21. U.S. Congress, House, Committee on Appropriations, Subcommittee on Foreign Operations and Related Agencies (1982), pt. 1, p. 39.

22. The French aid program is analyzed by Arnold (1982), pp. 11–30, Berthelot (1973), and Robarts (1974).

23. Arnold (1982), p. 32.

24. Netherlands, Ministry of Foreign Affairs, Development Cooperation Information Department (1980), p. 102.

25. Arnold (1982), p. 105.

26. In the early 1980s, Swedish aid programs to both Cuba and Tunisia were phased out because of the two countries' relatively high per-capita incomes.

27. Edgren (1984), p. 154.

28. "Aid Policy Review," Neil Marten's statement presented to the House of Commons, February 20, 1980.

29. Arnold (1982), pp. 172–73.

References

Arnold, Steven H. (1982). *Implementing Development Assistance: European Approaches to Basic Needs*. Boulder, Colo.: Westview Press.

Baldwin, David A. (1985). *Economic Statecraft*. Princeton: Princeton University Press.

Berthelot, Yves (1973). "French Aid Performance and Development Policy." In Bruce Dinwiddy, ed., *European Development Policies: The United Kingdom, Sweden, France, E.E.C., and Multilateral Organizations*, pp. 65–87. New York: Praeger.

DiGiovanni, Cleto, Jr., (1980). "U.S. Policy and the Marxist Threat to Central America." Heritage Foundation *Backgrounder* 128: 1–4. October 15.

Edgren, Gus (1984). "Conditionality in Aid." In Olav Stokke, ed., *European Development Assistance, Volume II: Third World Perspective on Policies and Performance*, 153–62. Oslo: The Norwegian Institute of International Affairs, and Tilburg: The European Association of Development Research and Training Institutes.

Eisenhower, Milton S. (1953). *United States-Latin American Relations: Report to the President*. Washington, D.C.: Department of State. Reprinted in the *Department of State Bulletin*, November 23, 1953.

Fontaine, Roger, Cleto DiGiovanni, Jr., and Alexander Kruger (1980). "Castro's Specter." *Washington Quarterly* 3 (Autumn 1980): 3–27.

Helms, Jesse (1984). Press release, February 7.

Holsti, Ole R., and James N. Rosenau (1984). *American Leadership in World Affairs: Vietnam and the Breakdown of Consensus*. Winchester, Mass.: George Allen and Unwin.

Hufbauer, Gary Clyde, and Jeffrey J. Schott (1983). *Economic Sanctions in Support of Foreign Policy Goals*. Washington, D.C.: Institute for International Economics.

Jordan, Amos A., and William J. Taylor, Jr. (1981). *American National Security: Policy and Process*. Baltimore: Johns Hopkins University Press.

Kegley, Charles W., Jr., and Eugene R. Wittkopf (1982). "Beyond Consensus: The Domestic Context of American Foreign Policy." *International Journal* 38 (Winter 1982–83): 77–106.

Knorr, Klaus (1975). *The Power of Nations*. New York: Basic Books.

LaFeber, Walter (1983). *Inevitable Resolutions: The United States and Central America*. New York: W.W. Norton.

Lillich, Richard B. (1975). "Requiem for Hickenlooper." *American Journal of International Law* 69(January): 89–102.

Marten, Neil (1980). British Minister for Overseas Development statement presented to the House of Commons. February 20.

Netherlands, Government of (1980). *Development Cooperation and the World Economy*. The Hague: Ministry of Foreign Affairs, Development Cooperation Information Department.

Robarts, R. (1974). *French Development Assistance: A Study in Policy and Administration*. Beverly Hills, Calif.: Sage.

Smith, Wayne (1985). Quoted in the *New York Times*. May 2, p. A10.

United States Congress, House of Representatives, Committee on Appropriations, Subcommittee on Foreign Operations and Related Agencies (1982). *Foreign Assistance and Related Programs Appropriations for 1983*. 97th Cong., 2d Sess. Washington, D.C.: U.S. Government Printing Office.

United States Congress, House of Representatives, Committee on Foreign Relations, Subcommittee on Inter-American Affairs (1981). *U.S. Policy Toward El Salvador*. 97th Cong., 1st Sess. Washington, D.C.: U.S. Government Printing Office.

United States Congress, Senate, Committee on Appropriations (1982). *Foreign Assistance and Related Programs Appropriations, Fiscal Year 1983*. 97th Cong., 2d Sess. Washington, D.C.: U.S. Government Printing Office.

United States Congress, Senate, Committee on Foreign Relations (1982). *U.S. Policy in the Western Hemisphere*. 97th Cong., 2d Sess. Washington, D.C.: U.S. Government Printing Office.

United States Congress, Senate, Select Committee to Study Governmental Operations with Respect to Intelligence Activities (1975). *Intelligence Activities*. Vol 7, 94th Cong., 2d Sess. Washington, D.C.: U.S. Government Printing Office.

Index

AEZ1961 10/16/90 econ EBCS

Women—*Cont.*
53; informal sector, 237–39, 241, 252;
land tenure, 235, 237, 239–42, 249–52;
politics and the law, 247–49, 251, 253;
ratification of selected conventions, 248–
49; recommendations, 251–53; summary,
250–51; wages, 237–38, 240, 242;
workplace, 237–40, 252

World Bank, 59, 264–66, 269, 344, 377,
388, 390, 400
World Neighbors, 143
World Wildlife Fund, 112, 131, 143
Wright, James, 414

Ydrígoras Fuentes, Miguel, 422

BM